THE ISLAMIC LAW OF BEQUEST
and its application in Saudi Arabia

THE ISLAMIC LAW OF BEQUEST

ABDULAZIZ MOHAMMED ZAID

SCORPION PUBLISHING LTD LONDON

THE ISLAMIC LAW OF BEQUEST

First published in 1986 by
Scorpion Publishing Ltd
Victoria House, Victoria Road
Buckhurst Hill, Essex, England

ISBN 0 905906 42 X

Designed and Produced by Scorpion Pica
Editor: Leonard Harrow
Design and Art Direction: Colin Larkin
House Editor: John Orley
Design and Production Team:
Chris Crossman, Dale Dawson,
Susan Pipe, John Orley, Peter Davey

Typeset by Scorpion Pica in ITC Garamond Light
Printed on 90gsm white book wove
Printed and Bound in England by
Ebenezer Baylis and Son Ltd

بسم الله الرحمن الرحيم

To
the memory
of
my dear father
and
mother

May Allah
bless them

ACKNOWLEDGEMENTS

I would like to express my heartfelt, deep and warm gratitude to all those who extended to me their infinite help, valuable advice and encouragement, wittingly and unwittingly, during my research efforts.

May Allah bless them.

Abdulaziz Mohammed Zaid

CONTENTS

INTRODUCTION

THE ORIGINAL LEGAL CONCEPT OF AL-WASIYA

The legal concept of *Wasiya* (bequest), like other matters related to the law, is derived either from the *Quran, Sunna* (tradition), *Ijma'*, (consensus) or *Qiyas* (analogy). Although *Qiyas* is one of the four main sources of Islamic law, on closer reading of these sources, we find that *Qiyas* is not regarded as an element which supports the institution of bequest at all. The principles of *Qiyas* do not take into account the idea of allowing the dead person to remain in possession of his estate or to exercise any power upon it. Thus at his death he loses the right to convey anything. This could have been the result of an Islamic principle which states that in the case of death all the deceased's estates or rights are transferred automatically to his heirs. However, by looking into the three other sources we find that the constitution of bequest has been created from these three other sources. In the *Quran*, at the beginning of its legislation comes the verse 'It is prescribed when death approaches any of you, if he leaves any goods, that he makes a bequest'.[1] In the *Sunna* comes the Hadith (tradition) from the Prophet saying 'What right has a Muslim having something which may be bequeathed, to sleep for two nights unless his bequest is written'.[2]

Also the jurists have been guided by what the companions of the Prophet said or did after the Prophet's death. An example of this is the case of the *Khalifa*, Abu Bakr. He bequeathed the *Khalifa* to Umar to be *Khalifa* after his death and Umar in his turn bequeathed it to a consultative body of the six companions called *Ahl al-Shura* to choose one of them to succeed as *Khalifa*. The making of such wills was universally acknowledged so that no Muslim ever refuted, rejected or denied the act of bequest.

The jurists, however, are not interested at all in this particular point from *Qiyas* so long as they can find evidence to support the *Wasiya* constitution from three out of four sources. These three are the *Quran, Sunna and Ijma'*. Therefore *Qiyas* would lose its weight beside those three because we are allowed to derive the legality of anything from *Qiyas* on one condition only, that is, the failure of those three sources.

So far we have seen the broad elements of the legal concepts of bequest based on the Islamic legal sources. It is now vital to understand how the jurists classify legacies in connection with the legal concepts of bequest as they have been deduced from these sources.

According to the *Quran*, it is incumbent upon everyone to bequeath, but to whom? The *Quran* states that it is necessary for the deceased to bequeath his estate to be distributed amongst his parents and his near relatives.[3]

This was the legal position at the beginning of Islam which was vital at that time as the Muslims were incredibly few and most of their relatives had not been converted to Islam and the people in general were not prepared yet for any major change in the system they had inherited from their ancestors, which was based mainly on the pre-Islamic *Jahiliya*. Women, for instance, had no rights whatsoever under that system to demand any part of their father's, son's, or husband's estate. Inheritance was the right only of the male, who was able to ride and fight enemies and gain booty. The woman had no such right, as she was considered incompetent to fight.

But here we should notice that the system which prevented women and children as a whole from inheriting from their relatives was very logical according to the people of the *Jahiliya*. It was fundamentally fitting to their way of viewing social life, to the time and to the way in which estate was acquired, i.e. by raiding and fighting to win booty. No child or women was able to do this. So it was logical to their way of thinking that the estate should not by any means be allowed to pass by inheritance except to those who exhausted themselves to gain it. But they failed to realise that that which is considered logical is not necessarily equitable. They failed, too, to realise that estates are owned by *Allah* (God) who is only able to bestow them upon those he chooses amongst his creatures. This fact was later regarded to be one of the substantial principles in Islam. Nor had they noticed that children and women were more deserving of help than men. They had also failed to apply pragmatically the strength of the relationships of the excluded women and children to the deceased. This omission marks another failure of their system since their social existence was based entirely upon this relationship.

Under such a system it was not necessary for the law to change suddenly but to make people accept change gradually, in the same way as the *Quran* had done when forbidding wine, i.e. to take three steps towards achieving that aim, thus preparing them psychologically and socially to accept the change to come. That is why at the beginning it was left to a person to decide how he wanted his estate to be distributed after his death i.e. 'It is prescribed when death approaches any of you, if he leaves any goods, that he make a bequest to the parents and near relatives'. He was, therefore, able to make bequests to whomever he chose regardless of sex or belief. The reason was to take him away from applying the customary *Jahiliya* system.

Then the second revelation was revealed to the Prophet Muhammad to tell Muslims of another change in the system of inheritance. This is seen in the verse which says 'From what is left by parents and those near related, whether the estate is small or large, a determinate share shall be for both men and women'.[4] We have seen how the *Quran* started changing the system of inheritance of the *Jahiliya* in the verse mentioned earlier, where *Allah* set up the first stage by imposing the *Wasiya* to be made for parents and the nearest relatives without mentioning limitations in respect of 'sex'; the earlier rule was then regarded as a preparatory stage. In the second verse *Allah* announces that a woman has the right to inherit in the same capacity as a man from what is left by either parents or relatives. Nevertheless, in the meantime, despite the revelation of the woman's right, in order not to upset them too much by breaking their inherited system completely at this stage, it did not explain clearly the women's position in comparison with men's, nor did it state their portions.

However, as usual *Allah* (the Legislator) left them for some time to absorb his instructions. Sometime later Muslims were in great need and there were some cases where it was disputed whether women and children should have any part of the deceased's estate, and if so, how much. It was not clear; should they just continue to apply their old customary system. It was very confused indeed.

Men preferred to keep up the old system because it gave them priority over women and children, as the women and children's position was left undefined. Women on the other hand brought their rights before the Prophet, as in the case of the wife of Sa'd b al-Rabi' who, on behalf of her two daughters, went to the Prophet to present their claim before him and said: 'Oh, Messenger of God, here are the daughters of Sa'd. Their father was killed at the battle of Uhud as a martyr and their (paternal) uncle took their estate without leaving anything for them.' The Prophet said God would solve it. So later the verse of inheritance was revealed and the Messenger of God told their uncle to give two thirds of the estate to the daughters, one eighth to their mother and keep the residue himself.[5] In this decision the Prophet was applying the verse which states: 'God thus directs you as regards your children's inheritance; to the male, a portion equal to that of two females: If only two or more daughters their share is two-thirds of the inheritance; if only one, her share is a half . . .etc.'[6] This was meant to finalize the intended change and stop the controversy between people relating to matters of succession. That is to say the revelation of this last verse completely abolished the *Jahiliya* system of inheritance. This was the stage at which Muslims were instructed as how to behave regardless of what rules they had been used to following. This also abrogated the 'Brotherhood' Legislation made by the Prophet immediately after his immigration to Madina, because this new situation had to be coped with in order to gather the strength of different believers and make use of them by putting them into the one stream of Islam, which needed every effort of the Muslims to strengthen its position rather than splitting them up amongst the different Arab tribes. So when it was found necessary socially, as well as economically and politically because their position at Madina was not stable enough, they were enabled to inherit from each other, but this was cancelled when the necessity was over.

When the inheritance verses, with their magnificent discipline of distributing the estate among its beneficiaries are put beside the bequest verse, some confusion may be caused especially when a question about the parents and nearest relatives is raised. Would they have the right to accept a bequest (*Wasiya*) as well as the fixed portions given in the inheritance verses?

Muslim commentators on the *Quran* agreed that those who have fixed shares should not by any means take anything from the praepositus's estate by bequest and they referred to the *Hadith* laid down by the Prophet, which says that 'God had given to each what he deserved so that there is no bequest in favour of an heir'.[7]

Hence most of the *Ulama* (scholars) said that the bequest verse was abrogated by the *Hadith* for those who were entitled to fixed shares by the *Quran*. As stated above, the inheritance verses superceded the bequest verse, for both dealt with succession matters and the latter (the inheritance verses) were more accurate in dividing the estate by giving fixed portions rather than by leaving it to the person's discretion, for the person may feel more inclined towards the people he favours, so giving them a greater portion of his estate, perhaps even more than he gives to his nearest relatives. This would make the whole act look unjust because some relatives may be in great need. This was particularly the case with women and children where there are some legatees who have been given the bigger shares.

This weakness in the pre-Islamic system may be one of the reasons why the *Quran* confines mention of shares to those of the women mostly, but on the male side specifying the father's uterine brother or husband's. For men, or in other words agnatic relatives, were mostly strong enough to demand their shares and to take them.

Nevertheless, when we say that this Tradition *(Hadith)* abrogated the Quranic verse, it does not mean that the latter was no longer considered to be a source for the constitution of *Wasiya*. The inheritance verses abrogated the right of the person to distribute his estate amongst those of his near relatives who were entitled to the fixed Quranic portions. It did not, however, abrogate the whole legal concept of *Wasiya* in connection either with other distant relatives, not regarded as heirs, or with non-relatives. If the testator felt that they had done something beneficial for him and it was impossible to recompense them during the course of his life it was found more suitable under the constitution of legacy to recompense them by making a bequest to them after his death. This also applied if he wanted to make a benevolent bequest.

Besides these verses the *Quran* confirms the legal concept of *Wasiya* even in the inheritance verses themselves. This was when it repeated four times the verses, 'The distribution (of inheritance) in all cases is after the payment of legacies and debts'. This is because the bequest is still valid for the rest of the people who were not mentioned or allotted any share.

And in addition, of course, many *Hadiths* affirm the legality of the principle of the *Wasiya* (bequest) either by recommending people to apply it or by quoting cases that related to it.

Even when we look at the verses saying: '(distribution of inheritance is to take place) after the payment of legacies or debts', we will find that it gives priority to the carrying out of the deceased's will even before the distribution of his estate amongst his heirs. This was meant to give more emphasis to the importance of bequest in comparison with the importance of debts. The emphasis becomes even more precise when we see that the *Quran* mentions bequest before debts. It was considered just to put some pressure upon Muslims to feel that the immediate settlement of bequest is as important as the settlement of a debt.

Some of the Sunni *Ulama*, and the Zahirites in particular, said that the *Wasiya* verse was abrogated by the inheritance verses only for those parents and near relatives entitled to the fixed portion and that it was never abrogated for the more distant relatives who were excluded from inheritance by the next-of-kin. Hence the rule is still, according to them *Fard*, which imposes upon Muslims the duty to bequeath to distant relatives.

Therefore, according to their interpretation of the bequest verse, the contemporary law of Egypt states its preference for this unpopular view when it says 'It is necessary for every person to make a bequest to those near relatives excluded from succession, such as the two main lines ascendant or descendant whether grand-parents or grandchildren, who have the super agnatic male line, without including the daughter's children.'

On the other hand the interpretation of the abrogation question by the majority of jurists, especially the four *Ulama* who were the leaders and founders of the Sunni schools of law and the Shi'a both Imamites and Zaidites said the *Wasiya* was neither *Fard*, imposed, nor *Wajib*, incumbent, unless it released the testator from obligations and rights to both God and people. Otherwise it would be *Mandub*, or praiseworthy, only where performance brings reward from God, but omission does not entail punishment.

The *Wasiya* is therefore divided, according to the Sunnis and the Shi'a views, into two parts:

a. *Wajib* or incumbent to satisfy the rights of God as *Zakat* or alms-tax, and *Hajj* or pilgrimage, etc, and the rights of people – which rights would be unknown unless indicated through bequest, i.e. debts, deposits, borrowed objects, etc.

b. *Mustahab.* praiseworthy act. This relates to whatever is given out voluntarily or graciously by way of *Wasiya* after death. Therefore, the Hanbalis for their part (concerning the recommended *Wasiya* for classification according to their point of view) divided bequest into four parts having different rules, as follows:

1. *Mandub*, praiseworthy. As part of the Sunnis, the Hanbali jurists have derived this rule from their interpretation of the verse 'It is prescribed upon you when death approaches any of you . . .etc'. They said the then existing law had been abrogated, so the only remaining rule was the *Mandub* *(Mustahab)*. They have also seen this rule as the outcome of the

interpretation of the *Hadith* stated by the Prophet which said *'Allah* the Glorious said, O child of Adam, I have given you a portion of your estate when death approaches you to purify and sanctify you'.[9] This they said implies the giving of alms, for a person to bequeath to a poor relative such a bequest was strongly recommended to them. If there were no poor relations, it was to be made to a poor person, say an alien who was unrelated to the testator or a learned or pious person etc. on one condition that the testator be well off or that his heirs be well off.

2. *Makruh*.[10] This is where it is reprehensible for a poor person to make a bequest at all, either when he is poor and his heirs are poor too, or when he is rich but his heirs are poor, since the estate that they inherit will in neither case be sufficient to make them rich. So in this case, to leave it to the heirs is strongly recommended for the *Hadith* says 'To leave your heirs rich is better than to leave them in need, begging from other people'.[11]

But it is not, as we stated above, disapproved of for the person whose heirs are rich, because the *Hadith* confined it to the benefit of the heirs. Hence every act against the heirs' benefit is considered ultra vires and thus subjected to approval or disapproval. But at the same time, it is considered reprehensible if the testator ever makes a bequest to those who live in sin or debauchery.[12] It will, however, be regarded as praiseworthy if he thinks they will spend it in ways which will prevent them from committing sins; otherwise it will be *Mubah*, inconsequential. In either case it depends on the legatee's position and on the testator's motives and intentions.

3. *Muharram*. Forbidden which probably needs to be subdivided into:

a. Those who leave heirs of blood relatives, i.e. other than a husband or wife, are forbidden to bequeath more than one third of the whole estate or to make a bequest in favour of an heir, for the *Hadith* says 'No bequest in favour of an heir' though the prohibition is to be lifted when it is approved by the heirs.

b. To bequeath anything at all which is more than the allowed one-third to a non-relative whether it is made while the testator is healthy or on his deathbed,[13] for the *Hadith* states when Sa'd ibn Abi Waqqas asked the Prophet if he could bequeath 'All of his estate, or half of it,' the reply was negative until he said 'Or the third.' The Prophet agreed but said 'The third and the third is excessive'. Then Ibn Abbas said, 'One of the major sins is to do harm through your bequest.'[14] This is what is called *Wasiyat al-dirar* or the detrimental bequest.

c. To bequeath something which will promote religious disobedience such as a bequest for the building of a bawdy-house, and so on. To bequeath to a non-relative or to an heir with the solid intention that the testamentary act meant to harm his heirs through reducing their portions of inheritance. This is denounced in the *Qur'an* where it said, at the end of what is called the Golden Rule in the verses of inheritance, 'After any bequest that may have been bequeathed or debt not injuring the heirs (by willing away more than a third of the heritage) hath been paid . . .etc.'[15] And in addition to this we refer to the above stated saying of Ibn Abbas.

4. *Mubah*, inconsequential for the testator to make a bequest in favour of a. rich relative or a non-relative, on the condition that he has enough estate and his heirs are not in need. b. a person who has no heirs, neither Qur'anic heirs, agnatic relatives nor even cognatic relatives however remote, is permitted to bequeath an unlimited quantity out of his estate, even to give away the whole estate by *Wasiya*. He is also permitted to bequeath the residue after the portion of the heir who is not a blood relative (such as a husband or a wife) has been allocated.

NOTES

1. *Quran* II (the Cow), 180.
2. Bukhari & Muslim. See *Al-Mu 'jam al-Mufahras*, Vol. 7, 229.
3. *Quran*, II (the Cow), 180.
4. *Quran,* IV (the Women), 7.
5. Reported by Ibn Hanbal & Ibn Majah. See *Al-Mu'jam al-Mufahras,* Vol. 6, 307, Vol. 7, 182.
6. *Quran*, II (the Women), 11.
7. Al-Bukhari. See *Al-Mu'jam Al-Mufahnas*, Vol. 7, 187, Vol.1, 485.
8. Moh. Al-Kishi, *Al-tarikah wama yata'allqu biha min al-huquq*, 151.
9. Reported by Ibn Majah. See *Al-Mu'jam al-Fahras*, Vol. 6, 312.
10. *Al-Insaf*, Vol. 7, 191.
11. Bukhari & Muslim. See *Al-Mu'jam al-mufahras*, Vol. 7, 188.
12. *Muntaha al-iradat*, Vol. 2, 552-553, Vol. 2, 558, and Mughni, Vol. 6, 532.
13. *Sh. Muntaha al-iradat*, Vol. 2, 540.
14. Ibn Daqiq Al-Eid. *Ahkam al-Ahkam*, Vol. 4, 4.
15. *Quran*, II (the Women), 12.

Part I

THE CAPACITY OF THE TESTATOR

INTRODUCTION

The testator is the one who decisively makes a bequest. Therefore, in order for his action to be validated, he must beside being free, be an *'Aqil* or be in a mental state which enables him to appreciate the nature of the bequest and the responsibilities it entails. This puts his mental state in the forefront of the qualifications required to validate the act of making a testament, since the lack of mental faculty is the most vulnerable point allowing any vitiation.

What makes the mental state such an important issue is the fact that coming of age is not necessarily indicative of mental maturity. The law allows the validation of the bequest of a child who is defined as *'Aqil* or sane.

Since the attainment of absolutely suitable mental faculty can not be precisely defined, there was a great need to discuss it in relation to age or physical signs to see at what stage a testator's bequest should be considered valid.

CHAPTER I
THE AGE OF DISCRETION

It is difficult to know exactly to what degree the human mind has developed at any given stage. However, for the purposes of law, Islamic jurists found it inappropriate to treat people of different age groups equally. Due to this principle jurists sought a ruling on this point in the *Quran* and the *Sunna*. Also they observed the development of a human being at different stages of his life.

These jurists defined the age of seven years as the age of discretion.[1] This was derived partly from the reported *Hadith* 'Ensure that your children pray when they are seven'.[2] This *Hadith* shows by implication the importance of this age. Further, the jurists observed that the acts of a child of seven relatively co-ordinate with his mental faculty. One therefore assumes his understanding to be sufficiently developed to cope with the demand of his age in a remarkably different way from those infants who are still below that age.

These results are compatible with the findings of the modern psychologists. This idea is substantiated by C.I. Sandstom, who considered the age of five as being very important for the stability of the mind that would develop at the age of seven: 'A new period of integration begins, during which the various processes of development combine in the creation of the whole personality. But not until the age of seven years . . ., has the early childhood phase been passed. Before then the child usually passes through a period of disorganization and anxiety'.[3]

It is often at this point in his life that the child begins to use his mind and to make use of what he has already experienced. In early childhood he becomes fairly capable of absorbing correct statements and reacting logically. He also starts to adapt to his environment and gradually begins to cope with the difficulties of life.

Realizing these facts, scholars, came to a decision from the *Hadith* in which a father and a mother disputed each one's right to embrace their boy came before the Prophet to settle their dispute and the Prophet said 'O, boy this is your father and this is your mother so take the hand of the one you choose,' and the boy chose his mother.[4] Thus such a child, if found to be *'Aqil* or sane when the custody period expires, could be given the right to opt freely between his father and mother (or their representatives).[5] As a result of this principle if the male child opts to live with his father, he would continue to live with him day and night. If however, the child chooses his mother, he would be allowed to stay with her only at night. For the rest of the day he would stay with his father and be brought up and educated in the right and proper way.[6]

The application of this principle in Saudi Arabia is shown in the case of *A v. D.*[7]

After the divorce, the defendant retained her children *Y*[8], and *Ab*[9]. But *A*, the father and thus the guardian, raised the claim that the children should be in his custody. So we may consider the fact that the level of maturity of minors of this age is such that they may be considered mature enough, within certain limits, to opt for one of their parents. In other words they can decide, prompted by their feelings, which parent they choose to live with. In the case in question, the court granted *Y* and *Ab* the right of option. As they had both been brought up by their mother, they chose to live with her.

But for the girl, as she needs to be in the custody of an older person to protect her purity and morals, the right was given to her guardian (the father of his representative). Thus the girl of seven will not be granted the same right of option but will be given into the custody of her guardian, who must be a *Mahram*, (one forbidden to marry the girl), to remain in his care until she marries.[8] An illustration is seen in the case of *H v. S.*[9]

When *F's* mother remarried, leaving her daughter in the care of her maternal grand-mother, *F's* paternal uncle, *H*, applied to the court for the custody of his niece. Since *F* was over seven, the uncle was granted the right he had demanded.

THE ROLE OF *'AQL* (MENTAL STATE) IN DETERMINING THE AGE OF DISCRETION

The most indespensible stipulated condition which determines the age of discretion (*Tamyiz*) is that the child should be *'Aql* (rational). However, the best definition so far to test and describe the state of *'Aql* in a child is that of the author of *Al-Muttali'*, 'It is the child who comprehends what is said and gives a sound response to it'.[10]

As to the commencement of such a state, Ibn al-Qayim saw it as a possibility that the state of *'Aql* and the age of *Tamyiz*, discretion, could be attained below the age of seven.[11]

However, in contrast to the above opinion, the late Hanbalis[12] considered the set age of seven to be the onset of the age of *Tamyiz*, and this is the opinion held by the Saudis.

THE RANGE OF THE *MUMYIZ'S* CAPACITY

The *'Aql* is regarded to be the main qualification that the *Mumayiz* child must possess before his bequest becomes legally valid. At this age the child is still not considered mature enough, either mentally or socially, to carry out the responsibilities of an adult and it is felt that he must be kept under close and direct supervision of mature people (this supervision is called interdiction). The legality of some of his acts performed in the course of his training or preparation for the coming adult life becomes, apart from the major actions, reasonably and fairly endorsed. The same is true for mere rights with no bearing on his property.

Selling, buying and dealing with minor articles and objects, sueing someone or raising a claim and the presentation of his evidence to the court with or without the guardian's approval, are examples of the minor's capacity at this age. Application of this in Saudi courts is illustrated by the case of *Kh v. S.*[13]

Kh, a girl, had appointed her uncle, *D*, as an agent to present to the court the evidence which confirmed her being of full age, mature and competent to receive her entrusted property from her guardian and to demand accordingly the termination of the guardian's power over her.

This action was accepted by the court and in the light of the irrefutable evidence submitted, the court ordered the termination of the guardianship despite the denial of her other uncle (the guardian) that she had reached such an age.

This is also illustrated by the case of *A v. H.*[14] *A*, a boy, brought his mother, who was also his guardian, to court to obtain a decree to terminate his mother's guardianship over him. After the judge heard the boy's claims and his uncle's counter-claim, the judge subjected the boy to an intellignece test in which the boy failed to prove his alleged maturity. Accordingly the boy's claim was dismissed and his guardian (the mother) was allowed to keep the unterminated guardianship over her son.

In the case of *A v. Aq,*[15] the boy *A,* claimed that the 2 SR. maintenance, which had earlier been adjudicated in a grand court to be sufficient, had now, due to altering times and needs, become insufficient. He, therefore, asked the court to order his*Wasi* (guardian) to increase his maintenance. Consequently the judge asked the boy to estimate the amount of maintenance he thought adequate for his needs and subsequently ordered it to be paid to him.

Al-Mirdawi, a leading jurist, has also validated the *Mumayiz's* right to accept a gift and a bequest and to deal with minor objects so long as it does not preclude or violate his benefits and interests, even without obtaining the guardian's permission.[16] However, there is a tendency in Saudi Arabia for the guardian (*Wali* or *Wasi*) to accept a gift or a bequest on behalf of his ward. This tendency is demonstrated in the case of *F* and her boy *U.*[17]

F, the mother and the appointed guardian of *U*, had donated her share in the house of her deceased husband to her child *U*. In court, in her capacity as the child's guardian, she acknowledged that she had accepted and received such a donation.

In another case a generous man made a donation to provide lodging for X's children in his house for five years. The mother who was their testamentary guardian accepted this donation on the children's behalf.[18]

The testament of a *Mumayiz*, who has been proved sane, will not be considered 'ipso facto' invalidation just because he was under age. It will not even be subjected to the approval of his guardian so long as he is known to be aware of the nature of the bequest and shows no defiance in this bequest towards the laws of the *Wasiya*. This has been hinted at by the statement of al-Hijjawi and al-Futuhi when they were considering the validity of the bequest of the *Mumayiz*, who had not yet been proved *'Aqil* or sane. These statements were taken by al-Buhuti to imply that the ones who understand the nature of the act and the meaning of *Al-Wasiya* can make a valid testament.[19] This view stemmed from the concept that the principle of the imposition of interdiction over the child was introduced only for his personal benefit, thus protecting him from concluding harmful dispositions. Whereas *Wasiya*, it is said, would not be in any way harmful to him, but was assumed to be beneficial to him and others.

This, it was also said, would not prejudice the principle of interdiction since the imposition of it was a protective measure to preserve his property from being lost or damaged, whereas neither of these two dangers could be sure to be avoided if the child were to make a bequest. The reason for this is that the property bequeathed would remain in the possesssion of the child as long as he lived. Accordingly, the validation of his bequest would only give him a chance to obtain religious rewards in the hereafter as it would be considered as alms given in accordance to the *Hadith* which states that, 'Be aware that *Allah* has given you the third of your property at your death to increase your deeds so invest it in the way you like'.[20]

AL-BULUGH, PHYSICAL PUBERTY AND ITS PECULIARITIES

As a child grows older, it becomes less difficult to recognize with any accuracy the stages of his development. At this particular stage in the child's life, various aspects of his development can be observed. Puberty can easily be discerned if the child is kept under close and constant observation.

Al-Bulugh, puberty, has always been considered significant. It is the turning point physically between a child's body and an adult's body.

The jurists believed that *al-Bulugh* is associated with profound and widespread physical changes in the child. The signs of *al-Bulugh* as defined by the jurists were to be divided into non-physical and physical signs, which in their turn could be sub-divided into the signs in 1. boys, 2. girls, both having an ultimate age of puberty.

The physical signs are relatively easy to observe because there can be a sort of fluid discharge from the body. When it occurs for the first time, the beginning of a new and a significant stage in the child's life is said to have been reached. Different sexes have different signs.

Thus, for a boy such a phenomenon could be marked either by having what is technically called *Ihtilam*, or wet dreams, i.e. by ejaculating semen somehow, or by growing of thick pubic hair round his genitals and displaying secondary sexual characteristics.

A girl will not be considered to have obtained the age of puberty only by showing similar signs as those of a boy. But she will attain it with the onset of one or two more physical conditions, menstruation and/or the ability to procreate.

As far as the age of puberty is concerned the jurists have stated that it can never occur below the age of nine.[21] They also emphasize puberty would not necessarily occur at this age in all children as there are numerous factors which might delay such a process of physical maturity. Therefore, a great number of jurists such as al-Awza'i, Imam Ahmad, al-Shafi'i, Abu Yusuf and Muhammad, all considered fifteen years as the latest age at which anyone can become legally *Baligh* or physically mature, irrespective of the non-appearance of physical signs.[22]

Should a controversy in respect of the attainment of puberty arise between the adolescent and his guardian, it may be resolved, as agreed by all jurists, by the judge subjecting the adolescent to examination by ordering two trustworthy people to look under his or her clothes to see whether or not the signs of puberty exist.[23] This has recently been applied in the Grand Court of Makkah in the case of *A*, would be held reponsible for such an accident, his attainment of *al-Bulugh* or physical maturity had to be established first. Therefore, the judge ordered some trustworthy men to look for the signs of puberty under the boy's clothes. Having found that the boy had not developed the necessary thick pubic hair to be considered physically mature, the judge acquitted the boy of responsibility for the accident, since such responsibility was based only on his confession which was invalidated by lack of maturity.

However, in a case where the matter was not so serious as it was in the above case, the method of determination prescribed by the court would be quite different. Instead of stripping the adolescent to confirm *al-Bulugh*, the judge would usually ask the witness, who knew the adolescent well, to testify that he or she had become *Baligh*, physically mature, and capable of sensibly managing his or her own affairs.

This is to be demonstrated by the case of *Kh v. S.*[25] *D, Kh's*, agent, who was also her uncle, applied to the court for his neice to be declared *Baligh* and *Rashid* in order to terminate the power of her guardian (her uncle S) and oblige him to surrender her property to her.

When the guardian disputed such a claim and insisted that she was still an immature girl, the court requested the plaintiff to prove his allegation. The testimony of two witnesses who testified that *Kh* was fifteen years old and that she was *Rashid* and competent to manage her own property outweighed the guardian's claim of immaturity. Accordingly, the court declared *Kh* as *Baligh* and *Rashid* without having to resort to looking under her clothes.

The adherence of Saudi courts to the majority view which set fifteen years as the latest possible age of *al-Bulugh* or physical maturity is seen in the case of the boy *A*,[26] the motor cyclist who had an accident on his motor cycle causing the death of the pillion passenger, *S*. When the local authority of Makkah received the decision of the court in respect of this case, an urgent message was sent to the court enquiring about the word *Baligh*, which was used in the court's decision, whether it meant that the boy was physically mature or meant something else. The court's reply indicated that the word *Baligh* meant that the boy was physically mature. This was also explained by adding that when the court asked the boy during investigation about his age, his answer was that he was fifteen. So the court considered him *Baligh* or physically mature. This was clarified further by indicating that it was the court's habit to refer to a boy of physical maturity by using this word *Baligh*. For a boy who is not physically mature, the word *Ghair Baligh*, or undeveloped is used.

AL-RUSHD OR MENTAL MATURITY

The law also attaches great importance to the attainment of *al-Rushd* as the complete attainment of both *al-Bulugh* and mental maturity constitutes the whole faculty, *al-'Aql*. Its importance, as we shall discuss later, becomes apparent in relation to bequest in many respects, from invalidating the appointment of a guardian by the prodigal over his children, to the stipulation that *al-Rushd* is obligatory in anyone who is to be appointed a *Wasi*.

One who attains *al-Rushd* is clearly set out by al-Futuhi as, 'The one who recognized the essentials in theory, (what is necessary or otherwise), what is possible and what is not, what is often deemed to be in the person's favour and interests and what might be harmful'.[27]

Maturity of mind cannot be as easily ascertained by applying some practical tests as other signs might be. However, one can appreciate the usefulness of the method which the jurists provided to estimate the development of the child's mind when nearing adulthood. This was done by observing his level of accomplishment in whatever field he was good at and in whichever sphere was appropriate to his position in the community.

Such methods vary from one person to another according to each one's activity and his position in the community; A farmer's son, for instance, has to have some skills in farming, some knowledge of plants and seeds and the seasons of planting etc. He must also be able to take the product to market, sell it without much loss and prudently save and spend his earnings. The carpenter's son and the merchant's son must also acquire the basic skills in their areas of activity. The application of this principle is seen in the case of *A*.[28]

A, whose father died leaving him in the care of a *Wasi*, applied to the court to declare him *Baligh* and *Rashd* with particular emphasis on the termination of his guardian's power over him and the claim that the guardian hand over his property to him.

Being the son of a merchant who was expected to continue his father's business, *A* was requested to present sufficient proof not only of his attainment of *al-Bulugh* but also, by producing the precise evidence upon which *al-Rushd* is based, to confirm his suitability and ability to deal with his merchandise. Two trustworthy witnesses testified that *A* was able to manage his own property, to deal without loss and earn enough to prove his *Rushd* adequately.

A young girl has also the same rights as those of a boy, we must use adequate methods to test her abilities of adjustment to her community such as her ability to pay for her domestic commodities, buy her knitting wool and clothes, manage her house and to look after her father, mother, brothers and sisters, etc. This is the case of *F*.[29]

Two witnesses testified that she was *Baligh* and able to manage her own property herself and that she was actually in charge of her house. This testimony was apparently the kind of qualifications needed to obtain the court's declaration of her *Bulugh* and *Rushd* and this was followed by her release from the care of her guardian and the order that he should deliver her property to her. It is interesting to note that the same decision was taken for both *F* and *A* who were brother and sister.

A criterion was established to ensure that when applying the principle of *al-Rushd* we do not go as far as to demand perfection in all actions conducted by the young and the interdicted prodigal but to accept adequate and fair conduct, as it was stated by the jurists that: 'The under-trained person ought not to be observed to be defrauded by an excessive loss.'

The original idea of proving the *Rushd* of the young and the prodigal before validating their actions was initiated by the text of the *Quran* in the following fragments of two verses, 'But do not give up the fools (and the prodigals) their property which *Allah* has made you to stand by; but maintain them from it, and cloth them, and speak to them with reasonable speech' and 'Prove orphans until they reach a marriageable age, and if you perceive in them right management, then hand over to them their property, and do not devour it extravagantly in anticipation of their growing . . .'[30]

The meaning of the quoted verses is so clear that it need not be mentioned that the ruling does not just apply to orphans but includes every immature person, whether the abnormality occurs after the coming of age because of a defective mind or merely because the age of maturity has not yet been reached.

Meanwhile, the law takes considerable care to clarify the person's position as to capacity, ability and suitability which have a great effect upon his or her conduct. It is even more indispensible, in respect of voluntary and bilateral acts, to take into account the adequacy of each person's state of mind, since this is a principal factor in such deals.[31] As it is a maxim in law that the person's state of mind is the most vulnerable to any criticism intended to invalidate the deals a person involved himself in,[32] it is the defects in the donor's personality, more than anything else, that we should discuss fully.

THOSE WITH DISORDERED MINDS

Mental handicap and abnormality occur mostly as a result of injury to the brain to cease growing or functioning properly. It might also stem from an infectious attack on the central nervous system or from physical or emotional shock. A brain deficiency might also be the outcome of mental retardation or heredity.

As mental deficiency varies considerably in its manifestations, we must carefully consider the effect of it on the legality of conduct.

For a person whose insanity is utter and complete his conduct in all circumstances is considered null and void. The same is true when considering the irrational behaviour of a person during attacks of lunacy. But when the affected person's conduct is proved to have occurred during a lucid interval, such conduct will be validated as he will be considered sane at the time of lucidity.[33] However, controversy has resulted with regard to an already executed bequest made during a pre-insanity period, as to whether such a bequest should be granted the law's approval as a de facto or not; discussion of this will follow later.

As for other less chronic states of deficiency of the *Ma'tuh* (idiot), whose conversation, if coherent at all, is studded with those inaccuracies and improbabilities that are described as confabulation. This is because of the amnesiac disturbances which can swing abruptly between the two parameters of acuteness and temporary remission leading to the situation that a person acts or makes statements without purpose or sense of direction because of the inability to remember what he has done before. These reasons lead to the principle of interdiction being imposed on the idiot and senile person as it is thought to be in his interest to protect him and preserve his property.

These were exactly the reasons which induced the Grand Court of Makkah to impose interdiction of 'A, in the case of *H v. 'A*.[33]

H, the son of 'A, had applied to the court to impose interdiction and appoint a guardian to his father 'A who was confirmed by the testimony of two witnesses to be *Ma'tuh*, or idiot, it being said that he was confused and that due to his old age he was not able to manage his property and was not aware of what he was saying. The court agreed with this and appointed his son, *H*, as his guardian, to look after him and his interests.

From this case it is apparent that the court does not only treat a senile person as a *Ma'tuh* (idiot) but also refers to him as *Ma'tuh*. This is because both have lost the sense of direction and purpose.

The position of the *Ma'tuh* (idiot and senile person), who is subjected to interdiction varies according to the acuteness or the degree of temporary remission of the deficiency. If such deficiency hinders *al-Rushd* entirely causing a serious threat to his status in society, he will be treated by his guardian as a non-discretional infant and thus prevented entirely from engaging in any business at all. Such is illustrated in the case of *'A v. S.*[35]

'A, the niece of *S*, had appealed to the court to appoint a guardian to her uncle, whom she claimed to have been *Ma'tuh* for twenty years, on the grounds of his inability to deal prudently with his property and his inability, also, to care for himself. As her claim was supported by adequate proof and as she was confirmed to be trustworthy and able to look after her uncle, *S*, he was declared *Ma'tuh* and she was the appointed financial guardian to deal with all his property.

However, if deficiency is so mild that it does not seem to hinder *al-Rushd* entirely, then the imposition of interdictiion will not be absolute but will be relaxed in a way comparable to that of the prodigal whose bequest will be validated so long as it disposes only of his property but which, if it disposes of the power of guardianship over his children, the bequest will be null and void.[36]

Prodigality is a state which is defined not from any apparent or conspicuous defects of the mind since the manner of finding out the scope of prodigality is not through discovering a fault or defect of the mind, but rather through simple observation of the manner in which a person spends his money and disposes of his property. This is based on the unanimous opinion of the jurist that an over-extravagant person or one who persistently wastes his propery on trifling things and reaps no benefit, or who spends it on sinful ways, is to be classified as prodigal or *Safih*, and thus to be eligible for the imposition of interdiction.

If such a prodigal is subjected to interdiction, he will be treated in the same way as a child and not as an infant as would be *Ma'tuh* whose deficiency is more serious. Thus, as far as the bequest is concerned, the prodigal will be deprived only of the power to appoint a guardian for his children while his other bequests relating to the disposition of his estate will be validated.

The general meaning of *'Uth* or idiocy might be extended to cover prodigality, and thus to regard prodigality as a less serious form of mental deficiency. Such a link was indicated by the case of *M v. 'A.*[37]

The former petitioned to the court against what she regarded as ultra vires act of divorce carried out by her husband whom she alleged to have been suffering from senility. The court carried out an intensive investigation into the allegation about the state of *'A's* deranged mind at the time the divorce was known to have been effected. At the end of the examination, the court issued a decree declaring the divorce null and void and confiming that the husband was feeble minded. He was also declared as *Ma'tuh* (prodigal) and *Safih*. Thus his wife was restored to the status quo of matrimonial life and he was subjected to interdiction with the appointment of his son, *A*, as a guardian to manage his affairs.

THE EFFECT OF INTOXICATION ON THE ACT OF BEQUEST

Many factors contribute to excessive drinking and excessive drinking leads to intoxication. Where a person's normal behaviour is inclined to aggression this can be aggravated. The natural healthy fighting spirit which enables us to battle with adversity, can be transformed by alcohol into violent outbursts of temper, extreme intolerence, quarrelsomeness and deeply-felt resentment against all. An excessive drinker of alcohol generally suffers from a personality disorder which often shows itself in other forms of anti-social behaviour.[38]

Because personality disturbance distinguishes the drunkard in the throes of intoxication, the jurists tend to nullify any bequest made by him. A testator who is drunk at the time the bequest is being concluded cannot have the necessary sense on understanding as to the nature of bequest. Further, the bequest made during intoxication could harm his heirs according to his feeling towards them at the time.

As many drugs were probably unknown or untested by the old jurists we are left without specific and recognizable rules in respect of the drug addict.[39] Nevertheless, the drugged person could be treated, with regard to his ability to bequeath and the validity of his bequest, similarly to a drunken person.

The analogy is fitting since, the profound effect of drugs on the individual mind is almost comparable to that of alcohol in the sense that, firstly, it makes the user more passive and, secondly, it doubles his sensitivity and, thirdly, its effect is faster than alcohol.

It is a fact that almost the entire world has come to realize the side effects of drugs on the drug addict himself and on his society. This explains the determined effort to stop the growing of drugs and their smuggling into countries. It explains also the foundation of special hostels and clinics to help cure drug addicts. Saudi Arabia has contributed to the efforts to halt the spread of drugs into Arabia by imposing severe penalties, (imprisonment of up to fifteen years), for smuggling, dealing in and use of.[40]

CERTAIN CASES CONCERNING MOTIVES

The Prophet is reported to have said: 'The blame is lifted from my people for whatever they do mistakenly, from absence of mind or under coercion.'[41]

WITHOUT CONSCIOUS CONTROL

A person without conscious control is, in all circumstances, unaccountable for the unguarded and thus unintended statements he makes in regard to any contract he seems to approve.

The same rule also applies to the sleeping person where we should not hold a dreaming person accountable for what he says. However rational the statement or the bequest of the unconscious or the sleeping person may be, it is to be of no legal validity at all.[42]

THE ABSENT MINDED PERSON

This is the person who acquires the necessary legal capacity having prudent judgement and being of sound mind but who is classified as a forgetful person. The frequency is of no matter to us; what concerns us more, is the effect this has on him and on others.

It is not odd or unusual for anyone to say or even do certain things which he, in actual fact, does not intend, because of a slip of the tongue or a mental lapse. This is natural since there are situations everywhere in our daily life, no matter how trivial and insignificant, that may easily divert our attention from the prime objective thus causing us to say something other than that which we really meant and would have said had we not been distracted.

Both in a common sense and in a legal sense, unless such absence of mind constitutes a hardship on the part of others, no rational legislation would present a logical reason to hold a person accountable for his mistake.

The *Shari'a* for its part, does not hold a man liable for his mistakes.[43] Within the scope of this comes the bequest which will have no value in reality nor in law, as the testator, if unsatisfied with a bequest made, can in due course revoke it.

DURESS AND UNDUE INFLUENCE

The case of a compelled person is utterly unlike any of the above cases. The mind of the person concerned is properly functioning. The person is aware of what is going on, unlike a man who is unconscious. Undue influence is a novelty for it is a factor which does not originate within the mind itself but is rather, extrinsic. In this instance, the person would not act according to the merits of his pure action but would act in accordance to the forcibly dictated wishes of the person exercising duress who intimidates or threatens to inflict some kind of violence to cause injury to the person concerned or to his interests.

In order for the law to nullify the effect of an action made under duress, the threats must be genuine and be made by a person capable of putting them into action.[44] However, the equitable doctrine is that where a person enters into an agreement or makes a disposition of property under circumstances which give rise to the presumption that he has not been allowed to exercise a free and deliberate judgement on the matter, it will be set aside and the act done under duress will generally be invalidated, for the Prophet says: 'The blame is lifted from my people for whatever they do mistakenly, from absence of mind or under coercion.'

Although the Hanbali doctrine prima facie invalidates such actions, nevertheless, it still leaves an option open for a disposition under duress to be validated if the person concerned, subsequently, approves it.[45]

In respect of bequest, the likelihood of coercion prevailing upon the testator is slim, because a major principle in the law of bequest gives liberty to testators to revoke any bequest made under any sort of duress. Yet, the importance of this rule cannot always be illuminated by the principle of revocation. This is because a testator, after being compelled to write his bequest or to utter it in front of witnesses, might die without having had access after the event to papers or to trusted witnesses in front of whom he could repeal the compelled bequest.

THE JESTING PERSON

Although, jesting is desirable, humour might sometimes become undesirable in relation to law. This matter is quite distinct from the previous cases. In the first two cases, the person could be said to utter statements which he neither understood in essence nor had any intention of implementing. However, in the third case, he has the necessary intention to make himself liable for the agreement he has entered into but the *Shari'a*, realizing the weakness of man in the face of fear, deems these actions invalid unless the person concerned approves of them afterwards, for the Prophet (peace be upon him) says: 'The blame is lifted from my people for whatever they do mistakenly, from the absence of mind or under coercion.'

The case of a jesting person, though distinguished from those above, has one feature in common with each of the preceding cases. For instance, the joker has no intention of carrying out his words and putting them into effect although he has pronounced them consciously and not in fear, but in accordance with his free will. Owing to all these facts, the legislator in his attempt to preserve the *Shari'a* and keep it from becoming the subject of derision or being treated facetiously gives the joker's words legal effectiveness.

This is thought to come from a precedent set by the Prophet by stating 'entering into marriage, divorce and emancipating slaves are to be taken seriously, (be legally binding), when they are done in earnest. They are also to be taken seriously and to be legally binding when they are done jokingly.'[46]

It is clear that giving the joker's words their full effect, is meant to be a kind of punishment, thus to deter people from making fun of others and joking at the expense of others.

An attempt to clarify the attitude of the *Shari'a* towards the joker's statements was made by Ibn al-Qayim. He defended such attitudes by analogy on the grounds of the relationship between cause and effect as such, 'A joker's actions will be considered to be legally binding as if they were of serious consequence and he has no power of retraction. The joker by his words meant to instigate the cause but he overlooked its effects. However, as a matter of law, when one instigates causes one has to expect (and abide by) the rules, whether one likes it or not'.[47]

Of course, if one's statement has been recorded in a sort of written document, one's intention will be presumed and thus will prevail in the absence of evidence to the contrary and be validated whether the document be an ordinary contract or a bequest.

NOTES

1. *Sh. Muntaha al-Inadat*, Vol. 1, 142.
2. *Al-fath al-rabbani* (a commentary and rearrangement of Al-Musnad of Ibn Hanbal), Vol. 2, 237, and also reported by al-Tirmithi and Abu Dawood. See *Al-Mu'jam Al-Mufahras*, Vol. 4, 325.
3. *Childhood and Adolescence*, 53.
4. *Al-Muharrar fi Al-Hadith*, 187.
5. *Sh. al-muntaha*, pp. 265-266, Vol. 3 and Kash, Vol. 3, 330.
6. *Al-muntaha*, Vol. 2, 338, and *al-Tanqih al-Mushbi*, 260.
7. G.C. Makkah, Vol.XV, (138OAH/1960AD), 55. Dr M.I.A. Ali Thesis, 120-121, London University, 1971.
8. *Al-muntaha*, Vol. 2, 338 and *Al-Tanqih al-Mushbi'*, 260, *Sh. Muntaha*, Vol. 3, 264/266.
9. G.C. Makkah. P. Reg. of Sh. Fatani, Vol. XVI, (1379H/1959AD), 115. M.I.A. Ali Thesis, 132, London University, 1971.
10. Matalib, Vol. 1, 277 Vol. 5, 669 and *Sh. Munt.*, Vol. 3, 545 and K. Vol. 3, 335.
11. Ibn al-Qayim, *Tuhfat al-mawdud*, 291.
12. Al-Futuhi, *Al-muntaha*, Vol. I, 51.
13. G.C. Makkah No. 88, Vol.I, 138OH.
14. G.C. Makkah No. 26, Vol.3, 1380H.
15. G.C. Makkah No. 106, Vol.1, 1376H.
16. *Tanqih*, 122-123.
17. G.C. Makkah No. 27, v. I, 1381H.
18. G.C. of Jedda, No. 64. v. 6. Joint Reg. of 1360-61-62H.
19. *Al-Iqna'*, Vol. 3, 47.
20. Reported by Ibn Majah. See *al-Mu'jam al-Mufahras*, Vol. 6, 316.
21. *Sh. Munt*, Vol. 2, 290.
22. Ibid, Vol.2, 289.
23. Ibid, Vol.1, 141.
24. G.C. Makkah, No. 109, Vol. 6, 1378H.
25. G.C. Makkah, No. 88, Vol. I, 1380H.
26. Makkah Court of first instance, No. 2/2768, file B/24 1386H.
27. *Al-Muntaha*, Vol. 2, 657 *Sharh Muntaha al-Iradat*, Vol. 3, 545.
28. G.C. Makkah, No. 84, Vol.6, 1378H.
29. G.C. Makkah, No. 84, Vol. 6, 1378H.
30. *Qur'an, II (the Women), 5-6.*
31. Mustafa Ahmad Al-Zarqa, *Al-Madkhal al-fiqhi al-amm,* Vol. I, 591.
32. Abdulmajid al-Hakeem, *Al-Wasit fi nazariyat al-'aqd,* 102-103.
33. *Sh. Muntaha,* Vol. 2, 539, and *Kashaf,* Vol. 4, 336-337.
34 .G.C. Makkah, No. 90, Vol. I, 138H.
35. G.C. Makkah, No. 178, Vol. I, 1380H.
36. *Sh. Munt*, Vol.2, 539, and *Munt.*, Vol. 2, 303, and *Kash*, Vol. 4, 336.
37. G.C. of Makkah, No. 181, Vol. 6, 1378H.
38. Lincoln Williams, *Alcoholism explained*, 42/47.
39. Ahmad b. Mohammad Al-Mangur, *Al-Fawakih al-'adidah*, Vol. 2, 84-86.
40. Royal Decree No. II, date 1/2/1374 H. Article (2). The regulation of drugs.
41. Reported by Ibn Majah, see *Al-Mu'jam al-Mufahras*, Vol. 6, 6/443.
42. Ibn Qudama, *al-Rawdah*, 27.
43. *Muntaha*, Vol. 2, 302, and *Al-Rawdah*, 27 and *A'lam*, Vol. 3, 39-40, 91, 137.
44. *Munt*, Vol. 2, 302/684, *Insaf*, Vol. 4, 265, and *A'lam al-muwaqqi*, Vol. 3, 159, and *Al-Rawdah*, 27.
45. *Insaf*, Vol. 4, 265.
46. Al-Muwatta'. See *Al-Mu'jam Al-Mufahras*, Vol. 4, 126.
47. *A'lam al-muwaqqi'in 'an rabb al-'alamin*, Vol. 3, 137-139, 160.

CHAPTER II
FORMATS OF BEQUEST

As in the case of contracts *Al-Wasiya* can be formed in three ways: 1. verbally, 2. in writing, 3. by gesture.

1. The usual manner of things is that a bequest is of a verbal nature. Speech is the main form of communication which binds people in their dealings and deeds. A bequest is only relevant when it has been introduced in audible words which avoids any obscurity and ambiguities.[1]

2. Writing is another method of making a bequest. Writing is, supposedly, to be a substitute for speech when speech is not possible but this is, in fact, not the case in bequest. A written bequest would be accepted as an equivalent to verbal one,[2] despite the fact that the testator is still able to talk. Thus any readable form of writing on any material can be produced for approval. However, if a foreign document is to be submitted to probate in Saudi Arabian courts it is required to have an Arabic translation attached to it.[3]

3. Gesture is the third form of bequest. According to the opinion of certain jurists a bequest formed in such a way could only be regarded as valid as long as a person shows his inability to talk or even to write. The gestured bequest of a person who appears to be temporarily dumb will not be validated but would rather be deferred until he dies when it would be realized that he had become permanently dumb. In the former case, for instance, it became a controvercial point between jurists as to whether a dumb person knows how to write or not.

No one, however, has objected to the right of a dumb person to form a valid bequest by gesture if he is an ignorant person. But there is disagreement between the jurists as to the ruling when the dumb person has the capability of writing. Certain jurists, most of whom are late Hanafis, are of the belief that such a person has to produce his bequest in writing thus making certain his intentions. The Hanablis,[4] on the other hand, accepted a bequest originated by a mute person regardless of the knowledge he possesses because both are ways of expression accepted and adopted by Muslim scholars.

Only a mute person whose state obliges him to use gesture to form a bequest can be considered as equivalent to speech or writing, for it is the only means of expression he has.[5]

However, the Hanbalis, despite their leniency in this respect, seem to have refrained from admitting a testimony made by a mute person unless and until he produced it in writing.[6] This seems to condradict their previous dicta. The Hanbalis, therefore, realizing this, took care to deny that there was any contradiction between the two statements on the grounds that, in the latter instance, a witness is meant to 'Preserve the property, honour and the souls of all people from unlawfully being infringed.'

Thus, a witness has a special responsibility to be devoid of any motive to indite the other party. Likewise, he must be of a vigilant nature. An acceptable attestation has to come from a mature, rational person with the ability to talk, etc., because it requires intelligibility and genuine motivation when he makes his testimony, for it involves the rights of other people, whereas the mute's testimantary action involves merely his own rights. His gesture could be accepted of necessity if it indicates clearly his intentions. This makes the testimony of a witness who is unable to talk unacceptable unless it has been certified in writing.[7]

PHRASES AND CLAUSES ACCEPTED AS BEQUESTS

The format requirements, in this respect, are relatively simple. The formula of bequest, generally speaking, must consist of those phrases agreed upon by the jurists which bear the genuine meaning of the allotment of a property or power by the testator to his *Wasi* or legatee after the death of the said testator.

Some example of the preferable phrases of bequest are as follows: 'I bequeath such and such to Ali', or 'I give him such a thing after my death', or 'It is to him after my death', or the like. But if the testator, when talking about a particular object, should say, it is Ali's without providing the explicit clause, i.e. after my death, it would not be construed as a bequest matter but would rather be interpreted as an *Iqrar*, acknowledgement, or a kind of intevivos donation which is liable to take effect and be discharged prior to death. It has been accepted that the intention to bequeath is also inferred to by the addition of this clause, 'from my estate', following any of the above forms.

There has never been a particularly rigid obligatory form of bequest to be followed strictly. This means that the law is flexible enough to enable the testator to utilize his own vocabulary to the maximum, and he may use such expressions he deems suitable so long as he clarifies that such a disposition is never to take effect prior to his death.

However, despite what is stated above, it is reported that certain companions of the Prophet pursued a rather strictly worded form with slight variations in their holographic testaments. An example of a pattern of form of documented bequest which has been widely adopted lately is as follows:

'In the name of *Allah*, the most gracious most merciful'
This is the testament of so and so who bear witness that there is no God except *Allah*, alone with no associate; Muhhammad is his slave and Messenger; Paradise is true so is Hell; doomsday is (no doubt) coming and *Allah* resurrects those in graves.
I enjoin my family to fear *Allah* and to reconcile their differences, to obey *Allah* and his Messenger if they are to remain believers, I prescribe to them what *Ibrahim* 'the Prophet' prescribed to his children and *Jacob*, 'O my children *Allah* has chosen for you the religion, do not die unless you are Muslims'.[8]

The end of the processed preface marks the embarkment on the subsequent stage where the testator states his intention to bequeath by inserting thereafter the chosen phrases which establish his commitments and commands.

Nevertheless, it should not cross anybody's mind that the adoption of certain forms could be obligatory. For the jurists realizing this fact emphasised the fact that, any form, phrase or clause that states positively the intentions of the testator will be sufficient. Henceforth, the adoption of the above form of document would merely be *Mustahab,* or praiseworthy.[9]

However, the Saudi courts, although they are known for their adherence to the precedents and traditions for some reason or another do not apply the aforementioned form. In authenticating a bequest they usually omit the recommended preface.The contemporary bequests issued by *Katab al-'Adl* are usually witnessed as to the identity of the testator. This is followed up by the detailed items of the bequest. The document is then concluded with the testimony phrase that such a document was read to the testator and signed by him in the prescence of the undersigned witnesses. Such tendency is demonstrated in the case of *Ibn 'A.*[10]

STIPULATION TO ACCOMPANY THE FORM OF BEQUEST

The common bequest

A bequest could either take the form of restricted bequest or be left bare of any sort of limitation. However, if no limitations are mentioned in the form then the bequest will be of a general nature, for example 'I bequeath such and such to *Zaid* after my death,' or 'I leave a third of my estate to *Zaid* when I die.' This is when the bequest has no conditions attached at all. On the other hand restricted type of bequest falls into two categories. These are as follows:

Al-Wasiya al-mu'allaqa or the restricted bequest

The restricted bequest is a bequest which contains a stipulated condition. If such a condition exists, it prevents the whole bequest from coming into effect until that stipulated condition is fulfilled. This kind of restricted bequest, according to its condition, becomes either a *Mu'allaqa* (suspended) or *Mudafa ila Waqt* (time related) bequest, as follows:

a. Al-Wasiya al-mu'allaqa *or suspended bequest*

This is a bequest the validity of which would be suspended till the contingent condition be satisfied. A bequest as such becomes suspended when the testator makes a bequest whilst ill, travelling or when he happened to be doing something or expecting something to happen in the future. In such a situation the testator suspends the validity of the thing he desires until the condition be fulfilled.

In order for a testator to suspend his bequest until the occurrence of an event, that event or condition bequest must be a probability, or at least a possibility. The satisfaction of this requirement is of substantial significance to the validity of such a bequest.

The testator has, of course, a right to state the time at which the event he made conditional is expected to take place. Accordingly, the testator may make the efficacy of his bequest dependent upon something happening during his life time, such as his saying: 'I donate the sum of £100 to the local pensioner's home in my town if I die from this illness or if I die during this journey, etc'. This sort of bequest will be carried out only when in the former case the mentioned illness constitutes the causation of his death or, in the second case, when his death occurs during that particular journey.

However, should the testator in the former bequest, first recover from his illness and then die, such a bequest will become null and void for the condition he put upon it was unsatisfied. So it will be in the latter case when his journey ends prior to his death.

To exemplify this sort of bequest from the Saudi practice we cite a case in which a father had bequeathed 3,000 SR. to his youngest daughter to be delivered to her when she married a *Kuf'* or competent person. This was intended to be equivalent to the assistance he had given to her sisters when they had married.

However, to be fair to his other daughters, he enclosed a conditional cancellation clause upon which the validity of his bequest depended. This was that if his daughter should marry during his life, the bequest was to be revoked. This, therefore, prevented her from taking twice as much of his favour as her sisters did.[11]

A bequest will also be validated when the testator says: 'I bequeath the third of my property to Hasan but if he dies before me, the third goes to Bakr'.

The testator may also make the efficacy of his bequest dependent upon an event which may not occur before the testator's death.[12] An example of this is if a person bequeathes money to send his nephew abroad for further education after graduation. This kind of bequest will be held valid for as long as the said graduation remains probable. But the bequest will be annulled if the condition (i.e. graduation) can no longer be expected to happen. This is because the validation in this case would be disadvantageous and harmful to the testator's heirs through their long and indefinate wait.[13] To show how this has been the practice of Saudi courts we present the following illustrations.

A testator had appointed as executor to adminster his property and to take care of his under age children. He also also appointed another person to act as a *Mushrif* or overseer to supervise all the actions taken by the appointed executor in all matters related to the bequest. He put a suspending condition on the supervision clause that the supervision of the *Mushrif* was to be effective so long as he remained in Jedda. The supervisor would thus terminate the supervision right automatically whenever he lives outside Jedda.[14]

In another case a testator had bequeathed to his wife the right to reside in his dwelling all her life provided she remained unmarried after his death and stayed with their children. Here, it is obvious that the wife's right to the bequeathed residence would stand so long as none of the vitiating conditions effecting such right existed. If for example the wife got married or left her children this would be a vitiating condition.[15]

However, when no time has been stated in a bequest by when an event is expected to take place or where the emphasis is instead put on the suspensive condition itself, the bequest will still be adjudicated valid pending materialization of the suspensive condition. This is in keeping with the principle of freedom conferred on the testator by the *Hadith* which states, 'Conditions made by Muslims are to be respected except a stipulation to turn into permisible what is forbidden or to forbid what is permisible'.[16]

Applying the rules of this *Hadith*, the jurists all agreed to give maximum effect to the suspensive condition in the testator's bequest such as: 'I bequeath my house to Bakr but it is to Zaid when he comes back from his journey'.

Thus, according to the suspensive condition the house becomes Zaid's absolute right if he comes back from that journey any time prior to the testator's death. According to the opinion of certain Hanbali jurists[17] the delay of Zaid's return till after the testator's death would not affect his right in the will. The condition put upon the will would have been satisfied by the return of Zaid. Hence Zaid ought to retain the right to inherit the house whenever he comes.

The majority of the jurists took the other view which was phenomenal to their refuting statement that 'The later coming of Zaid would not by any means be adverse to the right of Bakr in the will which would have been confirmed by the testator's decease'.[18] This view was apparently based on the fact that the right in the will and the time of the will's implementation and distribution is determined by the testator's death rather than by any other factor. The death itself is the condition upon which *Al-Wasiya* will be fulfilled.

Therefore, the transfer of ownership should not be permitted as if Zaid has not actually returned.

The reason given for this is that, at the time of the implementation of the bequest, there was no impediment to it. Hence, the existence of the stipulated condition afterwards has no effect whatsoever as it lost its efficacy by the testator's death before the return of Zaid.

The suspensive condition in the following case is also an illustration of the principle in question. Here the testatrix designated an executor to manage her property, to take the disposable third, to pay out of the third for her funeral expenses and for whatever needed paying and to spend the remaining on benevolent purposes. As the hereditable two-thirds had no legal claimant, she directed the executor to share it equally between himself and her maidservant.

Preparing for the unexpected, the testatrix rearranged her bequest with the inclusion of a new clause: But if an unexpected heir were to appear after the making of this bequest or after her death, then the disposable third is to be halved, spending one half on her funeral rites and whatever is needed to be paid and the remainder is to be shared equally between her executor and her maidservant. Thus, leaving the other two-thirds to be delivered to the heir who had appeared.[19]

As regards the last clause in which the testatrix said 'But if the unexpected heir . . . etc', the difference between the jurists in the case of Zaid and Bakr is applicable here too. This because the executor's and the maidservant's rights in the bequest are to be confined to the remainder of the diposable third at the appearance of a legal heir to the testatrix whether such appearance takes place prior to or after the testatrix's death. This applies, according to the view of the majority, even if the heir vanishes after his stipulated appearance.

Another case could also be taken as illustrative to the above where the testator had designated his wife to administer his estate, to pay for his funeral rites out of the fixed sum of 500 SR and spend the rest on benevolent deeds. She was also designated guardian to look after his children, their upbringing and the preservation of their estate.

To prepare for the unpleasant eventuality of his wife getting married to a stranger with the consequent effects on his children, the testator made the bequest conditional upon her not remarrying. If she remarried the judge would be empowered to execute his bequest.[20]

b. Al-Wasiya al-mudafa ila waqtin mu'ayyan *or the bequest related to a particular time*

As the former instances invariably refer to an unspecified time of occurrence, it is the tendency of such clauses to take into consideration both the outset time attached to the bequest and in another type of restricted bequest, the duration and termination of the period mentioned.

An example of a bequest delayed till a specific time is the testator's saying 'I donate my car to X a month after my death'. The handing over of the specific bequest (the car), to the beneficiary is to be delayed, accordingly, pending the lapse of the preconditioned time to following the testator's death; the conveyance of the bequeathed article is to be postponed for the period of time the testator imposed in the form of stipulated condition. It is a desire that must be respected with reference to the expiry of that period.

The acceptance by the courts of the principle of freedom given to the testator to insert whatever legal conditional clauses he wishes into his bequest is demonstrated by *Katib al-'Adl's* ratification and validation of the kind of bequests in which the testators have utilized such a principle. The following case illustrates this.

All his sons being under age and thus unable legally to carry out his bequest, the father (the testator) appointed a non-related executor to manage his property and carry out his bequest as regards the disposable third. As it was his wish that one of his sons should be able to execute his bequest, he inserted a conditional clause enabling anyone of his sons to take over the execution when possible, i.e. whenever any one of his sons became of full age and mature as the time at which one of his sons became of full age and mature as the time at which the appointment of the designated *Wasi* would be terminated. Thus he made use of the *Wasi's* services while making sure that his bequest would eventually be transferred to one of his sons.[21]

This is also obvious from the case where the testator had conferred the power of the marriage of his daughters to his wife and at the same time he inserted a conditional clause in which he debarred his wife (the marriage guardian) from giving in marriage any of his daughters before she reached the age of majority. Only then could the wife exercise her delegated power.[22]

As for the duration of the time the bequest is to run for, the testator may attach to it a conditional clause limiting such duration: 'I grant the use of my house at . . . to Zaid for the period of one year', or 'I bequeath to my two nephews, Aziz and Ali, the right to live in my house until they attain the age of majority, etc.'.

Such a phrase relating to time must be respected as it is the free will of the then owner of the estate and should not be taken to constitute an intervention or a violation as to the rights of the prospective inheritors who, in any case, would certainly find a way in the *Shari'a* to satisfy their rights from the allocated two thirds of the bulk of the estate.

This assumed to be generally applicable though not strictly confined to usufruct bequests, which do not concern the transfer of the article itself but only benefits and the manner in which it is therefore to be used. Thus such bequests do not affect the ownership in any way. In some ways they are similar to the *Waqf* or trust, in another way they are dissimilar. This matter will be discussed fully later.

Application of this is seen in the case where *Katib al-'Adl,* permitted the testator to limit the duration of his bequest when in his bequest he said: 'I, the testator, grant my wife the usufruct of residing in my house for the duration of her life'.[23]

The ownership of the bequeathed article itself will not be transferred to the possession of the legatee as a consequence of such a bequest but only the revenue or the use during a fixed period of time. At the same time, the benefit which was made the subject matter of such a bequest becomes returnable to the collective possession of the testator's heirs at the expiry of that defined period.

The following case is also an indication of such application where the testator, seeing the importance of his wife being with their minors in the same house and the loss to them if she were to leave them, granted his wife the right to reside in his house as long as she remained with them.[24]

The same is also extendable to the conferred power of executorship and the guardianship as illustrated in the following case.

The testatrix bequeathed the remainder of the disposable third (after the payment of funeral expenses and the discharge of her debts), to a girl minor. For the same reason she designated her daughter as executor to preserve the bequeathed property for the minor only while she was still under age. This prevented the *Wasi* from retaining such power over the girl after her becoming of full age, even though the girl might need such help because she had not attained sufficient maturity to deal with her own property. The power of the *Wasi* was limited up to the advent of puberty. In such a case the power would devolve upon the girl's *Wali* if there was one or to a suitable *Wali* appointed by judge.[25]

THE DEGREE OF PROOF REQUIRED TO PROVE A BEQUEST

It is a natural thing that the only way to prove an oral bequest is through the testimony of witnesses. An accepted testimony where the bequest is related to property is that of two male persons or the testimony of one male and two female witnesses where the appointment of guardians to look after the testator's minors is concerned, the only attestation acceptable is that of two male witnesses.[26]

A witness whose testimony is acceptable must be a person who is generally known to be trustworthy or one who is not known to have committed any offence or sin which is likely to damage his reputation and to violate the *Shari'a*.

The compliance of the Saudi judiciary to this principle is well illustrated by the statement of the late *Mufti* of Saudi Arabia who, in reply to an enquiry from *Katib al-'Adl* of Mecca, had made it clear that the acceptability of the witness's testimony does not depend on him being proved suitable or competent before bearing witness. His suitability can be judged from the observation of his previous engagements and commitments.[27]

The law does not ignore the significance of the act of writing as another means of proof. Indeed the precedent has been set for this by the authoritatively reported *Hadith* of Ibn Umar, 'What right has a Muslim having some property which may be bequeathed, to sleep for two nights, unless his bequest is written'.

A holgraphic bequest, although considered to have an identical role to a spoken one, is preferable to that of the verbally established one according to the jurists. Writing is more definite in making clear the actual motivation and meaning of the testator. Once the written bequest has been ratified and construed, this must serve as an ascertaining factor against any possible dispute.

The degree of proof required for the confirmation of a propounded bequest differs substantially from one case to another, whether a bequest be oral or written.

A testator who wishes to conclude a bequest in a verbal form has to bear in mind that his bequest could not be carried out without it being presented to whoever acquires the capacity of bearing a testimony. For an intended bequest which lacks witnesses will be inconsistent and useless. However, there are four ways to ensure and secure the ratification of any orally made bequest admitted to probate after the death of the testator.

a. The witnesses have to testify that the will they witnessed was, to the best of their knowledge, the will of such and such a person. They have also to testify that the bequest was accomplished with the testator's full knowledge and capability. Demonstratory evidence of the application of this principle in Saudi courts is offered to us in the case of *D v. R.*[28]

Q had made a bequest and appointed a *Wasi*. The agent of the plaintiff, who was the daughter of the testator *Q*, sought to exploit this principle thus to nullify such a bequest on the grounds that the father was allegedly a *Ma'tuh*, mentally deficient and consequently that he was unfit to bequeath as he would not know what he was doing.

This claim entails a tacit accusation against the witnesses of the bequest the validity of which depended on their trustworthiness. The court therefore summoned the witnesses of the bequest and those of the plaintiff and subjected them to an extensive and thorough examination which resulted in the confirmation of the ability and the soundness of mind of the testator. So in view of the unsubstantiated nature of the allegation and the established competency of the bequest's witnesses, the court dismissed the case. Consequently the bequest was declared valid and *R,* the designated excutorix, was ordered to carry it out.

The same principle also influenced the confirmation of the case of *Z*,[29] who on an ordinary piece of paper, undersigned by witnesses, had bequeathed the marrying of his daughters and the *Wisaya*, or guardianship, of his minors to *N*. When after the death of the testator, the *Wasi, N* propounded such a bequest to probate, he was requested to present the witnesses of the bequest. The witnesses were ordered to testify that the will was that of *Z* and that he when dies with his wishes had been inscribed on it. Thus, this bequest was declared valid and operative.

b. A bequest claimed by the legatee which has the support of the testator's heirs.[30] However, the prominance of the heir's status as the prospective beneficiaries will prevail. This will tend to minimize the role of the testimony.

The testimony of only one heir is also considered sufficient to certify a bequest. But in order for such a testimony to be acceptable, the law requires the heir to satisfy two conditions: to be trustworthy and to support his testimony on his oath. However, the refusal of the heir to take his oath as required would neither invalidate the bequest entirely nor relieve such an heir of the consequence of his testimony. Thus the testimony will be turned into *Iqrar* or an acknowledgement on the part of the testifying heir. Accordingly he will be ordered to surrender certain proportions of his hereditable share to the legatee. The proportion is to be equivalent to the difference between his share when the acknowledged bequest is operative and his share when it is not, leaving the other heirs to take their full shares.

The subsequent retraction of the testifying heir will have no effect on this rule whatsoever as he will not be allowed to retract his acknowledgement. This principle has ostensibly influenced the court's decision in the case of *S*,[3] as follows:

S, one of the heirs who had survived his grandfather, testified that his grandfather had dedicated his house in perpetuity to the mosque he had earlier donated as *Waqf* or trust. As his co-heirs all denied that such a trust had been made, *S* retracted his testimony (later known as his acknowledgement), and alleged that his acknowledgement stemmed from his misunderstanding and that he was plainly mistaken.

Unable to convince the court, he was held responsible for his acknowledgement and an order was made for his share in the house to be taken over by the trustee of the Public *Awqaf* (plural of *Waqf*).

c. A bequest pronounced by a travelling person just before his death in the presence of Muslims or even non-Muslims who are capable of bearing witness is accepted as a valid bequest by the *Shari'a*. The witnesses present at the death bed of a person are obliged to carry his bequest and chattels to his relatives or to the nearest *Hakim* (judge or *Amir*), to be dealt with accordingly.

However, to confirm a bequest made in such a situation where the heirs have a growing suspicion that the conveyors have altered the original bequest, or where there is an item missing from the deceased's chattels, the judge is orderd by the text of the *Quran*, to take their affidavits in the form of oaths after prayer time. They (the conveyors) must swear that they have not betrayed, lied, altered nor suppressed any of it and that they have conveyed the testator's bequest precisely as he told them to do.

The heirs have then to resign themselves to the fact that their suspicion was unfounded. But in the event of the discovery that the conveyors of the bequest were liars and misappropriators, the heirs are permitted to re-present the charge supported by the new evidence they have against them before the judge who seeks as a means of confirmation the plaintiffs' oaths, after which a decree is issued commanding the defendants (the conveyors), to satisfy the heirs with adequate recompence and remedy.[32]

The case of *Ibn Z* demonstrates the operation of these principles in the Saudi courts.[33]

In this case *Al-Y* who was on his way back to Yeman after performing the ritual *Hajj* (pilgrimage), had fallen ill. *Ibn Z* had volunteered to nurse him. After *Al-Y 's* death *Ibn Z* informed the court of what had happened and that *Al-Y* had bequeathed to him and to his wife the total of twenty-four sheep and that he had the property the deceased had with him in his custody.

Going over the inventory of the deceased's property, the judge ordered *Ibn Z* (the supposed conveyor of the deceased's property), to swear the required oath that he did not keep or know of any property of the deceased except that mentioned in the submitted inventory.

In the light of the presented testimony which established the alleged bequest, the court approved the two bequest totalling twenty-four sheep and ordered the rest of the property to be delivered to the Amir of Rufaidah to pass on, in his turn, to *Bait al-mal* (Public treasury) of Abha pending the emergence of an heir to the deceased, or failing that, it was to become the absolute property of the Public Treasury.

d. Verbal bequests might, in certain situations, be put into writing before or after the testator's death. Such a way of certifying a bequest is mostly done in a state of illness. However, although the testator might himself ask for his verbal bequest to be recorded in writing, the witnesses are, generally speaking, the initiators of the bequest for writing. In doing so they are therefore required to include the full name of the testator and the legatee in such a way as to describe the position of the testator indicative of his state of mind and to record the words of the testator as precisely as they possibly can and print their names with their signatures, seals or thumbprints.

This type of ordinary certified bequest is illustrated in the case of *Al-Y's* bequest to *Ibn Z*,[34] as follows:

In this case five people came to pay homage to the ill *Al-Y*. Before the visitors walked out of his room, *Al-Y* asked them to bear witness of what he bequeathed to his host *Ibn Z*. When they left, they printed *Al-Y's* verbal bequest, witnessing it with their names and signatures or thumbprints on a piece of paper and delivered it to the legatee, who had nursed the testator for almost a year.

(The death of a foreign subject has to be made known to the authorities according to the legal regulations, in order to investigate the cause of his death. As to the estate of the dead, the regulations make it the obligation of the director of *Bait al-mal* to appropriate it waiting his legal heirs to ascertain their relationship to the dead and claim it).[35] *Ibn Z*, the host of *Al-Y*, complying with this regulation hurriedly informed the authorities of *Al-Y's* death and appealed to the court to ratify the bequest made to him of the nineteen sheep.

Following the usual processes in such a situation, the witnesses were examined by the judge and their testimony was accepted. Also two witnesses testified that the deceased had bequeathed five sheep to the wife of *Ibn Z* for her services and their testimony was accepted too. Consequently, the director of Bait al-mal, was ordered to appropriate the assets of the deceased with the exception of the twenty-four sheep which the deceased had left to *Ibn Z* and his wife.

The confirmation of an illiterate mute's bequest by witnesses is hardly different from the above mentioned verbal bequest. But should the mute testator be capable of writing and wishes to draw up his bequest, the confirmation of his bequest will then be no different from that applied to the written bequest.

THE WRITTEN BEQUEST

The holographic bequest

A holographic bequest is a bequest which is entirely prepared and drawn up by the testator himself, dated and signed in his own handwriting.

People, usually, tend to keep their bequests away from other people. They do so by avoiding attestation of their deeds, because they therein explicitly detail their personal affairs, which for some reason or other, they prefer to preserve in secrecy.

The legislature appreciating this attitude and the weakness of man has validated this type of holographic bequest (despite the risk of forgery), in the famous recited *Hadith* of Ibn Umar, viz, 'What right has a Muslim, having something to be bequeathed, to sleep for two nights unless his will is written.'

However, in the application of this *Hadith* the jurists, particularly Imam Ahmad b. Hanbal, realizing that the risk of forgery has always existed, restricted the validity of a holographic bequest by permitting it only for the testator whose handwriting is recognizable.[36]

The bequest under seal

In contrast to the verbal bequest is the written one, which has different modes of preparation and confirmation, i.e. written by witnesses, lawyers etc. A holographic bequest, under certain circumstances, requires no attestation at all. In this way the *Sharia* attempts to alleviate the inconvenience and hardship and to further ease the application of the last desires of the deceased. To discuss these forms of written bequest we first proceed to consider the most common formats of the written bequest.

The commonest one in this category is the bequest written in the testator's own hand. Here he is likely to use his own expressions, which are so significant in indicating the testator's real intentions and elucidating implicitly his motives or *animus testendi*. In addition to all this the testator, by so doing, avoids his private life, pious dedications and business secrets being revealed.

Taking into consideration these reasons *Katib al-'Adl* apparently ratified this type of bequest, as is illustrated in the case[37] in which the testator detailed the unsecretive clause such as the designation of an executor by name to manage his property, to pay the funeral expenses and to distribute the unbequeathed portions of his estate between his legal heirs. His published bequest also declared the executor to become a guardian of the testator's children with the appointment of two other named overseers to the *Wasi* to advise him on the best ways of carrying out the bequest. However, the testator refrained from revealing all items bequeathed in this published authenticated document. Instead he contented himself with the insertion of a clause in his documented bequest in which he referred to another secretly written bequest containing other dispositions. This he signed and delivered to his *Wasi* whom he instructed to implement it precisely.

A more precise case which illustrates the above reasons for such action is the case of *M*,[38] which was also authenticated and validated officially by *Katib al-'Adl*.

The testator, *M*, had designated two executors to jointly provide him with suitable grave clothes and bury him in ordinary Muslim tradition. As to the proposed dispositions in the way of bequest he did not think it wise to record it here nor wished it to be disclosed simply because, as he stated, 'It contained some pious dedications and also contained the secrets of his business which were related to the N B of Trade.' Accordingly, he had written a separate bequest which contained such dispositions and secrets and attested it, finally instructing his two joint executors to execute and follow that secretly written will literally.

In short, three reasons might have been behind *Katib al-'Adl's* approval of such bequests; to sustain testator's right to avoid disclosure of his private secrets; to avoid causing loss to the testator if his bequest involves his trade secrets, or it might have stemmed from the wish to encourage as many testators as possible to authenticate their bequests themselves thus to avoid any controversy arising about it afterwards. It could perhaps have been the combination of all these factors. These points are, in addition to *Katib al-'Adl's* approval of it, perhaps an acceptance of the aforementioned classical principle which accepts recognizable hand writing and the signature of the deceased.

Position of the testator's signature

In the case of a holographic bequest the testator is not bound as to where to sign the testamentary document, whether it be at the foot or the end of such document or elsewhere. This issue has only recently been posed. Traditionally, Muslims have maintained the habit of writing their names in the middle or more frequently at the start of the deeds they sign.

The rule governing the deeds of the illiterate man who cannot write his bequest himself is determined by the usage. He is to be asked to put his seel or thumbprint at the end of the document either before or after the signatures of the witnesses.That is in addition to his name being recorded in the forefront of the document itself.

Is the testator's signature required?

An unsigned passage which appears on the face of it to be a bequest, if found by the death-bed of a person, will be taken to represent his last will, provided the writing is known to be his. Also, a statement containing an acknowledgement of a debt or a claim of a debt can be heard provided that such a claim or acknowledgement is found in an account book known to have been used by the deceased. Reference to the above are seen in certain statement of the old jurists where they, tacitly, legalized an unsigned testamentary document. This has also been hinted at in the aforementioned *Hadith* of Ibn Umar, 'What right has a Muslim having something to bequeath, to sleep for two nights unless his bequest is written,' where there is no reference to either signature or witnesses being required, provided, of course, that the handwriting is well known as we have said earlier. Applying this principle *Katib al-'Adl,* permitted the testator in a case to insert in his bequest a clause that he had presented his named executor with a list of outstanding debts which he had instructed him to discharge from the disposable third.[39]

Ibn al-Qayim, on his part, had contributed to this when he made it legal for an heir to go so far as to swear that so and so owes such and such to the deceased. That is so when the heir finds that such a claim is recorded in the deceased's written accounts provided, Ibn al-Qayim added, that the handwriting is known and the deceased was a trustworthy person. In the same manner as a means of defence to a petitioner's claim the heir, Ibn al-Qayim also stated, may swear that a debt has been paid if from the deceased's accounts the heir is convinced that the deceased had discharged the claim.[40]

Such views indicate the minimal role, if any, the courts attached to the signature being personally signed in a document. The only envisaged rule a signature could play to certify a document is where the document has been drawn up by someone else and we can be sure that such a document was drawn up with the testator's knowledge only if it is signed by him.

The above view of Ibn al-Qayim was followed by *Katib al-'Adl,* in a case presented to him.[41] The testator in his bequest had instructed that the named executor was to discharge whatever debts he owed and also to receive his due credits which he found recorded in his business accounts.

The unofficially attested bequest

This is more definite bequest than the holographic bequest. A holographic bequest might be covered under this heading but, since this would only be if a new element had been adduced, (i.e. witnesses), which has the power to eliminate uncertainty, we prefer to place it under a separate heading.

Included, also, under this heading, is a bequest written under the testator's direction by one who then reads it to him (the testator). This applied also when the bequest is later read to witnesses who sign it. The importance of the signature of the testator then is reduced, because probate will be granted according to the testimony of the witnesses and not to his signature.

The position of the witnesses

The jurists demand from a man who is to be a legal witness that he must know the contents of the document he signs (a bequest for instance), otherwise his testimony is totally unacceptable. Equally unacceptable is a document which is supposed to have been signed and sealed by the testator, if without the witnesses being aware of its authenticity and contents the testator puts it in an envelope and waves it in his hand asking them thus to witness his bequest. Testimony of this sort will also, be unacceptable. For the jurists insist that the document is to be read to the witnesses or to be read by them. Nonetheless, the document might gain the required approval through other means, say, the recognition of the testator's handwriting as we have previously stated.

To assess the effect of the above ruling upon the practice in Saudi Arabia, the following case was recently presented to *Katib al-'Adl*. A man added a codicil to a previous bequest he had made in which he said that he had written a bequest and kept it unattested in his safe. He gave as the reason for his action that it contained some items which were of a confidential nature and a trade secret. Thus he was eager not to disclose them to anyone. He also concluded with an order clause that he wanted his named executor to follow precisely his directions, as written therein.[42]
Usually, an ordinary ascertained document, i.e. a bequest with witnesses, is acceptable in the courts unless some of those concerned dispute either the authenticity of the document or the status of the witness the latter being classified as undignified or unworthy. An illustration of this in Saudi courts is the case of *D v. R*.[43]

R (the testator's germane sister), had been appointed a *Wasi* to dispense her brother's third for pious purposes. The agent of the testator's daughter petitioned to the court that the testator was insane at the time of the alleged bequest. Also she condemned the attestation as biased.

However, following an extensive examination conducted by the court, the allegation was decided unfounded and the witnesses were confirmed as trustworthy men. The bequest, which had been unofficially made and witnessed was thus approved of by the court as legally binding. Had the allegation been approved, the ultimate decision of the court would have been the nullification of the entire bequest.

The attestation clause

No special attestation clause is required. But in normal practice the contractor usually includes a tacit call for witnesses to come forward to testify to the document he has concluded, viz, 'I hereby call and permit whoever wishes to ascert this deed (or bequest), in which God is the best of all witnesses'.

It is not obligatory on the part of the witnesses, however, to begin their testimony with the following clauses, 'We, the undersigned witnesses, affirm the correctness of this document, (or acknowledgement, sale, bequest, etc)', or in the form 'We (the undersigned witnesses), affirm and bear witness to whatever is mentioned above in the deed'. These phrases are deemed desirable but a simple signature of attestation will suffice. Such a clause, if included, assures us that the witnesses knew the contents of the deed they were asked to affirm.

The presence of the witnesses at the signing ceremony or their ability to see the two parties to a contract actually draw up the document and sign it, is not a matter vital to the validity of the document. This view has been adopted as the official doctrine of the Hanbali school.

However, Al-Qadi, a prominent Hanbali jurist insisted not only on the witnesses knowing the contents of the agreement but insisted on them seeing the document in the process of its completion,[44] which coincidently resembles the rule on this point in English Law.[45]

Although, the opinion voiced by Al-Qadi is a very good safe-guard against forgery, the rule, if applied, will no doubt cause hardship to the lonely person who may die without his desires being recognized or to a testator without access to legal authorization. It will also cause hardship to the prospective witnesses through their long wait for the document to be drawn up and will in a way contradict the agreed principle which validates the orally made bequest. Not only could this have been regarded a premature move. But in practice even nowadays it would still be hard to apply such a scheme in countries where illiteracy is widespread. And further, the presence of an illiterate witness to the document will not add to his knowledge of it any further than he otherwise would know from the deed being read to him by the parties concerned. This principle has been suggested by the majority of jurists as an alternative to Al-Qadi's view.

The authenticated bequest

The accepted method to authenticate a bequest before the establishment of the court department of *Katib al-'Adl,* was by the pronouncement of one's bequest in front of a judge and the recording of its contents in the registry. This can be seen in the case of a chaste woman or an ill person for whom the judge himself or his deputy goes in person to their houses to obtain their wills.

This is illustrated in the case where *X* was a rich woman who was assumed to be living a chaste life. Through her agent she showed her willingness to make a bequest in the presence of the judge. Being the ultimate power of authentication the judge sent his deputy to the woman's residence to see her and her identifying witnesses and to record her bequest. It was subsequently read to the judge who approved it and ordered its registration in the court's records.[46]

In an attempt to rearrange the judiciary's administration, the task of authenticating bequests was now lifted from the shoulders of the judge to a court department known as *Katib al-'Adl,* by the Royal decree known as a summary of the regulations for the judiciary.[47]

The task of *Katib al-'Adl* with regard to the authentication of wills

One of the numerous tasks entrusted to *Katib al-'Adl,* is to receive testators and help them make valid their bequests. As a means of authenticating the validity of a bequest he has to ask the testator to put down the details of his beneficiaries and their degrees of relationship to him. He is instructed to copy the testator's bequest coupled with his references and witnesses into his records only when he is convinced that such a bequest is in accordance to the law.[48]

In certain circumstances *Katib al-'Adl,* may at the request of the person concerned, draw up the bequest himself on behalf of the testator, but if he, does so it has to be done according to the directions of the testator, or to be more precise, he should recast the instructions of the testator into legal language and put questions to resolve any ambiguities. Notwithstanding, *Katib al-'Adl,* is prohibited by the Royal decree, to alter or make expression with variable meanings from that of the contractor (or the testator).[49]

As to the legal rules and principles he is to rely on in the process of authenticating a bequest, he was confined by the Royal Prerogative regulating the judiciaries' responsibilities, to draw them according to the Hanbali doctrine only.[50]

The advantage of this form of authentication is that it removes the need to prove the bequest, and it is a great help for the illiterate persons who can not personally draft their own bequest. Its only disadvantage is the number of people involved (in drawing up the bequest) and the loss of privacy. This has lead some people, as we have seen, to register only the clauses from which they think no harm will ever come to them. Thus leaving unregistered the confidential clauses relating either to their business or private life, which are confined to a separately drawn up codicil to be known only to the parties concerned.

The testator's subsequent loss of capacity

The loss of capacity through insanity, idiocy or feebleness lasting over six months prior to the testator's death is a reason in the *Hanafi* view to nullify an otherwise valid bequest (made before insanity). A sceptical analysis used to support this idea stems from the ever present possibility for the testator to revoke the bequest had he recovered consciousness before death.

The other jurists, mainly, Malikis, Hanablis and the Shi'as refused to give a second thought to the theoretical assumption adduced by the Hanafis. They argued that it was impossible to repeal a bequest legally concluded by a then willing and capable person. They consider that it is not in their power to vitiate a decent and authentically prepared will, which contains no impediments to the legislation of bequest.

Finally, the jurists compare their stand with that of the Hanafis as the choice between certainty (the continuation of the validity of bequest), and hypothetical (the nullity of the bequest). They also see that common sense does not allow certainty to be dispised for the sake of hypothetical assumptions which have no foundations in reality.

To sum up the jurists' positions: when insanity occurs in a mature person and continues without interruption for six months, or imbecility develops and continues till death, a bequest would be null and void, according to the view held by the Hanafis. In contrast to the former view, the Hanabalis, Malikis and Shi'as uphold the validity of a bequest made prior to insanity. This is due to their firm belief in the legal maxim that succeeding events do not vitiate the earlier conduct and transactions.[51] Accordingly, only the sort of dealings which are known to have taken place during insanity are to be subjected to such nullity.

NOTES

1. *Sh. Muntaha*, Vol. 2, 539.
2. *Muntaha*, Vol. 2, 37, and *Kash*, Vol.4, 337, and *Sh. Munt*, loc. cit.
3. Resolution of the Council of the Deputies No. 19, (1358H). Also recorded under No. 122, Shari'a decisions. Institute of General Administration. Riyadh.
4. Al-Mirdawi, *Al-Insaf*, Vol. 7, 187-188.
5. *Kashshaf*, Vol.4, 336.
6. *Al-Tanqih al-Mushbi', 315. Sh. Muntaha al-Iradat*, Vol. 3, 545.
7. *Sharh Muntaha*, Vol.3, 545, *Kashaf*, Vol. 6, 416-417.
8. *Mughni*, Vol. 6, 490-491, *Kash*, Vol. 4, 338, and *Sh. Munt*, Vol. 2, 539-540.
9. *Kash*, Vol. 4, 339.
10. Taif Kakib al-'adl, No. 1200, Vol. 5, (1390).
11. Jedda Katib al-'adl No. 1122, Vol. 3, (1383H).
12. Ibn Qudama, *Al-Kafi*, Vol. 2, 482.
13. *Kashshaf*, Vol. 4, 351.
14. Jedda Katib al-'adl, No. 1257, Vol. 4, (1385H).
15. Jedda Katib al-'adl, No. 2459, Vol. 7, (1386H).
16. Al-Bukhari. See *Al-Mu'jam Al-Mufahras*, Vol. 3, 99.
17. *Al-Tanqih*, 195
18. *Sh. Munt*, Vol. 2, 546, *Kash*, Vol. 4, 351, *Insaf*, Vol. 7, 218, *Al-Sharh al-kabir*, Vol. 6, 460.
19. Jedda Katib al-'adl, No. 986, Vol. 3, (1379H).
20. Jedda. Katib al-'adl, No. 1247, Vol. 3, (1380H).
21. Jedda Katib al-'adl, No. 2701, Vol. 7, (1383H).
22. Jedda Katib al-'adl, No. 66, Vol. I, (1378H).
23. Jedda Katib al-'adl. No. 1577, Vol. 5, (1385H).
24. Jedda Katib al-'adl, No. 2459, Vol. 7, (1386H).
25. Jedda Katib al-'adl, No. 2535, Vol. 7, (1385H).
26. *Sh. Munt*, Vol. 3, 556-557.
27. Regulations of Katib al 'adl. of 1364 H/1945AD, p. 28.
28. G.C. Makkah, No. 162, Vol. I, (1380H).
29. G.C. of Mecca. Private minute of Shaikh Abdulmalik b. Duhaish, No. 1375, Vol. 8, (1391H).
30. *Sh. Munt*, Vol. 3, 548.

Sh. Munt, Vol. 2, 539, and *Al-Athb al-fa'id*, Vol. 2, 176.

31. G.C. Makkah, No. 22, Vol. 3, (1380H).
32. *Quran*, Al-Ma'idah, 106-108 and *the Commentary* of Ibn Jarir al-Tabari, Vol. XI, 174-5, and *Sh. Munt*, Vol. 3, 546, and *K*, Vol. 6, 417-8. Ibn Al-Qayim.*Al-Turaq Al-Hukamiya fil-siyasa Al-Shariya*, 197-209.
33. Ahad Rufaidah, No. 59, (1392H).
34. Ahad Rufaidah, No. 59, (1392H).
35. Regulation of Bait al-mal, articles 206-207/212, part 7. The summary of the Judiciary's regulations No. 109 (1372H), 3rd Ed. 1387H, Makkah.
36. *Mughni*, Vol. 6, p. 488.
37. Jedda Katib al-'adl, No. 669, Vol. 2, (1376H).
38. Jedda Katib al-'adl, No. 1018, Vol. 4, (1384H).
39. Jedda Katib al-'adl, No. 1001, Vol. 3, (1384H).
40. *Matalib uli al-nuha*, Vol. 4, 445.
41. Jedda Katib al-'adl, No. 1257, Vol. 4, (1385H).
42. Jedda Katib al-'adl, No. 1939, Vol. 5, (1380H).
43. G.C. Makkah, No. 162, Vol. I, (1380H).
44. *Matalib*, Vol. 4, 445, and *Kash*, Vol. 4, 337, and *Insaf*, Vol. 7, 188, and *Sharh muntaha*, Vol.2, 539.
45. P.W.D. Redmond *General Principles of English Law*, 278; Sir Barry (David Hughes), *The Law of Succession*, 18.
46. Jedda Katib al-'adl. Joint Reg. No. p. 82, (1344-45H).
47. Summary of the responsibilities of the judiciary. Art. 194, pt. 7, p. 24.
48. Arts. 14-15-16, p. 6 and also section 2, subsection G, p. 4. Regulation of *Katib al-'adl*. Royal decree No. 11083, (1364H). Ed. Makkah 1387H.
49. Summary of the Responsibilities of the Judiciary of 1372H. Article 183, p. 22, Part 6.
50. Accumulation of Saudi Regulations. Article 203/206/207. Chapter 1, Part 7, p. 94.
51. Jawad Maghniya, *Al-ahwal al-shakhsiya*, 180.

CHAPTER III
VOID BEQUEST

The Prophet (peace be upon him) said, '*Allah* has given you the third of your estate at your death, so invest it in the way you desire'.

Although we cannot deny that the testator has been given much freedom of choice as to the value of the subject matter and the beneficiaries, the fact is that the testator's desires will not be allowed to go beyond what the law permits. Thus he is to adjust and adjudge his actions according to the inspired spirit and principles of the *Shari'a*. In the following we discuss certain restrictions and conditions set up by the law as guidance to testators in this respect.

ILLEGAL PURPOSES

The prime purpose of the law introducing the following restrictions is to help the testator to conclude a valid will which will not defy the spirit of the *Shari'a* and thus be invalid. Thus, a bequest which is directed towards matters forbidden in Islam, e.g. to those who are employed for deep mourning, to houses of amusement, bingo clubs and casinos or to dance halls, etc. thereby encouraging people to waste their money, will be null and void. This is because the *Shari'a*, in its drive to purify people and protect them from any sort of exploitation, considers such things to contravene its objectives. Accordingly the law, in such a situation, acts firmly to make a legacy of this sort a prima facie reason for invalidity.

A similar consideration applies where the bequest appears to be properly made by a sound and capable testator to a beneficiary whose right to possess is unquestioned. Though the legacy may appear lawful, the court in its investigation would not count on its appearance but would rather look into the motives and objectives of the testator which urged him to formulate such a bequest. If the motive behind his action is found illegal, i.e. if the testator bequeaths to those who become dissipated (a brothel for instance) to help them continue their immoral business, such a bequest will be invalid. The same will be true if a person donates a legacy to a man or a woman to persuade them to continue their sinful relationship with him.

The motive for this type of bequest has caused considerable controversy among jurists. Some are of the opinion that they should ignore the search for motives altogether so long as it is not mentioned in the wording of the bequest. This opinion is supported mostly by a statement attributed to Hanafi jurisprudence that 'Consideration is paid to the meaning but not to the words and constructions'. Shaykh Abu Zahrah said that this statement must be comprehended in connection with the statement found in the commentary of *Al-Jami' al-Saghir*, 'Consideration should be paid to the meaning with regard to the laws of God, but the rules concerning the affairs of the slaves (human beings), must be obeyed to the letter of the law.'

To show in a more explicit way the Hanafis' disregard for motive as a basis on which to judge the validity of contracts, and that the former statement does not really represent their point of view, Shaikh Abu Zahra draws our attention to the numerous contracts which the Hanafis did not invalidate in spite of their purposes and motives. He also explained that what they really meant by such a statement was that to be legal the motive for a gift must not be to receive some compensation, such a motive turns it into a sale and not a gift.[1]

A somewhat similar view was apparently held by some Hanbalis, one of whom was Al-Bahuti, who validated a bequest made to an heir's son even though the testator meant thereby to give indirect profit to his heir. He stated that 'The responsibility of the testator's motive will be left to his own conscience (God)'.[2]

Unlike the Hanafis, who ignore motive completely, Al-Bahuti in his statement takes the middle course between the Hanafis' and his contemporarily influential colleagues, Ibn Taimia and Ibn al-Qayim, who clearly recognised the significance of motive in the case. Instead of giving it its full force in law, he accepts the testator's motive knowing that he will be faced with this problem in his second life if the motive is suspect.

The second opinion in this respect was led by Ibn Taimia and Ibn al-Qayim. The latter especially stood firm on condemnation and invalidation of evilly motivated bequests (as of all other kinds of contracts).

In his creative scheme he does not reject any contract of this sort bluntly. On the contrary, he furnishes the way for jurists and judges to safeguard them by turning their attention towards the concept of the persuasive elements within the circumstantial evidence. The application of this concept, which he sees as the way to uncover a motive hidden between the lines of the contract, is summarised as follows:

The motive of a contractor should appear to conform with the terms of the contract. Otherwise, in order to obtain such conformity, priority as stated is to derive his motive from the actual words he used, i.e. consideration is to be directed towards the related context and presumptions within the text of the contract. If by then, he adds, the aim and motive was still unclear it is resolved by considering the surrounding circumstances at the time.[3]

To assert the significance of conformity of motive with the terms of the contract he also said, 'Literal or apparent meaning is to be accepted only if no confirmation to the contrary was lodged. Thus if a hidden meaning was ascertained, no regard whatsoever will be paid to the apparent meaning'. In this respect too he referred in support of his view to the juristic concensus of opinion which makes it unlawful for a judge to decide on a case which contravenes his real knowledge of that case.[4] Further, he advocates the acceptance of a testimony by trustworthy men to either counteract or confirm a suggested motive by the use of extrinsic evidence. This is also seen to have been the view of both Ibn Rajab and Al-Mirdawi, who had to give a decision in cases where conflict with regard to the intended beneficiary arose. In such cases there was a pressing need to clarify who the testator meant to benefit under the will.[5]

IMPROPER MOTIVE

Improper motive usually stems from lack of responsibility on the part of a predecessor who is supposed to act responsibly towards his heirs and not to attempt to harm them with his evil ways. There are two types. First, the irresponsibility of the deceased is seen in a bequest concluded by the testator with the prior intention to lessen the entitlements of his natural heirs. For instance, if the testator encloses a clause which says to his heirs, 'I wish to disinherit you' or 'I bequeath a third of my estate to Ahmad and I wish to dispose of the whole of my estate and leave nothing to my heirs'. This, if established, could be a cause to repeal his disposition entirely on the grounds of improper motive and the desire to be of detriment to his heirs.

Further, if a deceased allocated to a legatee a bequest of more than the disposable one third, his action will arouse wide condemnation. For he commits one of the greatest sins, known as *'Wasiyat-al-dirar'*, or injurious legacy. This sort of bequest is considered *ultra vires*. The *ultra vires* principle also operates in a case of excessive bequest (even though the legacy was not meant to harm) if the extension of the legacy beyond the one third of his estate is interpreted as an actual violation of the rights of the legal heirs. Thus it is *ultra vires*, though it may become operative should the legal heirs subsequently approve of it.

The relevant rule is derived for the *Quran* viz., 'If there are a number of Uterine brothers or sisters then let them share in a third after payment of what he bequeaths and of his debts – without prejudice'.[6] In this verse God has, says Ibn al-Qayim, relieved from sin the one who removes injury from a legacy and who refrains from equating the testator's harmful instructions to the level of the text of the *Quran* or *Sunna*, which cannot be disagreed with.[7] Accordingly, a bequest, without reference to the motive behind it, is alterable by the heirs' approval or disapproval.

An improper motivated bequest can also include a bequest made to an heir. The testator's attempt to favour a particular heir is seen as defiance of both the divinely fixed shares of inheritance and the moral rights of the co-heirs and constitutes a material loss of their portions of inheritance by the allocation of a part of their due rights to that heir without their consent. The jurists anticipate that such a bequest could cause rivalry and hatred and so upset the unity of the Muslim family, which the *Shari'a* endeavours to preserve.

However, when no heir exists, then the bequest of the entire estate will be validated since it constitutes no violation to anyone. This principle is shown in operation in the case of *A v. Bait al-Mal.*[8]

Having no heirs, *Am* disposed of her entire estate in such a way that the estate was to be divided into two parts; one third was bequeathed for benevolent deeds and the other two thirds were bequeathed to the testatrix's executor, *A*.

As the bequeathed estate was seized by *Bait al-Mal*, following the death of the testatrix, *A* brought a legal complaint against the *Bait al-Mal*, demanding a court order against it, forcing it to surrender the deceased's estate to him in his capacity as a legatee and as an executor to the third.

On making his decision to order the surrender of the entire estate bequeathed to the plaintiff, the judge sought reference to this principle in the authoritative books of the Hanbali doctrine, all of which validated such a bequest.

THE UNINFORMED APPROACH OF THE TESTATOR, HOWEVER WELL-MEANING, RENDERS A BEQUEST VOID

A bequest which has the wrong approach cannot be saved from nullity though the original motive was good. An example is a bequest to someone who reads the Quran and devotes the outcome (the religious rewards) to someone else such as the testator's father or mother.

A new phenomenon as such usually attracts learned people who then subject it to detailed dissertation, argument and counter-argument and give it the ruling it requires. The reading of the Quran for reward met with fierce resistance from latter jurists of the Hanbali school of law as a bad innovation. Ibn Taimia, for instance, saw it as a bad innovation because 'None of the old Muslims read the Quran and then dedicate the religious rewards they got to the souls of dead Muslims, so we should not renounce their habit.' He also added that, 'Bequest for the mere reading of the Quran and hiring the readers, as such, causes degeneration towards the merits of the Quran, such as, diverting people from pious reading and causing people to read the Quran rather for the sake of earning money.'[9]

As for the transfer of rewards to the dead. The author of *Al-Ikhtiarat* (Ibn Taimia) states the decision of the scholars that no reward is obtained from reading the Quran for the sake of money. He pointed out that if no rewards could be earned then what rewards could be conferred upon the dead. None of course.

Also Ibn Taimia says, 'None of the scholars permitted it'.[10] However, the disciple Ibn al-Qayim has come up with the same conclusion as that of his teacher Ibn Taimia. In his book *A'lam al-muwaqqi'in*, he devoted an explicit chapter to what he called the illegal conditions stipulated by the donors. In it he commented that, 'In order for the religious rewards to reach the dead, the reader must be able to earn rewards as the dead person is regarded as an extension of the reader'.[11]

A judge of the grand court of Makkah reflected this reasoning when in pronouncing his verdict in a case concerning a *Waqf* (charity trust) dedicated for, inter alia, the hiring of readers to read the Quran continuously in the grand Mosque of Makkah, the rewards obtained from such reading being transferred to the donor, his ancestors and to the Prophet. The judge, in his judgement regarding the above case, annulled the reading provision and ordered the revenue to be shared, instead, amongst the donors needy relatives as they had been made second class beneficiaries.[12]

The above judgement, also, reflects the views of the official Saudi judiciary's adherence to the view of the later Hanbali jurists. Evidence of this attitude was produced by the head of the Grand Court of Makkah, Shaikh Abdullah b. Duhaish. He referred to a letter he had previously received from Shaikh Muhammad b. Ibrahim, the late Mufti of Saudi Arabia in which he let it be known that he had followed both Ibn Taimia and his disciple in nullifying both *Wasia* and *Waqf* (trust), dedicated for reading the Quran, because this implied the hiring of readers in order to donate their rewards to the dead.[13]

This rule will not, of course, be applied to the dedications devoted to those who take on the teaching of the Quran or knowledge in general. On the contrary, spreading knowledge and whatever leads to it is regarded as the most desirable thing to do because the Prophet states, 'The learned and the learner share goodness and there is less goodness in the others,' and 'Knowledge is incumbent upon every Muslim, male and female,'[14] and 'Seek knowledge even in China.' Such an attitude is illustrated by the *Waqf* of *Hadia* to the jurists of the Hanafi school. This *Waqf* was ratified by the court of Makkah which allowed the *Nazir* to sell part of the ruined *Waqf*, to receive the price on their behalf, and use it to rebuild the other part thereof.[15]

CONDITIONS RELATED TO THE LEGATEE

The legatee is another function of the main elements of bequest. It is known beyond doubt that without the legatee as a recipient, we cannot imagine a bequest as being effective. We find it therefore necessary to consider the question as to whom the bequest should be offered, in what state he must be and what qualifications he must have. All are matters of immense importance which are dealt with in the following.

a. Existence of the legatee

'There can be no bequest to a non-existent legatee.' This is a principle agreed upon by the majority of jurists. Implementation of this principle debars from bequest an unborn child if that child cannot have been known to exist at the time the bequest was made.

Disqualification of such a child from bequest is two-fold. First, the foetus is to be discounted if the bequest is later known to have been made with no positive sign of pregnancy. This bequest will be nullified as no worthy recipient is expected to emerge. Secondly, if a mother, who is co-habiting with her husband, delivers a child after the elapse of six months, such a child will be deprived of the bequest. Deprivation of such a child was caused by the jurists employing in their argument the presumption that the co-habitation of the mother with her husband could result in the pregnancy occuring after the bequest had been made.

Nevertheless, if the beneficiaries of a bequest or a *Waqf* were unspecified, i.e. it were made to any group of people, then any child born within that group will be eligible to a proper share of such a disposition.[16] An illustration of this is found in the case of *N*.[17]

A, the creator of the *Waqf*, stipulated the revenue of the *Waqf* to be distributed between his offspring (the male line only). Males and females amongst the direct descendants of the male line were to have equal shares. In the year AH 1380 (9/6/1380) *N*, a direct female descendant of the dedicator, was born having *lb.* as her father, who was himself a direct beneficiary in the *Waqf*. *N* was a direct descendant of the male line of the *Waqif*, dedicator, and, according to the principle which states that if a person makes a *Waqf* (or bequest) to his descendants or the descendants of another person only, his sons' children however distant in relationship will be included. Excluded are, of course, the children of his daughters and their children because genealogically, they are affiliated not to him, but to others, i.e. they do not carry his name.[18] The other principle states that the *Waqf* or bequest to his offspring covers the children of his sons however distant in relationship, whether they existed at the time of the disposition or after.[19] The girl's father demanded a share of the revenue to be given to her for a part of the year she was born in, but the *Nazir* or trustee of the *Waqf*, refused, claiming that the girl was born a month and a half later than the date stated by the father and that that year's revenue had already been distributed to the beneficiaries.

The father, on behalf of his girl, filed a legal suit against the *Nazir* and brought adequate evidence to support his claim that *Nadia* was in fact born on 9/6/1380 AH. As the judge was satisfied with the proof offered, he ordered the *Nazir* to settle the claimed share from the revenue of that year. The judge's decision was based on the girl being born within the first six months of that year which indicates the certain existence of the girl in the womb at the time the revenue became available.

The uncertainty of the duration of pregnancy in relation to the time the bequest was made compels us to consider the time of the child's delivery as the point at which judgement can be made. It also induces us to consider the minimum and the maximum period of gestation.

The decision to wait till the delivery date is of utmost importance since the due rights could be disturbed even further if the foetus was stillborn or there was a miscarriage.[20] The minimum and the maximum period of gestation is thus considered to be the determining factor in law.

In the Islamic law of inheritance, much importance is attached to the pre-natal stage where the foetus becomes a potential heir. So according to the jurists, the foetus must be in existence at the time of praepositus death.[21] To consider the state of the foetus, the jurists were obliged to look at the conditions causing pregnancy and the likelihood of a live birth. In this way certain rules were laid down.

1. The usual time of birth is nine months after conception.
2. It is possible for pregnancy to last as long as four years according to the Hanbali jurists.[22]
3. The ruling for shortest period of gestation was derived from two verses of the Quran which state '. . . and his weaning is for two years', and 'His mother carried and suckled him with reluctance for thirty months'.[23]

The scholars interpreted the first of the two verses to mean that the period of weaning the child from his mother's milk was two years and the second verse to mean that the total period of weaning and gestation was two and a half years. From this the shortest period of gestation leading to a live birth was deduced to be six months.[24] The adherence of Saudi courts to such a view can be illustrated in the case of *Ab.* and *'A.*[25]

In this case after *'A* revealed that she had been raped, her uterine brother, with the consent of their mother, duly contracted the girl to marry *A* who, she claimed, had raped her, when the case came before the court and all the necessary investigations were carried out, the court ordered the dissolution of the marriage. She was pregnant and there was no way to determine whether it was caused by the alleged rape or during the vitiated marriage. Considering the unborn child's status in relation of *A*, the court, in conformity to the above principle, took the minimum period of gestation as the basis for deciding such status. The court ruled that *A* would not be considered to be the legitimate father of the child if *'A* delivered it before the expiry of six months after the consummation of the vitiated marriage. But should the birth come a moment after the expiry of six months (the minimum period of gestation) from that consummation, then the child will legitimately be his.

In conformity with the principle of the period of gestation, this constitutes no infringement to the rights of any of the recipients, i.e. the heirs and legatees, since all have the right to be allocated the undisputed proportions in what is left of the estate. However, as far as the amount of property to be retained for the unborn child is concerned if compared with that which the heirs and legatees have actually received or with the net of the estate, we will find that it amounts, in general, to a negligible amount.

Retention is not in all cases harmful to the heirs or legatees, though their shares would be decreased proportionately to the minimum as a means of protecting the anticipated infant's interests. If the anticipated child is born within the stated period (minimum and maximum period of gestation), the delivery would alleviate the anxiety that accompanies heir and legatees throughout such pregnancy, since his birth makes him eligible to possess the retained portion.

Also, there is no reason to justify the anxiety shown by the excluded heirs, because their chance to step in into the beneficiaries' rank is so rare and is limited to cases of miscarriage of the foetus or stillborn or, rarest of all, phantom pregnancy.

b. Doubt related to the legatee

The identity of the legatee must not be left in doubt. A provision in this respect, makes it essential to state the appropriate potential recipient of the bequest. Also it is convenient to mention here that if a bequest is to take effect at all, the identity of the legatee must be stated with sufficient certainty to enable us to implement the terms of the bequest. The jurists state that the failure of a person to answer the description forfeits his becoming a legatee to such a bequest. To exemplify the sort of bequest which fails through lack of clarity, we resort to hypothesis, viz. 'I bequeath my car to one of these two persons'. This type of bequest is also held invalid on the grounds that the testator here has deliberately concealed his intention, which we will treat, therefore, as if there is no intention at all. It is true that the legatees are limited but still the uncertainty created by the testator's failing to make a responsible decision forfeits both legatees. This is because no one has the right to decide for someone else without authority. This is also so in the case where the testator leaves a blank or omits a word in the middle of his will unless its meaning is obvious from the passage.

If the testator says 'I bequeath one-third of my property to my neighbour Ahmad b. Salih,' his bequest, prima facie, is valid. But to maintain its validity to execution, we must find someone to fulfil such a description or name. However, if after the testator's death no one is found eligible to fulfil the description or to hold that title, or if two persons or more share the same name in such a way as to make it impossible to identify the intended beneficiary, such a bequest will fail.

The rule of invalidity will not be carried out before all avenues available for deciding the right legatee have been explored. In this direction we try to solve the uncertainty with the help of apposite circumstances 1. an effort will be made to find out which of the two was known to the testator at the time of the bequest, 2. if all of them were known to the testator and doubt remains , extrinsic evidence of the deceased's intention will be admitted, to decide the one with whom the testator had dealt much or the one who had done a favour to the testator, etc. 3. if after all possibilities are exhausted, the result still remains negative and it is impossible to ascertain the legatee's identity, then the bequest fails.

Nevertheless, doubt and uncertainty as to potential legatees of a bequest made to a big group of people will not affect the validity of it. If the revenue of the bequest or *Waqf* cannot be made available to all the beneficiaries simultaneously, the law has granted the *Wasi* and the *Nazir* the right to resolve such doubt or uncertainty by preferring some of those who answer the specified description against others in the same group. He is also permitted to give the whole lot to one person only, just as if the bequest or *Waqf* were made to a big tribe or to the inhabitants of a town or to students of law. This ruling was made as it is apparent that the intention of the testator or the *Waqif* was set to grant his disposition to whoever fits his description where an individual person is said to fulfil these conditions.

A LEGATEE'S ELIGIBILITY TO POSSESS AN ESTATE

Eligibility for possession is one of many provisions governing the legatee's right. It is conceived that if such a right is to be infringed or defeated by the subsequent occurrence or incapacity, such as death, for instance, a bequest previously made will become null and void. Accordingly, if a bequest is made to a person who pre-deceased his testator, the bequest will be void for it will find the potential beneficiary incompetent to hold the estate. This is equally true as if the will had been initially made to a dead person.

Furthermore, an angel is considered incapable of possession possibly because of its supernatural essence which renounces as immoral any attempt to reduce it to the level of humans in their greediness and associated wickedness. Thus an action which by bequest confers ownership of an earthly object on an angel is an irresponsible and illegal act.

Animals are to be exempted from bequest too, where they are to be favoured at the expense of humans. Ibn Qudama, the prominent Hanbali jurist, in his elaboration on ownership, linked the right of ownership to human beings specifically. He also contributed by adding his own version which limits the capacity of ownership by stipulating man as the essence of all possession, viz., 'Human existence is a provision for ownership and life is a requisite of human existence.'[27]

An embryo, though, during that state is considered imperfect or not yet existent, will not be compared with the status of animals which are considered perpetually incapable of ownership. The potentiality of ownership, in anticipation of a live birth sometime in the foreseeable future, is a reason for not including it under such a heading.

EXCEPTION OF THE ABOVE RULE

The principle of restricting ownership to humans has been slightly modified by the application of the prevalent usage or *Urf*, whenever it was found that such a maxim could become an obstacle to certain beneficial movements of estates *Urf* makes such conveyances lawful. Such modification is seen in the attitude of some jurists with regard to the exclusion of horses from the restriction imposed upon animals in respect of legacy. The exception of horses was entertained because of the vital role they play to help foil any attempt to attack Muslims or to wage a holy-war. To ensure that this interpretation would not cause further disruption to the law of bequest and ownership Al-Mirdawi, a Hanbali jurist, when he faced the choice between the latter interpretation and the former one, favoured the latter juristic intepretation. In a conciliatory manner he legalized a bequest for the benefit of a horse but restricted it to the horse whose use was confined to serving in war efforts. To show his subscription to the old view he noted that the testator should not transfer the ownership of the bequeathed object to the horse itself. He therefore obliged the testator to indicate that the bequest is to be used for the benefit of the horse. If the above two provisions are satisfied the bequest made to the horse will thus be valid and operative even, as he said, without acceptance by its owner being necessary. The portion bequeathed will accordingly be spent on provender for the horse. Part of the middle-course between the various views taken by Al-Mirdawi appears in his decision that whenever the horse dies, the unconsumed bequest is not left to the horse's owner but to return to the testator's heirs.[28]

INSTITUTIONS AND THE ISSUE OF POSSESSION

The main problem raised by the introduction of the eligibility of the legatee to possess as a condition is the issue of an institution being made a recipient of a bequest. A solution to such a problem was therefore urgently sought and needed. It was not long before a theoretical body was introduced. This body was called the public utility and was capable of receiving whatever estate had been conferred. The breakthrough is supported by the Quran which in many verses ascribes ownership of all estates to *Allah* (God) alone. Thus it is proper to leave merely the benefits of estates to be the subject of possession, which can be vested either in humans or the public, or alternatively can be deemed to pass over to the institute even without the assumption of the theoretical body.

The question of form threatened to put the whole settlement in jeopardy. The views of the various schools of law with regard to the application of such a basic doctrine are divided into two parts. Abu Hanifa, for instance, regarded the inclusion in the bequest of the sort of phrase 'To be spent thereupon', of utmost importance. He therefore treated any bequest made to institutions, i.e. Mosques, and which did not mention a method of disposal, as null and void.

But the majority of jurists, i.e. Malik, Al-Shafi'i and Ibn Hanbal, on the other hand, made a very constructive suggestion. In this respect, they regarded the inclusion of the phrase presented by Abu Hanifa in the bequest as unnecessary and having no practical value since people tacitly know what the bequest is to be spent on. The latter view could be regarded as having helped to remove and overcome the last obstacle which might seriously have hindered the disposition of properties. It not only made it possible to carry out the wishes of the testators fully but also promoted the drive towards more and more dispositions for pious purposes. It has also introduced a new dimension by recognising the importance of the testator's intentions behind their dispositions.

Running water, building bridges, hospitals, pensioners' homes, orphanages and universities, etc., owe their existence and maintenance mostly to the above interpretation. Donations from parts of people's fortunes to such establishments have become an accepted fact whether in the form of a gift or trust made during life or as a bequest or *Waqf* (trust) after death.

In recent times, some testators and dedicators in Saudi Arabia have drawn up their wills in accordance to the majority view of jurists. That the Saudi courts have adhered to such a view is apparent in their approval of the bequest made in the manner illustrated in the following cases:

In a certain case a person made a dedication involving his entire estate which following his death would go to a group of beneficiaries each of whom are mentioned in the document of his dedication and after their death he made it a *Waqf* to Madrasat al-Falah, a private school in Jedda, designating the headmaster as *Nazir*.[30]

In another case, the testator bequeathed one-third of his estate for good and benevolent deeds. With the bequeathed third he instructed his executor to build or buy a house or to select one of the houses he owned and make it a *Waqf* on his behalf for Madrasat al-Falah in Jedda.[31]

Also in a further case, the testatrix instructed the executor to exercise an annual *Adhiya* (immolation of slaughtered sheep to the glory of God) from the disposable one-third and also to build a house and dedicate its use to the glory of God.[32]

The principle of rewards in after life has also played a major role where more religious deeds have involved the giving of a great variety of alms. Thus the existence of such a link has facilitated a way for larger establishments to be erected, not forgetting the old Universities such as Al-Azhar, Al-Qairawan, the schools attached to the Umayyad Grand Mosque in Damascus, the Universities of Al-Andalus (Spain), which aspired to shed light upon the whole world in not one but in all areas of knowledge, from religion and philosophy to medicine, chemistry, mathematics, algebra, architecture, and so on.

ATTENTION PAID TO THE SOCIAL STATUS OF THE LEGATEE

The recipient's social position is an element to be born in mind for if ignored it could nullify the whole testamentary disposition. The motive of the testator is an inseparable factor in this respect too. The prospective use of the bequest is also to be taken into consideration as to whether it would broaden the sphere of knowledge, bring happiness and prosperity or whether it is likely to create chaos and confusion or to hamper social progress. Such factors are the subject of the following discussion.

a. The inter-communal relationship

Strengthening the inter-communal relationship is one of the tasks which Islam as a religion and as a law too, has set itself to achieve and maintain. Thus it is understandable that it legalizes all acts that help to promote such an objective. The bequest, therefore, was not only made legal but was considered recommendable too. With this objective in mind the legatee's state of need could be disregarded. This is because a bequest to an unrelated friend invokes the most hidden feelings in the recipient both psychologically and sentimentally, broadening and strengthening their relationship which in turn furnishes a basis for society's own true and social existence.

b. The inter-family relationship

The significance of the family structure comes from it being taken to reflect (though on a small scale) the whole of society. The family structure, for instance, demonstrates the most characteristic features of mankind and still dominates the scene especially in the third world countries. The interests of a Muslim inner-family have been secured by the law of succession without abandoning that of the other relationships. Paternal uncles and their children have been placed in this category if the inner-family relatives, for any reason, are excluded or none of them survived. *Dhawi al-Arham* or cognates, are also considered as a third choice when none of the above mentioned relatives exist.

In regard to bequest, Muslim jurists in general do not prescribe giving bequests to non-heir relatives. But they are all in agreement that the inter-family relationships must be preserved and strengthened by all means not least to bequeath to the poor amongst them. Bequest as such was considered not only advisable but praiseworthy as well.

The maintenance legislation for poor or dependent relatives and for a divorced woman is another means of tying the family closer together. To this end, Islam, in addition to giving power to the law to enforce its decrees, has at the same time classified such actions, if given voluntarily, as a life-investment bringing the donor some religious rewards in the hereafter. This is literally indicated in the Hadith '... It is better to leave your heirs rich than to leave them in need of other people. All that you dispense in maintenance is charity, even the mouthful which you carry to the mouth of your wife.' From a practical point of view if the above methods were fully applied this would greatly help combat poverty and eliminate misery from the family and extend this benefit to other families.

In reference to the bequest to the non-heir's poor relatives, certain jurists, mainly the Zahiria, sought to present it as obligatory, although to come from an unspecific portion of the estate. The Shi'a for their part have departed further from this premise. They say that if the testator's son or daughter predeceases his or her own children then these grandchildren who would have been excluded by the presence of their uncles are to be given a share equivalent to that which would have been their parents.

Recent Egyptian and Syrian legislation has adopted the above widely controversial point from the Sunni jurists. But to their disadvantage they departed a bit further from the original view and now hold a minority and unrecognizable view. This requires a testator to give the surviving relative, whether ascendant or descendant, if excluded from inheritance an equivalent amount to the disposable third or the remainder of it. Although this attitude might be seen as a genuine attempt to help in meeting the needs of the family, it disregards one of the prerequisite elements of the law of bequest, i.e. the need to have clear instructions from the testator prior to his death. It also contravenes the law of inheritance and ownership in that it gives them an unfounded and unprecedented right to compete with the legal heirs. Thus it upsets the basic principles of ownership which state that 'No transfer of estate is to take place unless with the consent of its owner.' And as it works against the consent of both the heirs and the deceased, it definitely breaks many laws. These laws in fact render this statute illegal. Also it constitutes a threat which could hinder the law of bequest from being applied.

However, the Saudi courts have not overlooked the significance of the alleviation of the poverty and needs of the family. Indeed, the courts have taken a practical step in this direction. Unlike the methods suggested by the Zahiria, Shi'a and the Egyptian and Syrian laws which grant the relative a share that neither the testator nor the law have accepted, the courts of Saudi Arabia have reached almost the same objective through their intelligent interpretation of the legal principles and the testator's wishes.

In a number of cases, for instance, when the bequest or *Waqf* was made for benevolent and good purposes or to the glory of God, the courts have acted positively. They have been motivated by the same objective of turning such dispositions into a family charity and place it in the hands of the deceased's relatives in general, whenever their poverty and need is established. The case of *N* and his brothers and sisters is an example of this.[33]

In this case the grandfather bequeathed a third of his house to be spent on benevolent purposes and assigned his son, *H*, to execute the bequest. The testamentary executor died suddenly before he had executed his father's bequest.

N, on behalf of his brothers and sisters (the grandchildren of the testator), claiming to have been more deserving than other people to obtain the charity of their grandfather, applied to the court to have the bequest granted to them exclusively. They offered as grounds for their claim their being the testator's relatives and in a state of need. Enough proof was presented to the court permitting such a claim. Granting their application, the court ordered the bequeathed portion of the house to be redistributed equally between the testator's four grandsons and the two granddaughters.

In the case of *H* and her daughter *N*,[34] each bequeathed for benevolent purposes one third of the houses they owned. Ultimately both houses were held in joint partnership with each one's respective heirs. When the two houses later fell into ruin and became uninhabitable, the executorix *Kh* tried unsuccessfully to sell the two houses amid stormy objection from the joint partners although someone had offered a good price for the two ruined houses. Thus in face of this coupled with her inability to implement the two bequests, she filed a complaint against the joint owners seeking a court order to sell the houses at the offered price.

In compliance with the court's request, she brought sufficient proof that the two houses were in a useless state and that the price offered at an auction was fair and beneficial to the two bequests and the joint partners. She was also to prove that it would be disadvantageous to the two bequests if the two individual thirds in the two houses were to be sold separately. To hinder the sale, the joint partners applied to the court, claiming that they deserved the two benevolent bequests since they were many in number, poor and also relatives of the two testatrixes.

However, a court order was issued allowing the sale and ordering the price to be handed over to the executorix to spend in the way directed by the two testatrixes. Taking into consideration the relatives' demand, the court instructed the executorix to consider the right of the relatives in the two bequests over others when the value of poverty had been established.

When the contestants showed their non-acceptance of such a judgement it was referred, as normal procedure, to the judicial Scrutiny Board to be reviewed and the appeal was dismissed by the Board.[35]

c. The legatee's social and religious status

That the bequest must not be given to a person who is going to use it against the well being of his society is a decision upheld by all jurists. The jurists treat as null a bequest to one who insists on committing sins or encourages immoral actions or allows destructive rumours to prevail or takes part in the corruption of society.[36] The same can be said about those who may use the bequest to pursue injustice.

The above principle could also be applied, though with some difficulty, against whosoever uses the influence he has upon others to discourage morals and good behaviour from being adopted. *Sadd al-dhara'i*, (prevention from making excuses), is taken as the jurisprudence source from which jurists have derived all the above rules. It is obvious that to apply such a rule one needs sufficient proof before any decision is taken. It is also obvious, however, that in spite of the many strings attached and the fact that proof is not easy to get hold of, it cannot at the same time be ruled out as an impossible task either.

If on the other hand, a bequest is to have the effect of converting an immoral person or to cause a sinner to abandon his sins or to make a person who causes injustices to behave justly instead, then as a reflection to the above juristic principle, the bequest will become a commendable one. The application of such a principle helps purify the community and, by providing wrong-doers with sufficient property to cause to refrain them from their defiance of Islamic laws, it prevents evil.

d. The status of the testator's heirs

The state of need or wealth of the heirs should be taken into consideration and should affect the testator's decision whether to bequeath or not. The law of inheritance should be looked at as a protector of the heirs' minimal interests and not as a hindrance. Thus to determine the dispositions the testator should settle his estate in any way which helps their interests to flourish rather than diminish.

Elements which determine what should be left to the heirs are the number of heirs, the degree of their wealth and the net sum of the testator's estate. Consequently, if the heirs are poor or if they are great in number and also if the estate to be left is not large enough to meet the needs of the heirs or if it is just enough to suffice, then to leave the property unaffected by any disposition is stated by the jurists as the most recommendable thing to do. Such action leaving the prospective heirs with the amount of property they need is also regarded religiously as if their relative had donated them with a prime gift[37] and therefore this act will be religiously rewarded in the second life.

The relevant points are in harmony with the advice of the *Hadith*, part of which is 'To leave your heirs well-off is better than to leave them dependent as begging people. All that you dispense in maintenance is charity, even the mouthful which you carry to the mouth of your wife'.

When the testator disregards the interests of his heirs and ignores the Prophet's and jurist's recommendations, his disposition is not void because such recommendations are not obligatory and enforcable. Thus the defiance of the above advice raises the testator's disposition only to the *Makruh* degree (blameworthiness),[38] unless his intention to harm them was manifest.

Two justifications to the testator's act would be considered. The first is that the testator is utilizing the right given by the law itself where neither of the former recommendations actually restrict his power by classifying it as a prohibition; the second is that the testator's disposition comes within the limit of one third up to which a testator is allowed to use his power to bequeath just as if the heirs are few, wealthy or the estate is extensive.

The non-existence of an heir removes the right of objection to a bequest no matter what amount it involves. Illustration of this is seen in the case of *A v. Bait al-mal*.[39]

Am bequeathed the disposable one-third for good and benevolent purposes out of which she directed the executor to meet the funeral expenses. To *A*, the designated executor, the testatrix bequeathed the remaining two thirds as she declared she had no legal heirs. Following *Am's* death, *A* sued Bait al-mal (public treasury), to release the bequeathed estate to him according to the express wishes of the deceased.

The court's verdict was as follows: 'As the above mentioned bequest and the death of the testatrix were all proved, from the text of the authoritative books of the Hanbali school, validity of the bequest with entire estate for the person who had no heirs, I, the judge, order the head of Bait al-mal, to release the deceased's estate and deliver it to the plaintiff'.

This verdict was later sent to the judicial Scrutiny Board, reviewed and ratified.[40]

e. Is being a Muslim a condition to become a legatee of a Muslim?

Islam has been seen to be an easily acceptable religion and has attracted many followers who have numerous relationships and ties with non-Muslims. To a newly converted Muslim who has come from a different background or has lived in a distinct society or who has a strong tie with his non-Muslim family or friends from whom he does not want to be alienated, he may find it hard had he been asked to terminate his relationship with them. Had alienation been necessary, an element of anxiety for the person and a problem for his new society could occur.

On a sensitive subject such as this, Islam has kept the momentum going and dealt cautiously with it. Thus apart from matters related to belief itself, Islam has opened the way for a wide range of relationships to ease the living conditions for its subjects. As to the new believer, the law has seen it more appropriate to make use of all the inter and the extra-family ties and communications both to strengthen and to widen the sphere of conversion to Islam.

The Prophet (peace be upon him) content with above, not only permitted transactions and ordinary dealings with unbelievers but allowed the donation of gifts to them too. A famous *Hadith* story in this respect is that of *Asma* whose mother had come to see her. *Asma* told the Prophet that her mother had come but was not at all interested in Islam and asked whether she should maintain her relationship with her mother (by donating her something). The Prophet's answer was 'Yes keep your relationship with your mother.'[41]

Another famous story in this respect is the story reported in the *Hadith* about the oriental cloak that the Prophet gave to Umar. The cloak was made of silk. As silk was forbidden for a Muslim male to wear Umar was astonished and inquired, 'You have given it to me though you commented about the cloak of *'Atarid* as you did.' The Prophet's reply was, 'I did not give it to you to wear.' Consequently, Umar, for his part, gave it to a non-believer brother of his in Makkah.'[42]

A bequest being of not much difference to a gift in the eye of the law has to conform with the above principle to validate legacies made to non-Muslims. The enactment of the law of bequest accordingly facilitated the way for a Muslim man to marry a non-Muslim woman. Thus a husband (knowing his non-Muslim wife is not entitled to a share of his estate after death through succession) can easily allocate to her a share of up to one third of his estate by the application of the law of bequest and vice versa, i.e. for a non-Muslim wife to bequeath to her Muslim husband. The same rule is also applicable in the case of a family whose members are a combination of Muslims and non-Muslims.

Notwithstanding, the jurists' unanimous decision not to allow a non-Muslim or a Muslim who renounces Islam to be assigned custody or guardianship would not in any way conflict with or lessen the significance principle of leniency towards non-Muslims for such a rule was merely intended to protect youngsters from being treated maliciously to their mortal detriment by their alleged protectors. The jurists even regard unfit for the post of custody or guardianship an adult Muslim who persists in defying the law and community orders by living in sin or indulging in immoral or irregular behaviour and insists that only a trustworthy person can have custody or guardianship over the ward.

The idea is to allow the child to grow up in a healthy atmosphere identical to that which the child presumably would have had under his parent's roof. To illustrate disadvantages and injustices done to the pre-mature child, the judge will usually retain the right to act as a supreme and general supervisor over custodians and guardians. The court will therefore act to dismiss them if the judge detects any dangerous change in the mental, moral or behavioural state of the custodian or guardian.

THE CRITERIA OF RECIPROCITY IN THE LAW BETWEEN MUSLIMS AND NON-MUSLIMS

The jurists of Malikis, Hanbalis and most of the Shafi'as have, since the formative years of the law, agreed to let a non-Muslim from a hostile country benefit under an operative will because of its similarity to a gift.[43]

Nonetheless, the jurists' resolution to hand over a bequest to the benificiary of a hostile citizen (the *Harbi*) stops short of being absolute. The subject matter of the bequest to be permitted to a *Harbi* or an enemy must be of non-aggressive nature. While if the subject matter constitutes a potential threat to the Muslim community or if it consists of a dangerous material such as arms, ammunition or documents or secret information, etc. the bequest beomes illegal entirely or in part according to the nature of its contents.[44]

Hanbali jurists made no distinction between the domicile of the testator, whether he was in a Muslim country or not when he drew up his will. Nor did they introduce any restriction as to the whereabouts of the legatee at the time the bequest was made. But the jurists are more absolute in allowing the free movement of the bequest or its value to an alien country. Since they do not demand that an alien beneficiary come in person to receive his entitlements.

Of course, such restrictions would be relaxed considerably whenever peace prevailed between warring countries and the threat to a Muslim country is over. So the state of enmity will give way to a more profitable and binding relation using the reciprocity of knowledge and necessary commodities thus to share equally the available fruits of peace and prosperity instead of belligerence and destruction.

DIFFERENCE OF NATIONALITY

The law has guaranteed the free movement of a gift from a citizen of one country to a citizen of another. This is a unanimous decision by all jurists. Using the method of analogy, Ibn Qudama, compared a bequest to a gift by stating that a bequest comes within the definition of a gift.[45] Accordingly, the Hanbalis authorize a Muslim or non-Muslim of any country to benefit from whatever has been left to him under a will or Waqf.

The Saudi Courts have long abided by such a view as is seen in the case where the testator bequeathed the sum of SR10,000 specified to be used to build a mosque or to supply water. He specifically left his executor free to invest his bequest in any location inside or outside Saudi Arabia. He also instructed his executor to buy sheep and sacks of rice for distribution to the poor of his village in Hadhramawt in South Yaman.[46]

A more positive application of the above principle is illustrated in the case of the *Waqf* of Zadah.[47]

This was brought about by *Sh's* application to the King asking for permission to reside in the *Waqf* of Zadah, since he and his son were readers of the Quran and thus fulfilling the conditions of the dedication (*Waqf*).

The document of the *Waqf* was found to contain an order of priority for the prospective beneficiaries as such. Produce of the *Waqf* is to be vested consecutively in the children of his sons, then in the children of his daughter, then in the children of his sister *A* then in her grandchildren and finally after they had all died, in those readers of the Quran.

The King, for his part, ordered the case to be presented to the court to enquire about the existence of any of the specific beneficiaries. The Court terminated its enquiries only when the lineage of those beneficiaries was ratified by the court of Erzerum in Turkey. The court thus ruled that the application of *Sh* was inapplicable since the existence of some beneficiaries had been traced and established.

Also in the case of *H*,[48] the Court agreed to give the heirs who were living in Kampuj (Indonesia), their due share from the deceased's estate. Nevertheless, apparently, expecting the heirs to come to Mecca and agree to the will of the deceased, the Court adjudged the share of those heirs to be handed over by the Public Treasury (Bait al-Mal), to his executor to keep until they came to Saudi Arabia.

Of course not all kinds of estate are permitted to pass into the possession of an alien person. The government of Saudi Arabia, for instance, for some reason or other, until very recently, banned foreign nationals from acquiring real estate in the country.

Although such a statute was not the reason for the decision in the above case, it certainly affects the courts' decisions when the matter involves the conveyance of an immovable property into an alien hand even if the person is the heir of a Saudi.

But instead it will be ordered to be sold on the alien's behalf and the value donated. Application of this statute is seen in operation in the case of *A v. Bait al-Mal*.[49]

B, a Saudi Arabian national died leaving *A,* the cousin of her father from Sudan. He petitioned to the Court to be given the estate of the daughter of his cousin, *B*, which consisted of an amount of money as well as two enclosed yards.

Since the deceased's estate consisted of immovable property and the claimant was a foreign subject, the court ordered the money to be paid to him by Bait al-Mal. But as regards the immovable property, the court resolved that it was to be kept until the claimant confirmed that it was owned by the deceased after which it would be dealt with according to the orders governing the ownership of immovable property by foreigners.

THE POSITION OF THE LEGATEE BEING AN HEIR

To make justice more accessible and to put an end to capital being accumulated by one group at the expense of others, Islamic law in its swift move against Jahiliya's (pre-Islamic) feudal system abolished their system of inheritance, which was built on the basis of personal strength and favouritism and operated against the weak and needy.

It was the law of succession in its final form that first hit that system hard, followed by the law of bequest with restrictions which were set to limit the testamentary power. Both effectively undermined the old system with its intrinsic social inequality. Such restrictions are derived from the main sources of the law, one of which is the *Hadith*. In one of the *Hadiths* of the Prophet there is an explicit pronouncement, viz., 'No bequest in favour of an heir.' This is, of course, one of the most important limitations on the testimentary capacity of a Muslim subject.

Muslim jurists in general accept this *Hadith* as the basic rule governing relationships between the testator and his inheritors. Jurists interpret the rule by arguing that the reason a bequest in favour of an heir cannot be allowed is that it would amount to giving preference to some inheritors over others, thus defeating the policy of the law which has allocated fixed portions to each heir in the inheritance. This situation would very likely give rise to disputes among related persons and lead to litigation. The *Ulama* have varying views as regards the issue of the co-heir's assent to a bequest made to one of the other co-heirs. Some jurists are of the opinion that bequest to an heir is automatically *ultra vires* and thus automatically invalid. Therefore subsequent consent of his co-heir will have no effect at all in altering a bequest which is already void.[50]

Nevertheless, the majority of jurists disagree with the above reasoning. They maintain that so long as his testamentary disposition does not violate or infringe the law and provided that the heirs give their consent to the testator's action, the law in that case upholds such a testament.

The right to bequeath, therefore, is seen by the majority of jurists not to constitute an infringement of the institute of bequest. They stated that any rivalry, animosity and viciousness which could arise from a disproportionate bequest to one of the heirs, will lose ground with all the inheritors having given their approval. Further, by the heirs waiving their outstanding claim over the will, the bequest ceases to be subjected to the proscription incorporated in the above *Hadith*; especially, when we observe that certain dependable reporters of the *Hadith* have recited it with an additional clause, 'God has given each all he deserves, therefore, no bequest to an heir unless other heirs so desire'.[51]

This is how it was reported by the Companion Ibn Abbas. Again, 'Unless heirs have consented to it,'[52] as was reported by 'Amr b. Shu'aib handed down to his father from his grandfather.

The above quotation of the *Hadith* denotes that bequest to an inheritor is indeed not void and therefore inexecutable but merely predicated and conditional upon the required consent of the heirs. If the other heirs assent to a bequest to one of them or to a bequest of more than one-third of the estate, the former reasons concerning voidance would no longer hold good and the bequest as made will be valid.

The adherence of the Saudi Courts to the majority view, which is also the view more preferred by the Hanbalis, is clearly illustrated in the case of a house which was bequeathed to be held in trust for the underage children of the deceased. The value of the house amounted to more than one-third of the bulk of the estate. The deceased's brother-in-law brought the case before the Court on behalf of his sister. He disputed the legality of the disposition on the grounds that 'the value exceeded the one-third and further, was made in favour only of his minors'. The judge, after examining the case thoroughly, informed the wife through her brother (agent) that she would not forfeit her right to the bequest because it was within her right if she so wished to withhold her consent on the accessive portion. Therefore, she would receive her full share in the estate from the two thirds and the shares of the other heirs, who had given their ratification would be reduced proportionately to meet the accessive bequest.

The wife who was then satisfied by the judge's explanation gave her consent to the execution of the testamentary trust to the minors.[53]

It is also evidence from the extract of the case above that the wife's objection to the bequest rested on the assumption that her husband, for some reason or other, might have intended to harm her by compelling her to abandon or to minimize her share of inheritance. Or she might have been induced to take such action by her objection to implied favouritism. A hypothetical question may be posed, 'If she was driven by her repugnance, why then did she later give her consent?' One may argue in reply that her suspicions of the husband's act were dispelled by the knowledge that it was legal for him to make such a will and also that it was her right to contest or object and that this was a necessary condition for the execution of the will. The knowledge that she had such a right might have been the main factor in her consent and the subsequent dismissal of the case.

It is also noteworthy that the above mentioned case shows not only the honest application of and the adherence to the views of the Hanbalis but it illustrates a significant aspect of the law. That is to say, an appropriation of *Waqf* becomes the object of the bequest.

However, *Waqf* or charity trust in law aims at prevention of alienation of ownership of an estate in perpetuity on behalf of the beneficiaries. If the *Waqf* as such becomes the subject matter of a bequest, then it should not exceed the one-third limit, but if it does it needs ratification by the heirs for the excessive part to pass over to its beneficiaries (as we have seen in the above case) or else it becomes invalid.

It is of cardinal importance to note that a testamentary *Waqf* generally (except for its validity to an heir) is subject to the same restrictions as an ordinary testamentary disposition. The bequest of trust should not exceed the third even when it is made in favour of an heir. The Hanbalis are of the opinion that *Waqf*, as such, does not necessarily require the stated consent of the other heirs. It was Ibn Hanbal's stated view that 'It is valid for a testator on his death-bed to bequeath his third on trust to his heirs' coupled with his answer to the question as to whether he agreed with the principle of there being no bequest to an heir. In answer, he agreed that the *Waqf* was distinguished from bequest for the former was not to be sold, inherited or to become the subject of absolute ownership of the inheritors.[54] All kinds of consent which were required, as we shall see later, can in Hanbali law be obtained only after the testator's death.

The question may be raised whether it is still necessary to have the heir's approval where the legatee is actually the sole inheritor. Would it not be ridiculous to ask his consent where he himself alone stands to benefit in both cases. In theory this may indeed be silly but in practice it is not so.

A simple example is when a testator makes a will leaving all his estate in trust for his sole heir. An option, of course, is open as usual for the heir to approve such entitlement. If the heir opts to go along with the wishes of his praepositus his position relating to the settlement will not be one of ownership but rather that of sole beneficiary. This means that he does not actually own the estate but continually enjoys the profits of the trust. Further, the appropriation immediately following the settler's death and/or after the consent of the heir the bequest becomes absolutely inalienable and tied eternally to the purpose the settler has stipulated.

But on the other hand, a greater freedom will be vested in the heir if he refuses his assent to the excessive bequest for he automatically acquires full and absolute possession of a two-thirds portion of the estate.

It could be said that the rule of option in its effect is a privileged concept set to counteract the odd impulses of the dying person who may take an advantage of his position to harm or blackmail his heirs. And it is another means of preventing extortion from being imposed on them by the deceased on his death-bed, forcing them to agree to an unbalanced deal, for fear that he will bequeath all his estate on trust; i.e. tie up his estate. This could in fact be one of the main reasons justifying the deference regarding ratification till after the death of the deceased.

Determination of the status of prospective heirs and legatees must, as a general policy of Islamic law, be postponed until the testator's death. It is a precautionary measure against a new situation which will probably upset the whole system. For instance, if the bulk of the estate was bequeathed by a childless person to his brother, the brother cannot enjoy being an heir if in the course of life the testator should have a child because the child will naturally displace the brother as an heir and reduce him to the status of a legatee.

NOTES

1. *Sh. Q. al-Wasiya*, 45.
2. *Kash*, Vol. 4, 340.
3. *A'lam al-Muwaqqi'in*, Vol. 3, 140.
4. Ibid, 170.
5. *Insaf*, Vol. 7, 232.
6. *Qur'an*, Al-Nisa (Women), 12.
7. *A'lam*, Vol. 3, 126. The jurists keep saying that the condition of the dedicator or the testator is binding as the Legislation text: which Ibn al-Qayim comments on by saying that the unjust bequest can be refused.
8. Makkah G.C. No. 71, Vol. 15, (1391H). Special Reg. of Shaikh Sulaiman al-Amr.
9. *The accumulation of the dictums (Fatawa) of Ibn Taimia*, Vol. 31, 215/316.
10. *Fatawa of Ibn Taimia*, Vol. 3, 316.
11. *A'lam*, Vol. 4, 233.
12. G.C. Makkah, No. 93, Vol. 7, (1377H).
13. G.C. Makkah. The letter is attached to the Case No. 93, Vol. 7, (1377H).
14. Reported by Ibn Majah. See *Al-Mu'jam Al-Mufahras*, Vol. 4, 332.
15. G.C. Makkah, No. 105, Vol. 17, private registry of Shaikh Sulaiman al-Amr, (1391H).
16. *Kash*, Vol. 4, 249, & *Sh-Munt*, Vol. 4, 495.
17. G.C. Makkah, No. 40, Vol. 1, (1381H).
18. *Kash*, Vol. 4, 287, & *Sh-Munt*, Vol. 2, 508.
19. *Kash*, Vol. 4, 278.
20. *Kash*, Vol. 4, 357.
21. *Al-Muntaha*, Vol. 2, 344.
22. *Al-Muntaha, Vol. 2, 340.*
23. *Qur'an*, Luqman, 14, & *Qur'an*, Ahqaf, 15.
24. *Sh. Muntaha*, Vol. 2, 43, & *Kash*, Vol. 4, 464, & Ibn al-Qayim, *Tuhfat al-mawdud*, 265-6.
25. G.C. Makkah No. 94, Vol. 3, (1377H).
26. *Kash*, Vol. 4, 290; *Sh. Munt*, Vol. 2, 550.
27. *Al-rawdah*, 25-26.
28. *Al-Tanqih al-Mushbi'*, 197; *Al-Insaf fi ma'rifat al-rajih min al-khilaf*, Vol. 7, 246.
29. Al-minhaji al-suyuti, *Jawahir al-'uqud*, Vol. 1, 452.
30. Jedda G.C. No. 774, Vol. 7, (1389H).
31. Jedda Katib al-'adl, No. 926, Vol. 3, (1384H).
32. Jedda Katib al-'adl, No. 1894, Vol. 5, (1386H).
33. Makkah G.C. No. 91, Vol. 1, (1380H).
34. G.C. Makkah No. 637, Vol. 10. Minute registry of Shaikh Abdulmalik b. Duhaish, (1391H).
35. Judicial Scrutiny Board of the Western Province No. 2409, (1391H).
36. *Matalib uli al-nuha*, Vol. 4, 483.
34. *Mughni*, Vol. 6, 416-417.
38. *Kash*, Vol. 4, 339.
39. G.C. Makkah No. 71, Vol. 15, (1391H). Sp. Reg. of Shaikh Sulaiman Al-Amr.
40. Decision of the Scrutiny board of the judiciary is attached to Case No. 71, Vol. 15. Special registry of Shaikh Sulaiman al-Amr, (1391HJ). Grand Court of Makkah.
41. Al-Bukhari and Muslim. See *Al-Mu'jam Al-Mufahras*, Vol. 2, 276.
42. Al-Bukhari. See *Al-Mu'jam Al-Mufahras*, Vol. 6, 17-18.
43. The prominent Hanbali jurist Al-Harithi qualified the legality of such a bequest to a citizen of a hostile country (*Harbi*) to be approved if it is to those who do not actively engage themselves in the war or campaign against the Muslims. *Sharh al-Muntaha*, Vol. 2, 547, *Kash*, Vol. 4, 353.
44. Ibrahim b. Abdullah b. Ibrahim, *Al-adhb al-fa'd sharh undat al-farid*, Vol. 2, 180. *Kash*, Vol. 4, 353.
45. *Al-Mughni*, Vol. 6, 531.
46. Jedda Katib al-'adl. Case No. 678, Vol. 2, (1382H).
47. Advisory Council's Resolutions No. 190, (date 4/8.1357H).
48. Makkah Grand Court, Case No. 38, Vol. 1, (date 16/2/1381H).
49. Makkah Grand Court, Case No. 74, Vol. 6, (date 8/3/1378H).
50. *Al-Insaf*, Vol. 7, 194, & *Al-Mughni*, Vol. 6, 419.
51. Reported by Al-Dar Qutni. See *Sh. Muntaha al-inadat*, Vol. 2, 541, *Kash*, Vol. 4, 340.
52. *Sh. Munt*, Vol. 2, 541, *Kash*, Vol. 4, 340.
53. Jedda G.R. Case No. 776, Vol. 6, (date 2/12/1389H).
54. *Kash*, Vol. 4, 312.

CHAPTER IV
FAILURE OF BEQUEST

LEGATEE PRE-DECEASING TESTATOR

Benefit of the legatee, in person, is a substantial objective of *Al-Wasiya*. His survival, therefore, is vital if the bequest is to be operative at all. The legatee who predeceases his testator becomes by definition unworthy to succeed to the bequest because he cannot meet the required conditions of a valid bequest.

The death of the beneficiary, as such, obstructs the movement of an estate into his (the dead person's) possession. Hence, the portion bequeathed if still unrevoked by the testator will fail because the person supposed to benefit is found incapable of possession. The reason, however, is that Islamic law demands the actual or at least the presumptive existence of the legatee a moment after the death of the testator. Thus there is no question of Islamic law permitting representation of the legatee's heirs in this matter as the bequest in such a case becomes immediately null and void.

UNCERTAINTY OF THE LEGATEE'S DEATH OR SURVIVAL

However, if a person is missing this is not like the case above and the due right of inheritance to the de facto missing person must be preserved until either he appears or is proved dead. In the cases of uncertainty, jurists dare not deprive him (the missing person) of the right to possess. For as long as his fate is not yet known, he has an equitable right to keep his title (though suspended pending his return, discovery or the establishment of his death) over his estate.

The position of the bequeathed share which is allocated to the missing person is a point of controversy amongst the Hanbali school. The jurists are split into two groups, one group maintains the idea that the estate of the missing person should be suspended for the span of his life which is considered to be the attainment of 90 years, for they say, people rarely exceed the age of 90 years, even during peaceful times, or be suspended for four years if his absence is during a period of danger.

The suspension concept, prima facie, is meant to protect the estate of the missing person from his prospective heirs. For this reason the jurists are assumed to activate the maxim of 'He who does not give, does not take: and loss goes with gain.' Also because of the suspension imposed upon the movement of the missing person's estate to his heirs, we find these are questioning his right to inherit alternatively from ancestors who die during this period. It is, as they see it, a one way traffic. So they question the right of a missing person to inherit from others while denying to others the right to inherit from his estate.

Bequest according to the jurists' analogy accords to the same argument, and, therefore, is inoperative, but suspended pending the return of the missing person or the Court's decree which determines his death. His estate, ultimately, is to be paid to him if he returns or to be handed over to his heirs if the court decrees that he has died.

The other group of jurists disagreed with the former's argument and say that the missing person is actually entitled to whatever right is due to him (such as inheritance) so long as his death is not yet known to have preceded that of his ancestor; for, they add, we cannot possibly determine the fact of his death except at the expiry of the waiting period.

The latter view was considered as more appropriate to the former one and was later to become the official doctrine of the Hanabalis. In a recent case the Grand Court of Makkah followed the official reasoning in preference to the former when in the *Waqf* of *D*[1] the share of *M* (the missing person) in his ancestor's *waqf* (trust) was kept for him pending his reappearance and when the Court declared his judicial death, the accumulated estate left aside for him was ordered to passover to his living heirs as part of his heritable estate.

Bequest as the sister of inheritance and the *waqf* by analogy, is bound to follow suit in the decision to allocate to the missing person whatever is due to him under bequest.

HOMICIDE AS A FORFEITURE TO BEQUEST

It is a matter of equity not to allow a criminal to benefit from his crime. Muslim law in general, has thus precluded a murderer from receiving profit in either a testate or intestate situation. The jurists have introduced a well known maxim to govern the application of the rules in the cases of homicide which says, 'He who hurriedly seeks to gain undue profit is punished by deprivation.' If, therefore, an unjustifiable killing has occurred to the testator by his legatee, such action will be interpreted, according to the maxim, to accuse the legatee of acting under an evil drive of greediness to acquire an undue right and profit from the will. Thus, by enacting such accusation he (the legatee) loses the right. The ruling on this point was derived according to Ibn Taimia and Ibn al-Qayim, from one of the sources of the Hanbali jurisprudence known as *Sadd al-dhara'a* or the prevention of excuses.[2]

The killing of an ancestor by his prospective heir causes the exclusion of that heir from inheritance. The same principle is to be applied to deprive a legatee of a bequest made to him in consequence of the killing of the testator. Similarly, if *Y* makes a will to *X* and *X* subsequently inflicts a mortal wound which later causes the death of the testator *Y*, the legatee *X* will forfeit his right to the testament.

The above rule, which is stictly enforced, is not only a deterent against whoever actually commits homicide against his ancestor and legator but has been extended to give an equal deterent to whoever offers false testimony and wild accusations leading to the death of either the ancestor or the testator.[3] The rule obviously would not include those with unsound mind nor infants, since they lack reasoning ability to form mins ria or criminal motive and at the same time they are unaware of the consequences which stem from their action. They are thus excluded from punishment.

The exclusion of infants from the relevant rule and their inability to form a mins ria was substantiated in the case of *H* and his son *'A*. *'A*, a young boy, was accused of carrying the rifle that shot his father who died as a result of his fatal wound. The Chief Justice intervened to repeal a decision taken by the original judge, before whom the case was brought, because that judge on the grounds of the minor's confession to having been part of the cause of his father's death, had made the minor son liable for the death of his father so he ordered him to be excluded from his father's inheritance. In his evaluation of the case, the Chief Justice's ruling was that the exclusion of the minor from inheritance is part of the conviction of that infant. Thus the Chief Justice decided that the minor's recall of the incident could not be witheld because he was under age. His exclusion, therefore, from inheritance would be suspended until he reached the age of puberty. Then and only then, he added, if the minor confirmed what he had said, his word was to be taken as a basis to his exclusion otherwise it would not.[4]

It is aparent, from the case above, that the Chief Justice adhered to the Hanbali doctrines on legal age by re-emphasising the attainment of puberty as one of the factors determining the responsibility of a person for his wrong actions.

Contrary to most jurists the Hanabalis validate a will in favour of the person who causes the mortal injury to the testator if such a will is made afterwards by the one who received that injury. They base their ruling on the grounds that bequest after the wound would be initiated by a person capable of exercising the right to bequeath to a legally capable recipient. Thus even if death follows it will not deprive the legatee of receiving such as bequest since the injury which caused death actually preceded the making of the bequest. Moreover, a legatee in such a case will not be accused of premeditation, according to the Hanbalis, to gain undue inheritance or bequest through the very denial of the life of its rightful owner. They also add that the mere awareness of the testator of the source of his injury contributes a lot to this reasoning for it shows the testator's willingness and insistance, after all, to benefit such a legatee,[5] and this will eventually become a persuasive element in deciding the validity of the bequest. The case of Al-H and Ibn D[6] shows these principles in operation. Ibn D, a good-hearted man and a friend of the family, offered Al-H his hospitality during the ritual month of Ramadan in the Holy City of Makkah. On their way the car turned over and the guest had his leg broken. Before he died a judge came to visit him in the hospital, recorded and validated his condonation and wish to release Ibn D from the responsibility of the accident.

Contemporary lawyers in their commentaries on the modern laws accept the Hanbali reasoning as more adequate and nearer to equity and justice. For instance the Hanbali approach in respect of homicide was accepted as a means of excluding a participant in homicide from becoming an heir or a legatee, by the Egyptian law of 1946 AD.[7]

The former view was held to assimilate an opinion voiced by the Hanbalis, that 'If a person who has received an accidental injury condones it and relieves from liability the one who inflicted that injury, the due amount of money which was supposed to be paid to him or the value, will be counted against the disposable one third to resemble donation made during a fatal illness.'[8]

The Hanbalis, in general, set as impediment to inheritance and bequest all kinds of homicide whether they be deliberate, quasi-deliberate or accidental leading eventually to the execution of the offender, the payment of the required compensation or blood-money or merely demands an expiation from the criminal, that is to say, the setting free of a slave (if there are any) or fasting continuously for two months.

Legal practice in Saudi Arabia recognizes the causation which was first found by the Hanbali jurists, e.g. a car accident where the driver is held immediately responsible, through negligence or recklessness, for the death or injury of the passenger. That is, of course, if he was in charge of the vehicle at the time of the accident. The same responsibility will be established against a person who was found to cause such an accident to happen.

The case of *Y v. Al-Sh* and *M*, provides us in their respect with sufficient illustration. The judge of the Grand Court of Makkah decreed that the actions of the two drivers (in a crash), *Al-S* and *M*, the defendants, were the cause of death of the two brothers who were passengers, and therefore the case was classified as homicide. The two drivers were ordered to pay blood-money to the petitioner *Y* for his dead brothers, However, as one of the two drivers was found to bear more reponsibility for the accident he was ordered to pay a greater part of the total compensation.[9]

ACCEPTANCE OF BEQUEST

Unlike the heir in inheritance, the legatee must show by action or verbal means some sign of enthusiasm and the willingness to comply with the will of the testator. The difference between succession and a bequest is substantial in that heredity in succession is natural and binding. Nonetheless, acceptance of a bequest on the other hand is far from obligatory; it confers an undue and utterly new proprietory right on the legatee.

To this extent Hanbalis considered the necessity of acceptance as an inevitable condition to the implementation of a bequest; and in this respect when we look beyond the Hanbali circle, apart from that of Zufar (a Hanafi jurist), who likened a bequest to inheritance which requires no acceptance we find this principle is generally accepted.

When acceptance is required

Unless a bequest is a contingent one, that is to say, was assigned to become operative at a particular time or at the occurrence of an event after the death of the testator, Hanbali jurists agree that acceptance will be ineffective unless it is made after the testator's death. Thus if a legatee should reject a will during the bequeather's lifetime, he will not be precluded from accepting it after the death of the testator.

Similarly, if the legatee should accept a will while the testator is alive he will gain nothing from such a bequest without the repetition of that acceptance after the death of the testator for bequest is operative only from death. Hence, no prior acceptance or renunciation, unless repeated afterwards, will be acceptable. The reason for this is that the main body of the Hanbali jurists liken a bequest to other contracts which necessitate acceptance. Alienation by contract will not be deemed to have been accomplished unless the other party to the contract has shown his willingness through the usual means of ratification.

Such a rule has its roots in the jurists belief that acceptance is an inseparable part of the cause, i.e. there must be an acceptance of the contract or the bequest without which execution of bequest cannot and will not take place. Or to use the juristic term, execution can never precede the cause. One of the strongest advocates of the above tendency is Ibn Qudama, who says 'Acceptance must either be a condition or a part of the cause (bequest, for instance), which in neither case can precede either its cause or its condition.'[10]

NO FORMATS ARE REQUIRED

As is a general phenomenon of testamentary law, no formats are required to subscribe to the legality of the bequest. Thus an informal sign or declaration (which indicates the legatee's desire to give his consent to the orders of the testator), is sufficient for the bequest to be operative.

THE LEGATEE'S RENUNCIATION OF THE WILL

If after his knowledge of the will the legatee eventually rejects the will made in his favour, the will then reverts to the heirs as the consent of the parties to any contract has always been regarded in law to be of vital importance to its validity. Another juristic principle states 'No estate is to pass into someone's possession without his consent.' These principles affirm the right of everyone to refuse the possession of an article which he thinks harmful or unwise to accept.

Succession is an exceptional case and the above principle cannot be extended to bring inheritance within its scope. This is because obligation in inheritance is imposed by the one who acquires the power, God, The Legislator Himself, and none else can claim such privilege or authority. Accordingly, the testator will have no authority to confer the ownership of the bequeathed object into the legatee's possession.

The legatee, therefore, will be said to enjoy complete freedom to renounce any bequest made in his favour. Many reasons have been put forward to justify and demonstrate the importance or the power to reject a bequest, one of which is that the bequest itself might be financially harmful to the legatee rather than beneficial. An example is the bequest of an old or a sick animal and so forth which incurs loss or trouble to the legatee. If this bequest were to pass into the legatee's possession without his consent, it would be very costly for him. Also morally he would have been denied the right to defend his interests. Thus, the legatee's right, according to the law of equity, to stop infectious disease spreading from the bequeathed animal to his own animals is of utmost importance.

But fortunately for law abiding people, the law which gives a person the right to defend himself against attackers by all means necessary makes available the means to reject a harmful bequest.

In the same way there is the possibility that the legatee may reproach the testator for the favour done to him because he resents the feeling of obligation imposed. However, it is only human nature that not many people would like to put themselves in a such a position of their own accord. The power to renounce a bequest, which has been vested in the legatee by the application of this principle, will ultimately help him get out of such a precarious and embarrassing situation.

THE LEGATEE WHO REFUSES TO ACCEPT OR RENOUNCE

The possession of an article bequeathed must not be left undetermined for a long time. The legatee is deemed to acquire the object by his acceptance or release it to revert back to the absolute possession of the testator's heirs by his renunciation of the bequest.

Nonetheless, if in the meantime the legatee refuses to accept the bequest or to renounce it, the law, through the office of the judge, will have to step in and order him to choose either way. But if after the Court's order the legatee sticks adamantly to his refusal to comply even with the Court's order, the judge will then act on the assumption of the legatee's renunciation. So, he, therefore, orders the article bequeathed to be allocated to those entitled to inherit from the testator.

THE DEATH OF THE LEGATEE PRIOR TO HIS ACCEPTANCE OR RENUNCIATION

If after the death of the testator and prior to his exercising the option of acceptance or renunciation, the legatee dies, the preferred doctrine of the Hanbali school holds that the right to accept or renounce does not lapse. It simply passes to the legatee's own heirs to exercise the outstanding option on behalf of their praepositus (the legatee).

The jurists' opinion in the above case resembles their views in the cases of a pre-emption sale, and the call-option (*khiyar al-radd*), or in another word, the right of an optional sale where the operation of such a sale is deferred to a later time by stipulation. In both pre-emption and call-option the right does not cease but is vested in the deceased's inheritors. A *Hadith* on this subject states 'An estate or a right left by a deceased shall belong to his inheritors'.[11] The rule to transfer the option of a bequest to the legatee's heirs, the jurists say, was also derived from the above *Hadith*.

OWNERSHIP BETWEEN THE TESTATOR'S DEATH AND THE ACCEPTANCE OF THE LEGATEE

Ownership of the article bequeathed following the death of the testator with no acceptance as yet by the legatee created a major controversy between *Ulama*, scholars, within the Hanbali school of law. The major point over which they differed and tried hard to resolve was the question of ownership and to whom ownership should be attached.

Three distinct possibilities were suggested. The first was the question whether the dead person could still be described as eligible to retain ownership so as to preserve ownership of the part bequeathed from both heirs and legatee alike. The second suggestion was that ownership of the subject matter of a bequest should be suspended to avoid giving the title to either till either the acceptance of the legatee or his renunciation had taken place. Or should it, in the final suggestion, descend automatically to the testator's successors who were supposed to hand it over to the legatee whenever it was accepted.

The majority of Hanbali jurists dismissed both the first suggestion and the second in preference to the third. Thus it would pass to the successors who were considered trustworthy and also needed to preserve the corpus. For instance, should the property be an animal, it would need protection and feeding, or money would be needed to be kept in a safe place, etc. No one is expected to look after someone else's property but the deceased's heirs who alone have the means of access to the estate by virture of their position as successors to the testator which was established by inheritance and also by the *Hadith* ascribed to the Prophet (peace be upon him), viz 'An estate or a right which is left by the deceased is allocated to his heirs.' After all, the ownership of the subject matter bequeathed to the legatee cannot be taken for granted but only after his/her acceptance which may or may not be obtained.

The majority claim that all Muslim jurists have unanimously resolved that acceptance need not be obtained immediately after the testator's death but could take some time. This rule influenced their dismissal of the idea of the bequeathed estate being left with no owner and their acceptance that it should pass over to the heirs pending acceptance or renunciation of it by the legatee. The same group of jurists have also, by analogy, reinforced their argument further by comparing bequest to the insolvent estate in that, as the insolvent estate passes to the heirs, so should property which is partly bequeathed, especially, they say, since the jurists have stated that a bequest cannot have priority over debt with its paramount and binding claim.

To demonstrate the kind of support the majority of Hanbali jurists have relied upon, we quote the words of Ibn Qudama, who stated their position in response to the arguments brought by the first suggestion, (which he himself said was a strong possibility.) He says that, 'Ownership of the deceased's estate is transferred to the heirs as a matter of natural course unless it is prevented by a legal ban.' He added that the verse, '(inheritance is given), after a property bequeathed or debt' referred to an accepted bequest. Hence, prior to acceptance by the legatee, the estate's ownership belongs to the heirs. And from the verse 'So to you a quarter after legacy' means that this was fixed and settled and could not be changed by doubtful ownership. So, debt does not hinder the ascertaining of ownership over the estate left by the deceased which in character is more secure than a legacy.'[12]

The Courts' invocation of the above rule is apparent in the case brought before the Court of Jedda where the judge ordered the debtor to hand over one third of the debt to the legatee after the legatee had given his acceptance of the legacy.[13]

THE TIME ESTATE AND INCOME PASSES TO THE LEGATEE

Though the jurists opinions varied from one group to another, their differences have never been pointless or merely a waste of time. The result of the jurists' arguments in respect of, the previous point, for instance, is highly beneficial. It opens a variety of alternatives before the students and new lawyers in particular, giving them a chance to examine and to choose from the different views what they consider a more equitable solution and more suited to their present needs. Such variations and benefit will help maintain the credibility of the jurists' saying 'Divergence of opinions is a mercy' which means, we all reach the same conclusion in the end even though we come to it by different approaches and thus it can only be described as a healthy sign within both the law and among scholars.

Thus in trying to discuss the time at which an estate as well as income or produce will pass into the ownership of the legatee, we find that controversy previously mentioned about ownership had a wider and more varied pattern of argument.

A jurist may sometimes persist in following his distinctive way of thinking to the end to form a parallel line with others. While on other occasions the jurist may keep to his original line but end up entangled with other points of view. For instance, if a person should bequeath a house, a garden or an animal and if any of these objects (after the death of the testator and prior to the acceptance of the legatee) should produce a profit or income, the new income will thus be subject to the aforementioned wide ranging controversy which can be summarised as follows.

First, the majority of jurists pursued a distinguished line of thinking and maintained it throughout. Their doctrine is that the deceased's estate, whatever it may be, is allocated to his successors. Thus all advantages or profits arising therefrom must appertain to the heirs as accessories to their estate. If this line had been followed by others, the point of dispute would then have decreased substantially or even be extinguished completely. But rather the problem became more complicated by the way the others looked at it, which is, as we said before, a healthy sign and of much benefit to students of law. For if it was not for the great variety of views, they would not be able to consider the advantages and disadvantages contained by each point of law.

However, the other jurists disputed the majority view that the estate bequeathed is allocated to the natural successors of the testator. This group also maintained the alternative, that is to say the ownership of the article bequeathed remains attached in some way or other to the deceased. Controversy, however, has crept into this group in respect of the matter of income (which is the product of the bequeathed subject matter). Here opinion divided into two. Some believe that on the legatee's acceptance, both the corpus and the income should pass over to the legatee because the legatee takes over directly from the testator.

Al-Qadi, though he had originally agreed with the view of this group, later adopted a different line of thought. He says in his book called *Controversy,* 'Although the corpus of the bequest is to remain in the deceased's ownership, the product prior to acceptance belongs to the heirs,' and as a supporting argument he revived the reasoning of the majority, i.e., 'Ownership of the legatee does not precede his acceptance. Thus, the disposable third (the subject matter of bequest), will not be increased.'

Al-Mirdawi, in his critical evaluation of the stand taken by Al-Qadi, disputed the above reasoning. He re-iterated that, 'If we say that the suspended bequest is to remain in the deceased's possession, the profit and income from it will then serve to increase the whole estate left by the praepositus, (and not only the estate inherited by heirs). This, therefore, helps to increase the third (the bequeathable third).

An example clearly demonstrating all the above varied views of the jurists is that of a testator who leaves his house (the only property he owns) as a bequest to Ali. Between the time of the death of the testator and the acceptance of Ali, the house is let for £300 and the real value of the house is, say, £9,000. In the meantime the heirs use their right to dispute such an excessive will so leaving the legatee with only one third of the house. Thus, according to the majority doctrine as well as Al-Qadi, none of the revenue (the rent of the house) will ever pass to the legatee; while the author of *Al-Muharrar* in one of his two views and also Ibn Rajab considered the revenue to be exclusively the property of the legatee, the heirs being entitled to none of it.

The £300 revenue, therefore, according to the former opinion goes to the heirs, and to the legatee according to the latter. But there is still a third opinion voiced on this matter which prefers to divide the whole (the house's value and its income) between the heirs and the legatee.

Still a fourth opinion was described as a possibility. It is regarded as the second version of Al-Qadi who says 'If by the legatee's acceptance we acknowledge that the possession of the bequest is the legatee's from the time of death, then possession of the income in addition to the corpus is established only when the corpus and the income (the rent, for instance) are both contained in the disposable third or can be extruded from the disposable third. Otherwise the excess amount over the third will then be reckoned to pass to the heirs.'[14]

The practice of Saudi Courts seems to sustain the opinion adopted by the majority of the Hanbali jurists. A demonstration of this tendency is the case of the daughters of *J, B and Kh v. the executorix*[15] which was presented before the Grand Court of Makkah. The record of the case tells that the two daughters *B* and *Kh* had alleged that their father had received on their behalf an annual gift from the King. In the process of the case, it was proved that the father acknowledged receiving such a gift in front of competent witnesses. The payment of that claim from the estate of the praepositus (their father), was, therefore, ordered. But since most of his estate had already been distributed among his heirs, the judge asked the executorix if any of the deceased's estate had remained undivided. The answer was positive, 'a house and some rents.' In his judgement, the judge, on this point, responded by pronouncing that the rent as such is not to be regarded as a revenue of the deceased's estate but rather the revenue of the heirs' property. Thus, he added, the daughters' claim must be satisfied from the house which remained undivided in the hands of the executorix. The judge also added that he would not object to a compromise between the guardian of the two minor daughters and the executorix being worked out to settle the claim out of the income rather than the corpus which would then be left as before (heridatable object).

This is clearly an application of the majority view and also to a certain extent an application of the principle which states that all incomes of bequest between the time of death and the acceptance of the legatee belong to the testator's heirs.[16]

EVALUATION OF THE DISPOSABLE THIRD AGAINST THE ENTIRE ESTATE

Controversy has never developed about the time when evaluation in regard to the subject matter of bequest shoud take place. As distinct from that of ownership, the opinions of all *Ulama* are united in singling out the time of the testator's death and not the time of acceptance as the time the real value of the bequest should be assessed and considered. This therefore prevents any foreseeable conflict about its value arising in the case where the legatee delays his acceptance of the object.

Another point similar in nature is the aim of the legislator to protect both the legatee and the heirs against sudden and unpredictable fluctuation of prices in respect of the bequeathed object. Such fluctuation cannot cause dispute if the moment of death is the time when the bequest becomes operative. Evaluation is also useful when we consider the revenue of the bequest.

FROM WHOM ACCEPTANCE IS REQUIRED

Of course not all beneficiaries are obliged to accept or renounce a bequest. The individual beneficiaries whose number can be counted without much effort and those who can answer to their description are those who are required to accept or renounce. For instance when a testator says 'I bequeath £16,000 to the sons of Hasan or to the population of a village', the efficacy of acceptance of Hasan's sons or the village's population is deemed to be on an individual basis if they are few enough to be known. Otherwise, acceptance will not be required if the bequest is made for instance, to the tribe of Shammar, a tribe which comprises countless people and numerous branches of families and clans. Nor will acceptance be required if the bequest is made for pious charity or intended for the welfare of the whole community such as building Mosques, bridges, hospitals, etc. The jurists in these cases are inclined to give immediate effect to the bequest from the time of the testator's death.

No intermediaries were proposed by the old jurists. Nonetheless in contrast to the above, some of the new legislation gives the administrators (who look after the foundations' interests) the right to accept any bequest made to them on behalf of those foundations. At the same time they attach considerable importance to this acceptance without which a bequest to such foundations becomes legally inoperative.

Contrary to the above the Saudi Courts have adhered to the juristic view. They, as far as the institutions are concerned, have never demanded acceptance from anyone on their behalf. Any disposition becomes binding the moment it is made.[17] This is exemplified in the case of *S*,[18] who acknowledged that his grandfather had made a *Waqf* of his house to the Mosque that he had dedicated earlier.

The response of the court of Makkah to this was that it carried out a thorough investigation into the case and as soon as it determined the validity of *S's* acknowledgement, it informed the department of the *Awqaf* (plural *Waqf*) that the house in question was held to be in *Waqf* and public *Waqf* was to seek the issue of an official document from the court and sue the person who had assumed ownership of the property concerned.

The reason why jurists insist on acceptance as a condition for ownership of a legacy for individuals, while utterly ignoring it for institutes, is the jurists' opinion that bequest has two fundamental features. First is its similarity to a gift (which voluntarily conveys the estate to the other party, no substitution being anticipated). Secondly, the bequest on the other hand is like inheritance (which due to succession has to be conveyed to the heirs after the death of their ancestor). Thus, if one considers its similarity to a gift, a bequest needs acceptance, whereas if we compare it to inheritance the bequest need not be accepted as the transfer of estate becomes automatic. Accordingly the jurists say that because the bequest's similarity to both a gift and inheritance, acceptance must be stipulated whenever possible. In the case of impossibility, acceptance becomes out of the question and bequest therefore becomes operative immediately after the testator's death.[19]

THE IRREVOCABILITY OF ACCEPTANCE AND RENUNCIATION

Jurists are inclined to give immediate effect to the legatee's acceptance or renunciation of bequests. Thus the legatee's action in this matter cannot be withdrawn and becomes ultimately irrevocable because, by the legatee's renunciation (after the death of the testator), we recognize that the legatee has dropped his claim to something he otherwise had the right to acquire had he wanted to. So no claim to the will should be brought afterwards by the legatee and he should not be granted any hearing, should he make such a claim. Likewise, after the acceptance of a bequest, the legatee cannot afterwards use the right of rejection to prevent the transfer of the ownership of the object bequeathed into his possession. By acceptance it implicitly becomes an integral part of the legatee's estate. Hence, should the legatee after acceptance wish to relinquish the object bequeathed to him and assign it to someone else, he has to follow the legal procedures used for a primary gift (with offer and acceptance).

THE CAPACITY OF AN INFANT OR PERSON OF DISORDERED MIND TO ACCEPT OR RENOUNCE

The capacity to buy and sell by a child or a lunatic is regulated by the general law concerning capacity to contract and to transfer and acquire property. Also, to acquire property donated or bequeathed to them, such a gratuitous act will be governed by a new factor which concentrates on their prosperity. The state of incompetence of the infant, the minor or the person who by reason of mental incapacity is unfit caused jurists and *Qadis* to consider the imposition of the principle of interdiction upon those persons and the like. Further, the jurists introduced the office of guardianship; i.e. a mature person was to act as a guardian to take care of an interdicted person, both in person and look after his interests, part of which is the acceptance or renunciation of a bequest, which can be made by the guardian, on behalf of his ward.

As to the question of prosperity, the guardian has to observe strictly the prosperity of his ward before proceeding to accept or renounce a bequest. If, for instance, the object bequeathed constitutes a loss in any way to the ward, the guardian is then obliged to utilize the new criteria the jurists have made available (as an alternative), to make his job easier through weighing loss against gain. If the loss then outweighs the gain to the ward, the guardian must reject it but if, on the other hand, gain is found to be more than loss, the guardian must accept. The law, otherwise, will be bound to intervene to condemn and reverse the decision taken by the guardian as being an *ultra vires* act and therefore, illegal, because such an act disregards the child's interests and prosperity.[20]

However, the illegality in the above case seems to have been disputed. An alternative rule in such a case has been ascribed to the jurist Ibn Nasrillah, in his book *Al-Hawashi*. He is reported to have ruled out the illegality of the guardian's act which was based on the allegation of the guardian's disregard to the interests of his ward. He instead holds the guardian liable to compensate for the loss the ward has suffered through the guardian's acceptance or renunciation of the bequest.[21]

Finally, the rule that gives the guardian the right to accept or reject a bequest on behalf of his ward does not conflict with the other rule allowing the ward, the prodigal, the lunatic or an infirm person to accept a bequest and gifts which appear to be in their favour, or even to accept a trivial thing with slight loss without the knowledge of the guardian because of the insignificance attached to the object concerned.

SUCCESSION TO THE *WILAYA* OR GUARDIANSHIP

To practise guardianship over an infant or a lunatic, one has to acquire the status of a legal guardian either by natural means, such as being the father, or one must get an order of appointment in a way acceptable to legal circles, i.e. the assignment of a guardian has to be obtained from the will of the father, at his death or before, or the assignee must obtain the order of assignment from the court.

The grandfather will not according to the Hanbali doctrine be allowed to enjoy the office vacated by the father. The Hanbali jurists regard the grandfather as being in a position inferior to that of the father and his executor and rather to be in a position equal to that occupied by the brother. The Hanbali's explanation of their stand is that both the grandfather and the brother are not directly related to the ward but through the mediary of the ward's father. The credibility of the grandfather is thus decreased considerably by such comparison which causes him to forfeit the right of succession to the *wilaya* or guardianship and vests it instead in the court to search for a trustworthy person to take over the ward's interests and care.[22]

The transfer of the office of guardian after the father to the court will not prejudice the grandfather's right to be chosen by the judge provided that the judge finds he is still competent and suitable in every way to succeed to the position of guardian and look after the interests of his ward. Otherwise, in practice, the trend in the courts of Saudi Arabia is to appoint a relative with whom the ward feels secure. This person is often the mother, the brother, an uncle or a cousin.

PROPERTY THAT CAN BE BEQUEATHED

In order for a bequest to be effective a number of conditions which the jurists have related to the subject matter of bequest must be satisfied, otherwise failure of such a bequest will be inevitable. Such conditions are discussed in the following:

1. It has to be a *mal*, (property)

The word *mal*, in its proper sense, has been designed to mean whatever can be possessed, i.e. paper-money, coins, gold and silver, animals, minerals, land, plants, houses, etc. But the application of the technical sense of the term used in the jurisprudence would limit its use and boundaries from generality to only what is considered beneficial in the eye of the *Shari'a*.

According to the legal definition the use of the term *mal* is limited and linked only to benefit. This will automatically lead us to the belief that there exist two types of property, beneficial and non-beneficial, both of which will be discussed in the following.

Beneficial property: or what the jurists call *Malun mutaqawwam*, includes everything that the *Shari'a* regards as useful to mankind. Or in other words, everything that the *Shari'a* has not spoken of as useless, harmful or forbidden.

The beneficial type of property is thus the only property that the *Ulama* have recognized as disposable. They also admitted as property things that can be valued as equivalent to property such as the service of animals etc. Accordingly, all property of a similar nature can be disposed of by testators in their testaments and will eventually be allocated to the legatees.

The non-beneficial property is called *Malun ghairu mutaqawwam*. Although the non-beneficial property can be included under the proper meaning of the word *mal*, or property to be disposable in the same manner as other properties, the juristic definition of *mal* has deprived such materials and objects of a non-beneficial nature from becoming disposable, valued or ever to be offered or accepted under the *Shari'a*.

Alcohol, pigs or animals that have died naturally[23] are not thus considered *mal*, in the *Shari'a* sense. So we can say that these three types or objects are not worthy at all of becoming the subject of bequest.

Notwithstanding, the law generally treats dogs as objects without value but because of the valuable services they can render mankind in many ways, an exception was made and they were given a special status in law which makes them (the useful ones) eligible for possession and bequest. The special status given to dogs does not make them *mal* (property) but rather a subsidiary so that their disposition is allowable only within the limits of their services. Therefore useless dogs are considered to be prohibited as non-beneficial. However, a Hanbali jurist considered that puppies which could afterwards be trained for some useful purposes, could be made the subject of bequest.

2. Attribution of ownership of bequests

In order to make a lawful testamentary disposition, the testator must attribute the ownership of the object he wants to convey under bequest to himself personally. That is to say, 'My law books are to be given to the central library.' If not the testator must refrain from ascribing the ownership of the object bequeathed to anyone not even himself such as 'These law books are to be given to the central library' or 'I bequeath a car to Y.' In such a bequest although the ownership of the bequeathed object is left unmentioned, it is still, however, valid. The right to ownership of the object by the testator is quite implicit.

Without exception, all the Hanbali jurists are of the same opinion; that is they reject the legality of a bequest where the ownership of the subject matter is ascribed to someone else other than the testator. For example, 'I bequeath the mansion of X to the disabled people' or 'I leave the use of Ahmad's car to Ali.

The jurists also invalidate the above bequest even if the mansion and the car subsequently come into the testator's possession. The illegality of such an act stems from what the jurist Al-Bahuti calls 'The corruption and the invalidity of the format.'[24]

3. The existence of the object bequeathed

Only a very precise and elaborate description of an object will the jurists accept as proof of the existence of the object at the time of bequest, such as 'My white house at such and such road and city.' Nonetheless, unlike the recipient's existence at the time the bequest was made, the object's existence is no condition to the validity of the bequest. Thus, if the testator bequeaths something, let us say, 'One of my horses', the bequest is legal. In such a case the subject matter of the bequest can be subject to a subsequent change of hands because the bequest is not actually tied to a particular horse yet the bequest remains valid.

Jurists, as a way of satisfying the instructions of the deceased, state that the heirs are to give the legatee one of the horses left by the deceased by using the preferred scheme of casting lots or to give the legatee whatever the heirs please.[25] Moreover the jurists have even permitted a bequest of something which the testator does not actually possess at the time he makes his bequest. This is done by the testator's instructions to his executor to buy, with a fixed sum of money or a portion of his remaining estate, something, say a house, to be given to a legatee or to be made *Waqf* on his behalf. Illustration of this is found in the following case.

The testatrix had committed a third of what she would inherit from her dead husband's estate as *Waqf*. She instructed her executor to buy a house to be dedicated to the glory of God from the bequeathed third and take an *Adhiy* (an annual immolation of slaughtering one sheep to the glory of God which would then wholly or partially, be distributed among the poor).[26]

It is also vital at this point to refer to the will where no object is specified or where the portion is unspecified. For instance, 'A quarter of his estate' or 'The same share as his daughter receives in her inheritance.'

In the above two cases a tendency shown by the law is to hold them operative. Thus the law makes chargeable any estate owned by the testator not only prior to his death but even that which comes into his possession after death.

However, from what we have said above, we can deduce in this respect that the insistence on an object being in the testator's possession at the time that the bequest was made becomes entirely irrelevant because it could reduce the bequeathable share to a point below the fixed third.

4. The usufructory bequest

One of the prime reasons that has prevented the Hanbali jurists from stipulating the existence of the article bequeathed (at or shortly after the testator's death) is that had they insisted upon it, they could have contravened their analogical principles which permit the non-existent article to be included in a legacy.

Other than those aforementioned is the principle which legalises a potential service, a product or an income to be bequeathed. The legacy, for instance, of a goat's milk, its wool or the tenancy of land, a house, a car or the services of an animal or a farm's product though uncertain would, in the belief of most jurists, refer to periodically renewable products.

A legacy of this nature, or usufructory legacy, in the meantime, will lapse if in the future the product or income cease to exist, i.e. the milk, for instance, ceases to flow or the animal dies or the plants or the ground cease to produce crops or the house becomes ruined.

The same result follows at the expiry of a period of time set by the testator as a final date at which his bequest is to come to an end.. The termination of the bequest is to occur if an ox, for instance, whose service was bequeathed, dies. Should an indictable offence causing the ox's death be proved later, costs will then be payed at the choice of *Al-Kashshaf*, to the testator's heirs with nothing to the usufructory legatee. The plea in such a case is that the rights of the legatee in the ox are tied to the usufruct and not to the corpus.[27]

However, as the indictable offence concerning the bequest and incurring compensation has become a disputable matter between jurists, we find that the *Kashshaf* in the view it has adopted followed the reasoning of *Al-iqha'*, which is contrary to views held earlier by two of the most influential jurists in the Hanbali school. The first of these, the editor of the *Big Commentary* gave the above views as one of two possibilities.[28] The second, the editor of *Al-mughni*, came to believe strongly that compensation should be given to the legatee. The reason, he maintained, is that every right which is attached to the corpus must preserve its link with the replacement so long as the bequest is still operative.[29]

THE METHOD TO EVALUATE USUFRUCT AGAINST THE ESTATE

Jurists of the Hanbali school adopted two different methods in their efforts to find a way to evaluate the usufructory bequest as against the disposible third.

The first of the two methods is to evaluate the corpus (together) with its usufruct and then to compare the appraised amount against the value of the disposable third of the estate. If the act of comparison results in the value of the usufructory object being equal to or less than the appraised value of the third the bequest will then be immediately operative. But if it is found to exceed the amount of the disposable third, the bequest will be operative only within the limits of the one third and will be suspended for the excessive part upon the assent of the deceased's heirs. Such a scheme is applicable in all cases whether the period of the usufructory legacy is limited or perpetual.

The second method speaks of two distinct schemes to be adopted when an estimation of the usufruct bequeathed is to be worked out. In this scheme two different objects are to be reckoned with separately, i.e. the corpus and the usufruct.

The duration of the usufructory legacy was a major factor which helped to bring about the distinction between the two schemes. Perpetuity of the bequest, for instance, suggests the solution adopted in the first method should be applied here too. But should the duration of time be mentioned in the bequest, then the above solution will be repudiated as inapplicable. Thus, the jurists' view is that both the corpus and its usufruct should have separate treatment.

The appraisement scheme forced us to appraise firstly the value of the corpus bequeathed with its usufruct and then to appraise the same corpus without its usufruct. Thus, whenever we get both appraisals established, we move to the second stage where we compare the two appraisals with each other. The difference we get will be the value of the usufruct alone which is later to be deducted from the disposable third. Here is an example to clarify all this. When a testator bequeathes the milk of his cow for a year to Ali, the milk will be our main concern. Thus in order to take it out of the bequeathable third the value of the milk has to be known. The process of evaluation must not be worked out without reference to the value of the cow itself. Accordingly the evaluation scheme will be done in three stages. The first stage is to find out the actual value of the cow itself including, of course, the milk. The second stage is to evaluate the cow as ordinary and a non-producer of milk. Then the third and final stage in this process is the comparison between the two appraisals, The result of the comparison is deemed to be equivalent to the value of the bequeathed milk which will eventually be deducted from the disposable third. Had the bequest been that of a house, a farm, trees, etc., it would have been dealt with in the same manner as above.

The two methods of evaluation we have demonstrated created divergence of opinion between the old Hanbali jurists and the latter jurists of the same school. On one hand, the editors of the two main works, the *Al-muntaha* and *Al-iqna'*, both supported the application of the first method, they insisted that the value of the object bequeathed together with its usufruct must, if the bequest is to be operative at all, come out of the disposable third.[30] On the other hand, Al-Buhuti, the commentator of the *Kashshaf*, preferred the unpopular view (the second method) which was mentioned in *Al-iqna'* without emphasis, and described it and presented it as 'the correct view'.[31] His opinion formed the core of the latter method in law circles. It was also as seen in the commentary of the *Muntaha* in contradiction to what the *Muntaha* itself had adopted thus allowing the possibility of a second opinion.[32]

Such variation of opinions shows how the latter Hanbalis could, to a certain extent, move freely throughout the various views and contribute in the development of law by drawing their own conclusions free from the influence of the old jurists and sometimes even from the immediate authority.

NOTES

1. Makkah Grand Court Case No. 110, Vol. 6, (date 15/4/1378H).
2. Ibn al Qayim, 321, ed. A. Sharaf al-din.
3. *Al-Mughni*, Vol. 6, 164.
4. Makkah Grand Court, Case No. 109, Vol. 6 (date 20/4/1378H).
5. *Mughni*, Vol. 6, 540-541.
6. This case ratified by Shaikh Abdulrahman Muhammad b. Huwaimil on 25/9/1389H, the Grand Court of Riyadh.
7. Sh. Q. Wasiya. pp. 62-63. Abu Zahra. Also M. Shalabi *Al-Waqf Wasiya*, 254.
8. *Sh-Munt*, Vol. 3, 290-291, *Kash*, Vol. 5, 546-547.
9. Makkah General Court, Case No. 26, Vol.6 (date 7/1/1378H).
10. *Mughni*, Vol. 6, 441.
11. Reported by Al-Bukhari, Ibn Hanbal, Abu Dawood and Ibn Majah. See *Al-Mu'jam Al-Mufahras*, Vol. 7, 187-188, Vol. 6, 50.
12. *Mughni*, Vol. 6, 442.
13. Jedda Grand Court, Case No. 218, Joint Reg. 1344-45H, p. 157.
14. *Insaf*, Vol. 7, 208.
15. Makkah Grand Court, Case No. 100, Vol. 1 (date 8/3/1380H).
16. *Kash*, Vol. 4, 346-347.
17. *K.* Vol. 4, 252, and *Sh. Munt* Vol. 2, 543.
18. Makkah Grand Court, Case No. 22, Vol. 3 (date 23/1/1380H).
19. Mohammad Mustafa Shalabi, *Al-Waqf w-al-Wasiya bain al-figh w-al-qanun*, 222.
20. *K.* Vol. 4, 346.
21. *Kash*, Vol. 3, 451.
22. *K.* Vol. 3, 447, *Sh. Muntaha al-Iradat*, Vol. 2, 291.
23. The jurists made an exception to this rule for the skin and hair of unslaughtered animals.
24. *Sh. Munt* Vol. 2, 555, and *Kash*, Vol. 4, 367.
25. *Sh. Munt*, Vol. 2, 557, and *Kash*, Vol. 4, 358, 370, 372, and *Tanqih*, 197.
26. Jedda Katib al-'adl, Case No. 1894, Vol. 5, (daste 1386H).
27. *Kash*, Vol. 4, 375.
28. *Al-sharh al-kabir*, Vol. 6, 514.
29. *Mughni*, Vol. 6, 482.
30. *Sh. Muntaha*, Vol. 2, 559, and *Kash*, Vol. 4, 373-374, *Insaf*, Vol. 7, 267.
31. *Kash*, Vol. 4, 373-374.
32. *Sh.Muntaha*, Vol. 2, 559.

CHAPTER V

INTERPRETATION OF BEQUESTS

The question of interpretation of a will is as important as the bequest itself in as much as the effectiveness and execution of the bequest depends on it. The intention of the testator as laid down in the will is the pivot upon which interpretation is usually centred. It is obvious that the subject of interpretation are the words and phrases therein. However, failing this, every other effort will be exerted to reach a suitable interpretation by all other means. The application of extrinsic evidence (i.e. the surrounding circumstances affecting the testator or the concommittant circumstances of the legatee) will be used to ascertain the testator's intentions and to make clear any obsure or vague or misused words in the bequest.

However, although both the context and the extrinsic evidence are applied to help interpret an ambiguous bequest, the former supercedes the latter because it is considered an inseparable part of the text. After all, it is in the nature of things that the testator's words should not be altered but be allowed to be self-explanatory before outside help is applied for. The extrinsic evidence therefore, will be a subordinate factor so it will not be resorted to unless all avenues for interpretation of the bequest without it have been exhausted. Attention must therefore be given first to the terms of the bequest as follows.

THE MEANING OF WORDS AND PHRASES

The jurists' attitude to the interpretation of wills is to observe as strictly as possible the intended meaning of the terms used by the testator. Further, they try not to abandon such a course unless an insoluble contradiction appears, for the jurists realise that the testator may have made his bequest from a motive which is unknown to them. Thus in the absence of certain indications that the deceased used the word in a special sense, the accepted meaning prevails and should never be departed from except in a few cases where the jurists themselves think it necessary.

THE OPERATION OF CONTEXTS TO INFER A TESTACY

When the testator uses terms that do not plainly show his intention to dispose of by testament, such as 'give' or 'this is a gift to him' or 'I make over to him such and such' or 'I make or confer the possession of such and such to him' etc. the law will not regard such statements as effective in the testacy sense. The recognition of those terms to relevant effect depends entirely upon the existence of contexts in the same instrument or passage to defer the disposition till after death, i.e. 'after I have vanished from the face of the earth or after my death and so forth'.

THE INTERPRETATION OF CERTAIN AMBIGUOUS WORDS WHERE NO HARM OCCURS BUT ONLY PROFIT IS ACHIEVED

The jurists, in certain circumstances, in their interpretation of the bequest may depart from the obvious meaning of the word used by the testator in preference for a rather more obscure synonym. That is simply because if such orders were carried out precisely, they would contravene the Islamic principles and their main purpose of ownership. Still the jurists will not abandon the obvious or intended meaning unless there is a possible ambiguity with a common element connecting the two meanings. A good example of this is the testator who orders the executor to bury his estate or to burn SR 20,000. Obviously, if these orders were to be followed precisely, the consequence of such orders would be grave and certainly harmful both to the testator's hopes for religious deeds in after-life and also to his family and to society as a whole.

The jurists' tendency in an apparently foolish will such as this is to act swiftly to re-interpret and direct the will in a more meaningful and profitable way. The jurists favoured approach to apply the terms of the will as strictly as possible is still adhered to. For instance, in their attempt to remove the harm from the former bequest, the jurists opted to overlook the approximate meaning in favour of a comprehensible and rather anticipatory one which is also covered by the general meaning of the word (bury). Thus, burying of the estate will be implemented but in a beneficial way, i.e. to hire labourers or to buy grave clothes for the poor, it will be extended to digging graves for the people's use.[1]

For the other example (the latter), 'The burning of the sum of money', the jurists' solution is to spend that sum on buying incense to burn in Mosques or as suggested by Al-Buhuti to buy oil for lighting mosques.[2]

The above tendency can be said to have succeeded as the jurists hoped in encountering what seems prima facie to cause such wills to be invalid and is helping to consolidate and develop the already established law.

CONSIDERATION IS PAID TO THE UTILITY OF THE OBJECT BEQUEATHED

If an indeterminate word is introduced into the will, the word shall remain general. The jurists have yet another consideration to introduce; when does a bequest constitute a harmful disposition and hence when should a limitation of option be brought about by the general term. That is to say, the usefulness or utility of the object is to be singled out amongst other things in the general sense. For instance, the bequest of 'A case to Salim'. If so many cases were left by the testator, say, a book-case, a suitcase, a brief-case and a violin-case, without reference to the purpose it should serve, the will can be ambiguous. Nevertheless, as the law makes inoperative a will motivated to promote illegal pre-occupation it may not permit the violin case to become the will's subject matter. But for other cases a surveillance is to be conducted to know if the testator in the context of his word or phrase or by the surrounding circumstances has disclosed a particular function or purpose for the object, i.e. case for his books, a case for his clothes or a case for his papers. Such an indication will be adhered to.

If, on the other hand, the uncertainty should stay with no sign of anticipation arising, then the operation of such a will will be referred to the testator's heirs to use their own discretion. The same rule should be followed if dogs were to be the subject matter of a bequest. Thus a bequest which consists of 'A dog to Ali' is ruled out as invalid unless it is of some use. Let us say, a hunting dog, a guard dog or a sheep dog, etc. Certain jurists, even regard as legal, a bequest of puppies which may be trained for such purposes in the future.[3]

Al-Bahuti, in *Al-Kashshaf*, endorsed the view of the *Muntaha*, that the legatee's position as a farmer (is an extrinsic factor to be borne in mind), will make him eligible to have an appropriate dog which he can make use of as a farmer.[4] Accordingly if for instance, the testator had three dogs, a hunting dog, a sheep dog and a farm dog, the former two dogs cannot be given to the arable farmer because they will not be of any use to his work. But the third dog and the third only (the farm dog), must in this case be given to him because in the context of his position as a farmer, the testator was assumed to have made a beneficial will where the legatee was supposed to gain a profit from the acquisition of such a dog.

However, if neither an indication in the bequest nor the position of the legatee is enough to settle the issue, it will be turned over to the heirs to settle.

TECHNICAL AND CONVENTIONAL WORDS

A technical word takes its technical meaning. Thus all legal terms with a technical sense if used in that sense must be adhered to. For when such a term is employed in the will the term is then presumed to bear that technical meaning. The same rule is referred to if we come across a word which has a special meaning in normal usage. This is true of the words used in the sphere of trade especially, for instance, by merchants and tenderers, etc. Thus, any alteration or distortion attempted will not be attended to by the law because in such a case the meaning is regarded as a primary one and so to be retained.

INTERPRETATION AS TO GRAMMATICAL OR CUSTOMARY MEANINGS

Controversy has been aroused between jurists about whether grammatical or customary meanings should be allowed to prevail in the course of interpretation.

Ibn Qudama favoured the more practical customary meaning of the term because he said: 'The customary meaning is the first to come into one's mind'. But the authors of *Al-Muntaha*[5] and its commentary both disputed such logic and in lieu of it they opted for the application of the proper meaning of the word of which they said, 'It has to be implemented because it is the original and grammatical meaning as well.' They supported their view by reminding the former jurists that, *Quran* and *Sunna* (Traditions), both predicated and depended upon the use of the proper meaning of their words. Hence, if a persons says, 'I bequeath one sheep to Ali' the sheep in such a bequest will be construed differently according to each of the above conflicting views. According to the former group of jurists, Ali (the legatee) will be given a ewe because it is the custom of people to regard it as so. By the latter view the legatee will be given either a ram or a ewe (which will then depend upon the discretion of the testator's heir), because the proper meaning of the word (*shah*), or sheep applies to both a male and a female sheep.

Contemporarily we could apply both simultaneously and acquire the benefit from both concepts. We should apply the latter view to those who have had a chance of obtaining much knowledge in the language field and the former to the majority of people who have little or no knowledge at all because it is unfair to construe a word in a will other than according to the usual meaning of the testator and that is to be determined by the degree of knowledge he has. In this way it is possible to take a middle course between the two views.

We could also apply as a matter of convenience the view adopted by Ibn Taimia which (though a little more lenient than that of Ibn Qudama), is not far from the view we stated above. He says that, 'The wishes of the testator and every contractor are subject to their usual language and the speech they use whether it agrees with classical Arabic, post-classical language or dialect or even if it is non-Arabic.' He added that, 'What is intended by words is indicative of the intentions of those who utter them.'[6]

Further, a bequest which is in the manner of 'give Salih something or a part of my estate,' will be left entirely to the discretion of the heirs. Here what Salih will actually get is not mentioned in the will and the term 'something' could mean anything at all. Thus, due to the terms of the will the heirs are not instructed how to satisfy the bequest. The law in such a case would dictate to the heirs neither the quality nor the quantity which they should allocate to the legatee.

Contrary to the above is the following case where the law does not give the heirs the liberty to choose what they think adequate. If the terms of the bequest are as follows: 'Give Hussain a portion or a share of my estate after my death,' the law, instead of being indifferent to the quality or the quantity of the bequest taken by the legatee, comes strongly in favour of giving him something of substantial or tangible proportion. They say, one sixth of the net estate is to be given when heirs are few and have big shares. Otherwise, the legatee should be given a share equal to the share of the least fortunate amongst the heirs.

INTERPRETATION WHERE THE SUBJECT IS NOT CLEARLY DETAILED

If a person should make a bequest in terms so ambiguous that the law affords no interpretation then the bequest must be left to the heirs to explain and be implemented as they think suitable. Example, 'Give Ahmad (the legatee) one of my cars after I die.' The heirs who are to handle such an imprecise direction will have to decide which car to give away, if there are several of them. The heirs' decision involves solving the problem about the kind of car, the model and the year of manufacture. If on the other hand, the testator has no car at the time of his death, the legacy lapses. If, however, only one car remained, it has to be handed over to the legatee as if the testator had singled it out. If the remaining car is later destroyed and compensation or damage was paid in settlement, what has been paid in settlement will be given to the legatee as long as it does not exceed the disposable quantity; however, if the destruction is then proved to be accidental and no order of damage is awarded, nothing will be given to the legatee because the legacy lapses.[7] On the other hand if the testator says 'Give Muhammad, out of my estate, a horse' is interpreted differently from the above for the jurists' interpretation of the term 'out of my estate' is as if the testator had ordered a horse to be bought for the legatee.[8]

INTERPRETATION OF A CONTINGENT BEQUEST

A bequest could be left subject to a condition depending upon the happening of some uncertain event, or subject to the fulfilment of a condition; in other words, the legatee who take the bequest must take it subject to the performance of some action, or the occurrence of an event. As for a condition which is impossible, the bequest shall be considered as unfounded. But if it is contrary to the law or good moral, such a condition will be grounds for annulling the bequest entirely. Therefore, the execution of a bequest depends on what we call a suspensive condition where such a condition would be honoured only if it were likely to happen. But where the condition is found unlikely to happen or merely a hypothetical one such as, 'I bequeath the third of Ali if he revives my dead son,' it would fail because of the unlikelihood of the revival.

Further, jurists would see in validating such a bequest a slight violation of the principle 'Do not do harm so as not to be harmed'[9] for they say: 'If that condition is to be legalized, then the interests of the heirs in the estate would be put at risk indefinitely.'[10]

The bequest, for instance, of sheep's milk, its wool or the tenancy of land, a house, a car or the services of an animal or a farm's produce, with no time limit set by the testator to terminate its course would, in the belief of most jurists, refer to the periodically renewable produce. A bequest of this nature, or usufructory bequest will lapse if in the future the produce or income ceases to exist (i.e. the milk, for instance, ceases to flow or the animal dies or the plants or the ground ceases to produce crops or the house becomes ruined).

The same result follows at the expiry of a future date set by the testator as a final date at which his bequest is to come to an end. The termination of the bequest is also to occur if an ox, for instance, whose service was bequeathed, dies. Should an indictable offence causing the ox's death be later proved, compensation will then be payed to the testator's heirs with nothing to the usufructory legatee. The plea of such a view is that the right of the legatee in the ox is tied to the usufruct and not to the corpus.[11]

BEQUESTS FOR CHARITABLE OR PIOUS PURPOSES

There are usually two reasons for the voluntary disposition of a bequest. Either it is an act meant to recompense the legatee for a prior favour or it is an expression of gratitude, or it is just a benevolent act for what the testator considers a charitable and pious objective.

As certain clarification is needed to make valid a disposition, jurists have interpreted terms and phrase cited to infer to the charitable and pious dispositions and how they solve any complications arising in connection with the subject, the object and the undertakings of the executor.

When a bequest is made for the welfare of a section of the community, i.e. the poor, in general or to a particular locality, the executor will not be under any obligation to try to find every needy person in the vicinity. Thus, giving the bequest to three people who answer the description in the will is considered conclusive evidence of the fulfilment of the testator's wishes because three is the smallest number of plurality according to the Hanbali jurist, Ibn Qudama.[12] Even giving such a bequest to one person only, according to some jurists, is sufficient to discharge the executor from the duty related to such a bequest. The above group of jurists arrived at this conclusion through analogical assumptions which compare the executor's role with the role of a person paying his alms-tax, which can be given to a single person only.[13] Adherence to this view is seen in the case of *K*[14], where Shaikh Ibn Duhaish, head of the Grand Court of Makkah declared in his judgement, 'If a person makes a *Waqf* (or bequest), with its revenue defined to be spent on the poor and needy people, and if amongst the children of the dedicator one is found to fit such a description, he or she is more entitled to it than the known poor or needy. Hence he is to be given only the amount considered to suffice his or her need.'

A bequest to foreign students, the blind or the orphans, etc., is the same except that unlike the former state where poverty is a condition, in the latter cases wealth plays no role at all. So it can be rightly said that whoever be a member of these groups will be eligible to be a beneficiary, regardless of age, sex or wealth. An illustration is in the case of *H*[15] where *Hi* had made a house *waqf* upon herself then to her children and after their extinction, to the jurists of the Hanafi school of law. Half that house was sold and demolished for the extention of the Grand Mosque of Makkah and compensation was paid.

M the agent of *H*, the *Nazir* of the Hanafi Waqf, applied to the Court to allow him to rebuild the second and ruined half, with the price paid being that which was ordered by the same Court. Satisfied with the application, the Court granted him his request.

However, if a bequest reads 'I bequeath the produce of my garden to Ali and the poor', then Ali must get a portion equal to that of the poor, i.e. 50/50, since the language in the text clearly emphasised Ali's position as an equal partaker. This rule was arrived at because the testator employed the word '*wa*' (and) in the instrument by which the literal sense is distinguished. Thus Ali is to have the same rights as a full and independent sharer. To show this principle in operation in Saudi Courts here is the case of *M* and *A v. Mu.*[16]

After the death of the testator, interpretation of such a testament was needed to define the share of each group of beneficiaries. Raising the matter in the Court of Taif, Shaikh Babusail cited the relevant principle of giving one third of the bequest to the testators' relatives and the other two thirds of it to the poor and humble people, being one third each.

Notwithstanding, the same *A* who was treated as an equal sharer with the poor in the above example would not be allowed under the same bequest to receive another portion from the poor people's share had he himself become poor, because he was singled out as a sharer and not a partner.

The jurists in another case permitted a beneficiary to have access to dual portions under one will which may appear to the layman as being contradictory to their opinion in the former case. But before we give our own decision in the case, here is a detailed illustration of such a case. Suppose that a testator drew up a bequest which consisted of two halves; one half to the children of H to be divided equally per capita amongst them, the second half to orphans in general. If amongst the children of H. there should be an orphan, he/she then has the right to obtain two shares, one to be taken from the first half as one of the children of H and one from the second half as one of the orphans.

The jurists' emphasis this time does not seem to have been dominated by the literal orders but rather by the definitions of beneficiaries thus permitting a legatee to have dual interests in one bequest when the legatee answers two or more descriptions in the bequest. Also to avoid being mixed up with the former case, a condition to be satisfied is that the legatee has not been singled out as a sole beneficiary in the same bequest as was the case in the former.

Interpretation of this case found its roots in the law of succession which allows the holder of dual kinship to the deceased to profit from both kinships. The jurists who saw the solution to this issue in that law had to utilise an analogical scheme they invented to compare the situation of one who answers two descriptions or more with that of dual relationships in succession.

BEQUEST TO THE NEIGHBOURS

If a bequest is made 'To my neighbours' there is a reported *Hadith*, by Abu Huraira, which has partly construed such a will and has limited the benefit to 'Forty houses in four directions.' However, the *Hadith* still does not clarify or detail how the distribution should be made. This point provoked a wide controversy as will be shown in the following. Some jurists wanted a census to be carried out to define beneficiaries and from it define the distribution of the bequest to be given away per capita in that particular area.

Others saw it more suitable to divide the bequest according to the number of houses in the vicinity of the neighbourhood. The share of every house will then have to be divided per capita between the occupants of each house equally. An even less popular view was voiced that the bequeathed portion should be distributed per capita to those who usually held prayer in the Mosque of that area where the testator often prayed.

As to the receivers who are supposed to benefit under the will whether they include whoever moved into that area up to the time the testator died or just those who were there at the time the bequest was made, the authoritative law books indicate that the concensus of the jurists favours the latter only where the legatees are those living in that area when the bequest was made and not thereafter. The jurists' decision obviously depends upon the assumption that the testator might have aimed to make beneficiaries only the very people, in person, who lived there at that time. The same will be applied if the bequest was to those who were living in his street.

BEQUESTS FOR BENEVOLENT PURPOSES

Such bequests being distinct from the previous ones in the way they are distributed and to whom is left unspecified. For this reason the jurist acted swiftly and decided, enlightened by the *Quran* and the *Sunna*, that what is made for good purposes or for God is to be spent on the welfare of his needy creatures. In a like manner they interpreted what the testator might say from the many phrases which are well known to all Muslims and which signify the testator's intentions. For instance, the testator's saying: 'I dedicate one quarter to charity or for good or benevolent purposes,' or 'To be spent to the glory of God,' etc.

The general implication of the above phrases makes it impossible for jurists to limit their application to a particular objective. Hence, they prefer to maintain generality as a way of flexibility, and thus to serve and so to suit all various puposes which are regarded as good in the eye of the *Shari'a*.

Priority in the spending of the bequeathed shares considered by the jurists to be given to *al-Jihad,* (holy warfare), and thereafter to the rest of what is considered *qurbah,* (the proximity of God) or to good and charitable purposes.

The jurists have, further, kept to this interpretation when a testator delegates the executor to carry out his directions according to his own discretion which is obvious from the following terms, 'Give, put or spend one third in the way God directs you', or 'Where God pleases' or 'In the way you think right.' In carrying out the deceased's order the executor has to distribute the bequest on the aforementioned *qurubat* or the proximity to the perfect being, as he, the executor sees fit. By so doing the jurists say that it is better if the executor chooses to spend the bequeathed sum upon the poor relatives of the deceased. With the exclusion of those who inherit as heirs, a bequest will take the form of alms to his relatives with the aim of strengthening their relationships. The Courts of Saudi Arabia adhere to such a view as can be seen in the case of *H.*[17]

Kh was appointed as executrix for the two bequests of her grandmother and her mother, to spend it on good purposes in the way she saw fit. In his judgement, the Judge upheld the bequests. Nevertheless, an appeal was submitted by the testatrix's relatives to grant them the two bequests, which were made for benevolent purposes, as their number was great and they were in need. The Judge's verdict supported the executrix's assignment to manage the two bequests as directed by the two testatrixes. But he added that the relatives are more worthy to receive the benefit of such bequests when their need is proved.

Also Shaikh b. Duhaish, former head of the Grand Court of Makkah concluded his decision in which he nullified the sort of *Waqf* (and bequest) to hire someone to read the *Quran* and confer the incurred religious rewards to the soul of someone else, as happened in the case of *K*, by saying, 'If a person bequeaths or makes a *waqf* with its revenue specified to go to the poor and the needy he or she is to be given only the amount considered to suffice his or her needs.[18]

If the testator, apart from his heirs, has no other relatives, then the executor, the jurists suggested, should distribute the sum amongst the testator's foster relatives if there are any, and if not, to his neighbours.

At the same time the jurists made it clear that they did not want to enforce their own view upon the testator's executor even though there is slight chance of reaching the aims set out in the testator's terms which will give his word their general meaning. Accordingly, the executor will not, in any way be bound to follow their suggestions because the testator gave him liberty to spend the bequest in the way he thinks fit so long as it is going to be spent on good things.[19] The latter view shows us the degree of respect jurists attach to the commands and instructions of the testator in so far as he does not commit a violation of testamentary law and the *Shari'a* as a whole.

It has been made clear according to the juristic opinion that a bequest to the Prophet or to God will be legally correct. However, a slight variation in respect to the spending of such bequests as compared to the above bequest has been introduced. Thus the amount is spent on public welfare and is by the use of analogy, the same as the portion of booty which is considered as part of the treasury or Bait al-Mal.

BEQUEST TO NEAR RELATIVES

A bequest to the testator's relatives could envoke a wide range of competition between the various groups of relatives as follows: If a bequest was made to the testator's 'Next of kin', or to 'The nearest to him', the jurists are of the opinion that unless the heirs ratify the will to their fellow inheritors the bequest will go to another class of legatees if any exist or ultimately go to relatives who are excluded otherwise from inheritance. In order to make such a scheme applicable the jurists borrowed one of the vital rules of succeession that says, 'The nearer in degree excludes the more remote.' Thus the father of the testator and his son are to exclude all other relatives and to be on an equal footing thus they shall share the bequeathed between them equally. Failing the existence of the father and the son or in the case of their exclusion the bequest will be passed on to the next in proximity so that a grandfather and a brother, whether he be germine or consanguine, will have the same footing and so on in regular succession. The shaky position of the uterine brother makes him unworthy to most jurists to compete with other relatives. Further, the germine brother defeats the consanguine in the competition for the bequest as in the case of inheritance.

However, a fundamental difference in this respect is that a female relative takes an equivalent share of the bequest to that of a male relative of the same degree. Hence a deceased's daughter and son or a brother and sister of the deceased are entitled to a share identical to that of the brother. The ruling of the Saudi Courts in the case of *N*, is an illustration of such a principle.[20]

After the grandchildren of *N* proved their need, the Judge ordered the bequeathed third of *N's* estate to be granted to his grandchildren. As a basis to the distribution, the Judge emphasizes that such a bequest was to be shared between the males and females, equally.

Also in the absence of a condition, the beneficiaries of a general *Waqf* are to be governed by the same principle as shown in the case of *M v. A.*[21]

In this case, a long chain of beneficiaries died after the making of the *waqf*. No provision in respect of the distribution of the *waqf* could be traced to have been made. Faced with the absence of the *Waqif's* directions and the need to define the share of each of the beneficiaries, the Judge decided to give all beneficiaries equal partnership in the *waqf* regardless of sex.

INTERPRETATION OF BEQUESTS IS THE TASK SOLELY OF THE COURT

It is inherent in the notion of freedom of testamentary disposition that a testator may make a bequest as he wishes and in terms so obsure that he will be deemed to have been unwise in doing so. The task of interpreting words used by the testator in his will is, of course, to be shouldered by the courts. The court's interpretation must be enlightened by the ways and means that have been made available by the jurists.[22]

It is worth noticing that there is no contradiction whatsoever between the work of the judge and *Katib al-'Adl,* though a department of the court, and a probate officer whose task is concerned mainly with the making of a valid will by making all the necessary enquiries and arrangements to that effect. However, the meaning of the terms and the effect thereafter is the task of the judge in the court, as ordered by the Chief Justice.[23] To see how this has been applied see pages 99 infra and 101 infra

REVOCATION OF BEQUEST

A bequest being a voluntary disposition and non-operative before the testator's death caused jurists to agree, without exception, to it being of an unbinding nature and therefore subject to revocation, amendment or even replacement. Of course the right of revocation is left entirely to the free will of the testator.

The action of revocation will not be regarded as a breach of promise since the will is merely a proposed act the revocation of which incurs no harm whatsoever nor will it cause any loss to anyone. Thus a proposed act as such, where no acceptance has not occurred, can easily be withdrawn by the testator at any time before death. A commitment in the form of a bequest is only held to be legally contracted when the testator persistently affirms his intention up to his death.

The chief principle ruling revocation is seen in the inclination of the jurists to express their consensus of opinion by giving the wish of the testator the maximum juristic consideration and by approval of the express desire of the said testator to revoke a former bequest.

As to the formats of repeal, there are no recognized and rigid forms of revocation available. But the jurists, evidently, are of the opinion that a testator should be allowed to show his desire to prevent a bequest's fulfilment by any means possible. However, the manner in which revocation can be made is limited to:
a. express revocation; b. implied revocation.

a. The testator's Express Revocation

Express revocation, despite the fact that we may find some wills containing ambiguous statements, is generally the most simple and distinct method of revoking bequests. The law of bequest does not prescribe any form in respect of the language used in revocation; thus no special forms or words are necessary and it is immaterial which language is used, provided the words used make apparent the intention to revoke, amend or replace a former will.

Preferred words such as revoke, repeal, abrogate or retract, if used, give immediate indication of the wish. Other expressions, however, need to await the interpretation of the jurists and judges. If for instance, a testator bequeathes an article to one person and by a subsequent will or codicil gives it to another, the former bequest does not become invalid but is to be equally and jointly shared between the two legatees since there was no intention indicated in the latter to revoke the former one; however, if he says that what I gave to 'Amr I now give to Yasir, then the former one is revoked for it cannot be given to Yasir without revoking the bequest to 'Amr. Similarly, if the testator defines an article he previously bequeathed, e.g. this article is to go to my heirs, it ceases to become a bequest because the abrogation intention is so plain that the testator does not wish to uphold his bequest.

To demonstrate this from the Saudi practice, here is a case with particular emphasis on the way the bequeathed shares and the appointment of a *Wasi'* are abrogated.

In this case the testator made several bequests: two of them were the bequest of the share of a son to his grandchildren and the appointment of four persons to execute his bequests.

In a subsequent will, the testator abrogated the bequest in its entirety and its details, particulary that of a son's share to his grandchildren and appointed four executors.[24]

Also the testator in another case who had made several legacies in his bequest and designated one person as a *Wasi'* to execute his bequest and to look after his children, had subsequently followed it with a codicil in which he revoked his earlier bequest in respect of the designated *Wasi'* and appointed his wife and two sons to replace him (the former *Wasi'*) in executing his bequest.[25] Finally, in another case the testator who had appointed his brother a guardian to his young daughter, dismissed the appointee and informed the court of his decision.[26]

Express revocation as regards the subject matter of a bequest is of two kinds: pecuniary and non-pecuniary.

Pecuniary legacy, i.e. an unspecified sum of money, requires a verbal revocation by the testator. However, if the sum so bequeathed is specific, i.e. I bequeath the money in this sack or the money I keep in the safe, then it may implicitly be revoked by the emptiness of the sack and the safe. When the testator bequeaths a share of his estate, say a third, eighth or a portion equal to that of his son, revocation can only be done expressly; in a similar way the revocation of a *Wasi'* must be expressed. The same applies in the case where the testator states that the bequest left by him to A or B is void, or if he merely says it was forfeited or unlawful (Haram), it will have the effect of revoking the will. But if on the other hand, the subject matter of the bequest is neither pecuniary nor a general share, the bequest could then be revoked either expressly or by implication by the conduct of the testator.

Revocation in all cases must be voluntary and if the testator gets drunk or suffers from mental derangement, his original bequest cannot be revoked whilst in these states because voluntary revocation must always be accompanied by animus revocandi. It is only when a person, having made a bequest, subsequently suffers from incurable unsoundness of mind that his bequest can become irrevocable according to the Hanbalis.

Although the revocation of a testamentary deposition by a written document is not yet widely practised, it is gradually gaining ground in all parts of Saudi Arabia where illiteracy is obviously giving way to literacy. The introduction of the office of *Katib al-'Adl* in its present state is an encouraging sign towards achieving that goal.

A written codicil to abrogate all or part of a former bequest is a way of expressing revocation but should the testator tear burn or otherwise destroy the written document, revocation of this sort could then be considered as implied revocation. However if the testator authorizes someone else to do it for him or if the testator writes a cancellation clause across or underneath the will, such a clause will affect the bequest as an express revocation. Similarly, if the testator appeals to the court or to *Katib al-'Adl* seeking to repeal his former bequest that also will amount to an express revocation.

Revoking part of a written will in a subsequent will or codicil is not an unusual feature in the practice of the Saudi people, who are famous for their conformity to Islamic principles. As an illustration here is the case of a man who legated a quarter of his estate to meet first his funeral expenses and then to pay out of the quarter an unspecified amount as alms to be distributed as the executor saw fit. Also SR 10,000 to his ex-slave, SR 1,000 for the repair of a particular Mosque, etc. and the residue to go to the executor.

At a later date, the testator, for some reason or other made another will dismissing the executor of the former will, his nephew, and appointing another to replace him in all functions stated in the former will. Further, the amount allocated to his ex-slave was also cancelled leaving the rest of the will intact.[27]

There is also a case where the testator, who had made a bequest and designated a number of executors to carry it out, subsequently applied to *Katib al-'Adl* to allow him to make a codicil. In this codicil the testator abrogated his bequest in its entirety replacing it with another. But as to the designated executors, he added a clause by which he relieved all executors in the abrogated bequest leaving only his son and wife to execute his new bequest.[28]

b. Implied Revocation

The option of testimentary disposition and the revocation of such acts is a personal right of the testator. As regards the option of revocation, it must be effected in appropriate terms such as shown in express revocation or by conduct which represents the intention of the testator to revoke the subject matter of the bequest by occasioning a change in the name, ownership or a substantial modification to the nature and the use for which it was destined.

The recognised conduct which indirectly indicates the intention of the testator to retract his former will is divided into the following according to the nature and substance of change to occur in the subject matter of the bequest:

1. Alienation of the property by the testator

Through sale, gift or any other means is held to serve as an indication to alter the disposition formerly proposed; for jurists of all schools of law maintain that alienation of property as such is bound to revoke the testator's bequest, i.e. when the subject matter of the bequest has actually passed from the possession of the testator by sale, trust gift or other form. If the testator should, subsequently, regain the ownership of the article set aside for bequest, this would not avert the revocation any more than if he had not repossessed it.

Also, if without using any expression to revoke, the testator contracts to sell the subject matter of the bequest or to give it away in a marriage dowry as a gift or as a pledge etc., such an act would still amount to revocation. The act of the testator, even if not accepted by the recipient, i.e. it is a mere proposal to sell, remains an act of revocation for it demonstrates a change in the testator's intention. This latter point is in accordance with the approved doctrine of the Hanbali jurists.[29]

2. *Consumption and the destruction of a specific bequest*

Destruction or consumption of the bequeathed property either by the testator or otherwise would be considered equivalent to revocation. For instance, if the testator bequeaths the vegetable or the wheat produce of his farm which is afterwards destroyed by storms and flood or if he gives his stored wheat to a person in anticipation of death or not within the duration of his life, he is considered to have either consumed it or allowed others to consume it. The bequest thus lapses in accordance to the jurists' unanimous opinion.

The slaughter of sheep the testator had bequeathed either personally or under his direction is an obvious and convincing indication of retraction from his prior will. For both destruction and consumption of the subject of the specific will dictate the inevitable failure of the bequest.

Contravention of the above principle is seen for instance if an animal is the subject of bequest and afterwards is killed by an offender, the legacy does not fail according to some jurists but is executed from the compensation money received for the animal's killing. Also the loss of the subject matter will not cause the revocation of the bequest but should the legatee fail to find it (if it is a specific legacy) after the testator's death such a lost or perished legacy will not be compensated for from the deceased's estate. Moreover, liability is vested in the heirs if the subject's loss is proved to result from their default.

A testament is not only revoked by the testator's conduct but a bequest could become void on the occurrence of a certain qualified event such as the arrival of Hasan from his long trip or from his disappearance.

The inclusion of matrimonial status in a contingency bequest is no bar, according Ibn al-Qayim, who envisages the revocation of the bequest if the recipient of the bequest (the testator's widow or any other woman at all) is later to get married. In this view Ibn al-Qayim stands against the main body of the Hanbali jurists who in their uncompromising opinion regard the widow's marriage as a defiance to the deceased's orders and his outstanding aim thus causing the inevitable failure of such a bequest. However, as in most of his ideas Ibn al-Qayim, on this point has gained the admiration of contemporary lawyers.

3. *Substantial change of the character of the property bequeathed*

When the subject matter of a bequest is altered in substance whilst in the possession of the testator, such as the change of the article's title, this will amount to a revocation of the will. For example the fabrication of the cotton bequeathed or the tailoring of a piece of cloth into a shirt or making a piece of gold into a ring or a piece of wood into a table or grinding wheat to flour; all these sorts of changes while in the hands of the testator would constitute a retraction on the legatee's part of his former will and be a reason for invalidating his legacy. Nonetheless the demolition of a house, whether it was subsequently re-erected or not, will not be taken as an indication of an intention to repeal. Some jurists add to the point above that revocation should be made certain only if the former title ceased to exist. Support by the author of the Commentary of the *Muntaha* to the latter view has given it more weight and prevalence, especially in recent years, with the opportunity of being applied in Saudi Arabia's courts.

4. *Changing or mixing the bequeathed object with another*

Changing or mixing the bequeathed object with another material, whether of a similar nature or not, operates as a revocation where the thing added is so connected with article bequeathed that the latter cannot be separated or delivered without it. Thus if the testator mixes two kinds of oil or mixes oil with flour or sets forestry on a bequeathed land, the act itself will be reckoned as constituting revocation in the view of the majority.

In the same manner, the act of erecting a building by using bequeathed bricks or stones or to hammer bequeathed nails into a wooden door, etc. operates to retract a bequest previously made of the flour, land, etc. as the case may be. Each of these indicates a departure from the former bequest because all relevant acts are meant to remain indefinitely.

5. *Permanent change as a means of revocation as opposed to a temporary one*

Although a major change in the nature of an object bequeathed, i.e. planting trees for posterity or turning the bequeathed land into a vineyard causes the bequest to be retracted. Nonetheless minor changes such as the plastering of a house where there is little destruction or modification will not amount to a revocation of the will. But adding, say, a new room to the house will neither repeal the bequest nor allow the added room to pass to the devisee under the bequest. This is because it was not in existence at the time the bequest was made. Hence, the extra room passes into succession to the heirs.

An exception to this principle was decided by the Court of Makkah. This is where the extention is covered by a conditional clause. Then as in the case of *T*,[30] the Court upholds the condition made by the *Waqif* or dedicator. This condition was 'If God blesses me with the means to build more on the dedicated house, it shall become a *waqf*. Also, whatever is to be built with the revenue of the *waqf* shall be included in the *waqf*.'

A resemblance to the former principle is the case of a house which in its present state becomes the object of a bequest but is later demolished and then the testator afterwards decides to rebuild it. The rebuilding of the delapidated house, though, may not bring much change to the interior arrangement or certain materials and tools might be used in the new project and although the new house may retain its former style, some jurists tend to regard that the act of change, which is of a major nature, is sufficient to condemn this bequest into extinction.

6. *Dissolving conditions or* Shartun Mubtil

This is where the occurrence of an event proposed by the testator causes all due rights conveyed under a will to be terminated. The onset of such a stipulated event will count as equivalent to a revocation.

For instance, if the testator says. 'I bequeath the sum of SR 10,000 to 'Amr. But the same amount must go to Zaid if he returns from his journey'. The right of 'Amr in this bequest is not final, but because of its nature as a qualified bequest, can at any time be retracted by Zaid's presence before the testator's death. Still some jurists maintain that Zaid retains the right in the will whenever he comes after the testator's death but it is much harder for them to maintain this stand when the acceptance of 'Amr is satisfied.

A similar case is where the testator says, 'I bequeath to Salih but should he pre-decease me, to Yasir'. Although Yasir has no claim on the bequest if Salih survives the testator, he will automatically step in as the sole beneficiary of the bequest if Salih pre-deceases the testator.

7. *A bequest where revocation by conduct cannot be applied*

Revocation by conduct, in no way, can be applied where the subject matter of the bequest is not specifically itemized, i.e. 'The fifth of my estate,' or 'Give a share of my estate to my aunt'. These types of legacies are not specific but general ones, for the testator did not direct a legacy to be taken out of a particular item or a corpus such as a house or a camel where by conduct or contract the testator may alienate, consume or subject it to certain changes.

In the absence of precise orders that a legacy is to be discharged from a particular piece of his estate, one third of the then existing estate (at the date of the testator's death) must be given or one third of whatever enters into his estate even after his death, e.g. blood-money or a pensioner's allowance, etc. Such could be illustrated in the case of *F v. M*[31] where *M* received the deceased *Al-Sh's* pensioner's allowance. As such allowance becomes part of the deceased's estate, *F*, the deceased's wife and their children who were left under her care, raised a claim to a share of that allowance on behalf of their children. The Court being satisfied with this claim, an order was issued for such a share to be paid and the defendant complied with this and paid it in the Court.

As blood-money is attributed to the deceased, it passes to the heirs, and legatees if any, as part of the deceased's estate as illustrated in the following case.

A man died in an accident leaving his wife and children, some of whom were still minors. The minors' mother was appointed to be their guardian to look after them and their interests.

The father's accident proved to require blood-money to be paid to his heirs as part of his estate by the responsible party. However, an agent of the wife, together with the mature children of the deceased, waived their right to the required blood-money. But as the right of the minor's share in the blood-money or otherwise cannot be waived, the agent of the guardian of the minors demanded their share of the blood-money to be paid. The Court, which upheld this right, ordered the payment of the minors' share from the adjudicated compensation.[32]

From all characteristics attached to the general legacy we may describe it as a special and distinct legacy in comparison to the specific legacies where revocation does not occur as a result of the testator's conduct. Moreover, the subsequent loss or alienation of all or part of the testator's estate will not affect the general legacy and rights given in it will be revived and remain attached to the estate which the testator may subsequently acquire.

Further, other conduct which is not seen to amount to a revocation is described, rightly, as small indiscretions or conduct that does not impair the transference or delivery, change the character substantially, change the name or destroy or consume the subject of bequest; thus the letting of a house, wearing a jacket or even cultivating the soil bequeathed will not constitute a revocation. These forms of conduct, have a limited character and objective and cannot be made permanent.

8. The testator's denial of his testament

It is a doubtful question whether the mere denial of a bequest amounts to a revocation in law. Al-Nazim, a Hanbali jurist, stated that, 'If the testator knows he has executed the will he denies, the bequest is then repealed'. But others maintain that the mere denial does not and will not cause a revocation of his former bequest, because the other jurists, in their view, liken the denial of a bequest to that of a contract where the contractor's denial of it will not affect the validity of the contract. The latter view accords with the official doctrine of the Hanbali school.[33]

NOTES

1. *K.* Vol. 4, 366, and *Sh-Munt*, Vol. 2, 558.
2. *Sh-Munt*, Vol. 2, 558, and *Kash*, Vol. 4, 366.
3. *K.* Vol. 4, 369, and *Sh-Munt*, Vol. 2, 556.
4. *Kash*, Vol. 4, 371.
5. *Kash*, Vol. 4, 369, *Sh-Munt*, Vol. 2, 556-557.
6. Ibn Taimia, *Fatawa*, Vol. 31, 47.
7. *K.* Vol. 4, 370, and *Sh-Munt*, Vol. 2, 557.
8. *Kash*, Vol. 4, 371, and *Sh-Munt*, Vol. 2, 557.
9. Rep. by Ibn Hanbal, Ibn Majah and In Al-Muwatta. See *Al-Mu'jam* al-Mufahras, Vol. 3, 497.
10. *K.* Vol. 4, 351.
11. *Kash*, Vol. 4, 375, *Sh-Munt*, Vol. 2, 559.
12. *Al-Rawda*, 121.
13. *K.* Vol. 4, 558.
14. Makkah Grand Court, Case No. 93, Vol. 7, (Date 26/2/1377H).
15. Case No. 105, Vol. 17. Makkah (Special Reg. of) Shaikh Al. Amr. (date 12/7/1391H).
16. G.C. of Makkah, No. 118, Vol. 1 (1380H).
17. Case No. 637, Vol. 10. Makkah Minute Registry of Abdulmalik b. Duhaish (date 1391H).
18. Makkah Grand Court, Case No. 93, Vol. 7, (date 26/2/1377H).
19. *K.* Vol. 4, 559.
20. Makkah Grand Court, Case No. 91, Vol. 1, (date 7/1/1380H).
21. Makkah Grand Court, Case No. 151, Vol. 1, (date 18/6/1377H).
22. Article (1), p. 136. Accumulation of the Judicial Regulations, (date 27/2/1352H).
23. Regulation of Katib al-'adl, 28, (date 1364H).
24. Jedda Katib al 'adl, Case No. 974, Vol. 3, (date 1379H).
25. Jedda Katib al-'adl, Case No. 1409, Vol. 4, (date 1384H).
26. Jedda Katib al-'adl, Case No. 731, Vol.2, (date 1382H).
27. Jedda Katib al-'adl, Case No. 274, Vol. 1, (date 1379H).
28. Jedda Katib al-'adl, Case No. 323, Vol. 1, (date 1380H).
29. *Kash*, Vol. 4, 349, and *Sh. al-Muntaha*, Vol. 2, 545.
30. Makkah Grand Court, Case No. 29, Vol. 1, (date 23/2/1380H).
31. Makkah G.C. Case No. 72, Vol. 17. Sp. Reg. of Shaikh Al-Amr (date 19/5/1391H).
32. Jedda G.C. Case No. 208, Vol. 2, (date 15/4/1390H).
33. *Insaf*, Vol. 7, 213.

Part II

AL-WISAYA

INTRODUCTION

Al-Wisaya is the act of delegating the right and power of one person to another thereby substituting him as an agent. The former person is called *Musi*, (testator); the latter or the substitute is called *Musa ilaih* or *Wasi* (executor). He may also be called a guardian when his commission consists of taking care of minors.

Al-Wisaya is a contract starting with a proposal. An absolute acceptance has to be made by the person to whom the power is given. In case of dispute, enforcement can be granted only to the true *Wasi* for the *Wasi* receives his power directly from its original possessor (the testator) himself. His actual presence is necessary for assuming the delegated post since he assumes the continuing capacity of the testator.

In performing his commission the *Wasi* must observe all the instructions and restrictions laid down by the testator. He must show tenderness and care, if he is a guardian, towards his wards in every sense. He must refrain from any act which exposes them to danger in person as well as property.

Appointees in a joint mission must stick to their orders and no one is allowed to deviate from his assignment unless singled out to accomplish another duty or made a preferred *Wasi*, i.e. general *Wasi* or supervisor.

CHAPTER I

WHO HAS THE POWER TO APPOINT A *WASI?*

The power to appoint a *Wasi* does not belong to a privileged class of people to the disadvantage of others. Possession itself is the criterion for deciding delegating capacity. Accordingly, a *Safih*, (prodigal) who is a spendthrift upon whom interdiction had been imposed for his own benefit (*Hajr lihaqqi nafsih*) and whose monetary affairs are managed by a *Wali* or guardian, could be allowed to nominate his own *Wasi*, guardian or executor. This is a view held by certain jurists. As a basis to their view they said that because the *Safih* had been given the right to bequeath in the first place, he should not be deprived of it now.

In contrast to this view the majority of jurists speak of two distinct capacities as follows: 'A *Safih* may bequeath estate and nominate an executor, but not nominate a testamentary guardian over his children.'[1]

It is noticeable from the above statement that the majority of Hanbali jurists have, in respect of the *Safih*, distinguished between having the power to appoint an executor and the power to appoint a testamentary guardian. They permitted the first and nullified the second. The basis for their decision is that the power which the *Safih* could not retain in the course of his life should not be allowed to be regained afterwards because his minor offspring were being looked after by a guardian other than himself.

No interdiction of any kind can be applied against a woman of full age and who is also mature. Interdiction from a father, a husband or anybody else to prevent her from managing her own affairs personally or through an agent is not acceptable by law. She alone may plan what she wants to be done with her estate after she dies. This freedom entitles her to arrange for an executor (who may have no relation to her whatsoever) to take over the administration of her estate after her decease as equally she may assign a person as an agent during her life.[2]

The modern Saudi woman enjoys as much freedom of conduct over her estate as that enjoyed by Muslim women of the past. Thus, in her bequest a Saudi woman is capable of disposing of any part of her estate and appointing anyone to administer it in the same way as she is able to do so during her lifetime. This is demonstrated in the following.

Here, the testatrix designated her uterine brother as an executor to administer her estate. She directed the executor to take charge of her funeral and pay for the incurred expenses. She also commanded him as a means of confirmation to the step she had taken in the past, to set free her slave girl and here she bequeathed her bedroom to the thus freed slave girl. Finally she authorized the designated executor to distribute the rest of her estate between the legal heirs.[3]

As for the transfer of estate or control over it during the woman's life, the Saudi woman enjoys this freedom as part of her overall control, as is plainly seen from the case where a rich woman appointed a man as her agent to manage her entire estate. She gave him the power to appoint and dismiss agents. In the meantime, for the previous services he had rendered to her and to her dead sister, he was released from any responsibility to any estate that might have remained in his possession and thus allowed to retain it as his own.[4]

Ostensibly, the only limitation to the above principle is the mother being deprived from nominating a guardian to take care of her children, this responsibility devolving solely upon the father.

Such limitation is understandably, in Muslim society, for two reasons. The first, concerning the father, is that he is responsible for the mother and the children and while he is alive the children will need no guardian other than their father, since the father is capable of looking after them and supplying all their needs. The second, concerning the mother, is that the mother herself is a recipient of maintenance. Also, once the mother gets remarried there will be dilemma as to her status concerning what responsibility she owes to her husband and her children. The new husband, as a non-relative to the children, is most likely to refuse to bring up another man's children under his roof. Thus as a protective measure, it makes it most unworthy and unwise for them all to attach the fate of the immature children to their mother who does not herself know what her position will be.

THE PERSON WHO MAY ACT AS A *WASI*

Only an adult mature person is regarded as capable of assuming the power of *Wisaya*. Nonetheless, *Adala* or competency is a required qualification as well. The maximum standard of competency is not what the law demands. It is sufficient for an individual who is to become a *Wasi* to acquire and maintain a modest minimum but proven standard of competency. *Adala* or competency stipulated is not proved by applying the positive proof. In this sense the negative proof only matters since the jurists place a person of concealed private status of *Mastur al-hal*, who is not known to have been in an open confrontation with the *Shari'a*, to be a suitable *Wasi*.

Apart from the awaited or substituted *Wasi*, all the previous qualifications must be in existence at the time of bequest for it is comparable to an agency contract whose conditions have to be made available at the time of conclusion. The same qualifications have to be in existence, too, by death because only then may a *Wasi* attain the post of executor and guardian.

THE RIGHT TO ACCEPT OR REFUSE THE ASSIGNMENT

The mere fact of assignment does not oblige the nominated *Wasi* to keep up his office since it constitutes a burden on the nominated *Wasi*. He may refuse to act either expressly or by implication as by refraining from entering upon his duties. Refusal of such an assignment may occur during the lifetime of the testator. This has been upheld in practice by the Courts in Saudi Arabia. It is demonstrated in the case where a man was designated executor in a judicial document. Unwilling to carry out his assignment, the assignee informed the testatrix of his intention to relinquish his duty. Afterwards he went to the Court and offically registered his self-dismissal from the office of executor.[5]

Hanbali jurists, in contrast to the Hanafis, even gave the right to the *Wasi* to relinquish his assignment after the testator's death. This is since the duties vested on assignment were analytically compared to those of agency where no responsibility is incurred by the act of refusal.

The strict compliance of the Saudi Courts with this view is clearly illustrated in a case where the deceased's brother was designated guardian to his children. Due to his old age and his many commitments, the guardian thought himself unable to supply the required care so he applied to the Court to be officially relieved of his duty which was granted.[6]

Also from the Court of Makkah the case of *H* can be taken to illustrate the above principle.

H, who was made the executor of his father's and grandfather's bequests, on reaching old age, thought himself unable to carry them through and applied to the Court for dismissal. On the grounds of the executor's right to resignation, the Court granted *H* an immediate dismissal and appointed another executor to replace him.[7]

Also the guardian of the children who was also the trustee of their *Waqf*, used the right of relinquishment of the two posts he had held, went to the Court to confirm his acquittal and was subsequently released of his obligation.[8]

The act of refusal will never be allowed to disrupt, prevent or to affect in anyway the relevant duties from being carried out. At all events, the power of appointing an executor or guardian following the refusal or relinquishment of the *Wasi* nominated by the testator or following the death of a praepositus who dies intestate falls upon the Courts. Nonetheless, if the refusal to comply with testator's nomination has taken place during the lifetime of the testator, then the power of appointment will naturally revert to where it originally belonged (to the testator).

RETIREMENT FROM *WISAYA*

Although retirement from the *Wisaya* is not an act of refusal as such, for the purpose of consistency, it is deemed appropriate to be included under the refusal heading. After all the *Wasi* who refuses to enter into the duties of executorship and guardianship, and the retired *Wasi* who gives up after acceptance, have something in common.

It is a well known fact that by his refusal, a prospective *Wasi* saves himself the trouble of entering into a commission in the first place. This is different from the case where a *Wasi* seeks to repudiate a previous commitment and thus retire from his commission after he has already carried out and accomplished part of that commission.

Continuing to carry out his duties until they are fulfilled assumes no perpetual obligation to the *Wasi*. This, in actual fact, is the result of a juristic consensus. The *Wasi*, they say, acts in the capacity of an agent whom they consider to have acquired the capacity of self determination, either to stay with his commission or to withdraw from it peacefully and gracefully. The courts of Saudi Arabia have complied with this principle as we can see in the following case.

H and *M* were appointed joint executors to administer and execute the bequests of two dead testators. After carrying out the two bequests jointly for some time, *H*, who was becoming old and felt that continuation of these duties might hinder his other business, decided to vacate his post and applied to the Court for dismissal. His request was granted and a replacement was appointed.[9]

A *WASI* WITH A SPECIFIC OR GENERAL FUNCTION

An executor may in certain cases act in the capacity of a limited executor while in some other cases he acts as a general one. In neither case, it is not the choice of the executor himself to decide in what capacity to act. It is an assignment which needs to be delegated directly by the testator himself either in the original will or in a subsequent will or codicil. That is to say that the testator is the prime initiator of all powers and duties conferred upon the executor.

No special formulas are recommended which make acceptable any term or expression used by the testator. Notwithstanding, the limitation of such assignment is usually denoted by the testator's instructions, viz. 'I delegate the collection of my assets to *A*.' or 'I assign *B*. to pay my debts and distribute my estate to my heirs,' or 'I appoint *X* to receive the disposable third and to distribute it among the legatees' or '*Y* is my executor to perform the *Hajj* (pilgrimage), to Makkah on my behalf for £500.'

A special assignment may be attached separately to two or more people to carry out the testator's assignment without being subjected to any influence from anyone. The courts of Saudi Arabia will not interfere with this sort of bequest other than to affirm it. This is illustrated in the case where the testator in his bequest could be said to have made two bequests to two executors. The first is the designation of two general executors, his son and his wife. He put the two collectively in charge of the entire estate he left. They according to his instructions, were to extrude the disposable third pay for his funeral rites and then divide the rest into two equal parts. The second bequest was that each of the two executors was commissioned individually to administer the spending of one half of the rest of the disposable third on good and charitable purposes.[10]

The designated guardians are to be treated in the same manner as above, in that the testator may appoint two or more guardians and leave each to manage the affairs of some of his children as is seen in the following case.

Here one of the two wives of the testator was designated as a general executor. However, as to the guardianship of the testator's children, each of the two wives was entrusted to take care of her own children respectively and to educate them and to preserve their estates.[11]

A more illustrative case in this respect, which also shows the attitude of Saudi courts, is where no administrator is known to have been appointed, the court will take it upon itself, represented by the head of Bait al-mal, to distribute the deceased's estate between the prospective beneficiaries as is illustrated by the case of *'A*.

'A's bequest was confined to the disposition of the third of his estate and how it was to be spent. It also contained the appointment of an executor to supervise the way the disposable third was to be spent. Nevertheless, no indication was made to extent the executor's power to administer the deceased's estate or to distribute it between the legal heirs. Nor was anyone else appointed to carry out that task.

Bait al-mal appropriated the deceased's estate as is usual in such a situation. When the heirs and the executor of the disposable third applied to the court for the return of the deceased's estate the head of Bait al-mal was ordered to assume the task of distribution of the deceased's estate. Thus to give each one of the petitioners, heirs and executor, their entitlements.[12]

As a limited appointee each of the above executors shall undertake his own assignment alone. None of them should under any circumstances try to interfere in the duty of others or to tell how it should be performed regardless of whether a duty has already been delegated to an executor or not. The case of *F v. M* is an illustration of this principle.

In this case *Al-Sh*, who was working in the government, died leaving four children born of two wives each of whom he had designated as guardian to her own children. As a person working for the government, he was eligible for any arrears of his retirement allowance and this was paid to *M* on behalf of the deceased's children.

F, on behalf of her children, applied to the court to order *M* to pay a share for her three children from such an allowance, leaving the share of *K*, the fourth child, unclaimed since she had no authority to claim such a right. Thus, since there was no objection to her claim, her request was granted.[13]

Another case also illustrates the relevant principle where the testator had commissioned different persons to perform different tasks in relation both to his estate and to his children. He firstly appointed his wife as guardian to her own children. Secondly he appointed his other wife as guardian to her son. Thirdly he appointed his first son as a supervisor over the two guardians and fourthly, he appointed his second son as executor to supervise his funeral rites and pay their expenses.[14]

The duties of the universal executor however, are usually vested in him by the exact expression of the testator. Examples, 'I appoint X after me to be my universal executor', or 'Y is to administer all my affairs after my death,' or 'Z should do everything necessary in respect to the management of my assets.' Also, in addition to the above, a universal executor should be installed by a mere implication which is denoted by the use of an unspecific term, For instance, if the testator should say: 'I appoint L as my executor', without further limiting his duties nor adding any of the words which normally indicate generality, like general or universal executor or an overall executor (the supervisor), etc., then the generality indicated by the above unspecific term should be maintained and strictly observed. The Saudi application of the above is illustrated by the case of *A*.[15]

In his bequest *A*, the testator, appointed his daughter *M*, his executorix to take the disposable third from his entire estate to pay for his funeral rites from the third and to spend the remnant on benevolent purposes.

Though such a bequest seems limited, the use of the term, *Wasi*, as well as the order to his *Wasi* to take the disposable third from the entire estate left by him, are both indicative of the generality of the appointment of *M* as a general executorix to administer his estate. She had to distribute the remaining two thirds between his heirs. This came about since the ordered extrusion act of the disposable third from the entire estate depends on the fact of her being an administrator as well.

THE JOINT EXECUTORS AND GUARDIANS

The number of *Awsiya* sing *Wasi* cannot be limited since no rule exists to restrict the number of appointees. In practice we do not find it unusual, for a number of reasons, to appoint more than one *Wasi* to hold jointly the office of *Wisaya*. These reasons stem from the testator's desire to make sure that his estate, his children and their estates are all cared for and properly looked after.

However, although the testator endeavours to choose the most appropriate and the best person to his knowledge, one can never be certain what the situation will be after his death. The nomination of a single person as the sole *Wasi* could turn out to be a disastrous choice. The *Wasi* might become greedy, a selfish exploiter, which would eventually lead to negligence and mismanagement, since the testator's absence is permanent. This would upset the entire arrangement. The *Wasi* might, also, turn out to be unworthy, socially or morally, or might become mentally unfit which will further expose his estate as well as his offspring to danger. The testator who appoints two or more *Awsiya* to the same duty might be said to have attempted to prevent the undesirable and awkward situations mentioned above.

Adopting the above method is a means of ensuring that the responsibility, delegated jointly to the *Awsiya* whom the testator has chosen to represent him, rests in safe hands. Thus, once any of the appointed *Awsiya* simply quits, dies or becomes unfit mentally morally, socially or commits an unreasonable act to endanger the estate or the wards, the unfit *Wasi* can easily, without affecting the foundation of the original power of appointment, be removed and his duty conferred upon his co-*Wasi* if this has been so directed by the testator. But in the absence of any directions the unfit *Wasi* will instantly be removed and replaced by an order of the court.

The courts of Saudi Arabia in general, recognize the wishes of the testators and act to allow them to be fulfilled in their entirety. Accordingly, in a situation where the testator puts his trust in two *Aswiya* believing that they are the best two to fulfil his bequest, these courts respect his wishes. Therefore, whenever either of the two becomes incapacitated for any reason, the court can intervene to appoint a substitute. Such a situation is demonstrated in the case of *H*.[16]

H was designated as a joint *Wasi* with *M*. On the grounds of his old age and other commitments, *H* applied to the court to relieve him of the *Wisaya* duties and his request was granted. But in recognition of the testator's desire to hold *H* as a joint *Wasi* with *M*, the court considered *M* alone, because of the joint *Wisaya*, unauthorized to perform the testator's *Wisaya* and therefore sought a replacement. Accordingly *Kh* was appointed to replace the retired *Wasi* with special emphasis that she was to undertake to perform her task jointly with the other remaining *Wasi*, *M*. Outlining the replacement's function, the Court instructed her not to act individually in anything related to the *Wisaya* but that she had to inform her co-*Wasi* of her intentions and obtain his consent first. Such a ruling ensures the collective nature of such a *Wisaya*.

Courts will act in the same manner when a joint *Nazir* (trustee of *Waqf*), dies or is dismissed leaving his partner as demonstrated in the case of *A* and *H*.[17]

The two brothers *A* and *H* held jointly the *Nazara* of the *Waqf*. *A* died leaving his brother alone in charge of the *Waqf* which was not recognized. The Court thus appointed *M*, the third brother, to replace the dead *Nazir* in all functions attached to him. Due to the *Waqif's* (dedicator) commands, the Court ordered each of the joint *Nazirs* to act in all matters related to the *Waqf* only with the knowledge and the agreement of each other.

The co-executors are usually appointed in the same bequest. The testator has been given the right to alter his will entirely by a subsequent will or codicil enabling him to cut out the number of executors he appointed in a previous will. Such is illustrated in the case where the testator, having made a bequest and nominated a number of persons, including his wife and son as executors, had second thoughts which led him to the cancellation of the property side of the bequest but not the *Wisaya*. He replaced it by another order, this time, the disposable third to be spent, after the discharge of funeral expenses, on good purposes, from which the sum of SR2,000 was to be paid to his ex-slave boy in addition to payments for his care and education.

But as to his previous bequest which referred to appointed executors, the testator had only partially cancelled it, thus dismissing all the executors mentioned except for his wife and son whom he authorized to conduct his estate and execute his bequest.[18]

However, if the testator instructs a co-*Wasi* in a joint *Wisaya*, to take over the *Wisaya* whenever his other co-*Wasi* became incapacitated, then the testator's wish will be respected without intervention from the court. An illustration is seen in the case where the testator had appointed three named men joint *Wasis* over his estate and children. The present amongst the three was to replace the absent (or incapacitated) in all matters related to the bequest.[19]

Also in another case the testator had appointed his son as a *Wasi* over his estate and children. He also appointed his daughter, his brother and sister collectively and separately to supervise his *Wasi* and to be consulted in all matters of his bequest.[20]

JURISDICTION OF THE COURT AS TO THE APPOINTMENT OF A *WASI*

We have already seen how a *Wasi* is appointed to the *Wisaya* (the office of executor or guardian) by the testator and with what qualifications he may assume his role. The absence of the testator or his appointed representative creates a problem as to who should succeed to the *Wisaya* and who should not. Will the grandfather, the brother or any of the *Asabat,* (male agnates in general) be in the eyes of the law acceptable to replace the deceased father or will it be someone else who presumably acquires a more predominant capacity.

All points in question as well as qualifications, powers and the right to the dismissal of the subsequent holder of the vacated post are fully discussed in the following.

POSITION OF THE GRANDFATHER AND *ASABAT* IN RELATION TO *WILAYA*

It is understood as a juristic fact that no power as far as the *Wilaya* or guardianship is concerned should devolve on the *Asabat* in general nor to the brothers in particular unless it has been assumed first to devolve upon the grandfather.

As the grandfather was the focul point of the jurists' controversy, he has been the subject of a profound contradiction and divergence between Muslim jurists. The Hanafis and Shafi'is, for instance, in their attempt to establish his right to *Wilaya*, veered to one side, while the Malikis and the Hanbalis veered to the other.

The Hanafis and Shafi'is both agreed in principle but disagreed when it came to the details of the order. The grandfather's rank is the second after the father's causing the father's *Wasi* to regress to the third rank in the view of the Shafi'is. But the Hanafis, for their part would not consider the grandfather having privilege which would allow him to step in between the father and his *Wasi*. This is because in their view the grandfather has been elected to assume the role of the father who has chosen otherwise and not to supercede him. The grandfather, according to such a belief will take up his post only after the father's *Wasi*.

On the other hand where there are those who have disputed the former status of the grandfather, the main difference amongst them is that the Malikis disputed any role whatsoever for the grandfather in relation to his grandchildren. Whereas the Hanbalis, although they formerly held almost the same view as the Malikis, nonetheless divided *Wilaya* or guardianship into three categories:

Wilayat al-nafs, or guardianship of person, is mainly concerned with the general welfare of the ward.

Wilayat al-mal, or guardianship of estate, is concentrated on the management of the ward's estate on his needs and the trading with his estate.

Wilayat al-nikah, or guardianship of marriage is confined to the guidance in electing the *Kuf'* or competent husband among the suitors and to arrange for the marriage ceremony of the ward.

In the lifetime of the father the three *Wilayat* are considered a single entity. The tripartite divisions of guardianship become noticeable only, either at the physical absence of the father, his mental incapacity or his death. The case of *M v. 'A*[21] is demonstrative of this principle. The latter was declared senile, after which his divorce from his wife *M* was vitiated and was subjected to interdiction.

The late *Mufti*, who was also the Chief Justice, reviewed this verdict and endorsed it. As to the expected appointment of a *Wasi* to the senile *A*, he ordered the Court to grant it to any among *'A's* sons, to be found fit to assume the responsibilities attached to his father which he (the Mufti) specified as the responsibility of the management of his father's affairs, providing the maintenance for his dependants and to be appointed a *Wasi* or guardian to his minors as well as to assume the *Wilaya* over *'A's* unmarried daughters (both of person and of marriage). The Court complied with this order and appointed *'A's* son, *Ah*, to the management of his affairs.

Moreover, such distinction is more observable when a mature person becomes mentally disturbed and needs the services of another mature person to act as a *Wasi* to handle his estate. If the father is still living, he does not automatically assume *Wasi*. This is demonstrated in the case where a mature girl became mentally disturbed and was adjudicated *Ma'tuh* or idiot. The principle states that the maturity of a person renders invalid all sorts of *Wilayat* over him or her except that of *Wilayat al-nikah* or guardianship of marriage. Thus the subsequent immaturity or mental disturbance of him or her will not give the former *Wali* nor anybody else the right to resume *Wilaya* unless and until authorized by the court. On the grounds of the girl's mental state and her need, in this case, for a *Wali*, and applying the above principle, the Court appointed the girl's father as her *Wali* and instructed him at the same time to keep a clear account of her estate and to record incomes and expenditures.[22]

Division, as such, could be invoked also by the father's orders to entrust each *Wasi* with one type of *Wilaya* in his bequest. He could also devolve the combined *Wilayat* to only one person to act as a universal *Wasi*. But should his absence or death be coupled with no appointment of an agent during the father's life nor a *Wasi* after his death, then the power of *Wilaya* will devolve onto the court to form the fourth category of *Wilayat*, which is called *Al-Wilaya al-'amma* or universal jurisdiction.

Out of the four types of *Wilayat*, the grandfather and the rest of *Asabat* or agnate relatives are considered to retain the *Wilayat* with family connections, such as *Wilayat al-nikah* or guardianship of marriage, provided someone else has not been delegated to act as a *Wasi* of marriage for the *Wasi*'s rights procede the *Wali* appointed by the court. As far as *Wilayat al-nafs* or guardianship of a person is concerned, the grandfather and the *Asaba* retain the right of education and moral behaviour and may also take the child into their care. Nevertheless, the Saudi practice has confined their right as to *Wilayat al-nafs* to mere observance and of complaint to the court if any of them notice a fault or negligence in the management of the child's affairs, education and morality conducted by his appointed *Wali* or *Wasi*. This thus gives the agnates no authority to act unilaterally without first consulting the court. Application of these principles by Saudi courts is illustrated in the following:

In the case of *Kh v. A*[23] the plantiff, claimed to have been the only *Wali* eligible to contract the marriage of his niece *M*. Accordingly he prohibited *A*, the defendant, to contract her marriage. Yet *A* contracted her marriage to *U* with her permission. Thus he complained to the court and appealed for the marriage to be declared null and void for the lack of a *Wali*. The court acted by ordering an investigation to these allegations.

In answer to the allegations *A*, the defendant, stated that *M* was mature, had been married before and had given him her permission, to act as a *Wali* for her to marry *U. M*, on her part, denied having any *Wali* in Saudi Arabia and claimed that she did not have relation with the plaintiff. The testification of two witnesses was turned down by the Court as insufficient to confirm the plaintiff's right to *Wilayat al-nikah*, or guardianship of marriage.

Nevertheless, the Court vitiated the marriage as being contracted without a legal *Wali* and ordered *M* to apply to the Court if she wanted to get legally married to *U* or otherwise she must observe *Idda*, the waiting period required after separation, from that day.

The tendency of Saudi Courts to the right of the guardianship of the person over the ward is indicated in the case of *M v. A.*[24]

M objected to *A* the testimentary designated guardian, as being a non-relative and thus unsuitable to become the sole guardian of his nieces, as his appointment would effect the relationship between him and his nieces. As an alternative he suggested the appointment of the maternal uncle of their father to be a co-guardian.

Consequently, though the court accepted the plaintiff's argument in theory, it rejected his nominee and installed the ward's mother as a co-guardian instead. As to the power supposedly held by the *Asaba* over the ward, the Court limited his power solely to the role of complaint whenever he noticed or suspected the guardian of having mismanaged the affairs of the estate of the wards.

But as far as the guardianship of the estate is concerned, none of the *Asaba* is eligible to hold it without prior authorization from the father, in his natural capacity, or the judge, in his general capacity and his universal jurisdiction.

Furthermore, three conditions have to be satisfied before the guardianship of estate is approved of by the court. These are trustworthiness, adherence to religious obligations and suitability or fitness.

These qualities have always been insisted upon by the Saudi Courts as is demonstrated in the case of *S.*[25]

On seeing his minor nieces being left without a guardian following their father's death, *S* appealed to the Court to grant him the guardianship of his three nieces. But before his application was accepted, he was requested to prove that he was trustworthy, adhered to religious obligations and capable of caring for his nieces. Only after he proved that he possessed such qualities was he installed as their guardian.

In another case the mother of a boy was nominated as his guardian and was requested by the Court to prove her *Salahiyah* (as has been used to indicate trustworthiness, religious adherence and suitability). When satisfactory proof was presented, the mother was appointed financial guardian to her boy. She was instructed to keep a clear account of her child's estate in which to record the income and expenditure.[26]

DOES THE RIGHT TO APPOINT A GUARDIAN COME FROM *WILAYA* OR *WISAYA*?

As we have already seen, none of the powers of the grandfather nor the rest of the *Asaba* (agnate relatives) is acknowledged by law nor will it be respected if any of them gains possession of the ward's estate or any part thereof. For none of them can, by his own merits, succeed to *Wilaya al-mal*. Thus, since they do not possess the right to become *Walis (Awliya, pl.)* themselves, they obviously will have no right to delegate as seen in the Arabian proverb, 'He who does not possess does not give.'

The only natural claimant to the *Wilaya* is the father. Consequently the father alone can confer it upon others whom he may consider as standing in a fiduciary capacity to him, to take over his place.

The power of appointing a guardian to the minors may also be delegated to the father's *Wasi*, though such a right cannot be claimed from his merits as a personal representative, for no right exists as such. However, if the relevant power is ever to be possessed by a *Wasi*, then in order to delegate it at his own will, he must secure beforehand precise instructions from the father to this effect such as 'My *Wasi H* shall have my permission to appoint after me anyone whom he shall think fit' or 'Whomever *H* assigns to be his *Wasi* shall be mine too'.

The Saudi stand on this particular point is clearly stated by the resolution of the Board of Deputies.[27] In this resolution, the Board had shown its conformity to the King's order to *Katib al-'Adl* to abandon the Hanafi doctrine in favour of the Hanbali one thus disallowing the uncommissioned executors or guardians to vest in someone else such rights and powers as they have in trust, i.e. to make someone a sub-executor or a sub-guardian.

Eventually the appointed *Wasi* can entrust the guardianship of estate as well as of marriage to anyone who stands in a fiduciary capacity to him. And only then the *Wasi* can rightly claim to have acted within his own rights and powers as a proxy to the natural possessor of such powers (the father).

The judge also has access to the *Wilaya* but his type of *Wilaya* is not as absolute and natural as that of the father. His *Wilaya* is also distinct from that of sub-*Wasi* who succeeds to it through someone else. It is fair to say that his right has been brought about by his position as a general protector of public welfare. The necessity of appointing a guardian could also be considered a principal factor placing *Wilaya* in the new type of universal jurisdiction.

The universality of the *Wilaya* of a judge is extendable beyond any limit. It might be used to remove even from the father, under certain circumstances, his natural guardianship by the imposition of the doctrine of interdiction if he be found unfit.

A busy person like a judge would not personally take over the guardianship but he will practice his authority through his proxy. Thus his task will be to select a suitable person to act under his supervision with the capacity of an agent to assume the name of *Wasi* or *Wakil al-Qadi* (the commissioner of the judge).

Finally, the power of assignment may be said to become transferable in two capacities. If the one who confers that power is the father or if he is the judge then it is right to say that such power comes from the *Wilaya*. But if the conferrer is the executor or guardian then the power comes from the *Wisaya* because the instructions to this effect came from him in a bequest.

THE TEMPORARY AND REPLACEMENT *WASI*

The temporary appointment.

A *Wasi* might be temporarily appointed. Nonetheless, during the course of his appointment the executor's credibility will not suffer a bit as a consequence. Many expressions may be used to convey the testator's intentions some of which are 'I bequeath the management of my bequest to *H* for a year' or '*A* is to become my executor to administer my state until he discharges my creditors' or 'until my absent or captured brother is back', etc. Such a *Wasi* will hold the same power and enjoy the same right just as if his appointment were indefinite.

The executor or the guardian of court may also be appointed temporarily to deal with the *Wisaya* and the minor's affairs. This is seen in the case of *Al-H*[28], a boy who for some reason or other possibly the illness or absence of the *Wasi*, was left with no one to care for him. When the matter was raised concerning the need of the boy for a temporary *Wasi* the Court requested proof of the fitness of the *Wisaya* candidate to be confirmed in the usual manner.

S was pointed out by the testimony of two witnesses to be suitable and fit to be a temporary *Wasi* for the boy. Thus, on the strength of the evidence presented, *S* was appointed a temporary *Wasi* to look after the boy's interests.

Such temporary appointment is also illustrated by the case of *A* and his co-beneficiaries in the *Waqf* of *K*.[29]

Two *Nazirs* were appointed to administer the *Waqf* of *K* jointly which makes unacceptable in law any act by one *Nazir* only without the consent of the other. Accordingly, when one of the designated *Nazirs*, *H*, was absent in Riyadh causing the Waqf's interests to be impaired with the consequent loss of revenue, *A* and his co-beneficiaries appealed to the Court to appoint a joint *Nazir* temporarily to replace the absent one. When the appeal to the Court of Riyadh proved useless since *H* did not report to either of the two courts the Court decided with consideration for the beneficiaries state and need, to appoint *Z*, who was confirmed fit, to become a temporary co-*Nazir* and advised him to comply with the provisions of the *Waqf* in conjunction with the other *Nazir*.

REPLACEMENT ASSIGNMENT

The testator may if he desires institute a person as *Wasi* and direct that another person be a replacement *Wasi* for that person. The *Wasi*, therefore, becomes susceptible to dismissal in no definite time but by the occurence of certain events. Such events could be the attainment of his son's maturity, if he is still young, or when he regains his mental faculty, if disordered, or recovers from his illness or becomes interested in trade (if the commission involves trading) or finishes his study (reaching a certain level or degree) or if he merely becomes reconciled with his mother or if he returns to live with his brothers or marries his cousin, etc.

A testator may assign his son *Wasi* but if the son is not yet of full age when the testator dies, then the testator's brother accedes to *Wisaya*. The substitute *Wasi* is then supposed to assume the office only on a temporary basis until the assigned *Wasi* meets or complies with the conditions laid down by his father. Then the son will become eligible to claim the *Wisaya*.
However, the substitute *Wasi* should not vacate his post until the instituted *Wasi* has been cited to assume his power by accepting his assignment because once the instituted *Wasi* accepts, the substituted *Wasi* becomes excluded. Still if the testator sees the services of whomever he has appointed substitute *Wasi* to be valuable to the *Wisaya*, then he might order his reinstatement as a limited *Wasi* to accomplish certain duties or he might reinstate him by appointing him a co-*Wasi* or give him a supervisory status over all executors and guardians.

The extent to which these rules are applied are shown in the case where the testator had appointed his father, his two brothers, his maternal uncle and three others as executors to administer, separately or collectively, his estate. In the same capacity they were to be guardians over his minors. He stipulated the right of any of his children to become a replacement *Wasi* and to take over the *Wisaya* whenever any of them became of full age and *Rashid* or mature. Since the testator considered the services of his appointed executors of value, he granted them the right of supervision after his son had become *Rashid* and therefore able to succeed to the *Wisaya*.[30]

In a further case the testator appointed his elder son his executor and guardian over his minors. Another man was appointed to supervise the *Wasi*. In another provision the right was reserved to the minors in that whenever any of them became *Baligh* and *Rashid* they would become joint *Wasi* under the same supervision.[31]

To ensure that the sudden death of the appointed *Wasi* does not hamper the implementation of his bequest, the testator may assign a number of *Wasis* in whom he puts his trust to replace consecutively the dead or unfit *Wasi*. The approval of such a bequest by the Saudi Courts is illustrated in a case in which the testator assigned his wife as an executrix to manage his estate, extrude the disposable third to meet his funeral expenses and use the rest of it for good and benevolent purposes, to distribute the hereditable two thirds among his legal heirs and to withold his minors' shares for them.

As life is always exposed to danger and also the testator wishes to make sure that his bequest is being carried out in the way he chooses, he designated one of his sons as a substitute *Wasi* and also designated another son as substitute *Wasi* to replace the second *Wasi*. If anything happened to his wife and his first son and second son, he gave the right to whoever among his other children should prove to be *Al-arshad* or the most suitable, to fill the vacated post of *Wisaya*.[32]

This is also indicated in the case in which the testator bequeathed the extrusion of one third of his estate to pay for his funeral and other expenses and to buy with the rest a house, a shop or part thereof, which would bring in indefinitely an income in order to pay annual alms.

He appointed his son as executor to adminster his estate and execute his bequest. Taking account of the unexpected (death, absence or unsuitability), he designated his brother *A*, his grandson *R* and then the most suitable of his offspring as a substitute executor to uphold this duty one after the other.[33]

HOW A *WASI* IS TO BE RELIEVED OF HIS DUTY

Relieving a *Wasi* of his duty takes different forms which depend on his original assignment. Thus the process of dismissal might be a peaceful one when the *Wasi* voluntarily concedes his power. Otherwise he could be subjected to a disgraceful removal when dismissal is the result of the *Wasi*'s abuse of his power.

The voluntary removal

Voluntary removal occurs when the *Wasi* has completed the task he was given. This occurs if the executor was commissioned to collect and distribute the testator's estate to his heirs, to reimburse his creditors, to receive the sum bequeathed or to pass the corpus over to those entitled. If the executor's commission consists of guardianship, then he will be relieved of it only when the deceased's minors come of age and become mature enough to manage their own affairs, or when he marries off his ward if he was appointed guardian of marriage. All the above assignments in addition to the temporary executorship are eventually terminated without any need to obtain an order from the court to this effect.

However, once a *Wasi* has been designated by the court on a temporary basis, the termination order of his duty has to be made by the court. This is illustrated in the case of *Z* in the *Waqf* of *K*.[34]

On the grounds of *H*, the joint *Nazir* of the *Waqf* being absent, the *Waqf*'s interests were impeded. Because of the benificiaries' appeal, the court appointed a temporary co-*Nazir* to replace the absent one. When the absent *Nazir* came back *Z*, the Court's designated temporary *Nazir*, applied to the court to be relieved of his temporary *Nazara*, a request which was duly granted his request for the same equitable reasons that entitle him to refuse

The executor who before he fulfils his task requests dismissal will be granted his request for the same suitable reasons that entitle him to refuse to enter into his duties of executorship in the first place. This is particularly relevant if an executor's desire to give up his commission stems from a feeling that he is unable to pursue his duties any further without harm to his assignment or hardship to himself.

Thus for an old *Wasi* or the *Wasi* whose ward and estate are at a distance from where he lives or one who is too busy or has too many people to look after, or simply the *Wasi* who for some other reasons does not wish to retain such an office because it demands too much of his time and emotions, the law has given them the right to relieve themselves of the burden which cannot be accomplished without much effort. For had the law insisted on holding a *Wasi* against his will it would be committing a self-contradiction, thus causing harm to those it tried to protect.

It is noteworthy that the replaced *Wasi* as well as the voluntarily retired one, though their *Wisaya* should, in theory, come to an immediate end, do in practice continue with the *Wasi* until they are judicially relieved of their commitments. The attitude of the Saudi courts to the termination of the *Wasi's* duty is only seen when another *Wasi* has been installed or shown his readiness to take over the post to be vacated. Such a tendancy is demonstrated in the case where immediately after hearing the guardian's plea for release from his commission on the grounds of his old age and engagements, a judge asked the petitioner if he knew of any suitable person to take his place. The mother was suggested and then proved fit for the post of guardianship. However, to ensure against the wards being left without a guardian for any time whatsoever the order for the uncle's release was postponed, pending the completion of the procedures for the installation of the mother. The release and installation were issued in one document.[35]

The case of *H* is another illustration of this point. *H*, being a joint executor to the two bequests, sought dismissal from the court on the grounds of his old age and his readiness to render a full account of the conducted bequest. Nevertheless, instead of ordering his release, the Court postponed it and started enquiries to find a suitable executor as a replacement. As *Kh* had shown her willingness to become an executrix and was proved fit, she was officially appointed exectrix to take *H*'s place jointly with the co-executor *M* in the same document that *H*'s release from his duty was issued.[36]

The forceful or involuntary dismissal

This is the judicial reaction to four major defaults in the executor's actions. These are: a defect in the mental faculty of the executor to a degree that it can never be tolerated, negligence in not taking good care of the ward, mismanagement of the estate he was appointed to take charge of or defiance of the *Sharia'a* such as wickedness, profligacy, postacy, etc, as well as *Fusuq*[37] (untrustworthiness). Disqualifying factors such as the above, whether individually or collectively, call for prompt action from the judge, as the supreme observer and supervisor of *Wilaya*, and the unsuitable executor or guardian will be dismissed.

Furthermore, the jurists agree that a guardian who contracts an infectious disease, is, as a protective measure, to be removed from the guardianship on the grounds of the danger that the ward might become infected by the same disease. Application of this principle can be seen in the case of *F v. M*,[38] in which the wife was granted the right to dissolve the marriage contract on the grounds of her husband's having contracted tuberculosis.

Application of this could also be inferred from the case of *A v. R*.[39]

R, the wife, proved that she had dissolved her marriage contract in accordance with the right conceded to her by the court when she claimed that her husband had contracted leprosy. The husband's agent's demand for the return of the wife was dismissed as not actionable.

The fact that even the close and binding relationship of marriage being able to be dissolved through an infectious disease having been contracted demonstrate that it is even more important for a helpless child, whether the guardian is a direct blood relation or not, to be protected from any disease contracted by the guardian. Prevention of contraction of the disease by the child is through the dismissal of his guardian, temporarily or permanently, and his replacement by a healthy and considerate person in conformity with the principle which states 'no custody (or *Wilaya*) for a person who contracts a disease which may endanger the ward's life'.[40]

NOTES

1. *Kashshaf al-Qin'a*, Vol. 4, 336, *Sharh Muntaha al-Iradat*, Vol. 2, 539, *Al-Tanqih al-Mushbi*, 194, and *Al-Insaf*, Vol. 7, 185.
2. *Sharh Muntaha al-Iradat*, Vol. 2, 296.
3. Jedda Katib al-'adl, Case No. 804, Vol. 2, (1382H).
4. Jedda Grand Court, Case, p.82. Joint Reg. 1344-45H.
5. Jedda Katib al-'adl, Case No. 153, Vol. 1, (Date 1378H).
6. Makkah Grand Court, Case No. 48, Vol. 1, (Date 27/2/1380H).
7. Mecca Grand Court, Case No. 130, Vol. 1, (Date 5/5/1380H).
8. Jedda Grand Court, No. 133, joint reg. (1344-1345H), p.140.
9. Makkah Grand Court, Case No. 130, Vol. 1, (Date 5/5/1380H).
10. Jedda Katib al-'adl, Case No. 2777, Vol. 8, date 1385H.
11. Jedda Katib al-'adl, Case No. 157, Vol. 1, (1379H).
12. Mecca Grand Court, Cass No. 131, Vol. 1, (1377H).
13. Makkah Grand Court, No. 72, Vol. 17. Sp. Reg. of Shaikh Al-Amr, (date 19/5/1391H).
14. Jedda Katib al-'adl, Case No. 1408, Vol. 4, (date 1380H).
15. Makkah Grand Court, Case No. 107, Vol. 1, (date 20/4/1381H).
16. Makkah Grand Court, Case No. 130, Vol. 1, (Date 5/5/1380H).
17. Makkah Grand Court, Case No. 62, Vol. 1, (date 3/3/1380H).
18. Jedda Katib al-'adl, Case No. 323 Vol. 1, (date 1380H).
19. Jedda Katib al-'adl, Case No. 1939, Vol. 5, (date 1380H).
20. Jedda Katib al-'adl, Case No. 408, Vol. 1, (date 1380H).
21. Makkah Grand Court, No. 181, Vol. 6, (1378H).
22. Makkah Grand Court, Case No. 546, Vol. 1, (date 2/3/1379H).
23. Makkah Grand Court, Case No. 59, Vol. 1, (date 7/2/1376H).
24. Makkah Grand Court, Case No. 1375, Vol. 8. The Minute Reg. of Shaikh Abdulmalik b. Duhaish, (date 1391H).
25. Makkah Grand Court, Case No. 61, Vol. 1, (date 9/3/1377H).
26. Makkah Grand Court, Case No. 14, Vol. 1, (date 24/1/1380H).
27. Deputies Office Resolution No. 95, (date 28/2/1348H).
28. Makkah Grand Court, Case No. 22, Vol. 1, (date 25/1/1377H).
29. Makkah Grand Court, Case No. 91, Vol. 6, (date 24/2/1376H).
30. Jedda Katib al-'adl, Case No. 226, Vol. 1, (date 1380H).
31. Jedda Katib al-'adl, Case No. 2258, Vol. 5, (date 1384H).
32. Jedda Katib al-'adl, Case No. 2592, Vol. 7, (date 1385H)
33. Jedda Katib al-'adl, Case No. 561, Vol. 2, (date 1382H).
34. Makkah Grand Court, Case No. 91, Vol. 6, (date 24/2/1376H).
35. Makkah Grand Court, No. 48, Vol. 1, (1380H).
36. Makkah Grand Court, Case No. 130, Vol. 1, (date 5/5/1380H).
37. *Kashaf al-Qina*, Vol. 4, 395-396.
38. Case No. 202, Vol. II, (1380H/1960AD), p. 115. Quoted from M.I. Ali's Ph. D. thesis p. 103. London University 1971.
39. No. 1821-7452, Vol. 1, (1377H/1959), p. 160 Fatani, from M.I.A. Ali's Ph. D. thesis *Social Responsibilities* pp. 102-103, London University 1971AD.
40. *Kashshaf al-Qina*, Vol. 5, 499, *Sharh Muntaha al-Iradat, Vol. 3, 267, Matatib uli al-nuha*, Vol. 5, 667.

CHAPTER II

APPOINTMENT OF THE GUARDIAN BY THE COURT

In the case of a conflict about to whom the *Wisaya* should be granted, the judge's discretion prevails in respect of the suitablility of the *Wasi* to look after children and the bequeathed estate provided it does not conflict with the intentions and the instructions of the testator.

The judge's role is to choose a trustworthy and competent person to succeed to the *Wisaya*. But in his judicial discretion the.judge is not bound to choose the next of kin provided that it is considered to be in the best interests of the child. However, when the judge decides that two persons, who have both offered their services, have equal merits of trustworthiness and competency, preference is to be given to a relative over a non-relative to be appointed as the guardian by the court. Although the judge usually consults the child's relatives first, it must be borne in mind that this is not a matter of right for the relatives concerned but a matter exclusively held within the discretion of the judge.

Nevertheless, the Saudi judges tend to grant the *Wisaya* to one of the child's mature relatives. This may stem from the belief that the relatives in generai are more intimate and concerned. Such preference was voiced by the late *Mufti* and Chief Justice of Saudi Arabia when he instructed the Grand Court of Makkah, in the case of *'A*,[1] who was found to be senile and thus in need of a *Wali*, that if among the sons of the senile *'A* one is found fit, he is to be preferred to others to be appointed as a *Wali* to his father, his adult sisters and also to the two other sisters who were still minors.

The sex of the minor must be taken into consideration when appointing the guardian by the court. For a minor girl must not be handed over to a a non-*Mahram Wali* provided there is a female in residence as well. In compliance with this principle the Court in the case of *Z*[2] restricted the power of the testamentary *Wasi* who was a non-relative to the girls by appointing the mother of the girls as a co-*Wasi* in agreement with the girls' uncle's objection to the designation by the father of the non-relative *Wasi* to his nieces.

A boy who is old enough to make a decision between prospective guardians should be allowed whenever possible to exercise such an option in order to go with whom he feels intimate and secure in conformity to the principle which states 'The male minor over seven years of age has the right to choose the parent he wants to live with in the case of divorce or separation. If he opts to choose the custodian (his mother or another close female relative) he will remain with her only at night. During the daytime he must live with his guardian (the father or his representative).'[3]

This principle was applied in the case of *A* v. *D*. After the divorce, the defendant retained her children *Y* (8) and *Ab* (9). But *A*, the father and thus the guardian raised the claim that the children should be handed over to him.

At this point, we may consider the fact that the standard of maturity of minors of this age is such that they may be considered mature enough, within certain limits, prompted by their own feelings, to decide which parent (or guardian) they choose to live with. In the case in question the Court granted *Y* and *Ab*. the right of choice. As they had both been brought up by their mother, *D*, they chose to live with her.[4] The jurists also thought the same principle is applicable to the seven years old girl, whose father is dead or unfit, to choose between two competing *Mahrams*.[5]

The *Wasi* who only seeks the grace of God by offering his services freely might be deemed to be the sort of *Wasi* whose commission is safe and would look after the ward and the estate better and could thus be favoured to a businessman as a *Wasi*.[6]

Finally a person who lives within the same vicinity as the ward or the estate bequeathed is preferred to one who lives far from where the minor or the estate is situated. However, the court, for some reason or other, may overlook this point when it is found to be in the interest of the minor or the estate as can be seen from the case of *Kh* v. *A*.[7]

The Court had appointed the latter guardian of his grandchildren, *N*, *R*, *I* and *M*. A dispute arose when *A* forced them to evacuate the house they had inherited and in which they were living with their mother, the plaintiff, on the grounds that it was too distant from his residence to supervise them properly. In return he allotted them a small apartment in his own house. *Kh* the mother, officially appointed co-guardian, petitioned the court to examine the situation of the children who, as she claimed, were ill-treated by their grandfather. She described the life with her ex-father-in-law as continuous humiliation and asked the court to revoke the grandfather's guardianship.

The court refrained from enforcing any decision and advised an amicable agreement in consequence of which the grandfather undertook to rent a separate home for the children and their mother in the proximity of his own residence but not without first consulting the co-guardian. Moreover, a committee consisting of representatives of the guardian and the co-guardian was set up to examine, under the supervision of the court, all allegations concerning income and expenditure and to act as an intermediary in paying the monthly maintenance.

In brief, the qualifications the court look for when appointing the guardian are, besides his trustworthiness and competency, that he be if possible, a relative to the ward and if a girl over seven years old, a *Mahram*;

the *Mumayiz* child (who has attained the age of discretion) should be left to choose between two or more competing relatives living in the same locality as the ward and who may protect the ward's estate from diminishing and that whosoever freely offers his services may preferably be chosen.

DIFFERENCE BETWEEN THE TESTAMENTARY GUARDIAN AND THE GUARDIAN ELECTED BY COURT

The testator is under no obligation to favour a relative over a non-relative to take care of his minor issues. He is undeniably the closest to the minors and most caring, too, among their *Awlya* or guardians and will thus be expected to choose a person of competence and trust to fulfil the obligations of *Wilaya*.

In such a position the father could assign to the *Wilaya* a less competent person if he thinks him to be more lenient to his minor child. *Al-fasiq*, for instance, (who is not usually trusted with money) can be appointed executor even with the testator's full knowledge of the executor's undesirable character because, as we said, the executor stands in a fiduciary capacity to the testator.

Also in the same category is the appointment of an incapable person to succeed to *Wilaya* whenever a stipulated condition is fulfilled. This is seen in the appointment of his premature or mentally disturbed son, who is to take over from the substituted executor whenever he regains his faculty or reaches the age of maturity or if he is reconciled with his mother.

Unlike the father, a judge is in no position to know who would best protect the minor's interests and his welfare. He is thus advised to entrust the guardianship of a minor to one of the minor's relatives if there exists among them a sympathetic and competent one. Accordingly, there will be no chance ever for a *Fasiq* to be entrusted as a guardian or executor by the court.

As a precautionary measure, the Saudi judges in an attempt to contain the possibility of conflict between the minor's relatives in respect of the appointed guardian and to waste no time in lawsuits often consult those who may feel obliged by their social custom to get involved with the affairs of the minor. Here is a case as an illustration of such an attitude. In this case a man died leaving in need of a guardian his three girls. When their case was raised in the Court, the three directly involved people, the minors' mother, their grandfather and their paternal uncle were present and were consulted about the person they thought suitable to be the girls' guardian. Both the minors' mother and grandfather gave their full approval to the appointment of the minors' paternal uncle as their guardian.[8]

Also in the case of *al-M*[9] he claimed, in the presence of his mother with the support of adequate proof, to have been appointed by his father a *Wasi* to his brothers. But before the brother was appointed the judge consulted the mother and got her approval.

There are two cases where the testamentary executor cannot be removed from executorship by the court. The first is a defect in his faculties which does not affect his mental capacity, e.g. blindness or deafness and dumbness which are likely to weaken the conduct of the executorship's affairs. The second is the mere suspicion of negligence and extortion by the executor.

When a judge is ambivalent about an executor, whether he is desiring to respect and observe the testator's instructions or to remove him as suspicious, he should seek the only way out which was recommended by the majority of the Hanbali jurists. This is to appoint a co-executor to help run the testacy. Thus, the benefit of the necessary protection by the co-executor is obtained while not deviating from the instructions of the testator by dismissing the executor in whom he had put his trust. As to the name, although, the safekeeping is done by the recently appointed co-executor, the official name will remain attached to the testamentary executor alone.[10] The application of this principle is exemplified in the case of *A* v. *H*.[11]

In this case the judge rejected the maturity claim brought by the boy. But when the judge learnt during the hearing that the boy's guardian (his mother) did not know the exact income of the ward's estate, he appointed the ward's paternal uncle as a co-guardian and insisted on his presence every year at the time the mother received such income and every month when she extracted out of it the maintenance of the ward, thereby obtaining precise accounts. The judge also compelled them to keep records of the ward's expenditure.

A different consideration was made the basis of appointing a co-*Wasi* in the case of *Z*.

The paternal uncle of the three girls objected to the confirmation of the testamentary designated *Wasi* to take care of their estate and their marriage because he was a non-relative to them (which he thought would cause friction and estrangement between him and his nieces). He thus suggested their father's maternal uncle to be a co-*Wasi*. Accepting the uncle's argument in theory, the judge appointed the girl's mother as a co-*Wasi*.[12]

When the objective of properly caring for the children is at risk, the court acts to ensure that adequate care is restored by its appointment of a co-*Wasi* such as illustrated in the case of *I* v. *A*.[13]

The former, also being the mother, was the testamentary designated *Wasi* responsible for the well-being of the minors in her care. The uncle who got alarmed by the absence of satisfactory care, resulting from the mother going out to work, took the children into his own care. The mother sued the uncle and promised to employ a servant to help care for the children when she was absent provided they were returned to her safekeeping. Taking into account the seriousness of the risk involved since the mother had no intention of giving up her work, the judge appointed the uncle a co-*Wasi* and ordered their return to their mother's custody. She was instructed to keep her promise to employ a servant to care for the children during her absence from the house.

Suspicion of negligence caused by the *Wasi* delaying the payment of maintenance to the custodian is taken as grounds for the appointment of a co-*Wasi* as shown in the case of *F.* v. *M.*

The latter was accused by the mother, who was the custodian of her own girls, of refusing to provide support for her children during the years 1378 and 1379 AH, causing immense hardship to the mother and demanded, therefore, the appointment of a co-*Wasi* to ensure the continuance of support. Her request was granted and she was appointed the co-*Wasi* over her children.[14]

DUTIES OF THE *WASIS* AND ADMINISTRATORS

There is no legal obligation existing in Islam which will force the legal representative to inherit the duties and the responsibilities of his praepositus. But that does not mean that the remaining liabilities will not be met. The law has made sure that in the absence of testamentary directions and a designated *Wasi*, the heirs themselves will have to bear the burden of administering the estate and ensuring that all the deceased's liabilities are met in full or in part according to the extent of the estate, no more and no less. This was illustrated in the case of the heirs of *M.* v. *the heir of A.*[15]

A was indebted to *M* and both died before the debt was recovered. Thus the two daughters of *M* sued the debtor's brother and his heir for their share in the debt. The defendant informed the court that his brother died destitute and he had no obligation to settle such a claim.

Nevertheless, the defendant desiring to release his dead brother from spiritual condemnation over this debt, reached an amicable agreement with the plaintiffs to pay out of his own pocket a sum of money, as he had also done with other claiming heirs, in return for the plaintiff's undertaking to release his dead brother from any moral blame related to the debt.

The court may intervene to limit such power by appointing one of the heirs executor or turn it over to the head of the department of Bait al-Mal, to carry out the task. Accordingly charges will be made against the appointed administrator instead of the heirs collectively as demonstrated in the case of *S* v. Bait al-Mal.[16]

The plaintiff used to work for *al-Sh* who died with the wages of the plaintiff unpaid. The appropriation by Bait al-Mal of the dead man's estate caused the wage's claim to be made against the Public treasury. As the claim was supported with adequate proof and that Bait al-Mal informed the court that the appropriated estate was sufficient to meet the asserted debt, the court ordered the claim to be settled from the dead man's estate.

The case of *F* v. *al-M*[17] is also an illustration of this. *F* was a *Nazir* of a *Waqf* and *al-M* was her agent. On behalf of his client, he received SR8,840 and died without it being paid to his client, *F*. Following her claim, the court ordered an investigation into *al-M*'s monetary state which revealed that he was also indebted to someone else and left only a share of two and two-thirds *qirat* in real estate.

A court order was served to Bait al-Mal to seize the two and two-thirds *qirat* and to sell it in an auction and pay the plaintiff and other creditors, who had sufficient proof to support their claims. If the price is insufficient to meet all debts, he is to allocate proportionately to each debtor an amount which will only partly meet the original debt.

The general task of the administrator is to collect the assets, to receive credits due to the deceased, to discharge owing debts, to settle all the outstanding liabilities and finally to distribute the remnants in accordance to the law of inheritance by giving each heir his entitlement. When a part of the estate is the subject of a will, the administrator's task will be to hand it over to the testamentary executor otherwise to the executor appointed by the court. An illustration of this is found in the case of *S* and *al-M* v. Bait al-Mal[18] in which the death of *A* resulted in the appropriation of his estate by Bait al-Mal. Following such action *al-M*, being a testamentary executor (to administer the deceased's estate and to extrude the disposable third out of which to pay for his funeral and to pay the remaining for good and benevolent purposes at his own discretion and to conduct the distribution of the two thirds between his heirs), applied to the court for the bequeathed third to be delivered to him. *S*, as agent of the heirs, also applied to the court to distribute and surrender to each heir his entitlement. As head of Bait al-Mal acknowledged that the deceased's estate was still in his trust the judge ordered him to hand over the disposable third to the *Wasi* and to distribute the remaining two thirds among the deceased's legal heirs.

It is the duty of Bait al-Mal, when more than one person claims to have been appointed the sole executor, to appropriate the bequeathed estate, until the dispute is solved, as occurred in the case of *Z* v. Bait al-Mal.[19]

Z's father, *A*, had given his daughter the authority to pay for the funeral rites and to distribute one third of the estate among the poor according to a provision in his will. After the death of *A*, a dispute arose between *Z* and her uncle who claimed the right of *Wisaya*. This resulted in the deceased's estate being entrusted to Bait al-Mal until the dispute was settled. As the uncle could not prove his claim and *Z*'s claim was supported by evidence Bait al-Mal was ordered to hand over the estate to her.

In his capacity as a testamentary executor with special instructions to receive debts owed to the testator, it will be an *ultra vires* for him to sue the debtor for the debt due to the testator. This is because the debt owed to the deceased testator is considered to have become part of the heir's property. Nevertheless, in his other capacity of administrator of the testator's estate, the executor may receive credits handed over by the testator's debtors. But contrary to the testamentary executor, the court's executor can sue for such debts since he (the court's executor) may be acting in the capacity of the heir's agent too.

As to the dischargeability of the executor to the bequeathed obligations and loans, the law has given him the right, in the face of the heir's refusal or denial, to carry out the bequest secretly from whatever property he has or from whatever property he may lay his hands on, with the only condition that the executor must be sure that the claimant's allegations are genuine.

The appraisal of the ward's maintenance is the court's task. The sum is fixed by the court according to the current standard of living, the social position of the ward and the financial capability of the ward's estate. However, should the fixed amount be too high for the ward's estate to bear or too low to suffice for the ward's needs, the court will reconsider its previous appraisal and replace it with an adequate amount. This is manifested in the case of *F* v. *M*.[20]

In this case the latter who was the court appointed financial guardian of his brother's children, failed to make the required regular payment of maintenance SR276 monthly on the grounds that the amount was too high. Therefore *F* and *M* petitioned to the court to order the guardian to fulfil his duty. Consequently two trustworthy men were appointed to estimate an adequate amount of maintenance. The guardian was ordered to pay the mother, SR80, SR70 and SR50 , i.e. a total of SR200 monthly in maintenance for the children.

The power of administration can never be extended beyond the management of the estate. Whereas the testamentary executor can, on the testator's special or general directions, become an administrating executor, a collector and distributor in addition to becoming a testamentary guardian over the deceased's children and a testamentary guardian of marriage. On his appointment as a *Mushrif 'ala-al-Wasiya*, (supervisor), an executor can exercise an extremely strong control both over the estate and the ward. Although, the *Mushrif* will not personally conduct the testacy, his control over the testament wil be unlimited since the final decision making lies in his hands. This means that none of the ordinary *Wasi*'s actions in relation to the executory are binding and legal unless the required approval of the *Mushrif* is first obtained by way of consultation.

The control held by the *Mushrif* is spelt out by a Saudi judge in the following case.

A man appointed his wife as *Wasi* to his minor daughter and assigned a trusted man as a *Mushrif* to supervise his *Wasi*. They both applied to the court to confirm their assignment. When authorizing this assignment, the judge instructed the appointed *Wasi* to seek advice from the *Mushrif* and stipulated that she was not to do anything in respect of the *Wasiya* until she first obtained the approval of the *Mushrif*.[21]

CALLING THE *WASI* TO ACCOUNT AND HIS LIABILITIES

Negligence and mismanagement by a *Wasi* will not be left unchecked, for the law cannot afford to let him, as an immediate controller of the ward's affairs, abuse his duties and get away with it. The law has, instead, set up a set of rules which if contravened will result in the *Wasi* being accused of negligence or mismanagement. Apart from offences against life and limb, none of the rules can be described as unqualified or uncompromising rules. They are all set in a non-arbitrary way to allow for the customary law and the judicial discretion to be incorporated in any solution.

However, various punishments have been suggested, in the case of negligence or mismanagement. The lowest is the disgraceful dismissal from the office of executorship and guardianship. If, for instance, negligence goes as far as committing the mortal sin of killing his ward or in aiding and abetting his death, then the guardian should not expect to be exempted from punishment or to be shown clemency, just by being the victim's guardian. The law is resolved to observe the equability of offence with punishment. Accordingly, the guardian will receive a similar punishment as that of an alien. That is to say, by retaliation in person if it has been proved deliberate or by paying compensation to the other heirs, if it has not. The heirs may commute the retaliatory penalty to blood money and they may also remit gratuitously both penalties.

But if, on the other hand, the loss of limb was the result of negligence, then no one is permitted to relinquish on behalf of the child and monetary compensation must be paid in full. Further, if the act is deliberate, an immediate dismissal is necessary, otherwise the repercussions are left to the judge's discretion.

As far as the property is concerned, the *Wasi* is expected to administer prudently and efficiently the property in his trust, as if it were his own. He is thus to invest the property in a lucrative way to compensate for the paid maintenance and *Zakat* (alm-tax), in compliance to the *Hadith*, 'Trade with the property of your ward so as it is not to be devoured by the *Sadaqa (Zakat)*.'[22] Nevertheless, the *Wasi* must not commit the property of his ward to an unsafe and unprofitable trade. He must not also take this property to a city which is unsafe or through a route which is threatened with perils.

Although the law permits someone to be contracted to trade with the child's property in return for a portion of the profit as a fee, the *Wasi* (or *Wali*) is not permitted to take a fee for trading with his ward's property himself and all the profit must go to the ward. This is because the validation of giving a fee needs the agreement of two separate contracting parties which cannot be obtained here. For if the guardian were to have a fee, his case would be likened to the guardian who sells to his ward or buys from his ward. Since he would make the offer of acceptance on behalf of his ward, it would be considered invalid.[23]

In adherence to the principle which recommends trading with the child's property, the Saudi Court has upheld the bequest in which a father had appointed his elder son a general *Wasi* (an executor and a guardian of the children) with instructions to maintain his trade. He also appointed two persons as overseers to provide his *Wasi* with their advice only in respect of his trade.[24]

In another case the testator, who was not known to have been a merchant, appointed his two brothers as executors and guardians to his children. He ordered them to trade with his children's property until they became of full age.[25]

Also the Saudi judges, in compliance to legal principles often recommend the guardians to purchase with the accumulated wealth some real estate giving revenues thus to assure its safety together with the continuous support for the wards. This is illustrated in the case of *Z*, who designated *A* as guardian to his children. In consequence of an objection raised by the children's uncle against the designated non-relative being the sole guardian of his minor nieces, the court appointed *M* the girls' mother, a co-guardian. In the letter of her appointment, the judge instructed both guardians to safe-guard the property of their wards and to invest it in a real estate. It enjoined both to act collectively in relation to their duties and warned both of them to act without first consulting the other and making sure that their action would be beneficial to their wards.[26]

The *Wasi* must avoid extravagance in dealing with the ward's property, pay no more than a reasonable price for the necessities and pay only a sufficient maintenance for the children. Such maintenance should be equal in amount to that usually required by his class and no more. In this, the Saudi judges have complied with principles seen in the case of *A*,[27] who pleaded to the court to name the amount of SR10, as maintenance for each of his wards per day. In answer to his plea, the judge requested proof that the suggested amount was required by their equals in addition to a proof that the property of his ward could bear that amount. The judge also requested proof that the amount to be ordered for maintenance be suitable and deductable from the income of the ward's property. This was to insure a lasting revenue for the ward as it necessitated an adjustment between the property owned by the ward and his needs.

A comprehensive case which is indicative generally of all points discussed above, as well as the trend in Saudi courts concerning preservation and spending of the ward's property, is the case of *A* and *Ab*.[28]

A and *Ab* who were guardians to two different groups of wards submitted an application to the court stating the needs of their wards to maintenance. Accordingly they sought authorization to sell the wards' common shares in three houses at the offered price they considered to be fair. The judge requested the two guardians to support their claim by presenting letters of their appointment, which gave them the right to speak for the children, coupled with a proof that the offered price was fair and of value to the wards.

After they had presented what was required of them, the judge delivered his judgement as follows: 'In accordance to the adequate proof presented in the usual manner and the assertion of their appointment, I (the judge) judicially confirm the correctness of their claim. I also permit the two *Awsiya* (pl. of *Wasi*) to sell jointly the shares of their wards as part of a whole sale of the three houses with a fair value offered for them since such a sale at the mentioned price is of benefit to the wards. I, at the same time, award the two *Wasis* the wards' share of the price from the three houses and enjoin them not to spend any of it except when needed for the necessary maintenance. I also enjoin them to expand and invest the children's property in lucrative schemes and avoid loss and fraud or alternatively, to buy real estate with potential revenues.'

As any excessive payment over moderate maintenance is an ultra vires act, the property of the child should bear none of it. The *Wasi* will be regarded as having gone beyond his authority by providing on a higher standard of living than the ward has been accustomed to.

The *Wasi* will in no case be permitted to pledge any of the ward's property for his own benefit. Also he must not gamble, bet or spend a single penny thereof in any sinful or unprofitable way. He must pay the *Zakat* or alm-tax regularly out of the ward's property.

Selling without need or apparent profit any of the child's property is illegal, thus the impending cost of the contract and consequent loss because of the invalidation of such a contract must be borne solely by the *Wasi*, for it is the result of an unlawful act.[29]

The responsibility for unauthorized or irresponsible actions in relation to the property of the child as determined by the Saudi courts in adherence to the principles, is illustrated in the case of *F* v. *S*.[30] The latter had committed the property of the children of his deceased brother to a sale on credit. Since *F* was unauthorized to contract such a sale, *S*, his other brother, who saw that such an action would incur some loss to the children since their property had become unattainable on demand, appealed to the court to invalidate the sale and issue an order for the defendant to return the children's property to the children's mother. The defendant was obviously expected to bear the consequences of the property having been sold or consumed or the buyer's refusal to hand it back.

If the *Wasi*'s act involves the letting of the ward's property with less rent than the usual market rent, the *Wasi* will be held liable for the loss incurred by the low rent. This is compared to the letting of a *Waqf* with less rent,[31] thus leaving the act of letting unaffected. This is, of course, unlike the act of selling without benefit to the ward, as the letting mistake with less rent can be corrected by later letting, while the act of selling cannot be undone since it involves the alienation of the ward's property.

If the *Wasi* trades in the property of his ward himself, the incurred profit should go exclusively to the ward. But if he contracts it to a merchant for a fee from the profit or if he deposits it, he will avoid liability only by lending it to a trustworthy person and if he knowingly gives the corpus in his trust to a dishonest person and the corpus is afterwards lost or perishes, the *Wasi* will then be obliged to compensate for the lost or perished corpus.

The *Wasi* will not be regarded as generous by giving generously from a property he does not own, thus if he pays the servants or agents more than their usual wages or remuneration for their services, he must bear the excessive part himself because in doing so the *Wasi* is considered to have exceeded his power. The property of the child will also not be affected by voluntary donations made by his guardian. Thus, if on behalf of the child, the guardian does so, donations will be deducted out of his own estate and not out of the child's. Nevertheless, a small gift is permitted provided that it satisfies two conditions, that it is a compensation for a prior gift to the child that it is a small one which does not affect his property.

Usually the maintenance of the child is spent on him by his guardian but if the guardian is to prepare his ward for on-coming adult life, he may pay his ward his usual maintenance provided he keeps him under close supervision to know how and on what things the child spends it. But if from past experience the guardian knows his ward to be a spendthrift, then he must not hand over the maintenance to the child every month, nor even every week, but every day, and if the child is very extravagant, then not even daily but meal by meal. When the guardian, without reason, persists in giving the extravagant child his maintenance, he will be committing an act of negligence and will thus be held liable for incurred loss of the child's estate. Nevertheless, if the court decides the time and manner at which the maintenance of the ward is paid, then no liability will fall upon the guardian. A demonstration of the Saudi attitude as to these principles is seen in the following cases.

In the case of *A* v. *Aq*,[32] the amount of SR2 daily had already been adjudicated as the sum of maintenance to the boy. As it became insufficient to meet his primary needs, the boy brought his guardian to court and appealed for an increase in his maintenance to a level sufficient to cover his primary needs. Showing an understanding attitude towards the problems facing the boy in view of his changing needs, the judge responded favourably. He asked the boy what amount he thought sufficient for his maintenance. SR120 monthly in addition to SR100 every three months for his dress was estimated by the ward to meet his growing needs. As this estimate fell within the revenue of the boy's estate, it was accepted as fair by both the guardian and the judge and an order was made for it to be paid and the first instalment for the month of Rabi' al-Awwal was actually paid to the boy by his guardian in the presence of the judge in the court.

Due to the relative maturity and understanding shown by the boy, the judge altered the previous arrangement ordering the maintenance of the ward to be paid to him monthly instead of it being paid daily.

Also in the case of *A* v. *H*[33], the former, an under aged boy, had applied to the court to declare him *Rashid*, mature and to terminate the guardianship of his mother over him. His failure in the test of intelligence carried out by the judge caused his allegation of maturity to be dismissed. Turning to his maintenance and how it was to be spent the boy's uncle, who was consulted by the judge, stated that the boy was not *Rashid* and was unfit to adequately conduct his estate because, he added, the boy did not have sufficient discretion to deal with his estate. So alternatively he suggested as a sufficient maintenance for the boy, the amount of SR1 per day, to be given to the boy in addition to whatever amount he might obtain in return for his services.

Apparently the judge seeing as unsatisfactory the latter part of the uncle's suggestion, ordered the amount of SR30 to be paid to the boy monthly at the rate of SR1 per day.

Of course, the court does not always order the maintenance to be handed over to the child but may order it to be spent on behalf of the child by the guardian. This is illustrated in the case of *A* and *S*.[34]

F, who was the mother of the two and also the guardian designated by the court, appealed to the court to specify an adequate amount for the maintenance of her two children and for permission to spend it on them. To estimate the amount regarded as adequate for their maintenance two witnesses were called to testify to the court that the maintenance needed for food, drink, residence and all other requirements was SR300 per month for *A* and *S* together. Satisfied with such a proved estimation, the judge ordered the above amount to be spent on the two children by their guardian (mother).

When this decision was submitted, as required, for ratification to the Judicial Scrutiny Board of the western province of Saudi Arabia, ratification from the Board's judges was granted.[35]

The principle of holding a *Wasi* liable for the disadvantageous conduct due to unalterable circumstances may become inapplicable when the court deems an action, however disadvantageous it may appear to be, as ultimately beneficial to the bequest or the ward. This occurs whenever the question facing the *Wasi* becomes a choice between the lesser of two evils. Such a situation makes the choice of the lesser of the two evils by the *Wasi* beneficial and advantageous. This is demonstrated in the case of *S* v. *al-B*[36] in which the plaintiff's daughter, *H*, died due to burns. According to an inventory enclosed with the case, the mother claimed the estate of her dead daughter to amount to SR2,150. In his answer, the defendant, being the husband of the deceased, alleged that most of the claimed estate was burnt with the plaintiff's daughter. Eventually, an amicable agreement was reached between the defendant and the heirs; the plaintiff (the mother), the deceased's young half-brothers, whose father acted on their behalf, as he was their *Wali* or guardian, agreed with the deceased's husband who undertook to pay in settlement of the claim the amount of SR600 and the mother and the *Wali* of the children in their turn undertook to drop any other claim against the deceased's estate and to regard such settlement as final.

Also the case of *B (agent Sh)* v. *N*,[37] stands as an illustrative case to the above trend where the latter, who was the *Nazir* of the *Waqf*, was accused by the former, the agent of the beneficiaries of mismanagement and extortion. *Sh*, conducted the case until it came to the crucial stage of agreeing to a reconciliatory solution, then *B* took over and pleaded her own case (as original plaintiff) on behalf of herself, her children, to whom she was guardian and as agent to all the beneficiaries of the *Waqf*, took over the case in which the defendant, the accused *Nazir*, undertook to pay SR14,000 in return for *B*, the original plaintiff and agent dropping the charge against him. Here the guardian of the children, on behalf of her wards, is considered to have accepted the settlement with less than the original claim rather than to allow the case to drag on and on to an unpredictable end. This had the backing of the court as it was apparently beneficial to the children and the beneficiaries as a whole.

Due to the principle which states that 'the guardian (*Wali* or *Wasi*) is assumed trustworthy until the contrary is proved',[39] then the guardian loses all responsibility. The assumption of the guardian's trustworthiness comes into question when his ex-ward accuses him of having committed a direct offence against his estate or of an act which requires compensation such as negligence causing loss, favouritism or donation from the estate of his ex-ward, etc. An accepted justification accompanied by the guardian's oath are considered necessary to cause the dismissal of such accusations against him. In the case of accusation against the ex-guardian which involves a dispute concerning the period of maintenance and the amount paid, he will not be liable to support his defence on his oath provided what he had done does not contradict an established tradition.

But if he is accused of underselling the estate of his ward or that such a sale was contracted for no obvious benefit, then his claim that he acted on the basis of the benefit and interest of the ward is to be accepted provided he supports it on his oath. If the sold property is real estate, then one of two justifications supported by his oath is to be accepted in defence against the accusation. These are that it was considered advantageous to the ward or that it was done out of necessity.

Nevertheless, the Saudi legislature has taken a protective step to prevent such a dispute concerning the sale of the ward's real estate developing between the ex-guardian and his ex-ward by obliging the guardians to apply to the courts for permission if any of them wished to sell the real estate of his ward and to state the reasons for it supported by two witnesses. An extra precaution that is deemed necessary in this situation is that the court must after issuing permission for the requested sale refer the case to the Judiciary Board of Scrutiny for further reconsideration.[39]

This is illustrated in the case of *F* who as guardian over her boy, applied through her agent, *M*, to the court for permission to sell a share of the boy in a real estate as he needed the sum for his maintenance and education. Consequently, due to the stated need and the adequate proof presented in support of the claim, the Court issued the requested permission which enabled *F* to sell the shares proved to be owned by the boy in the mentioned real estate. The Court enjoined the guardian to pay the obtained price on the boy's necessary maintenance, education and on whatever was considered necessary for him.[40]

In another case following the death of a father leaving a girl, the named

Wasi (guardian) and the named supervisor of the *Wasi* sought confirmation of their appointment from the Court and this was later granted in accordance with the adequate proof the two presented. Consequently, the Court enjoined the *Wasi* (the mother of the girl) to consult the supervisor in all matters concerning her duty. In conformity to the Royal Prerogative and also to reinforce the duties of the two *Wasis*, the Court ordered them to refrain from selling any of the girl's real estate before they obtained a permission from the Court.[41]

To avoid dispute between the ex-ward and his ex-guardian in respect of the payment of the ward's estate to him after his coming of age, the Quran advises the guardian to bring witnesses at the time of delivery.[42] With reference to the credibility of the ex-guardian who did not take witnesses when he is faced with the claim of his ex-ward that his estate was still undelivered to him, contrary to the aforementioned, the jurists, here, distinguish between the guardian who receives remuneration and the one who does not. They accept the defence of the latter on oath as he was considered trustworthy, and do not accept the defence of the former.[43] This is based on the analogy comparing the ex-guardian without remuneration to the depository in claiming to have returned the deposited object. Similarly the case of the ex-guardian who receives remuneration for his service is analogically compared to the person who borrows an object and later claims to have returned it. This is so because the ex-guardian as well as the borrower holds the orphan's estate and the borrowed object for his own benefit.

REMUNERATION OF *WASIS*

It is very unusual, though not entirely improbable, for a *Wasi* to be remunerated for his *Wisaya*. People have for so long undertaken the duties of *Wisaya* not only because they were appreciative and pleased that their services were badly needed, but also it was coupled with their desire to obtain religious rewards by dedicating their work to the glory of God.

However, on rare occasions, the testator himself sets apart a sum of money, a fixed share of the estate or an annual percentage which does not necessarily match the services rendered by the *Wasi*, as remuneration. This sort of action is exemplified in the case of *M* v. *Mu*[44] in which their father, *A*, bequested a number of houses and some productive lands as a *Waqf* to his relatives and the poor and the humble people. To remunerate the *Nazir* for his services he set aside one tenth of the entire produce after paying for mending, repairing and other necessary services.

Also in another case the testatrix bequeathed a fixed sum for the executor in return for his efforts in performing her bequest.[45]

Also there is a case where the testator stated that he agreed with the executor not to take or ask for remuneration in return for the execution of his bequest.[46]

On some other occasions, (the rarest of all) the *Wasi* (or the *Nazir*) may put his need for remuneration before the judge on whose discretion the decision to grant or refuse the request depends. The judge, therefore, may limit a sum paid to the *Wasi* or *Nazir* if he deems it to be beneficial, for instance, if the custom of the country's inhabitants requires it. An application of this rule is seen in the case of *S*, who as a *Nazir* to his grandfather's *Waqf*, felt a need for the work to be remunerated so he applied to the court for remuneration to be paid to him. As requested, two experts testified that *Nazarah* required the deduction of one twentieth from the income and the court ordered it to be paid to the *Nazir*.[47]

In another case the fixed remuneration of the income of the *Waqf* for the *Nazir*, *S*, was ordered by the Court to be one tenth when his claim for it was supported both by adequate proof and by the backing of the beneficiaries.[48]

In the case of services duly performed in cases of desperate necessity with the intention of claiming back or when something has been paid towards the safekeeping of the estate of the ward, the *Wasi* is entitled to reimbursement provided they are properly incurred expenses. Adherence to this by the Saudis is illustrated in the case of *F* v. *M*.[49]

When *F* claimed to have spent SR750 for the lodging and maintenance of her children with the expectation of reimbursement, the court ordered *M*, the *Wasi* of the minors, to settle that amount.

In reference to remuneration the Quran makes it permissible rather than a right to claim. The verse says: 'Whosoever (of the guardians) is rich, let him abstain generously (from taking of the estate of the orphans); and whosoever is poor let him take thereof in reason (for his guardianship).[50] The verse has restricted permission to the poor and has introduced, further, two other limitations; these are not to seek richness and not to extract more than his real need. Such restrictions are referred to from the word *Bil-ma'ruf* or benevolence, that is to say, to take as remuneration out of the minor's estate only what is reasonable.

The amount to be extracted from the ward's estate as remuneration by the poor *Wasi* is limited to the lowest amount between his need and the hire required for such a service since he takes it because of the two definitions; one for his services rendered and the other for his being in need. An order from the court is not necessary for this. But if the *Wasi* is rich he can only obtain remuneration when it has been ordered by the court.[51]

EXECUTOR DE SO TORT *(TUFAILY)*

Tufaily is in general a person who meddles in someone else's affairs without prior authorization. He is the one who, without being a *de jure Wasi*, deals with a dead person's property or children. The conduct of such a person, if seen to be beneficial to the property or the children, will be validated. In this case if someone pays out of his own pocket to protect or secure their properties or pays for the children's maintenance, he will be refunded. Also this is true in the absence of a *Wasi* or prior to the appointment of a *Wasi*; i.e. someone is allowed to sell perishable and trivial objects or borrows on their behalf if their maintenance is at stake.[52] This principle is illustrated in the case of *F* v. *M*.[53]

In consequence of the *Wasi*'s (the defendant) failure to provide the necessary maintenance of her children, *F* took the responsibility herself with the expectation of reimbursement. The defendant was enjoined by the court to refund it to the plaintiff.

But at no time will the *Tufaily* be allowed to sell the child's real estate or what is considered vital for him without authorization from the court. The unauthorized action of the *Tufaily* is penalized by the invalidation of the contract or by obliging him to pay compensation for the damage incurred or for the reduced value of the sold object or penalized for both, as he is described as having no rights but as being liable to penalty.[54] This principle is seen in operation in the case of *S* v. *F*.[55]

The defendant, who was the children's uncle, sold on credit some of the children's sheep before a guardian was installed. Since such sale incurred loss to the children and was conducted without authorization, the court held *F* (the seller) responsible for the return of the objects sold. To facilitate his task, the court called on the buyers to help in their return. The obligatory order on the *Tufaily* to return the sold sheep is an indication of his liability whereby the inability of the buyer to return the sheep since he had slaughtered them or the refusal of the buyer to return them on the grounds of increased prices in the meantime, will have to be settled and born solely by the defendant *F*.

Also in the case of someone being in the wilderness with a dying person or coming across a dead man, he may wrap the dead man's body in a modest cloth and claim reimbursement afterwards. He is allowed to sell perishable property and transfer the rest where there is a *Hakim* or judge. The *Tufaily*, in such a situation, escapes liability only by fully preserving without encroachment, the dead man's property.

NOTES

1. Makkah Grand Court, Case No. 181, Vol. 6, date 4/6/1378H.
2. Makkah Grand Court, Case No. 1375, Vol. 8. Pt. Minute of Shaikh Abdulmalik b. Duhaish, date 1391 H.
3. *Kashshaf al-Qina, Vol. 3, 330, Sharh Muntaha al-Iradat, Vol. 3, 264-265.*
4. Case N. H.C. Mecca Fatami Vol. XV (1380AH/1960AD) p. 55 from M.I.A. Ali, Ph.D. thesis *Social Responsibilities*, 120-121, London University, 1971AD.
5. *Sharh Muntaha al-Iradat*, Vol. 3, 266.
6. *Sharh Muntaha al-Iradat*, Vol. 2, 296.
7. Case No. 108, Vol. II, (1388H/1968AD), p.90, from M.I.A. Ali, Ph.D. thesis *Social Responsibilities*, 99-100, London University, 1971AD.
8. Jedda Grand Court, Case No. 33, Vol. 2, date 12/2/1390H.
9. Makkah Grand Court, Case No. 19, Vol. 30. Special R. of Shaikh Sulaiman al-Amr, date 7/10/1391H.
10. *Kashshaf al-Qina*, Vol. 4, 394, and *Tanqih*, 200.
11. Makkah Grand Court, Case No. 26, Vol. 1, date 22/1/1380H.
12. Makkah Grand Court, Case No. 1375, Vol. 8. Private minutes of Shaikh Abdulmalik b. Duhaish, date 1391H.
13. Makkah Grand Court, Case No. 184, Vol. 1, date 6/5/1376H.
14. Makkah Grand Court, No. 173, Vol. 1, (1379H).
15. Makkah Grand Court, Case No. 74, Vol. 1, date 23/3/1379H.
16. Makkah Grand Court, Case No. 34, Vol. 1, date 6/2/1380H.
17. Makkah Grand Court, Case No. 108, Vol. 1, (1381H).
18. Makkah Grand Court, Case No. 142, Vol. 1, date 8/5/1381H.
19. Makkah Grand Court, No. 905-3423, Vol. 1, p. 29, (1377H/1957AD). Sp. Reg. of Shaikh Ibrahim Fatani. See M.I.A. Ali's Ph.D. thesis, 139-140, London University, 1971.
20. Case H.C. Makkah P.R. Fatami Vol. XVI (1379AH/1959AD) p. 143, from M.I.A. Ali, Ph.D. thesis *Social Responsibilities*, 175, London University, 1971AD.
21. Jedda Grand Court. Case No. 866, Vol. 7, (1389H).
22. Reported by Al-Tirmithi. See *Al-Mu'jam al-Mufahras*, Vol. 3, 293. This was also reported in *Sharh Muntaha al-Iradat* to be the saying of Umar (the Khalifa); see Vol. 2, 292.
23. *Sharh Muntaha al-Iradat*, Vol. 2, 292.
24. Jedda Katib al-'adl, Case No. 68, Vol. 1, date 1378H.
25. Jedda Katib al-'adl, Case No. 708, Vol. 2, date 1379H.
26. Makkah Grand Court, Case No. 1375, Vol. 8. Private Minutes of Shaikh Abdulmalik b. Duhaish, date 1391H.
27. Makkah Grand Court, Case No. 27, Vol. 1, date 16/2/1379H.
28. Makkah Grand Court, Case No. 209, Vol. 1, date 15/6/1376H.
29. *Kashshaf al-Qina*, Vol. 4, 346, Vol. 3, 451.
30. Makkah Case No. 63, the court of second instance. Date 18/1/1391H.
31. *Sharh Muntaha al-Iradat*, Vol. 2, 506.
32. Makkah Grand Court, No. 106, Vol. 1, (1376H).
33. Makkah Grand Court, Case No. 26, Vol. 3, date 22/1/1380H.
34. Makkah Grand Court, No. 129, Vol. 15. Sp. Reg. of Shaikh Sulaiman al-Amr, (1391H).
35. Judicial Scrutiny Board, No. 2278 (1391H). Western Province.
36. Makkah Grand Court, Case No. 78, Vol. 1, date 23/3/1377H.
37. Makkah Grand Court, Case No. 32, Vol. 1, date 11/2/1381H.
38. *Sharh Muntaha al-Iradat*, Vol. 2, 296, *Al-Tanqih*, 153.
39. This is a resolution widely circulated by the Judiciary Dept. to the courts No. 2414/2/M, date 14/10/1386H.
40. Makkah Grand Court, Case No. 134, Vol. 1, date 23/3/1376H.
41. Jedda Grand Court, No. 866, Vol. 7, (1389H).
42. *Qur'an*, Al-Nisa (The Women), 6.
43. *Sharh Muntaha al-Iradat*, Vol. 2, 296, *Kashshaf al-Qina*, Vol. 3, 456, *Al-Tanqih*, 153.
44. Makkah Grand Court, Case No. 118, Vol. 1, date 14/3/1380H.
45. Jedda Grand Court, Case No. 211, Joint Reg., (1344-1345H), p. 153.
46. Jedda Katib al-'adl, Case No. 194, Vol. 1, date 1386H.
47. Makkah Grand Court, Case No. 45, Vol. 1, date 22/2/1380H.
48. Makkah Grand Court, Case No. 52, Vol. 1, date 25/2/1381H.
49. Makkah Grand Court, Case No. 57, Vol. 1, date 23/2/1377H.
50. *Qur'an*, IV, 6.
51. *Kashshaf al-Qina*, Vol. 3, 455, *Sharh Muntaha al-Iradat*, Vol. 2, 295.
52. Ahmad b. Mohammad Al-Manqur, *Al-fawakih al-adidah*, Vol. 2, 24.
53. Makkah Grand Court, Case No. 57, Vol. 1, date 23/2/1377H.
54. *Kashshaf al-Qina*, Vol. 4, 397-398.
55. Makkah Grand Court, Case No. 31, Vol. 15. Special Registry of Shaikh Sulaiman al-Amr, date 8/2/1391H.

Part III

SOME ACTIONS WHICH IN CIRCUMSTANCES ARE LINKED TO THE LAW OF BEQUEST

CHAPTER I
INTRODUCTION

An inter vivos gift made to another person, if met by acceptance and delivery, becomes effective immediately without restrictions. The donation made while dying is another type of gift. It is the gift made during the donor's illness. For this purpose the type of illness must be a serious one where death becomes a possible outcome of that particular illness.

The main condition in this repect is that an illness must constitute a menace and apprehension of death, be considered dangerous or be likely to cause death or death must be considered to be a direct result of it. Virtually, an illness proven as such has the effect of turning the donation made during death sickness into a degree between a gift inter vivos, (a gift made during health), and a testamentary gift. This position makes it more convenient for us to treat it separately.

Donation during death sickness is likely to incur a disastrous loss to the legatees. That is of course, since donation in death sickness has a priority over legacies and in terms of time is bound to be settled first. This is a move which will ultimately and effectively decrease the disposable third forcing a proportionate abatement of bequests if there is a number involved. Such precedence over a bequest owes much to the eligibility of the bequest to operate in a time stipulated in the future because the testator does not give up his rights until after his death when such rights have substantially ceased. While the gift, on the contrary has an immediate effect though its execution is deferred.

In order for it to avoid the application of the ultra vires doctrine for being excessive to the disposable one-third, the donation in death sickness whatever it is, (whether *Mahabat* or connivance, in sale, acknowledgement of debt to another, releasing a debt owed to him by others or merely a personal gift), has to gain, partially or fully the approval of the legal heirs if it is to become operative at all. This is based on the Prophet's (peace be upon him) rule in the case of the dying person who freed his only estate of six slaves. After his death the Prophet cast lots between them, freeing two of them and retaining the other four to the possession of the heirs as they represented two thirds of the estate of the dying person.

A dying person or, more precise terms, a person on his death bed (which matches the Arabic technical term *Al-marid marad al-mawut al-makhuf*), is a person who is suffering from a fatal physical disease, even without pain, such as haemorrhage where danger lies in the result of the continuation of haemorrhage. It can also be a person whose sole danger consists of him being subjected to live under the threat of death.

GIFT IN DEATH SICKNESS

A gift of any estate made during the donor's illness will not, under Islamic law, be treated as a gift made in health, whether the gift is in the form of a donation, an acknowledgement of debt or a connivance (in the character of selling an article for less than the real value or buying it with more than its normal market value). The reason for this is the fear that should the dying person be left to his own desires he might leave a token portion to his legal heirs or might even leave none at all.

The donation in death sickness is not under Islamic law the same as donatio mortis causa of English law. Though they both deal with the same object and serve the same objective besides the fact that the transaction according to both laws takes place during what each law considers to amount to terminal illness.

However, a fundamental difference between the two laws concerning donation in death sickness is the possible redemption of the donation in English Law if the donor recovers from his illness since it is made conditional on death.[1] But under Islamic Law, the donation is ultimately operative. Thus it will never be redeemed in the way it would under English Law since Islamic Law does not recognize any condition whatsoever as accompanying the donation.[2]

POINTS OF RESEMBLANCE TO GIFT INTER VIVOS AND BEQUEST LAWS

Donation in death sickness will not be featured as a bequest. Notwithstanding, a lot of the bequest's limitations are applied to it for in so many ways that it resembles the gift inter vivos. The resemblance with the gift inter vivos denotes how far apart donation in death sickness is from the testamentary gift. Below we set out evidence of resemblance which supports what we have said earlier; that is, compromise between the two laws. Here are the rules that it takes from the law of gift inter vivos.

Various gifts though made during a death sickness, unlike a bequest, will be effective according to the different times of their acceptance and the donation would not be subjected to redemption after delivery unless of course, as a measure protecting the rights of the heirs, when the donation in death sickness exceeds the disposable one third. Also acceptance of the gift has to follow immediately on the act of offer. It is noteworthy that the position is not the same as it is for the bequest where acceptance cannot in any way take place prior to the testator's death.

The other rules which the donation in death sickness take from the law of bequest consist mainly of limitations as follows.

The amount of the donation made during death sickness has to be within the one third limit. Anything in excess of the disposable third is subjected to the approval or disapproval of the parpositus' heirs. Also, just as in the case of a bequest, the gift will not be operative to an heir, who has a positive and fixed share in inheritance unless his co-heirs consent to it.

Donation in death sickness also resembles a bequest in the case where a number of donations are involved and there is simultaneous acceptance by a number of donees or by an agent on behalf of them all by verbal acceptance or receipt or otherwise. All these gifts are to be considered without priority in the disposable one third. As to the process of proportionate abatement of the accumulated gifts, if the third falls short of meeting all gifts, this can occur only after the death of the donor and not before.[3]

WHAT ILLNESS IS REGARDED TERMINAL?

Marad al-mawut or death sickness, generally speaking is an illness which brings with it a reasonable degree of certainty of death. Of course, from the definition of the jurists, one realizes that in order for an illness to be defined as terminal, it does not necessarily mean that death is an inevitable consequence. But there has in the meantime to be reasonable grounds for suspicion that death could follow as a result. This has to be the case because the jurists have described it as merely a dangerous illness. That is to say that *Al-marid marad al-mawut al-makhuf* is the ill person whose sickness is feared to lead to his eventual death.

The fact that Muslim jurists have concentrated much of their efforts on defining and examining the types of diseases to establish what may or may not lead to death would not meet with justification of any suggestion that they are to be blamed for ignoring or shifting the emphasis from the mental to purely physical state of the ill person. An evident confirmation of this attitude is the association of the ever present fear of a terminal illness or an ill person when referred to by the jurists. Such association is a convincing sign to substantiate to a certain extent the jurists' acknowledgement of the significance attached to the mental state which is accepted side by side with the physical state of the ill person. The whole concept centres around the word *Makhuf*, anticipated or serious.

Finally, to further reinforce what we have said above, we refer to some cases which the jurists considered to amount to death sickness. This is where the state of mental fear is deemed to be the determinate factor in a death sickness, with the exclusion of the physical factor, which may lead to eventual death. For instance, in the case of a healthy person who sails into unpredictable, stormy seas, the mental fear of extinction which must have arisen caused the jurists to consider him throughout the duration of the storm as a person in death sickness.

Our conjecture is that the juristic definition of the state of the dying person may have been a composite of the two distinct categories of dying person. They might have taken the word (*Marid*), diseased, to symbolize the physical state of illness; while the word (*Makhuf*), the fear for his life, to symbolize the mental side (such as a person going to war, sailing on high and vicious seas or awaiting execution) where a person would be living under a constant threat of death and thus in fear for his life.

This is in line with the attitude of the jurists who always seek to contain the whole idea they search for in as few words as possible.

Contemplation about a person contracting a fatal disease is meaningless unless death actually occurs. It will not be of much concern if heirs do not object to the dying transactions and the donees do not dispute illness or fatality. For if they do, all the ill person's previous conduct will be subjected to a retrospective review back to the point of time at which terminal illness is deemed to have started and from then on is reckoned to have steadily worsened.

The case of *al-Kh*[4] illustrates the relevant point in its practical sense.

In this case the heirs objected to the selling of part of the deceased's house to his wife. They claimed him to have been sick at the time and not to have known what he was doing. In the light of this claim, a lengthy investigation into the deceased's state of health was conducted by the Court. The investigation went back to the point of time before the disputed transaction was known to have taken place. The aim of this was to establish whether or not the alleged transaction was contracted in health or in sickness.

When the result of the investigation carried out by the court was found to confirm the deceased's sickness prior to the time of the alleged contract, the Court issued its verdict annulling the contract as an unfounded one, not only because it amounted to a fraudulant act since nothing was paid in return but because the alleged seller was certified incapable of alienation and was considered to be a dying person as he was suffering from what the Court termed to be death sickness.

Marad al-mawut al-makhuf is divided into two distinct groups, physical and anticipated.

The physical illness, which is regarded as fatal and might thus be the responsible cause of death, is in turn sub-divided into fatal diseases and non-fatal diseases:

The fatal diseases are the kinds of diseases which, once contracted, cause rapid fatality to the sick person because they are highly dangerous in themselves. Such diseases are defined as leprosy, plague, pleurisy, heart conditions, colitis, gall bladder and bile diseases, emphysema, other lung conditions and brain disease. The inclusion of the latter two illnesses may indicate the similarity of old medicine to the so called cancerous illnesses of our time.

Cholera is considered a fatal disese by the Saudis.[5] In 1971AD they sealed off the town of Al-Qatif, thus preventing any one entering or leaving it. This was an emergency measure because there was some suspicion of an outbreak of that disease. Such measures resemble what would have been done were an outbreak of plague ever to happen. They thereby stated in practical terms their adherence to the jurists prophylaxis.

However, the policy of preventative medicine in Saudi Arabia does not seem to approve of sealing off disease stricken areas but instead of implementing a different method of control. This is done by establishing medical points on the roads leading to the stricken areas, by insisting on inoculation of everyone going into or out of such an area and to trying at the same time, to fight the disease from within the area.[6]

Although the declared policy of preventative medicine seems to contradict what the government practiced in Al-Qatif, pragmatically the two policies might be considered to have been reasonable alternatives.

The measure of complete sealing off is applicable to villages or small remote towns which through their geographical position can strategically be sealed off. The other measure of conducting preventative medicine is applicable to big and vital cities or where the disease appears to be containable.

As cancer is considered a terminal disease which does not necessarily affect mental faculty in spite of its seriousness, a Saudi testator had to present medical evidence from his doctor stating his mental state and that he was capable of making a bequest before it could be accepted and registered.[7] Such procedure, in accordance with regulations, obliges *Katib al-'Adl* to ratify the contracts and the *Wasiya* of any ill person only when he is convinced personally, from the medical evidence or otherwise, of the ability of the ill person to do so.[8]

In the non-fatal diseases, the factors which influence the decision as to whether or not a disease is truly terminal, are continuous or recurring as follow.

Consumption or tuberculosis will not be considered a terminal illness at its diagnosis but only its continuation will cause it to come into that category during the final stages. Continuation is also a vital factor in leprosy as also in haemorrhage whether through the nose or otherwise, as in a wounded person. Senility had also been included by the jurists in the relevant illness simply because of its continuing character where there is no hope of recovery. When the patient becomes confined to his bed, it is also seen as a condition applicable to all cases above.

However, the only disease whereby continuation plays a contrary role is paralysis. The response of the jurists is that the paralysed person is regarded to be suffering from a death sickness at the onset of the illness. However, the constant state of such an illness avoids the ill person from being classified as a dying person.

Dysentry accompanied by blood or dysentry with inflamation, which requires an ill person frequently to visit the toilet and spend much time in it, is regarded to be a death sickness. But if neither blood nor frequency accompany dysentry, then it will not be considered as a death illness. *Humma al-rab'a* (Malaria), is a severe kind of fever which can be cyclical in that it comes one day, remits for two days and then comes back for another day and so on. This is considered a death sickness only when the contracted became a bed-ridden person;[9] continual fever is considered a terminal or death illness.

The diagnosis of dysentry and fever was held by the Saudi Court to be responsible for the death of *al-Kh*, which caused him to be bed-ridden and unable to talk for a few days before his death. This nullified his alleged selling of part of his house to his wife.[10]

For almost all the above diseases, apart from the plague, the Hanbali jurists presented rather easy criteria applicable to everyone's case, in that a person wil be regarded to have contracted *Marad al-mawut*, or death sickness whenever an ill person is confined to his sick bed. Thus all donations made by him in such a state are affected.

However, minor ailments which last for a day or so, such as a headache, simple types of fever, a little nose bleeding, opthalmia toothache, scabies and so on are ones which do not endanger the patient. A gift during such ailments is treated as an inter vivos gift even though, Al-Hijjawi stated, the ailment might develop and become more serious and actually cause death as a result. For this reason the jurists take into consideration only the origin of the ailment.[11]

ANTICIPATED ILLNESS

The word illness which is used in the former cases to denote the physical illness could only be mis-used here. Instead the word *Makhuf* (fearful or serious anticipation of death), which was mentioned as part of the definition is better used here to symbolize the second part of this topic.

Fear is the cardinal factor in this point. It could be provoked by subjecting an individual to terrifying and fatal situations whereby death becomes so close and near as to become an eventuality.

However, situations which provoke great fear thus effecting the disposing power of an individual are as follows: an engagement in an act of war where the strength of the opposing parties is equally matched, or where the person in question is with the losing side so that the chances of his death are relatively high. The same regard is given to a person fighting for his survival, including the one who has already received a mortal wound or a person sailing in hazardous conditions at sea.

Prisoners of war, whose fate has been engulfed by uncertainty, are treated as dying persons. In this case the jurists have restricted the rule of *ultra vires* imposed on a dying person to be applicable only to a person in captivity whose captors are known to kill their captive. This is also true in the case of a criminal who is awaiting his execution.

In addition to the above cases the jurists have rendered the case of a person still healthy at the outbreak of an epidemic disease, such as plague in his town as in danger; thus *ultra vires* doctrine will be applied in due course. Restriction of the donational power of a person who has not yet contracted a terminal disease has been justified as being a precautionary measure. Such a measure was necessary because no one can guarantee against the possibility of a person in a position of danger being infected by that disease.

The jurists also cited the case of a pregnant woman during labour, if it is accompanied by pain, as coming under the *ultra vires* doctrine though the state of the pregnant woman is usually safe.[12]

From the latter case we may draw an important conclusion in that the mere contemplation of apprehension of or the anxiety about death shown by the person concerned (who is subjected to a dangerous state) is not in itself the deciding factor. It is rather the objectivity of such a state being probable reason which may lead to the sufferer's death

THE WAY DISPUTE BETWEEN HEIRS AND DONEES IS SOLVED

In the case of controversy between heirs and donees concerning the illness itself, if it is such a simple one that the *ultra vires* doctrine is inapplicable then the donees claim to the donation is upheld; if it is fatal, then the *ultra vires* doctrine becomes applicable. Solution of this conflict will necessitate going all the way back to the onset of the alleged *Marad makhuf* or terminal illness to establish whether or not execution of the relevant donation by the deceased was made in the course of such an alleged illness or not. Such a step is vital to the decision as to whether or not to apply the *ultra vires* doctrine.

But when, on the other hand, no settlement can be found between heirs and donees, then, in the view of the latter jurists, the whole matter will be referred solely to two trustworthy doctors.[13] This stand has been evoked by the latter jurists to compare the two doctors' decision to the decision of the two other arbitrary experts. Nevertheless, the late Chief Justice of Saudi Arabia over-ruled this view and inclined to the earlier and more lenient view of Ibn Qudama and his nephew, who stated that it was sufficient for one doctor to decide.[14] Thus the Chief Justice, in a case brought before him, accepted the diagnosis of one doctor concerning the possibility of a convicted criminal as being able to bear the decided punishment or not. However, the Chief Justice insisted on a condition that the doctor to be consulted must be competent and trustworthy if his decision was to be accepted.[15] According to a third Hanabali jurist the matter should be adjudged from common experience to decide whether an illness is deemed to be counted as *Marad makhuf* or not.[16]

We sum up by giving a full account of the official stand of the Hanbali school of law on the *Marad al-mawut al-makhuf*, anticipated or feared death sickness. It comes in the form of rather practical criteria that make it easy to establish the causation of death. The death sickness, according to the official view, is always linked to whatever is seen as the immediate and responsible cause of death. It is apparent therefore that mere apprehension becomes a non-effectual factor in substantiating a death sickness except in the non-physical state of a dying person which will not alone, without a realistic assessment of the causation, alter a person's donational power.

Dismissal of such a notion has been explained in the words of the author of *Al-ikhtiyarat*, which has been held to represent the official doctrine, viz. 'The meaning of the fear of death is not what is normally meant by the apprehension of death. Nor does it mean that survival and death are equally probable, because our companions (jurists) took the contractions of labour as among the possibilities of a fatal illness. Although death of a woman is not frequently a result of labour and deaths are not more frequent than safe confinements. The purpose is to establish that death sickness is a responsible cause of death which must be attached to the illness and death must occur from that illness.'[17]

The motive behind the above criteria was apparently to help control the irrational, emotional and psychological fear suffered by the dying person and his family which was likely to excite an unfounded fear of death.

DISPUTE CONCERNING ILLNESS AND THE TIME OF DONATION

A conflict concerning the degree of illness during which the gift was executed may arise. The focal point is the donee's claim that the gift to him was executed during the donor's health contrasted with the heirs' counter claim that he was then a dying person. The subject of the conflict is whether the gift is to be withdrawn from the disposable third or from the net sum of the whole estate as has previously been explained.

The jurists' approach to this issue shows an almost solid stand behind the heirs' claim. Following the agreement of many old jurists the Commentary of the *Muntaha, Al-Iqna'* and *Al-Kashshaf,* in one of its two versions, all sided with the heirs in their denial of the allegation of the donee.[18]

A stand, as such, might have been brought about by the heirs nearness to the deceased or by the presumption that the heirs are in a position to know exactly when the illness started and how it developed. It might also be that their stand forms a part of an all out attempt to avoid and encounter possible fraudulent allegations, harmful to the heirs, and thus infringe the law as a whole. Therefore we cannot accept unfounded allegations unless supported by evidence.

The only reported exception to the above approach is the response given by al-Harithi who supported his claim by saying that, 'By nature man is supposed to be a healthy creature so the burden of proof will fall on the heirs to substantiate otherwise.' Also the author of the *Kashshaf*, having explored thoroughly al-Harithi's claim in another of his two versions, seemed convinced by the al-Harithi's reasoning when he finally commented on it, saying 'So far as we are concerned the view of al-Harithi is more suitable for our case.'[19]

On another point, the unanimity of the jurists' views could be seen by their support of the donee's claim so long as the time at which the gift was concluded, e.g. the first day of the month, is undisputed. This leaves only the dispute as to whether at that particular date the donor was ill or not. An illustration of this is when the donee says that the donor was healthy when he gave the gift but meanwhile the heirs say that he was then unhealthy.[20]

Unanimity regarding the above was reached by envoking the jurisprudential maxim, 'Non-existence of illness is by virtue of nature' or in another way 'By virtue of his origin, a man is supposed to remain healthy not to fall ill.'[21]

THE CONFLICT OF HEIRS AND DONEES ABOUT THE TYPE OF ILLNESS

The type of illness may provoke a controversy dividing heirs and donees into two conflicting groups. Each disputes the others right to the subject matter donated. Once this happens research into the reason for the conflict will find it presumably lies in the inability of either side of produce supporting proof to their claim. To offer an acceptable solution to both sides the law has to refer to a previous jurisprudential maxim of *Istishab al-hal* which speaks of referring matters to their state of origin and laying emphasis on the continuation of health; thus the case would remain the same as it was before. For although numerous ailments occur to an individual, recovery is almost guaranteed. However, it is noticeable enough that recovery from many of the so-called fatal illnesses, although rare, has never been impossible.

Accordingly, the jurists treat the healthy state and simple ailments as of nature and the state of fatality as the exception. Consequently the logic of the juristic maxim constitutes a heavy blow to the heirs' allegation while giving strong backing to a donee's claim that the donor was not seriously ill when he executed his donation.

PRIORITY TO THE APPORTIONMENT OF THE DEAD PERSON'S ESTATE

Mature voluntary donation is to be duly handed over to its beneficiary and has priority over bequest once they are both amassed and awaiting the distribution of the deceased's estate. The law permits rivalry of execution even within the voluntary donations themselves. Precedence of donations over each other will be abided by unless antecedence cannot be established.

Priority will also be maintained on the basis of the first one first even to the avoidance of the latter ones when unsanctioned donations in death sickness are confined to the disposable third. But when an untraceable antecedent between the donations in death sickness awaits execution, simultaneously wil be assumed to avoid uncertain preference to some of them. Subsequently, depreciation in assets due to the proportional reduction might be the result of the third being insufficient to meet all donations of death sickness. This will ensure a fair distribution.

THE DONEE BEING AN HEIR

The time to determine whether a donee is an heir to the donor or not is the time of the donor's death. This is a comparison to the case of the legatee and not the time of acceptance.[22] This is due to the time of death being, in fact, the time when the donation made in death sickness becomes operative.

Any change in the donees heriditable position is liable to bring the right to the donation to follow suit. Accordingly, if an heir near to the dying person were to be born inevitably excluding the donee from his share, then the donation to him will be effective. While, if alternatively, the nearer heir were to die clearing the way for the donee to succeed to inheritance, then such a privilege will cost him his right to the donation.

TRANSACTIONS IN SICKNESS ARE TO HAVE EQUIVALENT TREATMENT AS THAT OF A GIFT

Interdiction is inapplicable to restrict the financial conduct of a dying person but the party to any transaction made during the duration of sickness must bear in mind that in the event of death the transaction contracted might be considered partially or fully invalid. This would be brought about by the application of the *ultra vires* principle. Such contracts and the range of the above principles are explained in the following.

THE DISCHARGE OF DEBTS

A debt which is owed by someone is not, generally speaking, considered as estate in the law in the sense that the conditions applied to a gift cannot be applied here too.[23] Thus it must not be made the subject of a gift before being repaid. Nevertheless, as Islam in general encourages people to do good by all means, the law has no choice but to yield to the pressure exerted by such principles by showing signs of tolerance which have eased the way for creditors to release debtors from their debts. However, if release from the debt happens to have been made while the creditor was dying, then such an act will have to comply with the rules laid down concerning donation in death sickness.

Release from a debt is also acceptable when it comes in the form of *Iqrar* or acknowledgement. An *Iqrar* as such, when made during death sickness, may or may not refer to a time in the past. If it does and the time indicated is obviously before the onset of the death sickness, then the *Iqrar* will be upheld as a completed gift inter vivos. But when no time is mentioned in the past the *Iqrar* will then be liable to the application of the *ultra vires* doctrine as a donation in death sickness.

The same conclusion, as in the above, will be evoked if the dying person makes an *Iqrar* containing an acknowledgement that the debtor has reimbursed him from the loan or that he and his partner or agent had amicably settled any outstanding business.

THE ACKNOWLEDGEMENT OF DEBTS

The fact that the law has no power to enforce the dischargeability of an unproved debt is a major reason for the validating of a bequest. Testamentary law is thus designed to give a chance to a person, in whatever situation he is, to tell of anything he has or owes to others which he could not otherwise settle. It is also a major force behind the unquestionable acceptance of an *Iqrar* made by a dying person; be it an alm-tax, a loan, a deposit, an object borrowed, mortgage or any other commitment involving liabilities which the responsible party should have settled and has not yet done so.

Another reason for accepting the *Iqrar* of a dying person is that the time of death is considered to be an ideal moment to manipulate matters fully. This would put the dying person in the fear of God and make his conscience lean towards piety over evil thoughts and also make him desirous of ridding himself of his bad reputation. The acknowledgement is, therefore, a duty needing discharge. The law, accordingly, will not interfere, despite the amount involved. As an acknowledgement of this sort is a right and not a privilege, it will enjoy precedence over gifts and bequests. But should it be made in health then it is to be satisfied against the bulk of the estate left by the praepositus.

An acknowledgement of a debt or estate to an heir by the dying person such as the sort of *Iqrar* which the testators in Saudi Arabia habitually make to their wives is an exception to this rule. An illustration of this is as follows:

At the end of his bequest the sick person made an *Iqrar* to his wife that all his house was owned by her and no one else could possess any of it.[24]

Also in another case, after a testator had appointed his wife to carry out his bequest, he acknowledged a debt to her amounting to SR10,000 and added that she too owned the contents of their house.[25]

To encounter unjustifiable acknowledgements to the testators' heirs, a late Saudi Chief Justice instructed the court of Mecca in the case of *'A*[26] not to sustain such acknowledgements unless they were supported by sufficient proof of genuineness.

The Chief Justice's instructions were effective in shaping subsequent decisions issued by the courts. The efficacy of the Chief Justice's instructions were particularly effective in the case of *S* and *M v. Y's* estate.

Before his death *Y* acknowledged a debt to his wife, *S*, amounting to SR3,000 and to his other wife *M* SR2,000. After the death of *Y*, both wives applied to the court for an order discharging the debts owed to them. As they were both regarded legal heirs, confirmation to their claims was requested since the principles of law accept only a genuine and certified claim of debt. When adequate proof was presented, both were requested to swear that they had not received it or any part of it before the Court ordered the debts to be discharged from the deceased's estate.[27]

The jurists are also in agreement to accept as valid a donation which is made after an acknowledgement of debt though the debt is great and the estate is little or if the donor was insolvent simply because it is dischargeable after the settlement of the debt. Also there is still the possibility that the debt might be fully or partially remitted to render the relevent donation executable.

THE ACT OF CONNIVANCE OR *MUHABAT*

A Muslim is, in general, expected to act in a righteous and responsible manner. He is, therefore, supposed to leave whatever estate he has, with the exception of the disposable one third, to his heirs, to help alleviate their poverty. Accordingly, any act which gives rise to suspicion that a bequest is harmful to the heirs' interests in general is regarded an irresponsible act and thus will be met by the law's contingency plan called the *ultra vires* doctrine. Within this sphere comes any transaction which is falsely designed to benefit a non-heir by causing him to pay less or to receive more than that he should normally get at the market price, is an act of irresponsibility called *Muhabat* or connivance. Restrictions of the *ultra vires* doctrine are designed to protect and to consolidate the sacred unity of the family against elements of envy and rivalry which might lead to the disintegration of the family unity.

Nevertheless, when the one involved in connivance is not an heir, such connivance will then be upheld, be it in health or in death sickness. However, in both cases whether the beneficiary from *Muhabat* is an heir or non-heir, *Muhabat*, though it may exceed the entire estate, remains valid and operative so long as it gains the approval of the praepositus' heirs.

The types of *Muhabat* are numerous but below we shall demonstrate certain aspects of connivance to explain what it means.

a. The act of giving away an item for less or more than its real value. For instance, if a car worth £300 were sold by a dying person for only £100 or, alternatively, if a car worth only £100 is bought by the dying person for £300, the difference between the two prices in the above two instances is so high that the motive is obvious; the deceased in his death sickness had attempted to give the buyer in the first instance and the seller in the second, by way of gratuitous gift, something of value for nothing in return.

The gross difference between the agreed prices and the real market value which is deemed to be made in favour of an heir renders the deal inoperative except in as much as the price paid for the object or the received price may allow. This of course leaves two thirds of the value of the above car to revert back to the deceased's heirs. If, on the other hand, the subject of *Muhabat* should be to a non-heir the deal is valid pending the full approval of the heirs or the *Muhabat* coming out of the disposable one third.

If the transaction involving a non-heir consists of the whole estate held by the dying person, if for example, the car in the above example were the only estate the dying person owned, the buyer will then be entitled to two thirds of such a transaction (one third in exchange for the price and the other third being the equivalent of the disposable third) while the legal heirs will get only one third of the transaction.[28] This is of course in addition to the price already paid in transaction. The price paid with the remaining one third of the transaction will actually form two thirds which the heirs are entitled to under inheritance law.

b. Where *Muhabat* or connivance contained in a transaction is designed to operate by the manipulation of a *Hilah* or strategem, which is forbidden in Islam, the transaction will then be null and void. Transactions of this sort are demonstrated by the act of *Shuf'a* (pre-emption). Here is a dying person, having one of his heirs a partner in an undivided property and whom he wishes to benefit by going round the law knowing that he cannot vest any benefit to him otherwise, sells his common share to a non-heir for less what it is really worth.

If it is proved that the transaction had been designed as a cover in order to pass the unlawful profit to one of his heirs and if the heir has afterwards shown disapproval of this by exercising his right of *Shuf'a*, the sale will then be nullified.

Alternatively, if there has been no unlawful, hidden motive to profit his heir, the transaction will remain valid even if, afterwards, the heir should take over the transaction by implementing the law of *Shuf'a*.

c. The dying person hiring his animals or tools for less than the usual hire fee is considered *Muhabat* or connivance. Accordingly, the difference in the amount should be taken out of the disposable one third.

However, the dying person's action of hiring himself to do a job for an heir is not in the eye of law an act of *Muhabat* on the grounds that such an act does not involve or tie any of the dying person's estate thereby constituting a loss to the heirs' rights.

d. The fourth type of *Mahabat* consists of three other instances. The first is related to the efficacy of the period of time in contracting a sale. This exemplified by the act of sale where a waiting period in an option sale of, say, a month was stipulated to give both parties a chance to rethink. According to such a stipulation each of the two parties to the sale should have the same right to rescind the deal whenever they like, provided that the rescindment is made before the expiry of the agreed period.

If the party who granted the favourable sale becomes a dying person within the duration of the stipulated period and then dies leaving the optional sale unrescinded, the rate of *Muhabat* in such a sale will become operative only if it comes out of the third set apart to settle legacies, or was consented to by the heirs.

Sharh muntaha al-iradat, for instance, had upheld the above rule. It has also presented a supporting reason for it, viz. 'The leaving unrescinded of a favourable sale by a dying person will be interpreted as if he had, thereby, chosen to give the excessive portion in the sale to the other party. The amount involved will thus be compared to an act of gift during death sickness.'[29] This is then subjected to the *ultra vires* doctrine.

The second instance refers to the position of a delivered gift. A gift could become a redeemable gift if the donor gives permission for delivery of the object to an heir after he has become a dying person. It also becomes, partially, a redeemable gift when it is made to a non-heir and the heirs withold their consent to the excessive part beyond the disposable third. This was the result of regarding it an undesirable act of *Muhabat* because a gift without delivery, which needs delivery, is not a mature gift yet and thus remains redeemable until permission is given by the donor.

The third instance illustrates how a bequest can be the subject of *Muhabat*. It happens where a heriditable estate has been credited with an excessive legacy to someone and therefore required ratification by the heir who has been classified as being in a death illness.

If ratifications of the excessive part ot a non-heir was obtained from the heir during his death sickness, it will be reckoned as an act of *Muhabat* and will thus be counted against the third of the estate of the dying heir. This is so because he is considered to have forfeited his own heirs' pecuniary rights which he could have maintained by withholding his approval.[30]

NOTES

1. Anthony R. Mellows, *The Law of Succession*, 476.
2. *Sharh Muntaha al-Iradat*, Vol. 2, 549.
3. *Kashshaf al-Qina*, Vol. 4, 328, *Sharh Muntaha al-Iradat*, Vol. 2, 532.
4. Makkah Grand Court, Case No. 125, Vol. 1, 1377H.
5. Articles 5/13/14 Section 3, Regulations of Communical diseases No. 260 Royal Decree, (dated 28/12/1379H).
6. Declaration No. 207, (dated 19/2/1393H). A circulation from the Director of Health Affairs in Taif.
7. Jedda Katib al-'adl, Case No. 1408, Vol. 4, (date 1380H).
8. Article 197, p. 24. Summary of the responsibilities of the Judiciary. Ratified by the Royal Decree No. 109, (date 24/1/1372H). 3rd Edition Government.
9. *Kashshaf al-Qina*, Vol. 4, 324.
10. Makkah Grand Court, Case No. 125, Voi. 1, 1377H.
11. *Kashshaf al-Qina*, Vol. 4, 323, *Sharh Muntaha al-Iradat*, Vol. 2, 529
12. *Sharh Muntaha al-Iradat*, Vol. 2, 530.
13. *Kashshaf al-Qina*, Vol. 4, 323.
14. *Mugh, Vol. 6, 507, and Al-Sharh al-Kabir*, Vol. 6, 290.
15. Case No. 2251/26/74 Qunfudha authority, (date 1374H).
16. *Insaf*, Vol. 7, 166.
17. *Kashshaf*, Vol. 4, 323.
18. *Sharh Muntaha al-Iradat*, Vol. 2, 537, *Kashshaf al-Qina*, Vol. 4, 326.
19. *Kashshaf al-Qina*, Vol. 4, 326.
20. *Sharh Muntaha al-Iradat*, Vol. 2, 537, and *Kashshaf*, Vol. 4, 326.
21. *Kashshaf*, Vol. 4, 326.
22. *Sharh Muntaha al-Iradat*, Vol. 2, 542-543.
23. *Kashshaf al-qina*, Vol. 2, 486, Vol. 4, 304,*Sharh Muntaha al-Iradat*, Vol. 2, 528.
24. Jedda Katib al-'adl, Case No. 1345-1347, Vol. 4, (date 1379H).
25. Jedda Katib al-'adl, Case No. 493, Vol. 2, (date 1385H).
26. Makkah Grand Court, Case No. 181, Vol. 6, (date 1378H).
27. Makkah Grand Court, Case No. 20, Vol. 1, (date 9/1/1376H).
28. *Kashshaf al-Qina*, Vol. 4, 332.
29. *Sharh Muntaha al-iradat*, Vol. 2, 542.
30. *Sharh Muntaha al-iradat*, Vol. 2, 542.

CHAPTER II

THE LAW OF WAQF OR CHARITABLE TRUST

Waqf was first introduced in Islamic Law by two Prophecies; one is the *Hadith* of Uthman,[1] where the Prophet (peace be upon him) said: 'He who shall buy the well of *Rumah* shall dangle his bucket with any Muslim's bucket and shall go to heaven.' Nevertheless, the second is the most important of the two as it is known to have set up the basic rules of *Waqf* being the *Hadith* of Ibn Umar[2] which states that Umar acquired a property in Khaibar and came to the Prophet seeking his advice as to what to do with it and the Prophet replied, 'If you wish to make this a charity in perpetuity, the ownership cannot be sold, donated or inherited' and that Umar made it a charity to the poor, his relatives, for freeing slaves, to the glory of God, for wayfarers and guests. He stated in a provision that it was no felony for the one in charge to eat in reason or feed a friend in reason, i.e. it was not to be used for gain.

Ever since, Muslims have tended to employ this principle of making *Waqf* for charitable puproses in their widest sense. In practice, for instance, the inhabitants of Arabia have devoted *Waqfs* for public utilities ranging from the idea of providing food and water during the month of Ramadan for the poor and travellers and whoever wishes to break his fast in Mosques,[3] for repairing Mosques with help offered to those who lead prayers and teach children and for digging wells with all that is involved in making water available. This principle was used in providing meat for the poor, neighbours and relatives during the great feast of *Al-Adha* by dedicating the produce of an estate to buy *Adhyya* (sheep, goat, cow or camel to sacrifice to the glory of God). Offering sacrifice was considered a praiseworthy thing to do as it adhered to the example set by the Prophet who in *Eid al-Adha* (the feast of *Al-Adha*), after the *Eid* prayer was reported to have offered two sheep to God, one on behalf of himself and his family and the other on behalf of all his followers.[4]

The making of *Waqf* is identical to the bequest in many respects as it goes without saying that a great part of what is called *Waqf* comes, in fact, as a bequest and therefore is generally subjected to its rules and regulations. Accordingly it is considered wise to avoid repetition by stating below only a summary of the essential conditions and then the special regulations indicating whatever differences exist between the law of *Waqf* and the law of bequest.

The validity of a *Waqf* depends on the existence of four essential conditions[5] as follows: Firstly, that the subject matter of *Waqf* must be a specific corpus which could be utilized indefinitely such as books, lands, houses, animals, etc., by renting, cultivating or otherwise, without the corpus itself being exhausted, provided that it was eligible for sale at the time of making the *Waqf*. A share in an undivided property may also become the subject matter of *Waqf* as seen in the precedent of Umar's question to the Prophet in which he asked what to do.[6] 'My one hundred shares in Khaibar are the best ones I ever acquired and I wish to make a charity of them.' The Prophet told him to suspend its ownership (make it inalienable) and devote its produce to a charitable purpose.

Second, that the beneficiary of a *Waqf* must be either a specific person with an absolute right to possess or an institution.

Thirdly, that the *Waqf* must be for benevolent purposes.

Fourthly, that the *Waqf* becomes binding and implementable the moment it has been made. Therefore the *Waqf* becomes invalid if it contains a provision to delay the *Waqf's* commencement, or to limit its duration for any given time, or if it was made before the completion of a sale. However, the only exception permitted to accompany the form of *Waqf* is the provision which suspends its efficacy until the death of the dedicator. Such a vital link between *Waqf* and bequest is derived from the *Waqf* of Umar who said, 'This is what Abdullah (I, the slave of God), Umar, the Commander of the Faithful, declare if death occurs to me, Thamgh will become a charity . . .'

As regards the ability of a person to make a *Waqf*, a fifth condition was added to those above. This was that the dedicator must be of full capacity to manage his own affairs, i.e. of full age and a mature person.[7]

Although, generally speaking, the *Waqf* is like bequest in many respects and the *Waqf* itself could sometimes be considered partly a bequest, the aforementioned essential conditions reflect certain differences in character between the two, part of which is briefly stated in the following:

The condition which stipulated the coming of age and maturity of the *Waqif* (dedicator) resulted in the invalidity of a *Waqf* made by a child or a prodigal. However, one should consider this concept in the light of the other condition which regards *Waqf* as binding and implementable immediately after it has been made. The reason for the invalidity is because the child or prodigal may be harmed financially as a result of the immediate transference of ownership of their estate and the fact that neither of them was allowed to deal freely with their estate. Accordingly, one could conclude that no harm would come to either of the two if either were to bequeath the *Waqf* of his estate since the transference and implementation of his bequest comes only after his death.

The law of bequest permits the usufruct or income of a corpus to become the subject matter of bequest. Nevertheless, the law of *Waqf* stipulates that the subject matter eligible for *Waqf* must be a specific corpus, which nullifies the making of the benefit or the income of a corpus the sole subject matter of *Waqf*. This has been inferred by the *Hadith* which states that the corpus itself together with the rendered benefit is to be disposed of through the suspension of its ownership (to the glory of God) on the named beneficiary or institution.

The horse, though, deemed unworthy to own property, has nevertheless enjoyed an exceptional status under the law of bequest. This status was lost under the law of *Waqf*. The perpetuity of *Waqf* could have been responsible somehow for this change as the transferred ownership must be attached to a person or an institution worthy to possess. A horse, being an animal, has none of these qualifications to make it possible to validate *Waqf* to it.

Non-existence of a beneficiary was particularly mentioned as a cause to nullify bequest. Accordingly, the validity of a bequest to an expected child is to be suspended pending its delivery within the minimum period of gestation from the time the bequest was made so long as the expectant mother was known to be co-habitating with her husband. But if the availability of the expectant mother to a husband is ruled out, then the waiting period will be extended to the maximum period of gestation. Due to this, a bequest becomes invalid if made only to a potential child as no pregnancy was assumed when the bequest was made. This can be considered the same as if a person bequeaths to whoever might be born to so and so. However, the law of *Waqf* does not differentiate between expected and non-expected children. The *Waqf*, which is made specifically to an individual child, whether existent in the womb or not, is not valid, since such a child is not eligible to possess except from inheritance and bequest.[8] But at the same time it allowed both to benefit from *Waqf* provided they are related to a named beneficiary or a class of beneficiaries. Demonstration of this is that of a person who makes a *Waqf* to *X* and *X*'s children and their children generation after generation, however distant in blood relationship. Thus whenever a child is born to *X* it will become a sharer with the already existing beneficiaries whether the new child to be born to *X* is born immediately after the making of the *Waqf* or to be born to his children's children a hundred years later, see p. 56 infra.

The *Waqf* is the only part of law to recognise any proximity to God as an ultimate aim of the dedicator as it was made a condition upon which the validity of such an act must depend. In this the *Waqf* differs from *Wasiya* where proximity was not recognised as a condition by most jurists due to its ability to repay a favour or to be made to a friend without need. Accordingly, a *Waqf* for the rich (in general), the lighting or guarding or providing incense or curtains to a tomb is invalid as no benefication nor proximity to God is anticipated from such *Waqfs*. It is forbidden to build a Mosque on the site of burial or to turn a house which contains a grave into a Mosque for the Prophet in a *Hadith* stated that God has cursed those who build Mosques on graves or illuminate them (the graves).[9] This makes a dedication with such an aim null and void.

The *Waqf* to non-Muslim individuals is validated since they are eligible to benefit due to their assumed need, as the Prophet was reported to have said, 'Every soul is worthy of receiving alms.' Also there is the precedent of Safiya, the Prophet's wife, who was reported to have made a *Waqf* to her Jewish relative. Nevertheless, this type of benefit nullifies the *Waqf* if made for an apostate or for a *Harbi*, the belligerent in an enemy country.

One may also think that the nullification of the *Waqf* for the above apostate and the *Harbi* could be affected, too, by the application of the condition which makes *Waqf* effective and implementable the moment it was made and also because it runs indefinitely since neither of the two is to be left to enjoy the comfort of his estate. This is because both are supposed to be harassed and to lose their civil liberties, or even killed.

The acceptability of the provision suspending the implementation of *Waqf* upon the dedicator's death paved the way for the inclusion of such a *Waqf* under the bequest law. This, therefore, limits the regulations in that it becomes a *Wasiya* and therefore has to come out of the disposable third of the deceased's estate. Should the bequeathed *Waqf* then exceed the disposable one third, it has to win the approval of the heirs for that part,[10] i.e. it becomes partly operative pending such approval. An exception to this is that an heir could be made a beneficiary of a *Waqf* with his co-heirs having no right to disapprove of it, unlike that of a bequest, see p. 70 infra

One difference remaining between the *Waqf*, (the bequeathed *Waqf*) and the bequest itself is that, unlike the bequest which becomes operative only at the death of the testator, and is therefore subject to revocation, the bequeathed *Waqf* becomes operative also only at the death of the dedicator (testator). It becomes binding immediately and thus irrevocable after it was made thereby rendering ineffective the doctrine of revocation in respect of such a bequest.

As to the revenue between the time the *Waqf* was bequeathed and time the dedicator (testator) dies, it has been decided to let it go to the *Waqif* (the dedicator) or his heirs until the *Waqif*'s death. This is because it was considered the *Waqif*'s possession until his death since the implementation of it was postponed till the occurrence of that event.

As regards the form of *Waqf* it was stated that the *Waqf* could be made by word or by action. One of three terms, *Waqqaftu*, *Habbastu* or *Sabbaltu*, was stated to be used when one wishes to create a *Waqf*. It was also stated that one may also use as an alternative any other terms one wants provided such terms indicate the indefinite suspension of ownership of the corpus specified as *Waqf* with its produce only being vested in the named beneficiaries or the area of hardship.

Waqf can also be created by implication of an action such as building part of his house as a Mosque and opening its doors, calling for prayers or even hanging a board or a piece of paper on its door on which the *Waqif* states his permission for its use for prayers. Implication of a *Waqf* is indicated too when one builds lavatories and leaves their doors open or digs a well and leaves one section of it open to the public. Such actions are interpreted as indicating, by implication, the permission for general use by the public for an indefinite period.

NOTES

1. Reported by Al-Bukhari and Muslim. See *Al-Mu'jam al-Mufahras*, Vol. 3, 121.
2. Reported by Al-Bukhari and Muslim. See *Al-Mu'jam al-Mufahras*, Vol. 6, 312.
3. Ahmad b. Mohammad Al-Manqur, *Al-fawakih al-adidah*, Vol. 2, 22.
4. Reported by Al-Bukhari and Muslim. See *Al-Mu'jam al-Mufahras*, Vol. 3, 487. Also reported by Ibn Hanbal, Abu Dawood and Al-Tirmithi. See *Al-Mu'jam al-Mufahras*, Vol. 3, 488.
5. *Sharh Muntaha al-iradat, Vol. 2, 491.*
6. Reported by Al-Bukhari and Muslim and Al-Nasa'i, see *Al-Mu'jam al-Mufahras*, Vol. 3, 279, and Vol. 7,186, which mentioned that Ibn Majah has also reported it.
7. *Kashshaf al-Qina*, Vol. 2, 251.
8. *Sharh Muntaha al-Iradat*, Vol. 2, 495-496, *Kashshaf al-Qina*, Vol. 4, 249, *Al-Tanqih*, 186.
9. Reported by Al-Bukhari and Muslim. See *Al-Mu'jam al-Mufahras*, Vol. 1, 28.
10. *Sharh Mantaha al-Iradat*, Vol. 2, 541, *Kashshaf al-Qina*, Vol. 4, 340.

Part IV

RULES OF CALCULATION

CHAPTER I
INTRODUCTION

This topic is considered to be one of the major achievements of Muslim scholars. It has been a lucky thing, for them and for us all, that the *Qur'an* drew their interests to the importance of figures and fractions by imposing fractions to be the bases of the distribution of property where each heir shall have his share accordingly. Since then the scholars have reintroduced the figures and fractions to solve the problems of inheritance and bequest.

Complicated problems which maintained a need for a hypothetical solution have directly or indirectly lead to the invention and the practical use of algebra for the first time ever, and have also led to the invention of cipher (zero).

In respect to this particular point Professor N.J. Coulson in his excellent book, *Succession in the Muslim Family*, said, 'The law of succession is a solid technical achievement, and Muslim scholarship takes a justifiable pride in the Mathematical precision with which the rights of various heirs, in any given situation, can be calculated.'[1]

However, since solution of inheritance problems depends on figures, the jurists' objective was to achieve an answer with as few figures as possible. Thus they have introduced and developed a number of rules which they have set up as a basic pattern to follow in the solution of all problems of inheritance.

Below we present the four primary rules of calculation in detail with full illustration for each rule. Two more illustrations are made to exemplify these rules when they come together in one case.

THE FOUR PRIMARY RULES OF CALCULATIONS FOR MAKING A WHOLE NUMBER AS AN ANSWER TO THE PROBLEM (*MASALA*) OUT OF THE QUR'ANIC FRACTIONS

Making a whole number out of the fixed fraction shares each beneficiary is entitled to under Islamic law of inheritance is a very vital step towards achieving a solution to the problems of inheritance.

The fractional portions mentioned in the *Qur'an*, the so-called 'Qur'anic portions', are ½, ¼, ⅛, ⅔, ⅓, ⅙. The role of the fractions' denominator is the most vital thing for making a whole number from the problem (*Masala*). If only one fraction existed the denominator of it will be made the whole number of the *Masala*. If only one group of *Asabat* (agnates) sharers existed their per capita number will be made the whole number, the male equalling twice that of a female. But if the *Masala* contains two or more of the above fractional portions then one has to apply the following four rules:

1. First of the primary rules. The *Mutamathil*, (identical).

When the denominators of the fractions are equal one of the *Mutamathil* will be applied. In such a case one of the identical denominators is to be taken to form the whole number of the Masala and thus to become the basis of distribution, such as, from ⅙ and ⅙ we take 6, from ⅓ or ⅔ we take 3, and from ½ and ½ we take 2, etc.

Illustration: if a woman dies leaving a husband and a sister, the husband's share of her total estate then is ½ and the sister's ½. The denominator of the two fractions is *Mutamathil* (identical). So, according to the above rule, it is sufficient to set one of the two denominators as the whole number of the *Masala* thus giving the two heirs one share each, see fig. 1.

2 is the whole number.
2 ÷ 2 = 1 for the husband.
2 ÷ 2 = 1 for the sister.

2		
1	**H**	**½**
1	**Sis**	**½**

Fig. 1

This rule, (the *Mutamathil*), is also applied where the heirs inherit per capita shares, as if they are all members of one group which inherits the whole property equally between them as in the case of four sons only surviving their father.

The *Masala* is made 4. One share for each son as follows:

4 ÷ 4 = 1 share for each of the four sons. See fig. 2.

4	
1	S
1	S 4
1	S
1	S

Fig. 2

If the heirs are a son and a daughter then the *Masala* is made 3, (since the male inherits twice the female).

3 ÷ 3 = 1 for the daughter.
2 x 1 = 2 or 3 − 1 = 2 for the son.
See fig. 3.

3	
2	S
1	D

Fig. 3

2. Second rule. The *Mutadakhil*, (Concordent).

The fractions become *Mutadakhil* when the denominator of one fraction becomes part of the other and the smallest is capable of dividing the biggest leaving no fraction, that is to say, 2 and 4, or 2 and 8. Also, 3 and 6, or 2 and 6. In all the latter denominators the biggest is thus to be taken as the whole number of the *Masala*.

Illustration: when a wife dies, the husband takes ¼ the daughter takes ½, and the full brother takes the residue as the only *Asaba*.

Denominators of the fractions 2 and 4 are *Mutadakhil* because one of them forms part of the other. 4, as it is the biggest denominator, will thus be taken as the whole number of the *Masala*.

4 ÷ 4 = 1 for the husband.
4 ÷ 2 = 2 for the daughter.
1 + 2 = 3 the aggregate share of the husband and daughter.
4 − 3 = 1 for the full brother (the residue). See Fig. 4.

4		
1	**H**	**¼**
2	**D**	**½**
1	**FB**	**Res.**

Fig. 4

Another illustration: M when a person dies a mother receives ⅙, two daughters receive ⅔ together and the residue for the father. 3 and 6 are *Mutadakhil*, where 6 is divisible by 3 without fraction. Thus, according the present rule 6 is divisible by 3 without fraction. Thus, according to the present rule 6 will be taken as the whole number of the *Masala*, to be distributed between heirs as follows:

6 is the whole number.
6 ÷ 6 = 1 for the mother.
6 ÷ 3 = 2 equalling ⅓ for one daughter.
6 ÷ 3 = 2 equalling ⅓ for the other daughter.
1 + 2 + 2 = 5 the aggregate share of the heirs who have fixed shares.
6 − 5 = 1 for the father, (the residue).
See Fig. 5.

	6		
	1	**M**	**⅙**
4	**2**	**D**	**⅔**
	2	**D**	
	1	**F**	**Res.**

Fig. 5

3. Third Rule. The *Mutawafiq* (Compatible).

The fractions become *Mutawafiq* when two or more denominators can neither be described as *Mutamathil*, or identical, nor *Mutadakhil*, or concordent, but can be identified by having a common factor with the ability of dividing them all leaving no fractions. The dividing number is called the common factor, while the quotient of the division operation is called, *Wifq* or factor. For instance, 4 and 6 are *Mutawafiq*, their common factor is 2. The *Wifq* (factor), of the 4 is, 4 ÷ 2 = 2 and the *Wifq* of 6 is 6 ÷ 2 = 3.

Also the two numbers 6 and 8 are *Mutawafiq*. The common factor which divides them all is 2. The *Wifq* (factor), of the 6 is 6 ÷ 2 = 3.
And the *Wifq* of 8 is 8 ÷ 2 = 4.

When both figures 4 and 6 or 6 and 8 occur in one *Masala*, the *Wifq* (factor), of one of the two figures is to multiply the entire of the other, i.e. (2 x 6 or 4 x 3 = 12). So, the 12 will thus be the *Masala* whole number where 4 and 6 come together (3 x 8 = 24 or 6 x 4 = 24). So, 24 will be the *Masala* whole number when the figures 6 and 8 come together.

Illustration: the heirs are a wife, a uterine brother and a full brother.
As the wife's portion is ¼ the uterine brother's portion
brother's portion the residue (because he is an *Asabat* or agnate), thus according to the above rule the *Masala* whole number will be calculated as such:

2 x 6 = 12. The *Masala* whole number. See Fig. 6.
¼ equals 12 ÷ 4 = 3 for the wife.
⅙ equals 12 ÷ 6 = 2 for the Uterine brother.
3 +2 = 5 the aggregate share of those with fixed shares.
12 − 5 = 7 the residue for the agnate, full brother.

12		
3	**W**	**¼**
2	**UB**	**⅙**
7	**FB**	**Res.**

Fig. 6

The same *Masala* can also be worked out as follows:
the fractions have been reduced to a common denominator 2 x 6 = 12.

W. ¼	3⁄12
UB. ⅙	2⁄12
FB. Residue	7⁄12
	1

6 is multiplied by the *Wifq* or factor of 4. 6 x 2 = 12.
¼ of 12 = 3 for the wife.
⅙ of 12 = 2 for the Uterine brother.
The residue of 12 = 12 − (2 + 3) = 7 for the full brother.
But this method will not and cannot be applied in the long run as will be seen later.
Another illustration:

If a person dies leaving his wife, his mother and his son, then the wife will receive ⅛, the mother ⅙ and the son takes the residue.

Applying the above rule one finds the denominators of the two fractions in the *Masala*, 6 and 8 are *Mutawafiq*. To get the *Masala* whole number 8 will thus have to be multiplied by the *Wifq* of 6. (3 x 8 = 24).
⅛ equals 24 ÷ 8 = 3 for the wife.
⅙ equals 24 ÷ 6 = 4 for the mother.
3 + 4 = 7 the aggregate share of the heirs with fixed share.
24 − 7 = 17 the residue for the son. See fig. 7.

24		
3	W	⅛
4	M	⅙
17	S	Res.

Fig. 7

4. Fourth rule. The *Mutabayyn* or incompatible.

The fractions become *Mutabayyn* when their denominators have no common factor between them. This occurs where (2 and 3), (3 and 4) /or (3 and 8), come together in one *Masala*. As none of these denominators (2 and 3 or 3 and 4 or (3 and 8) are identical or concordent nor have a common factor), the whole number of the *Masala* will be worked out by multiplying the two numbers by each other to make the product divisible on all shares involved in the *Masala* as such:
3 x 2 = 6, or
3 x 4 = 12, or
3 x 8 = 24.

Illustration:

A person dies leaving only a full sister, two uterine brothers and an uncle.

Here the share of the full sister is ½ the two uterine brothers' share is ⅓. The residue for the uncle. The denominator of ½ and the denominator of ⅓ are *Mutabayyn*, have no common factor. To calculate the whole number of the *Masala* out of these two denominators one has to multiply the two denominators by each other. 2 x 3 = 6.

½ of the whole number 6 ÷ 2 = 3 for the sister.
⅓ of the whole number 6 ÷ 3 = 2 for the UB's (one share each).
2 + 3 = 5 the aggregate share of those with fixed portions.
6 − 5 = 1 the residue for the Uncle. See Fig. 8.

6	
3	Sis ½
2	2 UBs ⅓
1	Uncle Res.

Fig. 8

Another Illustration:

If a husband dies leaving his wife, two full sisters and a consanguine brother. The Quranic portion of the two full sisters is ⅔. The wife's portion ¼. The residue is for the consanguine brother. The denominators (4 and 3) are *Mutabayyn*, so the *Masala* whole number is worked out by multiplying the two denominators by each other.

3 x 4 = 12.
¼ of the whole number = 12 ÷ 4 = 3 for the wife.
⅔ of the whole number = 12 ÷ 3 = 4 for each sister.
4 x 2 = 8 the collective share of the two sisters.
3 + 8 = 11 the aggregate share of fixed portions.
12 − 11 = 1 the residue for the CB. See Fig. 9.

12		
3	W	¼
8	2 Sis	⅔
1	CB	Res.

Fig. 9

A third illustration:

A person dies leaving his wife with ⅛, four daughters with ⅔ and a full brother with the residue.

Applying the rules of calculation one finds that the denominators (3 and 8) of the two fractions are *Mutabayyn* with no common factor, thus to get a whole number for the *Masala*, one has to multiply the two numbers by each other. 3 x 8 = 24.
⅛ of the whole number = 24 ÷ 8 = 3 for the wife.
⅔ of the whole number = 24 ÷ 3 = 8 one third of the total.
⅔ of the whole number = 8 x 2 = 16 the collective share of the four daughters.

16 ÷ 4 = 4 for each of the 4 daughters.
3 + 16 = 19 the aggregate of share of fixed portions.
24 − 19 = 5 the residue for the full brother. See Fig. 10.

24		
3	W	⅛
16	4D	⅔
5	FB	Res.

Fig. 10

Two test cases to apply the aforementioned four rules of calculation

The first case is the *Masala* of a wife with ¼, a full sister with ½, and a mother with ⅓ is solved as follows:

Applying the four rules of calculation we find that the *Masala* contains three different fractions with two fractions we can apply one rule and another rule to the third fraction. The denominators (2 and 4) are *Matadakhil* or Concordent, thus applying such a rule we keep the biggest of the two denominators 4. The biggest denominator, (4 and 3 which is the third denominator in the *Masala*) are *Mutabayyn* or incompatible. So, applying such a rule for working out the whole number of the *Masala* we multiply the two incompatible denominators by each other 4 x 3 = 12.
¼ of the whole number = 12 ÷ 4 = 3 for the wife.
½ of the whole number = 12 ÷ 2 = 6 for the full sister.
⅓ of the whole number = 12 ÷ 3 = 4 for the mother.
3 + 6 + 4 = 13.

The allocated portions of the heirs from the whole number have inceased where the whole number cannot bear them all, so applying the Doctrine of *'Awl* (increase which we are going to discuss later), we put aside the whole number and replace it with the aggregate shares the heirs have taken from the whole number, so the heirs' shares will be reduced proportionally to suit the new situation (the new whole number), thus to refer shares to the new whole number as such:

$1/4$ which equal to $3/12$ is reduced to $3/13$ for the wife.
$1/2$ which equal to $6/12$ is reduced to $6/13$ for the sister.
$1/3$ which equal to $4/12$ is reduced to $4/13$ for the mother. See Fig. 11.
$12/13$ $\qquad$ $13/13 = 1$

Fig. 11

13	**12**		
3	**3**	**W**	**$1/4$**
6	**6**	**F Sis**	**$1/2$**
4	**4**	**M**	**$1/3$**

13 − 12 = 1 (deficit)

The second case is the *Masala* of a wife with $1/8$, a daughter with $1/2$, a son's daughter with $1/6$, (to form $2/3$ with the portion of the daughter), and a father with the residue is calculated as follows:

Applying the forementioned four rules of calculation to the portions of the *Masala*, we find the denominator 2 to be *Mutadakhil* with the other two denominators (6 and 8), in such a way that it forms part of both, thus according to such a rule 2 is to be ignored in favour of the other two (6 and 8).

By considering the other two denominators (6 and 8) we find them neither *Mutamathil* nor *Mutadakhil* but we find that they are *Mutawafiq* or compatible, in that they both have a common factor where both are divisible by 2, as the common factor, $6 \div 2 = 3$. The quotient 3, is called the *Wifq* or factor of 6. As the rule speaks of multiplying the *Wifq* or factor of one of the two denominators by the other to get the whole number for the *Masala*, then the whole number is thus:

3 x 8 = 24.
⅛ of the whole number = 24 ÷ 8 = 3 for the wife.
½ of the whole number = 24 ÷ 2 = 12 for the daughter.
⅙ of the whole number = 24 ÷ 6 = 4 for the son's daughter.
3 + 12 + 4 = 19 the aggregate share of the fixed portions.
The residue of the whole number = 24 − 19 = 5 for the father. See Fig. 12.

24		
3	W	⅛
12	D	½
4	Son's D	⅙
5	F	Res.

Fig. 12

THE DOCTRINE OF 'AWL (INCREASE)

The doctrine of *'Awl* or increase is, as defined by the jurists, 'An increase of the fractions and a decrease in the shares', that is to say, an increase in the number of allocated basic portions over the whole number of the *Masala* which eventually leads to a decrease in the value of each portion's share in the *Masala*.

This doctrine is a means of ensuring that an heir who is not exclusively excluded from inheritance should be given his or her respective share from the property left by the deceased even though the whole number of the *Masala* may not seem to be able to cover all the allocated portions.

A precedent case of this occurred at the time of 'Umar (the second *Khalifah*), calling on the learned among the companions of the Prophet (peace be upon him) to discuss the unprecedented problem, they adopted a scheme suggested by Al-Abbas b. Abdulmuttalib. According to such a scheme, which has unanimously been accepted by all jurists apart from Ibn Abbas, all portions involved in a problem of inheritance will be adjusted so as to formulate a whole number out of the existing portions, capable of containing and satisfying all the allocated portions. The whole number which for differentiation is called *'Awl* or increase, is not obtained by the process of multiplication but rather by aggregating all the shares withdrawn from the whole number of the *Masala* and committing such aggregate to replace the whole number thus making the shares of all heirs, as a final step, to be withdrawn from *'Awl* and also all shares to be referred to the *'Awl* and not to the whole number. To explain this doctrine here is an example:

A married woman dies leaving her husband who receives ½ as a Quranic heir and a full sister who also takes another ½ as a Quranic heir. If, besides these two Quranic heirs a half sister, who is also a Quranic heir with ⅙, also survives the deceased then according to the doctrine of *'Awl*, the half sister will be eligible to compete with her ⅙ against the two halves of the husband and the full sister as follows:

Applying the rules of calculation the whole numnber of the *Masalu* is 6. The division of the whole number according to the basic portions of the heirs is calculated as such:

½ of the whole number = 6 ÷ 2 = 3 for the husband.
½ of the whole number = 6 ÷ 2 = 3 for the full sister.
⅙ of the whole number = 6 ÷ 6 = 1 for the half sister.
The aggregate of shares withdrawn from the whole number of the *Masala* is 3 + 3 + 1 = 7.

Fig. 13

Awl	**W N**	
7	6	
3	**3**	**H ½**
3	**3**	**F Sis ½**
1	**1**	**C Sis ⅙**

7 − 6 = 1 (deficit)

One notices that the total of shares above exceeds the whole number of the *Masala*. This explains why the jurists say an increase of portions because the whole number has to be increased to match up the increase of shares. However, to offset the adversity of the *Masala* being unbalanced one is to replace the indivisible whole number by the aggregate of the shares withdrawn from the whole number, i.e. from 6 to 7. See Fig. 13.

Such increase in the whole number of the *Masala* leads inevitably to a change in the value of each of the basic portions as such:

The full sister who previously took a whole ½ which is equal to 3/6 from the whole number of the *Masala* should be reduced to take 3/7 from the *'Awl* or increase. The husband who took ½ equalling ¾ should take it reduced to 3/7. The ⅙ of the half sister should be reduced to 1/7. This is to explain what the jurists mean by saying, 'and a decrease in the value of shares' or '*Wa naqsun fi alansiba*'.

Another example:

A man dies leaving a wife, two full sisters and a grandmother. The basic portions of this *Masala* are the wife's ¼. The two full sisters' ⅔. The grandmother's ⅙.

Applying the primary rules of calculation a whole number for the *Masala* (a common denominator), form the basic fractions the whole number will be 3 x 4 = 12. Dividing such a whole number between the heirs according to their basic portions each one gets as follows:

¼ of the whole number = 12 ÷ 4 = 3 for the wife.
⅔ of the whole number = 12 ÷ 3 = 4 one third of the total.
⅔ of the whole number = 4 x 2 = 8 the collective share of the two sisters.
8 ÷ 2 = 4 for each sister.
⅙ of the whole number = 12 ÷ 6 = 2 for the grandmother.
3 + 8 + 2 = 13 the aggregate of the shares withdrawn from the whole number of the *Masala* 12.
13 − 12 = 1 the aggregate of the shares of the heirs exceeds the whole number of the *Masala* by one 1. See fig. 14.

Fig. 14

Awl	**W N**	
13	**12**	
3	**3**	**W ¼**
8	**8**	**2 FS ⅔**
2	**2**	**GM ⅙**

13 − 12 = 1 (deficit)

Therefore, to patch up such a difference the aggregate of shares 13 is to be used to replace the whole number of the *Masala* and thus be called *'Awl*. The ratio of each one's share is to be referred to the *'Awl* instead of being referred to the whole number. This is done by reducing the value of each share proportionally as follows:

W ¼ is reduced, to make the common fraction, to 3/12 and reduced again by *'Awl* to 3/13.

2 sisters ⅔	8/12	8/13.
GM ⅙	2/12	2/13.
	13/12	13/13 = 1

See Fig. 14 above.

THE DOCTRINE OF *RADD* OR RETURN

The doctrine of *Radd* or return is, the opposite of *'Awl*, a fewer basic portions followed by a surplus from the whole number.

As an *'Asaba* or agnate share is always the residue of the property after the Quranic heirs with fixed portions have taken their shares then it is essential for the *Radd* or return not to be considered wherever any of the *'Asaba* survives. This is based on a Hadith by the Prophet (peace be upon him), 'Give ____ heirs with fixed portions their shares and give whatever remains to the nearest male agnate (*Asaba*).' Thus it is essential for the doctrine of *Radd* to be applied that there must not be an *'Asaba* or agnatic relative existing. It is also essential for the doctrine or *Radd* to be applied to have a surplus from the whole number of the *Masala* after satisfying the shares of the surviving heirs.

The surplus as such has caused a controversy between jurists. Their controversy centres on whether the Public Treasury is considered an heir in the absence of all or some heirs who inherit as Quranic sharers or *Asaba,* thus to take over the left property or the surplus or not. The *Malikis* and the *Shafiis* have argued in favour of the Public Treasury because they said, 'one cannot be given more than his proper portion which was limited by the Quran'. But the late *Shafiis* have qualified their argument, that the Public Treasury must be 'properly administered for the benefit of Muslims'.

The *Hanafis* and *Hanbalis* have argued otherwise. They have based their argument on a verse of the Quran which says, 'And blood relatives are nearer one to another (than) from others'.[2] Also, their was, they said, no mention of the Treasury being an heir in the Quran. Thus the blood relatives are more deserving to succeed to the property of their relatives than the Treasury and muslims in general. Most of the latter *Shafiis* and some of the *Malikis* have inclined to prefer it to their former stand.

According to the *Hanafi* and *Hanbali* jurists the surplus which is the subject of *Radd* is to be redistributed on the pro rata basis of the shares of the surviving heirs. Thus with the exception of a husband or wife (who is not a blood relative to the deceased as well), the redistribution of the surplus by *Radd* is worked out as follows.

If the deceased was survived only by one relative then he or she will be entitled to an exclusive right to the entire property left by the deceased relative. But if two or more blood relatives survives, (without a husband or wife), then a whole number for the *Masala* with the use of the rules of calculation, should be worked out dividing it between them according to their basic portions and then adding the shares drawn from the whole number to each other. To reduce the unity to a figure equalling that of the shares withdrawn from the whole number one has to make use of the aggregate of shares to replace the whole number.

Illustration:

A person dies leaving only a grandmother and a uterine brother each of whom inherits ⅙ as a basic portion, the property of such a person is to be pro rata partitioned as follows:

The whole number of the *Masala* is 6

⅙ of the whole number = 6 ÷ 6 = 1 for the grandmother.

⅙ of the whole number = 6 ÷ 6 = 1 for the uterine brother.

1 + 1 = 2. The aggregate of the grandmother and the uterine brother's shares which they take from the whole number of the *Masala*.

The difference between the whole number and the aggregate, i.e. the surplus, is 6 − 2 = 4.

Fig. 15

Radd	W N	
2	6	
1	1	GM ⅙
1	1	UB ⅙

1 + 1 = 2 This aggregate becoming the Radd Masala.

To avert the surplus to augment the share of the surviving relatives one need not make another *Masala*. It is sufficient to use the aggregate share of the heirs they have withdrawn from the whole number which will thus be referred to as the *Radd*. See Fig. 15 above.

Another illustration:

If a person dies leaving a mother who inherits ⅙, a daughter with ½ and a son's daughter with ⅙. The doctrine of *Radd* will be applied to this *Masala* as such:

Applying the primary rule of calculation the whole number is 6.
⅙ of the whole number = 6 ÷ 6 = 1 for the mother.
½ of the whole number = 6 ÷ 2 = 3 for the daughter.
⅙ of the whole number = 6 ÷ 6 = 1 for the son's daughter.

Fig. 16

Radd	W N	
5	6	
1	1	M ⅙
3	3	D ½
1	1	SD ⅙

1 + 3 + 1 = 5 This aggregate becoming the *Radd Masala*.

Adding the shares from the whole number the aggregate is 1 + 3 + 1 = 5. The difference between the two figures i.e. (surplus), is 6 − 5 = 1.

To return the surplus 1 to the heirs according to the pro-rata of their shares they have withdrawn from the whole number, no other *Masala* is needed to be worked out but the jurists' method in such a case is to install the aggregate, (of shares the heirs have already withdrawn from the whole number) to replace the whole number and be called the *Radd*, which becomes the basis of the re-distribution.

Thus the mother instead of taking ⅙ of the property she will take ⅕ of it.The daughter instead of taking 3/6 of the property she will take 3/5 of it. The son's daughter instead of taking ⅙ of the property she will take ⅕ of it. See above Fig. 16.

Whenever one of the spouses exists besides the blood relatives one should consider making two or three *Masalas*, as needed. The whole number of the first *Masala*, (called the spouse *Masala*), is always the denominator of the fraction inherited by the existing spouse. Giving the spouse his/her share from the whole number leaving the remnant (including any surplus), for the blood relatives.

If there is only one blood relative he/she will exclusively take the remnant and there will therefore be no need to make a second *Masala*. But if there are two blood relatives or more then it is necessary to make another *Masala*, for them (called the relatives' *Masala*) and then a third one making a comprehensive *Masala*, which is a matter of necessity.

It is advisable that the three suggested *Masalas* be worked out in one table (three in one), if individually each relative succeeds to his/her *Quranic* portion. However, if a group of relatives succeed to inherit one *Quranic* share where the *Tashih* (redistribution), is needed then it is advisable to work out the three *Masalas* separately.

Illustration:

First a description of the table advisable to contain the three *Masalas* of *Radd* where the blood-relatives also survive with the spouse. We must draw a four sided table containing four columns inside it. From right to left, the first column will be occupied by the heirs' status and their basic portions. The second column is to be occupied by the shares of the heirs out of the whole number of the spouse *Masala*, leaving the top square for the whole number of it. The third column is to be occupied by the *Radd Masala* (the blood relatives' *Masala*), the top is to be left for its whole number.The fourth column is to be occupied by the aggregate of the relatives' shares from their *Masala* (the *Radd Masala*), leaving the top square for the aggregate of shares.The fifth column is to be occupied by the comprehensive *Masala*, the top square is left for its whole number. Horizontal lines equalling the number of heirs are to be drawn inside the table leaving each heir in a separate square, opposite each heir, his/her (on the far left in the comprehensive *Masala*), share out of the comprehensive *Masala*.

To work out the comprehensive *Masala* from the former two *Masalas* one has to make a comparison between the aggregate of the *Radd Masala* and the remnant (the collective share of the blood relatives from the spouse *Masala*). considering of course the application of the primary rules of calculation. If the comparison proves the two numbers to be *Mutamathil* (identical),then the whole number of the spouse *Masala* will be transferred to form the comprehensive *Masala*. Transferring, as well, the share of the spouse which he or she takes out of the whole number of the spouse *Masala* as it is, to the last column to form his or her share in the final distribution. Thus each of the relatives shares shall be given to him or her by dividing the remnant on the aggregate of the *Radd Masala*.

Illustration:

A man dies leaving his wife with ¼, the basic portion, his grandmother with ⅙ and two uterine brothers with ⅓, then the deceased's *Masala* is calculated as follows:

Applying the primary rules of calculation the whole number of the spouse *Masala* is 4.

¼ of the whole number = $4 \div 4 = 1$ for the wife.

$4 - 1 = 3$. The remnant is the collective share for the relatives.

Applying the primary rules of calculation the whole number of the relatives' *Masala* is 6

⅙ of the whole number = $6 \div 6 = 1$ for the grandmother.

⅓ of the whole number = $6 \div 3 = 2$ for the two uterine brothers.

$1 + 2 = 3$ the aggregate of the shares out of the relative whole number. The *Radd Masala* (the aggregate), is 3.

One of the aggregate for the grandmother. 2 of the aggregate for UBs. The comprehensive *Masala* is made by comparing the aggregate of the *Radd Masala* with the remnant (the collective share of the relatives out of the spouse *Masala*), which in this case proves to be *Mutamathil* (identical), meaning that the remnant from the spouse *Masala* is divisible by the *Radd Masala* without fraction that also means that the whole number of the spouse *Masala* is eligible to become the comprehensive Masala thus to be redistributed as follows:
See Fig.17.
$4 \div 4 = 1$ for the wife.
$4 - 1 = 3$ the collective share for the relatives from the comprehensive *Masala*.
$3 \div 3 = 1$ for the grandmother.
$3 - 1 = 2$ for the uterine brothers.
$2 \div 2 = 1$ for each of the two brothers.

Comp	Radd	WN	SM		
4	3	6	4		
1			1	W	¼
1	1	1		GM	⅙
1	1	1	3	UB	⅓
1	1	1		UB	

Fig. 17

Should the comparison between the aggregate of the *Radd Masala* with the remnant from the spouse *Masala* prove to be *Mutabayyn*, (incompatible), then the comprehensive *Masala* is to be the product of multiplying the *Radd Masala* with the whole number of the spouse *Masala*.

To divide the comprehensive *Masala* between all heirs one is firstly to multiply the wife's share out of the spouse whole number by the aggregate of the *Radd Masala*. Secondly as for the relatives' shares, they are worked out either by multiplying the remnant out of the spouse *Masala* by the aggregate of the *Radd Masala* then to divide the product of them according to their shares from the *Radd Masala*. Or to multiply the remnant by each one's share from the aggregate of the *Radd Masala*.
Illustration:

In a case where the deceased has been survived by his wife with ¼ as the basic portion, a grandmother with ⅙ and a uterine sister with ⅙. The Masala will be calculated as such:

Applying the primary rules of calculation the whole number of the spouse *Masala* is 4, (the denominator of the spouse's fraction).
¼ of the whole number = 4 ÷ 4 = 1 for the wife.
4 − 1 = 3. The remnant (including the surplus) for the relatives.
The whole number of the *Radd Masala* is 6.

⅙ of the whole number = 6 ÷ 6 = 1 for the grandmother.
⅙ of the whole number = 6 ÷ 6 = 1 for the uterine sister.
1 + 1 = 2 the aggregate of the *Radd Masala*.

Comparing the aggregate of the *Radd Masala* with the remnant out of the spouse *Masala* (2 and 3), are *Mutabayyn*. Thus the comprehensive *Masala* is to be the product of the whole number of the spouse *Masala* by the aggregate of the *Radd Masala*, (2 x 4 = 8).
Out of the comprehensive *Masala* the wife's share is 2 x 1 = 2.
Out of the comprehensive *Masala* the relatives' shares are 2 x 3 = 6.
The remnant of the aggregate of the *Radd Masala*.
6 ÷ 2 = 3 for the grandmother.
6 ÷ 2 = 3 for the uterine sister.

An alternative solution

The wife's share 2 x 1 = 2.
The relatives' shares are: The share of the grandmother is the product of multiplying the remnant by her share from the aggregate of the *Radd Masala* 1 x 3 = 3. The share of the uterine sister is the product of multiplying the remnant by her share from the aggregate of the *Radd Masala* 1 x 3 = 3.
2 + 3 + 3 = 8. See Fig.18.

Fig. 18

Comp	**Radd**	**WN**	**SM**	
8	**2**	**6**	**4**	
2			**1**	**W ¼**
3	**1**	**1**	**3**	**GM ⅙**
3	**1**	**1**		**U Sis ⅙**

1 + 1 = 2 Radd Masala

Another illustration:

A wife dies: a husband with his basic portion ½, a grandmother with ⅙ and a uterine brother with ⅙ is calculated as follows. The whole number of the spouse *Masala* is 2, the denominator of ½.

½ of the whole number = 2 ÷ 2 = 1 for the husband.
2 − 1 = 1 the remnant of the whole number for the relatives.
The whole number of the *Radd Masala* is 6.

⅙ of the whole number = 6 ÷ 6 = 1 for the grandmother.
⅙ of the whole number = 6 ÷ 6 = 1 for the uterine brother.
1 + 1 = 2 the aggregate of the shares of the relatives from the *Radd Masala*.

Comparing the remnant with the aggregate they are *Mutabayyn*. So, the comprehensive *Masala* is the product of multiplying the aggregate of the *Radd Masala* by the whole number of the spouse *Masala*, 2 x 2 = 4.

2 x 1 = 2 the husband's share from the comprehensive *Masala*.
1 x 1 = 1 the grandmother's share from the comprehensive *Masala*.
1 x 1 = 1 the uterine brother's share from the comprehensive *Masala*.
4 = the comprehensive *Masala*. See Fig.19.

Fig. 19

<table>
<tr><th>Comp</th><th>Radd</th><th>WN</th><th>SM</th><th></th><th></th></tr>
<tr><td>4</td><td>2</td><td>6</td><td>2</td><td></td><td></td></tr>
<tr><td>2</td><td></td><td></td><td>1</td><td>H</td><td>½</td></tr>
<tr><td>1</td><td>1</td><td>1</td><td rowspan="2">1</td><td>GM</td><td>⅙</td></tr>
<tr><td>1</td><td>1</td><td>1</td><td>UB</td><td>⅙</td></tr>
</table>

1 + 1 = 2 Radd Masala

A third illustration:

The *Masala* of a wife who takes ⅛ as her basic portion with a daughter who takes ½ and a son's daughter who takes ⅙ is calculated as follows;
The whole number of the spouse *Masala* is 8
⅛ of the whole number = 8 ÷ 8 = 1 for the wife.
8 − 1 = 7 the remnant for the relatives.
The whole number of the *Radd Masala* is 6.
½ of the whole number = 6 ÷ 2 = 3 for the daughter.
⅙ of the whole number = 6 ÷ 6 = 1 for the sons's daughter.
3 + 1 = 4 the aggregate of the relatives' shares from the *Radd Masala*.

The comprehensive *Masala*, because the aggregate of the *Radd Masala* and the remnant are *Mutabayyn*, is to be the product of multiplying the remnant by the aggregate. 4 x 8 = 32. See Fig. 20.

Fig. 20

Comp	Radd	WN	SM		
32	4	6	8		
4			1	W	⅛
21	3	3	7	D	½
7	1	1		SD	⅙

3 + 1 = 4 Radd Masala

4 x 1 = 4 the wife's share from the comprehensive *Masala.*
3 x 7 = 21 the daughter's share from the comprehensive *Masala.*
1 x 7 = 7 the son's daughter's share from the comprehensive *Masala.*

The application of the doctrine of *Radd* where the basic portion goes to a group and thus needs the application of *Tashih*

Should the comparison between the *Radd Masala* and the remnant prove to be *Mutadakhil* or *Mutawafiq* the view of the jurists detailed in the doctrine of *Tashih*, which will be discussed soon, shall be adopted in cases of this sort. Thus the *Wifq* or factor of the *Radd Masala* is to be used to multiply the whole number of the spouse *Masala* to make the product the comprehensive *Masala*. The share of the husband or wife from the comprehensive *Masala* is to be the product of multiplying the *Wifq* or the factor of the *Radd Masala* by his or her share out of the spouse *Masala*. While the share of each of the relatives is to be the product of multiplying his or her share from the *Radd Masala* by the *Wifq* or factor of the remnant out of the spouse *Masala*.[3] The *Mutawafiq* as such is deemed where the basic portion is inherited by a group or groups of heirs.
Illustration:

The *Masala* of a wife with ¼, two grandmothers with ⅙ and three uterine brothers who take ⅓ is to be calculated as follows:
The whole number of the spouse *Masala* is 4.
¼ of the whole number = 4 ÷ 4 = 1 for the wife.
4 − 1 = 3 The remnant for the relatives.
The whole number of the *Radd Masala* is 6.
⅙ of the whole number = 6 ÷ 6 =1 for the two grandmothers.
⅓ of the whole number = 6 ÷ 3 = 2 for the three uterine brothers.
1 + 2 = 3 the aggregate of the relatives share out of the *Radd Masala.*

Because the share of the two grandmothers is indivisible by their number without a fraction i.e. 1 ÷ 2 and the share of the three uterine brothers is also indivisible by their number without a fraction i.e. 2 ÷ 3 the *Tashih* become a necessity. Their shares and their numbers are *Mutabayyn*. Also as the number of heirs in the two groups 2 and 3 is *Mutabayyn* we first multiply the number of heirs in the two groups 2 x 3 = 6 thus the product which is called the segment of the fraction is to be multiplied by the *Radd Masala* to be then called the *Tashih* of the *Radd*. 6 x 3 = 18 the *Tashih* of the *Radd*.
The two grandmothers' share from the *Tashih* is 6 x 1 = 6.
The three uterine brothers' share from the *Tashih* is 6 x 2 = 12.

The comprehensive *Masala* is worked out by comparing the *Tashih* (in this case), of the *Radd Masala* with the remnant out of the spouse *Masala*. The comparison here proves 18 and 3 to be *Mutawafiq*. Accordingly the comprehensive *Masala* is the product of multiplying the *Wifq* or factor of the *Tashih* by the whole number of the spouse *Masala*, 6 x 4 = 24.
¼ of the comprehensive *Masala* = 6 x 1 = 6 for the wife.
The share of each relative is his/her share out of the *Tashih* multiplied by the *Wifq* or factor of the remnant as such:
6 x 1 = 6 for the two grandmothers.
6 ÷ 2 = 3 for each of the grandmothers.
12 x 1 = 12 for the three uterine brothers.
12 ÷ 3 = 4 for each of the uterine brothers. See Fig. 21.

Fig. 21

4	
1	W ¼
3	2 GMs ⅙
	3 UBs ⅓

1. Spouse *Masala*

2. *Radd Masala*

Tashih	Radd x 6	WN	
18	3	6	
6	1	1	2 GMs ⅙
12	2	2	3 UBs ⅓

1 + 2 = 3 Radd Masala

Comp	Radd M	SM	
24 = 6 x 4	18	4	
6		1	W ¼
6	6	3	2 GMs ⅙
12	12		3 UBs ⅓

3. Comp. *Masala*

Another illustration:

Two wives with ⅛, two grandmothers with ⅙ and eight daughters with ⅔. Complications as such are solved by the following methods of calculations:

The spouse Masala:

The whole number of the spouse *Masala* is 8.

⅛ of the whole number = 8 ÷ 8 = 1 for the two wives.

8 − 1 = 7 the remnant for the relatives.

As the share of the two wives is indivisible between them the *Tashih* will be considered as follows: The wives' share is *Mutabayyn* with their number 1 and 2. So to multiply the whole number with their number.

2 x 8 = 16 .

2 x 1 = 2 for the two wives,each takes one from the *Tashih*.

2 x 7 = 14 the remnant for the relatives from the *Tashih*.

The *Radd Masala*:

The whole number of the *Radd Masala* is 6.

⅙ of the whole number = 6 ÷ 6 = 1 for the grandmothers.

⅔ of the whole number = 6 ÷ 3 = 2. One third of the total.

⅔ of the whole number = 2 x 2 = 4 for the eight daughters.

1 + 4 = 5 the aggregate of the relatives' shares.

However, as the share of the grandmothers is indivisible by their number without fraction the *Tashih* will be considered (for the *Radd Masala*), as such:

Applying the doctrine of *Tashih* the result of comparing the share of the grandmothers from the*Radd Masala* with their numbers 1 and 2, is *Mutabayyn* so one keeps their number 2 in hand waiting the *Tashih* for the other group.

Also comparing the share of the daughters, which was indivisible by their number 4 and 8, one finds out that the two numbers are *Mutawafiq*, (according to the jurists' view in the doctrine of *Tashih*). The two numbers are *Mutawafiq* by both the halves and quarters but for the sake of keeping the *Masala* short, one is to compare the two by quarters 8 ÷ 4 = 2. The*Wifq* or factor of the number of daughters so to keep it in hand.

Then to compare the two numbers kept in hand (2 the result of comparing the number of the two grandmothers with their share and 2 the result of comparing the number of the eight daughters with their share), they are found *Mutamathil*, i.e. identical. So we take one of them and multiply it with the *Radd Masala*. The product will be the *Tashih Masala*. 2 x 5 = 10. Thus to be divisible between the relatives.

The shares of the relatives from the *Tashih Masala* are:

2 x 1 = 2 for the two grandmothers, 2 ÷ 2 = 1 for each.

2 x 4 = 8 for the eight daughters, 8 ÷ 8 = 1 for each.

The comprehensive *Masala*:

Here we recall the results of the spouse and the *Radd Masala* to make it easier to find the numbers in this case.
In the spouse *Masala* 2 for the two wives and 14 the remnant.
In the *Radd Masala* 2 for the grandmothers and 8 for the eight daughters.

The whole number of the comprehensive *Masala* is 5 x 16 = 80. Comparing the *Radd Masala* with the remnant out of the spouse *Masala* the two numbers 10 and 14 are *Mutawafiq* by halves.
10 ÷ 2 = 5 The *Wifq* or factor of the *Radd Masala*.
14 ÷ 2 = 7 The *Wifq* or factor of the remnant from the spouse *Masala*.
Multiplying the *Wifq* of the *Radd Masala* by the spouse *Masala*. 5 x 16 = 80.
5 x 2 = 10 for the two wives, their share out of the spouse *Masala* by the *Wifq* of the *Radd Masala*.
2 x 7 = 14 for the two grandmothers, their share out of the *Radd Masala* by the *Wifq* or factor of the remnant out of the spouse *Masala*.
14 ÷ 2 = 7 for each of the two grandmothers.
8 x 7 = 56 for the eight daughters, their share out of the *Radd Masala* by the *Wifq* or factor of the remnant out of the spouse *Masala*.
56 ÷ 8 = 7 for each of the eight daughters. See Fig. 22 below.

Fig. 22

<table>
<tr><th>Comp M</th><th>Radd M</th><th>SM</th><th></th></tr>
<tr><td>80 = 5 x 16</td><td>10</td><td>16</td><td></td></tr>
<tr><td>10</td><td></td><td>2</td><td>2 Ws ⅛</td></tr>
<tr><td>14</td><td>2</td><td rowspan="2">14</td><td>2 GMs ⅙</td></tr>
<tr><td>56</td><td>8</td><td>8 Ds ⅔</td></tr>
</table>

<table>
<tr><th></th><th>x 2</th><th></th></tr>
<tr><td>16</td><td>8</td><td></td></tr>
<tr><td>2</td><td>1</td><td>2 Ws ⅛</td></tr>
<tr><td rowspan="2">14</td><td rowspan="2">7</td><td>2 GMs ⅙</td></tr>
<tr><td>8 Ds ⅔</td></tr>
</table>

Spouse *Masala*

<table>
<tr><th>Tashih Radd</th><th>Radd
x 2</th><th>WN</th><th></th></tr>
<tr><td>10</td><td>5</td><td>6</td><td></td></tr>
<tr><td>2</td><td>1</td><td>1</td><td>2 GMs ⅙</td></tr>
<tr><td>8</td><td>4</td><td>4</td><td>8 Ds ⅔</td></tr>
</table>

1 + 4 = 5 This aggregate becoming the Radd Masala.

THE DOCTRINE OF *TASHIH* (REDISTRIBUTION)

The whole number of the *Masala* is to be redistributed on a pro rata basis between the different heirs in accordance to their basic portions to make the act of distribution final.

However, when the basic portion or the entitlement of a group of sharers with its equivalent share from the whole number of the *Masala* becomes indivisible without fraction per capita on the number of heirs in that group a problem has been created. The problem is how to increase the share of that group (out of the whole number of the *Masala*) to make it divisible per capita without disrupting the harmonious relation between such a share and the whole number of the *Masala*, on one hand and the ratio between such a share and the other shares (inherited by their co-heirs), on the other.

To solve such a problem one should not embark on increasing only the share inherited by that group but one should have a broader outlook to consider a scheme which covers the entire *Masala*, thus to make the anticipated increase go side by side with an increase in the whole number of the *Masala* along with a pro rata increase in the shares of other heirs.

One should also consider complying with the much stressed wish of the jurists to try to make the proposed increases as little as possible since their policy is to introduce in one *Masala* as few numbers as possible. To ensure this scheme working the jurists have proposed the following methods.

The method of distributing the indivisible share of one group on its members

When someone finds the share of a group of heirs indivisible on their number and he wants to find a way to make possible divisibility of that share between its beneficiaries he should look first to the ratio between the number of heirs in that group and their collective share which they have taken from the whole number of the *Masala*, using as a criteria the aforementioned, four primary rules of calculation, particularly, the *Mutawafiq* and the *Mutabayyn* rules.

If the two numbers were found *Mutawafiq* (compatible), i.e. having a common factor between them the *Wifq* or factor of the number of heirs in that group is used to multiply the whole number of the *Masala*, the product of such multiplication is called the *Tashih*.

But if the two numbers were found *Mutabayyn* (incompatible), i.e. with no common factor between them then the entire number of heirs in that group is used to multiply the whole number of the *Masala*.[4] The product of such a multiplication, which is called *Tashih*, is to replace the whole number of the *Masala* where pro rata shares of the different heirs is to be extracted.

Illustration:

A *Masala* with four full sisters and an uncle shall be calculated in accordance to the following rules.

Since the four sisters' basic portion is ⅔ and this is the only fractional portion existing in the *Masala*, 3 the denominator of that fraction is to form the whole number of the *Masala* thus to make the initial distribution as such:
⅓ of the whole number = 3 ÷ 3 = 1. One third of the total.
⅔ of the whole number = 2 x 1 = 2 the collective share of the four sisters.
The residue = 3 − 2 = 1 for the uncle.
2, the collective share of the four sisters from the whole number, is indivisable by their number without a fraction. To make a suitable increase to the whole number of the *Masala* one has to apply the primary rules of calculation beforehand to determine the ratio between collective shares of the full sisters and their number.

In our case we find that 4 the number of sisters and 2 their collective share which they extract from the whole number of the *Masala*, is *Mutadakhil* (concordent). As the function of the *Mutadakhil* rule is to ignore the smallest number keeping the largest in hand to be renamed 'the segment of the fraction'. 4, the segment of the fraction, shall be multiplied by the whole number of the *Masala*. The product renamed 'the *Tashih*', shall replace the whole number of the *Masala*. 4 x 3 = 12.
⅔ of the *Tashih* = 4 x 2 = 8 (the segment of the fraction by the collective share), for the four sisters out of the *Tashih*.
8 ÷ 4 = 2 the share of each sister from the *Tashih*.
The residue of the *Tashih* = 4 x 1 = 4 (the segment of the fraction multiplied by the uncles' share out of the whole number), for the uncle from the *Tashih*.
See Fig. 23.

	Tashih	**WN**	
Simplified	**÷ 2**	**x 4**	
6	**12**	**3**	
4	**8**	**2**	**4 Sis ⅔**
2	**4**	**1**	**Uncle Res.**

Fig. 23

The mathematical jurists with their policy of having, in one *Masala*, as few numbers as possible have done so precisely, as far as the *Tashih* is concerned, stuck to such a policy. As a consequence they have ignored entirely the *Mutadakhil* rule of calculation when they felt that it stood as an obstacle to their policy's accomplishment.

It is very bewildering and very unusual for the jurists to leave no explanation to such an act apart from repeating that 'only two rules (of calculation) are to be used'.[5] Thus they have ignored an important rule such as the *Mutadakhil* rule of calculation while confusingly letting its function be taken over by another rule, namely the *Mutawafiq*.

However, the author of *Matalib uli al-nuha*, has so far offered what seems to be the only justification available for the jurists' action as stated above. He explained that the *Mutadakhil* rule comes implicitly within the provision of the Arabic term *Mutawafiq* or compatible where he said: Only the *Mutabayyn* and *Mutawafiq* are to be taken into consideration, (in calculating the *Tashih*), and not the *Mutamathil* or the *Mutadakhil*. The reason, he said, is that when the number of heirs in a group and their shares becomes *Mutamathil* there will be no fraction, (so no need to apply the rule since the divisibility of shares between the heirs is possible). There will also be no need for such a rule where the number of heirs in that group forms part of the number of shares. Howeer, should the opposite become the case, (where the number of heirs becomes larger than their share), the jurist's consideration will be centred on the *Muwafaqah* (of *Mutawafiq* or compatibility), since each of the two numbers which are considered *Mutadakhil* are in fact *Mutawafiq*. Also, (another reason for such an act), the multiplication of the *Wifq* or factor reduces the whole number of the *Masala* than the multiplication of the entire number (of heirs).[6]

According to the jurists' scheme above, the *Masala* which we have already worked out, of four sisters who take ⅔ and one uncle who takes the residue shall be calculated as follows:
The whole number of the *Masala* 3, is the denominator of the fraction.
⅔ of the whole number = 3 ÷ 3 = 1. One third of the total.
⅔ of the whole number = 2 x 1 = 2 the collective share for the four sisters.
The residue = 3 − 2 = 1 for the uncle.

The collective share of the sisters is indivisible by their number to make the *Masala* so we need the following *Tashih*. The share of the four sisters with their numbers 2 and 4, are *Mutawafiq* by halves. The *Wifq* or factor of the number of sisters is called the segment of the fraction, 4 ÷ 2 = 2.
The *Tashih* is the segment mutiplied by the whole number, 2 x 3 = 6. The share of each heir from the *Tashih* is the segment multiplied by each one's share out of the whole number, 2 x 2 = 4 for the sisters.
4 ÷ 4 = 1 for each of the four sisters.
2 x 1 = 2 for the uncle. See Fig. 24 below.

x 2

6	**3**	
4	**2**	**4 Sis ⅔**
2	**1**	**Uncle Res.**

Fig. 24

However, despite the jurists' insistence in pursuing their new scheme of calculating the *Tashih* we find that Al-Bajuri, the author of a commentary on the commentary of Al-Shanshuri had supported the jurists' scheme, he also added that to work out the *Masala* by multiplying the whole number by the entire number of heirs in the group, (in accordance to the *Mutdakhil* rule of calculation), is acceptable.[7]

Anyway, it should be noticed that the number to be taken as the segment of the fraction in the case of *Mutadakhil* as well as *Mutawafiq* and *Mutabayyn* must always be the *Wifq* or the entire number of heirs in the group concerned (whose share becomes per capita indivisible by their number). It should be noticed also that the above scheme is to be applied only where there is to be a comparison between the share of a group of heirs and its number. But in the case of comparison between the different groups (when the *Masala* contains a number of groups), the four primary rules of calculation will be applied rather than the scheme of *Tashih*.

Illustration of the *Mutawafiq*:

The *Masala* of a mother with ⅙ as the basic portion, a uterine sister with ⅙ and six male cousins with the residue is calculated thus:

The whole number of the *Masala* is 6.

⅙ of the whole number = 6 ÷ 6 = 1 for the mother.

⅙ of the whole number = 6 ÷ 6 = 1 for the uterine sister.

1 + 1 = 2 the aggregate of the heirs' with fixed shares out of the whole number.

6 − 2 = 4 the collective share of the cousins (*Asaba*).

4, the collective share of the cousins is indivisible by their number (group). The comparison of these two numbers proves them to be *Mutawafiq* by dividing by two. The *Wifq* or factor of the cousins' number called the segment of the fraction is, 6 ÷ 2 = 3.

The *Tashih* is the product of the segment multiplied by the whole number of the *Masala*, 3 x 6 = 18.

The shares of the heirs from the *Tashih* is the product of the multiplication of each share from the whole number by the segment. So the final distribution will be settled as follows:

3 x 6 = 18 the *Tashih*.

3 x 1 = 3 for the mother.

3 x 1 = 3 for the uterine sister.

3 x 4 = 12 for the six male cousins.

12 ÷ 6 = 2 for each of the six cousins. See Fig. 25 below.

	x 3		
18	**6**		
3	**1**	**M**	⅙
3	**1**	**US**	⅙
2		**Cos**	**R**
2		**Cos**	**E**
2		**Cos**	**S**
	4		**I**
2		**Cos**	**D**
2		**Cos**	**U**
2		**Cos**	**E**

Fig. 25

Illustration of the *Mutabayyn*:

A *Masala* with a daughter with the basic portion of ½, a mother with ⅙, and three full brothers who receive the residue, is to be distributed as follows:

The whole number of the *Masala* is 6.
½ of the whole number = 6 ÷ 2 = 3 for the daughter.
⅙ of the whole number = 6 ÷ 6 = 1 for the mother.
3 + 1 = 4 the daughter and the mother's share out of the whole number.
The residue = 6 − 4 = 2 the collective residual share for the 3 full brothers.

The collective share for the full brothers out of the whole number is indivisible by their number. Comparing these two numbers we find that they are *Mutabayyn*, have no common factor (incompatible). The segment of the fraction is to be therefore, in order to get the *Tashih*, the entire number of brothers and will thus be used to multiply the whole number, 3 x 6 = 18. The share of each heir from the *Tashih* is the product of multiplying the segment by each one's share out of the whole number of the *Masala*.
3 x 6 = 18 the *Tashih*. See Fig. 26, below.

	x3		
18	6		
9	3	D	½
3	1	M	⅙
2		FB	RESIDUE
2	2	FB	
2		FB	

Fig. 26

3 x 3 = 9 for the daughter.
3 x 1 = 3 for the mother.
3 x 2 = 6 for the three full brothers.
6 ÷ 3 = 2 for each of the three full brothers

The method of distributing the indivisible shares of more than one group of heirs in one *Masala*

When the shares of two or more groups of heirs become indivisible by the number of heirs in these groups without fractions the following method of calculation will be considered which is in two stages.

Firstly, to make a comparison between the number of heirs in each group and their collective share applying the special juristic scheme for the *Tashih* which we have discussed before. Thus using only the two primary rules of calculation (the *Mutawafiq* and the *Mutabayyn* being kept in hand), to obtain the product of the comparison whatever it is.

Secondly, to make a comparison between the various products one kept in hand using the four primary rules of calculation. If the two products kept in hand are *Mutamathil*, identical, one should take the largest of them to be the segment of the fraction. The segment will then be multiplied by the whole number of the *Masala*. The product of multiplication will be called the *Tashih*. After having the *Tashih* the segment will be multiplied by the share of each heir or the collective share of each group thus to give each one or each group its share from the *Tashih*.

Illustration:

A *Masala* with four uterine sisters, who inherit ⅓ and eight full sisters who inherit ⅔, is to be calculated as follows:

The whole number of the *Masala* is 3.

⅓ of the whole number = 3÷ 3 = 1 for the four uterine sisters this is indivisible by their number.

⅔ of the whole number = 1 x 2 = 2 for the eight full sisters is also indivisible by their number.

Comparing the number of heirs in the first group 4, with their share 1, we find that they are *Mutabayyn*, that means we keep in hand the number of heirs in such a group 4.

Also comparing the number of heirs in the second group 8 with their share out of the whole number 2, we find that they are *Mutadakhil*, (thus we are supposed to keep the number of heirs in conformity with the *Mutadakhil* rule of calculation), but as we have said earlier a special scheme is to be followed in respect to the *Tashih* when the comparison is between the number of heirs in a group and their collective share as it is the case here. Accordingly the *Mutadakhil* in this case will be treated as if it is a *Mutawafiq* thus to keep in hand not the entire number of sisters 8 but the *Wifq* or factor of it, 8 ÷ 2 = 4.

Having reached this stage another comparison is to be applied between the two numbers 4 and 4 kept in hand from the previous two comparisons using this time, the primary four rules of calculation, *Mutamathil*, *Mutadakhil*, *Mutawafiq* and *Mutabayyn* rules.

The comparison shows us that the two numbers in hand 4 and 4 are *Mutamathil*. Thus one of these two 4s is to be taken as the segment of the fraction to be multiplied by the whole number and the heirs' shares out of the whole number as such:

4 x 3 = 12 The *Tashih*.

4 x 1 = 4 the share of the first group (the uterine sisters) out of the *Tashih*.

4 ÷ 4 = 1 the share of each heir in the first group out of the *Tashih*.

4 x 2 = 8 the share of the second group (the full sisters) out of the *Tashih*.

8 ÷ 8 = 1 the share of each of the eight full sisters in the second group out of the *Tashih*. See Fig. 27.

Another Illustration:

A *Masala* with two grandmothers who receive the basic portion of ⅙, three uterine brothers with ⅓ and one consanguine sister with ½ is to be calculated as follows:

The whole number of the *Masala* is 6.

⅙ of the whole number = 6 ÷ 6 = 1 the collective share of the two grandmothers is indivisible by them.

⅓ of the whole number = 6 ÷ 3 = 2 the collective share of the three uterine brothers is indivisible by their number.

½ of the whole number = 6 ÷ 2 = 3 the share of the consanguine sister

To increase the whole number of the *Masala* the indivisible share of the two groups of heirs to the minimal one the rules of calculation have to be applied in three stages.

First stage: Comparing the number of heirs in the first group 2 grandmothers, with their collective share out of the whole number 1, we find that they are *Mutabayyn*, therefore, we are to keep in hand the entire number of heirs in such a group (i.e. 2 grandmothers).

<table>
<tr><td></td><td>**x 4**</td><td></td><td></td></tr>
<tr><td>**12**</td><td>**3**</td><td></td><td></td></tr>
<tr><td>**1**</td><td rowspan="4">**1**</td><td>**US**</td><td></td></tr>
<tr><td>**1**</td><td>**US**</td><td rowspan="2">⅓</td></tr>
<tr><td>**1**</td><td>**US**</td></tr>
<tr><td>**1**</td><td>**US**</td><td></td></tr>
<tr><td>**1**</td><td rowspan="8">**2**</td><td>**FS**</td><td></td></tr>
<tr><td>**1**</td><td>**FS**</td><td></td></tr>
<tr><td>**1**</td><td>**FS**</td><td></td></tr>
<tr><td>**1**</td><td>**FS**</td><td rowspan="2">⅔</td></tr>
<tr><td>**1**</td><td>**FS**</td></tr>
<tr><td>**1**</td><td>**FS**</td><td></td></tr>
<tr><td>**1**</td><td>**FS**</td><td></td></tr>
<tr><td>**1**</td><td>**FS**</td><td></td></tr>
</table>

Fig. 27

Comparing the number of heirs in the second group (3 uterine brothers), with their collective share of the whole number 2 we find that they are also *Mutabayyn*, therefore, we are to keep in hand the entire number of heirs in this group to (i.e. 3).

Second stage: Comparing the numbers in hand 2 and 3 we find the two are *Mutabayyn*. The segment of the fraction is thus to be the product of multiplying the two numbers in hand by each other 2 x 3 = 6 and then this number 6 is to be multiplied by the whole number to give the *Tashih* 6 x 6 = 36.

6 x 1 = 6 the share of the two grandmothers out of the *Tashih*.

6 ÷ 2 = 3 the share of each of the two grandmothers out of the *Tashih*.

6 x 2 = 12 the share of the three uterine brothers out of the *Tashih*.

12 ÷ 3 = 4 the share of each of the three uterine brothers out of the *Tashih*

6 x 3 = 18 the share of the consanguine sister out of the *Tashih*. See Fig. 28.

x 6 = 2 x 3 The segment

36	6			
3	1	GM	⅙	2
3		GM		
4		UB		
4	2	UB	⅓	3
4		UB		
18	3	Con S	½	1

Fig. 28

NOTES

1. *Succession in the Muslim Family*, 3.
2. *Quran*, XXXIII, 6.
3. *Al-Iqna'*, Vol. 3, 94-95 and *Al-Kashshaf*, Vol. 4, 436.
4. *K* Vol. 4, 437.
5. *Al-Mughni*, Vol. 7, 36-37 and *Al-sharh al-kabir*, Vol. 7, 81-82,*Kashshaf*, Vol. 4, 437 and *Sharh al-muntaha*, Vol. 2, 602-603 and *Uddat al-bahith*, 53-54.
6. Mustafa al-Suyuti *Matalib uli al-nuha*, Vol. 4, 587.
7. *Sharh al-Bajuri*, 157-158.

CHAPTER II

THE CALCULATION OF LEGACIES

INTRODUCTION

The bequest is related to inheritance and is bound to be calculated in the same way that the basic portions and share of inheritance are calculated.

Certain divergences in the way the inheritance rules of calculation are being applied shall be stated in due course particularly where there are a number of legacies involved or where a number of legatees participate in sharing one bequest.

According to the *Quran* the bequest must be given away first before the distribution of the portions of inheritance. But as the Prophet's precedents have linked the efficacy of bequest to it coming out of the disposable one third there is in addition, the need to know the ratio between the share of the legatee and the collective share of all heirs on one hand, and between the share of the legatee and the share of each individual heir on the other. This might have inspired the jurists to develop a method whereby the legatee's share will be amalgamated with the heirs' shares to be calculated in one *Masala* whenever possible.

In the following is a discussion to the ways and means of solving the bequest problems as the jurists have proposed in addition to demonstrative charts with explanation to the applied processes.

BEQUEST WITH THE EQUIVALENT SHARE OF ONE OF THE TESTATOR'S HEIRS

Bequest with the share of an unspecific heir

A bequest could be made to be equivalent to the basic portion of a specified heir thus to consider the portion of the heir as the basis of comparison whereby giving the legatee an equivalent amount of shares to whatever amount of shares is given to that heir such as: 'I bequeath to Sa'id the same portion as that of my son, or to Muna the same portion which my wife is entitled to, or I bequeath a similar portion to so and so, or to a school as that of my father, etc.'

The validity of such a bequest depends on the status of the individual person whose portion has been referred to as the basis, being himself an heir. If under certain circumstances that person became excluded from inheritance, that is to say he was a slave, a non-Muslim, killed or participated in killing of his relative or has been excluded from inheritance by the emergence of another heir who is nearer in degree than the former one, then the legatee will subsequently lose the right to the legacy.

In this way by invoking analogy, he was considered to be no more than a branch to someone else and if that person, or say that root, loses his right to succession then by assumption the legatee (the branch) will follow suit. We can compare this to a tree with branches in so much that if the tree dies, the branches will die too.

However, should the portion of an unspecific heir become the subject of equivalence the jurists of schools of thought have agreed to respect the wish of the testator. Thus when the heir to whose share the legatee's has been made equivalent, becomes an equal sharer with others so as to inherit a per capita share the legatee wil be counted as one of them. The whole number of their *Masala* will be the total number of people including the legatee as such. When the deceased who is survived by two sons leaves a legacy equalling the share of one of his two sons the whole numbner of the *Masala* will be made 3.

$\frac{1}{3}$ of the whole number $= 3 \div 3 = 1$ for one of the two sons.
$\frac{1}{3}$ of the whole number $= 3 \div 3 = 1$ for the other son.
$\frac{1}{3}$ of the whole number $= 3 \div 3 = 1$ for the legatee. See fig. 29.

3	
1	**Son**
1	**Son**
1	**Legatee**

Fig. 29

The trend of bequeathing an unspecific share of a particular heir is recognizable by law as part of the freedom granted to the testator despite the difficulties of calculation it renders. A Saudi testator, for instance, took up such freedom in a case in which the testator among other things has bequeathed to his two sisters the share of one son to be equally distributed between them.[1]

But we find that the case of limiting the amount of shares to be given to the legatee or to which particular heir the unspecific legacy should be attached to where the shares of each heir in the *Masala* varies from one to another, according to their degree of proximity in their relationship to the deceased, has been characterized by divergence of opinions between the Maliki jurists on one hand and the majority of jurists on the other.

The view of the Malikis is that the legatee whose legacy has been made equivalent to the share of an unspecific heir shall get a per capita share, (taking count of the number of the beneficiaries including the legatee's, subtracting the legatee's share and leaving the rest to the legal heirs).

Application of this view ignores the variation of the heirs' basic portions thus shifting the emphasis to the number of beneficiaries so to regard the legatee as a per capita sharer with the heirs. This view of the Malikis' has provoked opposition from the jurists of other schools of law who logically consider this as impractical and inequitable.

To refute the Maliki view the Hanbali jurists said: 'Certainty is given preference over doubt. The logic of the Malikis to give a per capita share to the legatee regardless of portion variations contradicts even the basis of the testator's instructions, let alone that of the reckoning of such portion (in the way proposed by the Malikis), is not in actual fact a share of one of the heirs as it was instructed. The share of the lesser fortunate heir would and should in our (the Hanbalis) and in the majority opinion form the basis on which the unspecific legatee's share be compared to'. Moreover, the Hanbalis have added that, 'to adopt such a stance (as proposed by the majority of jurists), is better than inventing an irrelevant context to the words of the testator'.[2]

While the Hanbalis and the majority of jurists are inclined to give the legatee with the legacy of a share of an unspecific heir who takes fewer shares than his co-heirs, because they say it is the only share that we are sure of being included within the context of the testator's instructions.

Accordingly, if a person leaves a son, a wife and a legacy of the share of one of his heirs then according to the majority view it will be more equitable to give the legatee from the *Masala* a share equal to the share of the wife ⅛, since the wife's portion (in this *Masala*) is the lesser share.

Applying the rules of calculation the whole number of the *Masala* is 8, because it is the denominator of the only fraction in it. We start calculations by giving each heir his/her share from the whole number to see who amongst them takes the lesser share. When we have established this we add to the whole number a similar share for the legatee, thus to replace the whole number by the aggregate called the total of the *Masala* as such.

⅛ of the whole number = 8 ÷ 8 = 1 for the wife (the lesser sharer).
The residue = 8 − 1 = 7 for the son.
8 ÷ 8 = 1 for the legatee, as it is the lesser share.
The lesser share added to the whole number = 1 + 8 = 9 the total of the *Masala*

Thus the ⅛ of the wife is reduced to 1/9 to suit the total.
7/8 of the son is reduced to 7/9 " " " "
and 1/8 of the legatee is reduced to 1/9 " " " " See fig. 30 below.

	+1	
9	8	
1	1	W ⅛
7	7	S Res
1		Leg = 1 W = 1

Fig. 30

Another illustration:

If two wives ⅛ and a son survive the deceased who had made a bequest of an equal share as that of an heir the calculations of this *Masala* will be similar to the calculations of the above *Masala* except that the doctrine of *Tashih* has to be applied here because the collective share of the two wives is indivisible by their number thus.

The whole number of the *Masala* is 8.

⅛ of the whole number = 8 ÷ 8 = 1 for the two wives.

The residue = 8 − 1 = 7 for the son.

The *Tashih* 1 and 2 are *Mutabayyn* so the total of the *Masala* is to be the product of multiplying the number of wives 2 by the whole number 8,2 x 8 = 16.

⅛ of the *Tashih* = 2 x 1 = 2 for the two wives.

2 ÷ 2 = 1 for each of the wives, (the lesser share).

The residue = 2 x 7 = 14 for the son.

Adding the lesser share to the *Tashih* to form the total of the *Masala* = 1 + 16 = 17.

Thus the share of each wife from the *Tashih* 1/16 is reduced 1/17.

The share of the son from the *Tashih* 14/16 is reduced to 14/17.

The share of the legatee from the *Tashih* 1/16 is reduced to 1/17.

See Fig. 31.

	+1	x2	
17	16	8	
2	1/1 2	1	2W ⅛
14	14	7	S Res
1			Leg = 1 W = 1

Fig. 31

A third illustration shows the solution to a *Masala* where the above type of legacy existed in addition to the basic portions of the heirs which even without the legacy such portions have not only exhausted the whole number of the *Masala* but have also required the application of the doctrine of *'Awl* (increase), such as the case of a woman who had bequeathed to a person a share equal to the share of one of her heirs and was survived by her husband with 1/2, her germane sister with 1/2 and her consanguine sister with 1/6.
Applying the rules of calculation the whole number of the *Masala* is 6.
1/2 of the whole number = 6 ÷ 2 = 3 for the husband.
1/2 of the whole number = 6 ÷ 2 = 3 for the germane sister.
1/6 of the whole number = 6 ÷ 6 = 1 for the consanguine sister.
3 + 3 + 1 = 7 the aggregate of the shares taken out of the whole number so to use the aggregate of the *Masala* to replace the whole number is called *Awl* or increase.
Thus the share of the heirs out of the *Awl* are:
3/6 of the husband out of the whole number is reduced to 3/7.
3/6 of the germane sister out of the whole number is reduced to 3/7.
1/6 of the consanguine sister from the whole number is reduced to 1/7.

The lesser fortunate amongst the heirs is the consanguine sister who takes only 1/7, so the legatee's share 1/7 in our *Masala* will be equivalent to it where it will then be added to the *'Awl* to make the result the total, 1 + 7 = 8.

Accordingly the lesser share of the beneficiaries out of the total wil be as follows:
The 3/7 of the husband share is reduced to 3/8.
3/7 of the germane sister share is reduced to 3/8.
1/7 of the consanguine sister is reduced to 1/8.
1/7 of the legatee share is reduced to 1/8. See Fig. 32 below.

+1

8	7	6	
3	**3**	**3**	**H** ½
3	**3**	**3**	**GS** ½
1	**1**	**1**	**CS** ⅙
1			**Leg = c S = 1**

Fig. 32

The majority of jurists are also in agreement that the testator's reference to the minimal share taken by an heir such as 'I bequeath an equal share to Ali as that taken by the less fortunate heir', as to serve only to ascertain the legatee's position. They have also agreed that by such description the legatee will not be allocated more than he would otherwise under the former cases.

Allocating a legatee with the share of the most fortunate heir (who takes a share larger than others) such as 'I bequeath a share equal to the largest heritable share', is considered valid. Accordingly in a case as such with the daughter of the testator with ½, his wife ⅛ and his brother with the residue the legatee will be given an equal share to that of the daughter since she is the largest sharer in the *Masala* as follows.

The whole number of the *Masala* is 8.
½ of the whole number = 8 ÷ 2 = 4 for the daughter.
⅛ of the whole number = 8 ÷ 8 = 1 for the wife
4 + 1 = 5.
The residue = 8 − 5 = 3 for the brother.
Since the legatee's share is compared to the daughter's the total of the *Masala* will be an equal share as that of the daughter added to the whole number = 4 + 8 = 12. See Fig. 33 below.

+4		
12	**8**	
4	**4**	**D ½**
1	**1**	**W ⅛**
3	**3**	**B Res**
4		**Leg = D = 4**

Fig. 33

Thus the shares of the beneficiaries out of the total will become
4/12 for the daughter instead of 4/8.
1/12 for the wife instead of 1/8.
3/12 for the brother instead of 3/8.
4/12 for the legatee which the equivalent share of the daughter.

However where the testator (who has male and female children), has bequeathed the share of one of his children without defining to which of his children the legacy will be compared to, the legatee will be given a female share.

The Arabic term *Walad* or *Awlad* means child or children is in Arabic the same in English, to be regarded as a proper term for both the male and the female child.

The scrutineers of the Hanbali school have applied the juristic maxim 'Certainty is given preference over doubt'.[3] Thus they would not have to risk giving the legatee the share of a male child while they have an alternative choice to apply the same term to denote a lesser share, i.e. of a female child. The jurists can never be sure that the testator meant to give the legatee the share of a male child while they are positive that the share of a female child is meant, because the term *Walad* or child is also proper for the female child as it is clear in the statement of *Al-Sharh al-kabir*. 'We can never be sure that the testator has tended to give away (to the legatee), a male's share while we are certain that a female's share, if the intention is not explictly (made clear by the testator), is implicitly included within the frame of such a term.'[4]

Accordingly a legacy as such with a son and a daughter shall be calculated as to give the legatee 1/4 of the property as follows:

The whole number of the *Masala* is 3. We reach the number by taking into consideration that (the male takes double that of a female), since there was no fraction in the *Masala*.
Out of the whole number 1 for the daughter = 3 ÷ 3 = 1
Out of the whole number 2 for the son = 2 x 1 = 2.

As the legatee's share is equivalent to the share of the child (daughter) 1 is to be added to the whole number of the *Masala* to give the total 1 + 3 = 4. See Fig. 34 below.

	+1	
4	3	
2	2	S
1	1	D
1		Leg = D = 1

Fig. 34

From the total of the *Masala* the shares of the beneficiaries are
2/4 for the son instead of 2/3.
1/4 for the daughter instead of 1/3.
1/4 for the legatee instead of 1/3.

Many instances can be solved in the same manner as in the case where the testator bequeathes a number of various legacies to a number of legatees such as if the testator bequeaths 1/3 of his estate to a person, 1/4 to another, 1/5 to a third person and to fourth person a share equivalent to one of them. Applying the above reasons the legatee with the equivalent share will be given 1/5 as it is the lowest share bequeathed,[5] because this what we are sure to come within the context of the testator's term.

Also in a case where the testator bequeaths £100 to a person £60 to another person, £40 to a third person and an equivalent bequest of one of them to a fourth person, the fourth legatee will be given £40 an equivalent amount to the third legatee who gets the lowest amount in the legacy.[6]

When only a female heir survives the deceased and there is a legacy of an equal share of an heir, the estate will be divided between the sole surviving heir and the legatee equally. Also if a grandmother survives with the above sort of bequest, the estate will be divided into two halves ½ for the grandmother and the other ½ for the legatee,[7] unless the excessive legacy has been disapproved of by the surviving heir to cause the legacy to be reduced to the limit of one third as we shall discuss later.

Bequest of the entitlement of an heir to another person

Bequeathing the entitlement allocated to an heir by law without a hint as to any equivalence has provoked an immense controversy. Such a controversy has been forced upon other jurists by the *Hanafi* and *Shafi'i* jurists who have pronounced this type of bequest as null and void. A reason for such a decision is that they have compared it to the disposition with which the testator does not actually possess the right as if he (the testator) had bequeathed the property of someone else. Opposition to the valadity of an act of disposition as such has been caused by the testator's reference to the share of his heir.

The other jurists, mainly Malikis and Hanbalis (with the exception of Al-Qadhi, a Hanbali jurist), have agreed otherwise.

In their view it is not a bequest with someone else's property, on the contrary, it is a disposition which implicitly indicates equivalence to the share of the heir rather than being a disposition of the heir's share itself. As to the usage of language, they added, such implication is possible by the suppression of the first a genitive construction to replace it by the second, that is to say, a share equivalent to that of his heir.[8]

The Malikis and the Hanbalis have further supported their argument by referring to a related case where both the Hanafis and the Shafi'is will (by adopting their present view) be committing a self-contradiction. This is to validate the case in which the testator bequeathed his entire estate to someone, while invalidating the same disposition where it involves the share of one heir. Thus adopting the view of validating a bequest with entire estate (which is supposed to be owned by all heirs) makes it inevitable for anyone to validate a bequest with the share of an heir. Therefore, to regard the testator as if he had bequeathed a share equivalent to the share of his heir.[9]

The commentator of *Al-Muntaha* has contributed to the above argument with a new idea when he said, 'What is intended from referring to the heir is not an attachment to it but rather intended to appraise the value of the legacy. This means that the mention of the heir (or the share of an heir in the legacy) has no effect otherwise'.[10]

The following case shows the Saudi's adherence to the Hanbali view in the relevant point. The testator in this case made the portion, inherited by one of his sons, itself the subject of his bequest to be shared equally between his two germane sisters. Such a bequest was validated by the juidicial verification of *Katib al-'Adl*.[11]

THE PROPORTIONAL BEQUEST

The Arabic term *Di'f* means double, *Di'fain* means twice as much and so on could be used in a testament to appraise the shares to be taken by a legatee. As doubling has to be related to something known in advance the amount to be granted as a result will depend on the definition of the term *Di'f* or double. Defining such a term has caused difference in opinion to emerge within the Hanbali jurists as follows.

Two of the most influential Hanbali jurists, Muwaffaq al-din Ibn Qudama (the author of *Al-Mughni*), and his nephew Shams al-din Ibn Qudama (the author of *Al-sharh al-kabir),* are convinced that *Di'f* (double) and the dual form *Di'fain* (twice), denotes the same thing, i.e. to double. Accordingly, the legatee with *Di'f* or *Di'fain* of the share of an heir will be given twice the share of an heir (seeing no difference between the two forms). But when the testator bequeaths *Thalathatu ad'f* (threefold), the legatee will be given three times as much and with *Arba'atu adha'af* (fourfold), four times as much.[12] This was said to be the view of *Al-mujmal*, *Al-sihah*, *Al-qamus* and others of the Arabic dictionaries. This was also mentioned in the *Quran* and the *Sunna* and was defined as such by the majority of the former and latter mathematicians.[13]

The official Hanbali doctrine denies that the effect denoted by the term *Di'f* and the dual form *Di'fain* means the same thing, i.e. to double. Three *Quranic* verses have been invoked to support their interpretation that the *Di'f* is the very thing with an equivalent thing in addition to it. For this reason the official doctrine indicates that, *Di'fain* or twice means three-fold, i.e. the basic thing in addition to two times as much. As for *Thalathatu ada'af* or threefold, the basic thing in addition to three times as much, and so forth, each time you increase proportionally you add an extra one into the basic thing.

In adopting the official doctrine the latter jurists have sought to support such a view still further. They quoted the view of Abu Ubaidah Muammar b. al-Muthanna as saying, 'If, (the dual form) *Di'fain* or twice does not mean three times the amount then there will be no difference between the bequest with one *Di'f* and *Di'fain*, which he added, was clearly wanted and intended.'

They have also said, 'From the word, *Yudha'af*, in the verse, (The punishment for her will be double),[14] it is understood that twice is intended for the double of something is the addition of something to its equal. So to say, to combine two things to each other is called *Di'f* or double'.[15]

Thus, the testator bequeathing the *Di'f* or double the share of an heir will be adjudicated as giving twice as much as that heir to the legatee. Accordingly, if a person who has left one son only bequeathed to another a *Di'f* or double the share of his son then the legatee wil be given two thirds of the left property with one third to the son. But if the testator leaves two sons with the above bequest the legatee will take half the property left and the other half betwen the two sons, ¼ each.

When the heir to whose share the double bequest was likened was not specified then the legatee's share will be double that of the least fortunate heir.[16]

The bequest with *Di'fain* or twice will render three times as much to the legatee as if the testator who has one son only bequeathes a *Di'fain* or twofold the share of his son where their shares will, accordingly, be ¾ of the left property for the legatee and ¼ of it for the son,. The same bequest with two sons will be calculated as to give the legatee ⅗ of the left property and ⅕ for each son.[17]

THE HYPOTHETICAL EXISTENCE OF AN HEIR AS BEING THE BASIS OF THE APPRAISAL OF THE LEGATEE'S SHARE

Hypotheses are not an uncommon feature in Islamic law. It has helped tremendously in the developing stages of the law. In some stages it has in fact been the main source of enrichment that supplied the law with the necessary means of support particularly during the decline of the jurists' influence from the centres of powers and practice. However, hypotheses have been introduced to the law either in the form of purely fabricated cases where the jurists go back to consult the original sources of the law and try to secure appropriate solutions, or forced upon them in the form of questions or reported complaints where the jurist, after securing the appropriate solution, tries to draw from the original case other cases which he thinks are likely to occur and the right solutions to them in the same way.

Some of these hypothetical cases, though they might not have been of any practical value, are considered important to the lawyers and students of law because we can see tremendous value in them particularly since they will help to enrich the students' imagination with the kind of problems that are likely to occur in reality. Solutions of some highly complicated problems are of great intellectual and practical value that we the student of law cannot, at any time, afford to lose, Needless to say, the significance of hypotheses for the law of inheritence and bequest where the cases involve the calculations of figures and fractions, that is to say, without the use of so many hypothetical problems,, we will neither find proper solutions nor will be able to understand them. In the following we will be discussing a number of problems and their proposed solutions.

BEQUEATHING A LEGACY SIMILAR TO THE SHARE OF A PRESUMED HEIR

The presumptive existence of an heir and the likening of the legatee's share to the share supposed to be received by the presumed heir is another area of freedom of testacy granted to the testator. In adherance to this right governed by the old jurists the Saudi courts have also allowed the testator to practise such a right. To demonstrate this, here is a case in which the testator bequeathed to his grand children – the share of a son even if their father survives him or not.[18] Similar bequests are also found in the case where the testator in his will had bequeathed to his grand-daughters the portion of his pre-deceased son as if the son were alive at the testator's death.[19]

Solution of the share of the legatee whose share has been likened to the share of a presumed heir will be worked out as follows:

1. The supposition of the existence of the presumed heir alongside the surviving heirs.
2. Calculate the *Masala* giving each heir (including the presumed one) his share.
3. Give the legatee a share similar to that of the presumed heir.
4. Redivide the collective share of all heirs (including the share of the presumed heir), on the surviving heirs only.

Thus, to find the result in accordance with the statement of Ibn Qudama which is quoted from *Al-mughni* as follows: 'If a testator bequeaths a similar share as that of a presumed heir, then suppose the existence of such an heir and see what the legatee gets (from the *Masala*) with the presumption of the existence of that heir even though he is not in existence.'[20]

Illustration:

If a person dies leaving two sons had made a bequest to someone equalling the shares to be taken by a presumed third son, the *Masala* shall be worked out as follows:

Applying the primary rules of calculation the whole number of the *Masala* is 3. (the per capita number of sons, including the presumed one).

From the whole number of the *Masala*, $3 \div 3 = 1$ for each son. Thus the share of the prsumed son from the whole number is 1, therefore the share of the legatee (with the similar share of the presumed heir), is also, 1 so to add 1 for the legatee to the whole number of the *Masala* to get the grand total $1 + 3 = 4$.

Subtracting the legatee's share from this grand total results in the collective share of the heirs. $4 - 1 = 3$.

Since the presumed son has been used only to define the share of the legatee, which we have already done, then the subtraction or the collective share of the heirs above shall be redivided between the surviving two sons as such:

3 is indivisible by 2, the number of sons. Thus applying the doctrine of *Tashih*, we find that the number of sons 2 is *Mutabayyn* with their collective share 3 so to take the number of sons 2 as the segment of the fraction.

The *Tashih* is the grand total multiplied by the segment of the fraction $2 \times 4 = 8$.

The shares of all beneficiaries from the *Tashih* are reckoned by multiplying each single share from the grand total by the segment.

$2 \times 3 = 6$ for the two sons from the *Tashih*.

$6 \div 2 = 3$ for each son from the *Tashih*.

$2 \times 1 = 2$ for the legatee from the *Tashih*.

See Fig. 35 below.

	x2	+1		
8	**4**	**3**		
3	**3**	**1**	**S**	**2**
3		**1**	**S**	
X	**X**	**1**	**S pres**	
2	**1**		**Leg = 1**	

Fig. 35

Another illustration:

If a testatrix, who died leaving her husband and her sister, had left a bequest to someone equalling the share of a presumed mother, the *Masala* will be calculated as follows:

Applying the rules of calculation the whole number of the *Masala* is 2 x 3 = 6.

½ of the whole number = 6 ÷ 2 = 3 for the husband or ½ x 6 = 3.
½ of the whole number = 6 ÷ 2 = 3 for the sister or ½ x 6 = 3.
⅓ of the whole number = 6 ÷ 3 = 2 for the presumed mother or ⅓ x 6 = 2.
The aggregate of the heirs' shares (3 + 3 + 2 = 8), is more than the whole number of the *Masala* 6. So applying the doctrine of *'Awl* or increase we replace the whole number by the aggregate (called *'Awl*) to suit the number of shares drawn from the *Masala*.

As the presumed mother's share is 2, we give an equivalent share to the legatee thus adding two shares to the *'Awl* increase the *Masala* to 10, 2 + 8 = 10, the grand total.
Subtracting the legatee's share from the grand total leaves what is considered the collective share of the heirs (including the presumed mother's), to be redivided between the surviving heirs only.
10 − 2 = 8 the collective share of the heirs from the grand total.
8 ÷ 2 = 4 or 8 x ½ = 4 the share of the husband from the grand total
8 ÷ 2 = 4 or 8 x ½ = 4 the share of the sister from the grand total.
10 − 8 = 2 the share of the legatee from the grand total.
See Fig. 36 below.

Al-Buhuti's suggested method of solving bequests with a share equivalent to that of a presumed heir

Al-Bahuti, a latter Hanabali jurist, has suggested another way of solving the *Masala* in which the share of a presumed heir has been made the basis of the equivalent bequest. His method consists of three stages, two primaries and one final.

Fig. 36

Grand Total	**+2**		
10	**8**	**6**	
4	**3**	**3**	**H ½**
4	**3**	**3**	**Sis ½**
X	**2**	**2**	**M Pres ⅓**
2			**Leg = 2**

8 − 6 = 2 deficit

In the first stage one makes a subsidiary *Masala* which consists of the surviving heirs only, (Applying of course the rules of calculation to get the common denominator or the whole number of the *Masala* from the allocated fractions, and do also all other steps which need to be done such as, *Radd, Awl Tashih*, etc.

In the second stage one makes the main *Masala* consisting of the surviving heirs with the presumed heir (to get the common denominator or the whole number of the *Masala*, from the allocated fractions, and to do also all other steps which need to be done such as, *Radd, Awl, Tashih*, etc.

In the third and final stage one multiplies the subsidiary *Masala* of stage one by the main *Masala* of stage two using the product of such multiplication as the whole number of the final *Masala* in stage three. One then partitions the whole whole number of the *Masala* by the main *Masala* of stage two where the existence of the presumed heir was considered, the quotient is to be added to the product to become the share of the legatee while the product itself is to be divided among the surviving heirs.[21]

To exemplify Al-Bahuti's method by putting it into figures to test its accuracy we suggest the use of the table charts which the latter jurists developed to solve inheritance problems.

Here are two illustrations.

First illustration:

When a person dies leaving two sons and a bequest to someone equalling the share of a presumed third son the *Masala* applying the proposed method of *Al-Bahuti* will be calculated as follows:

2 is the whole number of the *Masala* of the heirs without the presumed one in stage I. 3 is the whole number of the *Masala* of the heirs with the presumed one in stage 2. Comparison of the two shows the two numbers to be *Mutbayyn* or incompatible. We therefore, multiply the two whole numbers of the two *Masalas* by each other 2 x 3 = 6.

6 becomes the whole number of the third *Masala*. Dividing such a whole number by the number of heirs produces 2/6, the share of the presumed heir.

As the legatee's share is similar to that of the presumed one we give the legatee an extra 2 = 2/6, thus leaving the whole number of the *Masala* to be allocated between the surviving heirs only.
The grand total of the *Masala* is 2 + 6 = 8.
From the grand total 2, for the legatee.
From the grand total 8 − 2 = 6 for the surviving two sons.
6 ÷ 2 = 3 for each one of the surviving sons. See Fig. 37.

Fig. 37

2	
1	S
1	S

Stage 1

3	
1	S
1	S
1	S pres

Stage 2

+2

8	6	=2x3
3	2	S
3	2	S
X	2	S Pres
2		Leg =2

Stage 3

Second illustration:

If a person leaves three sons and a legacy similar to the share of a presumed fourth son then applying the method of Al-Bahuti, the *Masala* will be calculated as follows:
3 is the whole number of the *Masala* without the presumed heir, in stage 1.
4 is the whole number of the *Masala* with the presumed heir, in stage 2.
The whole number of the *Masalas* are *Mutabayyn* so by multiplying them by each other we get the whole number of the third *Masala* 3 x 4 = 12.
Dividing such a whole number between the heirs including the presumed heir the share of the presumed son becomes 3.

The legatee who gets a share similar to the presumed son gets 3, to make the grand total 3 + 12 = 15, while the share of the presumed heir itself goes back to the collective share of the legal heirs to be redivided between the surviving three sons only as it is their share from the grand total.
From the grand total, 3 for the legatee.
From the grand total, 15 − 3 = 12 for the three surviving sons collectively.
12 ÷ 3 = 4 for each of the surviving sons. See Fig. 38.

Fig. 38

3	
1	S
1	S
1	S

Stage 1

4	
1	S
1	S
1	S
1	S Pres

Stage 2

	+3	
15	12	=3x4
4	3	S
4	3	S
4	3	S
X	3	S Pres
3		Leg=3

Stage 3

From the above two illustrations Al-Bahuti's method has proved to be reliably accurate when the presumed heir is being a member of a class which inherits the entire estate by their per capita capacity.

We consider Al-Bahuti's method to be also accurate where the presumed heir belongs to a group of heirs which inherit only part of the estate as we see in this illustration:

When a testatrix who leaves a husband, a son and a daughter was found to have made a bequest of a share equal to that inherited by a presumed second daughter the *Masala* shall be calculated as follows:
4 is the whole number of the subsidiary *Masala* in stage 1.
4 is the whole number of the main *Masala* in stage 2. However, as the collective share of those who take the residue is indivisible by their number 4, the application of the doctrine of *Tashih* was necessary 4 x 4 = 16, thus only the *Tashih* in this *Masala* will be considered.

Comparing the two *Masalas* of stage 1 and 2, we find the two numbers 4 and 16, are *Mutadakhil* or concordent thus applying such rule we take only the biggest of the two numbers 16, to be used as the whole number of the final *Masala* of stage 3.
From the whole number of the final *Masala*, 16 ÷ 4 = 4 for the husband.
From the whole number of the final *Masala*, 16 − 4 = 12 for the residuaries.
12 ÷ 4 = 3 for the daughter.
From the whole number of the final *Masala*, 12 ÷ 4 = 3 for the presumed daughter.
From the whole number of the final *Masala* 3 x 2 = 6 for the son.

An equivialent share as that of the presumed heir is to be the share of the legatee and will be added to the whole number to make the total,
3 + 16 = 19.

This will allow the whole number used in distribution to the heirs to be 16, (19 − 3 = 16), being the previous whole number to be redivided between the surviving heirs on the basis of their portions as such:
16 ÷ 4 = 4 for the husband = $4/19$.
16 − 4 = 12 for the residuaries.
12 ÷ 3 = 4 for the daughter = $4/19$
2 x 4 = 8 for the son $8/19$
And 3 for the legatee = $3/19$
$4/19 + 4/19 + 8/19 + 3/19 = 1$. See Fig. 39.

Fig. 39

4		
1	H	¼
2	S	Res
1	D	

Stage 1

x4

16	4	
4	1	H ¼
6		S
3	3	D Res
3		D Pres

Stage 2

+3

19	16		
4	4	H	¼
8	6	S	Res
4	3	D	
X	3	D Pres	
3		Leg = 3	

Stage 3

The inadequacies of Al-Buhuti's method

The cases we have presented to test the accuracy of the method proposed by Al-Bahuti have all proved it to be positively accurate and complete since the presumed heir takes his share as either a member of a class which inherits the entire estate or as a member of the residuaries. But should the presumed heir stand to inherit independently a fixed portion, then we will see no accurate result when we come to the end of the method proposed by Al-Bahuti. Certain defects in the method have been modified by suggesting a way on which to base the redivision of the whole number between the surviving heirs as is required as we shall see in this and the following Illustration:

When a testatrix, who had made a bequest equalling what should have been received by her father had he been alive, dies leaving a mother and a son only then without modification to the Al-Bahuti's method the *Masala* will be calculated as follows:

6 is the whole number of the subsidiary *Masala* in stage 1.

6 is also the whole number of the main *Masala* in stage 2.

Comparing the two *Masalas* using the rules of calculation we find them *Mutamathil* or identical, thus we take one of the two whole numbers to be used as the whole number of the final *Masala* of stage 3.

Dividing such a whole number between the heirs to define the shares of the legatee the mother gets 1, out of 6. $= 6 \div 6 = 1$.

The presumed father gets 1 out of 6. $= 6 \div 6 = 1$.

The son gets the residue $1 + 1 = 2$.

$6 - 2 = 4$. See Fig. 40 below.

Fig. 40

6	
1	M 1/6
5	S Res

Stage 1

6	
1	M 1/6
4	S Res
1	F Pres 1/6

Stage 2

	+1	
7	6	–6–
6	1	M 1/6
	4	S Res
X	1	F Pres 1/6
1		Leg=1

Stage 3

As the presumed father's share is 1 the legatee will also be given a share of one which is the equivalent of the father's thus to leave intact the whole number of the *Masala* 6, to be redivided between the surviving heirs only.

The whole number is 6. The basic portion of the mother is ⅙ and the son's portion is the remnant as he is a residuary. Here we are faced with a serious dilema because if we base our distribution on the basic portions of the heirs, the mother will get 1 from the whole number 6 which is exactly similar to the share she got when the presumed heir was supposed to be in existence. This will allow the son to get away with the remnant 5, which is obviously more than the share he would have got when the presumed heir was supposed to be in existence. This type of distribution is , of course, far from being just. Such a situation imposes a serious question. Was Al-Bahuti aware of what it would lead to and had overlooked it, or that he was unaware of it and was therefore caught unguarded?

As to the first part of the question, whether he was aware of the result and had intentionally overlooked it, is something that a great jurist (such as Al-Buhuti), who had written a number of books some of which were among the most authoritative law books and of high calibre, would certainly not have done.

We would rather consider that he was partly unaware of what it would lead to, because we think that had he been aware of it, he would have avoided it since he himself had proposed such a method. However, the truth about it lies as we see it with the fact that Al-Buhuti had perhaps found some examples from the old sources that he tried to formulate a pattern which led to a perfect solution. We have to say that he was partly successful. We say partly successful because it is apparent that he had not tested his method to prove the viability of its application in other cases.
The *Masala* as seen above had proved it to be defective and incomplete particularly at the end of his method. In the above *Masala* the possibility of basing the division of the whole number (after giving the legatee his share) between the surviving mother and son (with the heirs' fixed portions), would unjustly give the share of the presumed heir to the son only. This would not be accepted by most people.

So to complete the defective method we suggest the following steps.

Before repartitioning the whole number between the surviving heirs one has to work out the ratio between their shares which they have got from the whole number in the previous division when the presumed heir was supposed to be in existence. This is done by using the largest share as a denominator to the smaller share and simplifying them by dividing them in turn by a common divisor and to repeat it until one gets two numbers with no common divisor between them. So the ratio between the shares is as much as the ratio between the indivisible two numbers say 1:2 or 2:7 or 1:5, etc.

Add the ratios to each other and see if the whole number is divisible by the ratio or not. If it is then each heir will get from the whole number a share equivalent to the proportion he gets from the ratio and that will be the end of the *Masala*.

Alternatively, if the whole number is indivisible by the ratio then the ratio is to be used to multiply the total of the *Masala* to get what we may call *Tashih*. To give each beneficiary his share from the *Tashih*, multiply the collective share of the heirs (the whole number) by the ratio and divide the product on the ratio. Thus each heir shall get from the product a share equivalent to his proportion in the ratio.

And finally to get the legatee's share from the *Tashih* you simply multiply his share from the total by the ratio.

Accordingly, to divide the whole number of the above *Masala* 6, between the two surviving heirs, the mother and the son, equitably and fairly, we take the share of the mother from the whole number 1, and the share of the son from the whole number 4, 1 and 4 = 1:4, the ratio aggregate is 1 + 4 = 5.

The whole number is indivisible by the ratio so to make the *Tashih* we multiply the total by the ratio, 5 x 7 = 35.

The beneficiaries' shares from the *Tashih* are

5 x 6 = 30 for the mother and the son collectively, equal to every part of the ratio.

30 ÷ 5 = 6 for every part of the ratio from the *Tashih*.

1 x 6 = 6 for the mother from the *Tashih*.

4 x 6 = 24 for the son from the *Tashih*.

5 x 1 = 5 for the legatee, (his share from the total by the ratio).

See the chart below, Fig. 41.

Fig. 41

6	
1	**M ⅙**
5	**S Res**

Stage 1

6	
1	**M ⅙**
4	**S Res**
1	**F Pres ⅙**

Stage 2

	x5	**+1**	
35	**7**	**6**	**–6–**
6	**6**	**1**	**M ⅙**
24		**4**	**S Res**
X	**X**	**1**	**F Pres ⅙**
5	**1**		**Leg=1=5**

Stage 3

Another example of a practical modification of Al-Bahuti's method

If a person dies leaving a surviving son and a father and also a legacy of a share similar to the share of his presumed wife, the *Masala* will be calculated in accordance with the method of Al-Bahuti and the suggested modification as follows:

Applying the rules of calculation the whole number of the two *Masalas* 6 and 24 in stage 1 and 2 are *Mutadakhil* or concordent thus we take the largest of the two, 24, to be the whole number of the final *Masala* in stage 3.

Division of the whole number between the heirs (including the presumed one), gives each heir the following shares:
⅙ of the whole number = 24÷ ⅙ = 4 or 24 ÷ 6 = 4 for the father.
⅛ of the whole number = 24 ÷ ⅛ = 3 or 24 ÷ 8 = 3 for the presumed wife.
The residue = 24 − (4 + 3) = 17 for the son.

The legatee will be given an eqivalent to the share of the presumed wife 3 added to the whole number of the *Masala* 24.
3 + 24 = 27. The grand total of shares of all beneficiaries.

Deducting the share of the legatee from the grand total of shares leaves what will be the collective share of the surviving heirs 27 − 3 = 24.

The ratio of the heirs' shares from the whole number 4 and 17 = 4:17 have no lowest common multiple (L.C.M.), so the ratio is the aggregate of shares 4 + 17 = 21.

As the collective share of the heirs is indivisible by the ratio of their shares 24 ÷ 21 makes the *Tashih* a necessary thing which is obtained by multiplying the grand total by the ratio, 21 x 27 = 567 the *Tashih*.
The heirs' share from the *Tashih* are.
21 x 24 = 504 (the collective share by the ratio), for the heirs.
504 ÷ 21 = 24 the proportion equal to each part from the ratio.
4 x 24 = 96 for the father from the *Tashih*.
17 x 24 = 408 for the son from the *Tashih*.
21 x 3 = 63 for the legatee from the *Tashih*.

We could leave these figures as they are to be finale but as we are aiming to get as low a figure as possible in every *Masala* all the final figures (*Tashih* and the shares drawn from it), will be reduced by dividing them all by the L.C.M. (lowest common multiple), 3, that is to say,
567 ÷ 3 = 189 the aggregate of all shares.
96 ÷ 3 =32 for the father.
408 ÷ 3 = 136 for the son.
63 ÷ 3 = 21 for the legatee. See Fig. 42.

Fig. 42

6	
1	F ⅙
5	S Res

Stage 1

24	
4	F ⅙
17	S Res
3	W Pres ⅛

Stage 2

L W N	Tashih ÷3 L C M	G Total x21	+3	
189	567	27	24	– 24 –
32	96	24	4	F ⅙ 4:17
136	408		17	S Res
X	X	X	3	W Pres ⅛
21	63	3		Leg

Stage 3

An illustration to test the suggested modification on the method of Al-Bahuti

If a person dies leaving a daughter, a son's daughter and bequeaths a legacy similar to the share of the presumed full brother his *Masala* will be calculated as follows:

4 is the *Radd* of the *Masala* in stage 1 and 6 is the whole number of the *Masala* in stage 2. These two numbers are *Mutawafiq*, having a common factor. Applying the rule of *Mutawafiq* to the two numbers 4 and 6, the *Wifq* or factor of one of the two is multiplied with the other whole number, thus the whole number of the *Masala* in stage three is (3 x 4 = 12 or 2 x 6 = 12).

In distributing the whole number between the heirs, each heir will get the following:

½ of the whole number = 12 ÷ 2 = 6 or 12 ÷ ½ = 6 for the daughter
⅙ of the whole number = 12 ÷ 6 = 2 or 12 ÷ ⅙ = 2 for the son's daughter.
The residue = 12 − (6 + 2) = 4 for the presumed full brother.
An extra 4 for the legatee which is similar to the presumed full brother.
The grand total of shares are 12 + 4 = 16
The legatee's share from the grand total = 16 − 12 = 4.
The collective share of the surviving heirs from the grand total = 16 − 4 = 12 (previously called the whole number).
The ratio of the share taken by the surviving heirs from the whole number is 2:6 The two as such can be reduced 2/6 = ⅓ = 1:3. Thus the ratio between the daughter's share and the son's daughter's share is 3:1.
The ratio aggregate is 3 + 1 = 4.

Knowing the ratio between the two heirs we distribute their collective share 12, by the ratio giving each one a proportion equivalent to the shares he has in the ratio as follows:
12 ÷ 4 = 3 for each part of the ratio.
3 x 3 = 9 for the daughter.
1 x 3 = 3 for the son's daughter.
So from the grand total 16 the final shares are 9 for the daughter.
3 for the son's daughter and 4 for the legatee.

In this way the share accorded to the legatee, being that of the share of the presumed full brother, will also be distributed to the heirs according to their proportional shares from the whole number. See the chart below. Fig. 43.

Fig. 43

Radd	W N	
4	6	
3	3	D ½
1	1	S's D ⅙

Stage 1
3 + 1 = 4 The Radd Masala

6	
3	D ½
1	S's D ⅙
2	FB Pres Res

Stage 2

+4

16	12	= 2 x 6	
9	6	D ½	3:1
3	2	SD ⅙	
X	4	FB Pres	Res
4		Leg = 4	

Stage 3

Bequest of an heir's share with the exception of the share of a presumed heir

The jurists here talk about a bequest of a share of one of his heirs with the exception of the share of a presumed other one from the former, accordingly the share of the presumed heir is to be deducted from the legacy leaving it operative only by the difference between the two (the assumed and the presumed).

Illustration:

A person who has three sons bequeaths to someone a similar share as that of one of his sons with the exception of the share of the presumed fourth son.

Before we calculate this case we must refer to the fact that the jurists have decided that the legatee with the similar share as that of one of the heirs shall be given an added similar share. Therefore, in this case, the legatee will be counted as a fourth son so getting ¼ of the property. As this case also contains the exception of the share of the presumed fourth son from the legacy, the jurists have decided to apply the former presumption rule so the excepted share will not be the share of the fourth son but the share of a presumed fifth son

So to calculate this case it was thought better to be assisted by the method of Al-Bahuti with its three stages in addition to the application of the proposed method of the table chart as follows:

4 is the whole number of the *Masala* in stage one giving the legatee with the similar share as one son ¼.

5 is the whole number of the *Masala* in stage two counting the legatee as a fouth son and the presumed fourth son to be excepted as a fifth son thus giving him the ⅕.

To make the whole number of the final *Masala* in stage three we compare the whole number of the two *Masalas* in stage one and two. They are *Mutabayyn* so we multiply them or if the *Masala* is to become simpler we multiply the denominators of the share of the legatee by the excepted share by each other $4 \times 5 = 20$.

To define the legatee's share and the exception share from the whole number of the *Masala* we divide such a whole number by the two whole numbers of stage one and two thus to know the amount of shares each one of them gets.

$20 \div 4 = 5$ for the legatee.

$20 \div 5 = 4$ for the exceptioned.

Subtracting the exceptioned share from the legatee's share shows us the real legatee's share from the whole number of the third *Masala* $5 - 4 = 1$.

The total of the final *Masala* is formed by the addition of the real share of the legatee to the whole number $1 + 20 = 21$. The beneficiaries' shares from the whole number are

$21 - 20 = 1$ for the legatee.

$21 - 1 = 20$ for the heirs (the three sons collectively).

As 20 is indivisible between the three sons, we utilize the doctrine of *Tashib* as such.
20 is *Mutabayyn* with the number of sons 3, so 3 will be the segment of the fraction to be multiplied by the total 3 x 21 = 63.
Thus the beneficiaries' final shares from the *Tashib* are:
3 x 1 = 3 for the legatee.
3 x 20 = 60 for the three sons collectively.
60 ÷ 3 = 20 for each of the three sons. See the chart below. Fig. 44.

Fig. 44

4	
1	**S**
1	**S**
1	**S**
1	**Leg = ¼**

Stage 1

5	
1	**S**
1	**S**
1	**S**
1	**Leg Assumed**
1	**Presumed excep = ⅕**

Stage 2

	x3	**+1**	
63	**21**	**20**	**=4x5**
20	**20** {		**S**
20			**S**
20			**S**
3	**1**	**5**	**Ass H Leg 4=¼ By Subtract 5−4=1**
X	**X**	**4**	**Excep 5=⅕**
		1	**Resultant share of leg**

Stage 3

Another illustration:

The same course of calculation shall be followed if the person who has four sons bequeaths to someone an equivalent share as that of one of them with the exception of the share of a presumed fifth son.

The whole number of the *Masala* in stage 1 is 5 giving the legatee $\frac{1}{5}$ of it. $5 \times \frac{1}{5} = 1$ or $5 \div 5 = 1 = \frac{1}{5}$.
The whole number of the *Masala* in stage 2 is 6. Giving the excepted presumed son $\frac{1}{6}$ share of it. $6 \div 6 = 1 = \frac{1}{6}$.
The whole number of the final *Masala* in stage 3 is $5 \times 6 = 30$.
$30 \div 5 = 6$ the legatee's share from the whole number.
$30 \div 6 = 5$ the excepted presumed son's share from the the whole number.
$6 - 5 = 1$ the real share of the legatee.
$1 + 30 = 31$ the grand total of the *Masala* (the whole number plus the real legatee's share).
$31 - 1 = 30$ the collective share of the four sons from the grand total.
$30 \div 4 =$ the collective share of the four sons from the grand total is indivisible by their number and by comparing the two numbers they are *Mutawafiq* (have a common factor) so we take the *Wifq* or factor of the number of sons as the segment of the fraction for the calculation of *Tashih* $4 \div 2 = 2$.
$2 \times 31 = 62$ The *Tashih*.
$2 \times 1 = 2$ for the legatee (his final share from the *Tashih*).
$2 \times 30 = 60$ for the four sons (their share from the *Tashih*).
$60 \div 4 = 15$ the share of each one of the four sons from the *Tashih*.)
See Fig. 45.

BEQUEST WITH A DOUBLE PRESUMPTION WITH AN EXCEPTION

The double presumption occurs where the person who has two sons (for instance), bequeaths a share similar to that of an assumed third son with the exception of the share of a presumed fourth son.

The calculation of this *Masala* could be done in three stages as we have done before. The *Masala* of the first stage is for the legal heirs, the legatee and the presumed heir whose share was similar to a third son. Applying the *Tashih* the *Masala* is 8 in stage one. Out of it the share of the legatee is $2 = \frac{2}{8} = \frac{1}{4}$.

The *Masala* of the second stage is for the legal heirs, the assumed heir and the excepted heir whose share has been likened to the share of the presumed heir. Applying the *Tashih* makes the *Masala* 15. Out of it the excepted share is $3 = \frac{3}{15} = \frac{1}{5}$.

As the *Masala* is becoming simpler by multiplying the denominator of the fraction of the legatee's share from stage one by the denominator of the fraction of the excepted share from stage two we shall form the whole number of the final *Masala* by multiplying them by each other instead of multiplying the two *Tashihs*. $4 \times 5 = 20$.

Fig. 45

5	
1	**S**
1	**S**
1	**S**
1	**S**
1	**Leg = ⅕**

Stage 1

6	
1	**S**
1	**S**
1	**S**
1	**S**
1	**Leg Assumed Heir**
1	**S Excep Pres = ⅙**

Stage 2

	x2	**+1**		
62	**31**	**30**	**=6x5**	
15			**S**	
15			**S**	
15			**S**	
15			**S**	
2	**1**	**6**	**Ass heir** **Leg = ⅕**	**By Subtract** **6 − 5 = 1**
X	**X**	**5**	**Ex Pres = ⅙**	**Resultant share of leg**

Stage 3

¼ of the whole number = 20 ÷ ¼ = 5 or 20 ÷ 4 = 5 for the legatee.
⅕ of the whole number = 20 ÷ ⅕ = 4 or 20 ÷ 5 = 4 for the exception.
5 − 4 = 1 for the legatee as his real share.
The grand total of the *Masala* = 1 + 20 = 21.
21 − 20 = 1 for the legatee from the grand total.
21 − 1 = 20 for the two sons from the grand total.
20 ÷ 2 = 10 for each of the two sons from the grand total. See Fig. 46.

Fig. 46

	x2	+1	
8	4	3	
3	3	1	S — 2
3		1	S
X	X	1	S Pres
2	1		Leg = 2/8 = 1/4

Stage 1

	x3	+1		
15	5	4		
4		1	S	3
4	4	1	S	
4		1	S Leg	
X	X	1	S Pres	
3	1		Ex = 3/15 = 1/5	

Stage 2

	+1		
21	20	= 4 x 5	
10		S	
10		S	
1	5	Ass. heir leg. 1/4	By subtract 5 − 4 = 1 Resultant share of leg
X	4	Ex. 1/5	

Stage 3

The *Masala* could also be done in one stage only such as this. Counting beside the two sons the first presumed son as the third, counting the legatee as the fourth son and the exception presumed as the fifth son. The share of the legatee is to be taken from the *Masala* as if no exception existed in the *Masala*, giving him $\frac{1}{5}$ as if he were the fourth son. Then to consider the legatee as the fourth and add the exception as the fifth son to take from the *Masala* a fifth out of a fourth.

The whole number is the product of multiplying the two denominators by each other, $4 \times 5 = 20$.

$20 \div 4 = 5$ for the legatee.

$20 \div 5 = 4$ for the exception.

Subtracting the exceptional share from the legatee's, the difference is the real share of the legatee, $5 - 4 = 1$ $\frac{1}{20}$.

The grand total $= 1 + 20 = 21$.

	+1		
21	**20**	**= 4 x 5**	
10		**1.S**	
10		**2.S**	
X		**3.S.Pres.**	
1	**5**	**4 S.Leg. = ¼**	**By subtract**
			5 − 4 = 1
X	**4**	**5 S.Ex. = ⅕**	
	1	**Resultant share of the legatee**	

Fig. 47

From the grand total 21 − 20 = 1 for the legatee.
21 − 1 = 20 for the two sons.
20 ÷ 2 = 10 for each of the two sons. See Fig. 47.

Another illustration:

The *Masala* of a person who has four sons bequeaths a share equivalent to that of an assumed fifth son with the exception of the share of a presumed sixth son, will be calculated in the same way as we have done before as follows:

The *Tashih* of the *Masala* in stage one, with the four sons, the assumed son and the legatee whose share has been likened to the assumed is 24. Out of it 4 is the share of the legatee = $4/24$ = $1/6$.

The *Tashih* of the *Masala* in stage two, with the four sons, the assumed son, whose the legatee's share has been likened to, as the fifth son, the presumed sixth son, whose similar share is to be excepted from the legacy, and finally the legacy of the similar share of the presumed sixth son which will be the subject of exception, is 35. Out of it the share of the legacy to be excepted from the legatee's share is 5 = $5/35$ = $1/7$.

The whole number of the final *Masala* of stage three is the product of multiplying the denominators of the legatee and the excepted legacy $1/6$ and $1/7$ from the two *Masalas* of stage one and two, that is, 6 x 7 = 42.
$1/6$ of the whole number = 42 ÷ $1/6$ = 7 or 42 ÷ 6 = 7 for the legatee.
$1/7$ of the whole number = 42 ÷ 7 = 6 or 42 ÷ $1/7$ = 6 for the excepted share.
7 − 6 = 1 the real share of the legatee.
The grand total = 1 + 42 = 43.
43 − 42 = 1 for the legatee from the grand total.
43 − 1 = 42 for the four sons from the grand total.
42 ÷ 4 = the share of the four sons from the grand total is indivisible on their number to make the *Tashih* necessary.
42 and 4 are *Mutawafiq*. The *Wifq* or factor of the sons is 4 ÷ 2 = 2 to be taken as the segment of the fraction.
2 x 43 = 86 the *Tashih*, (the segment multiplied by the grand total).
2 x 1 = 2 the legatee's final share from the *Tashih*.
2 x 42 = 84 the collective share of the four sons from the *Tashih*.
84 ÷ 4 = 21 the share of each of the four sons from the *Tashih*.
See Fig. 48.

The same *Masala* could also be done in one stage only by counting beside the four sons the first presumed son as the fifth son, counting also the legatee as the sixth son and the exception as the seventh son. The share of the legatee is to be taken from the *Masala*, as if no exception existed in the *Masala*, is $1/6$, as if he were the sixth son. Then to consider the legatee as the sixth son and add the exception as the seventh son take from the *Masala* $1/7$ as if the exception is the seventh son.

Fig. 48

	x4	+1		
24	6	5		
5	5	1	S	4 Sons
5		1	S	
5		1	S	
5		1	S	
X	X	1	S Pres	
4	1		Leg = $\frac{4}{24} = \frac{1}{6}$	

Stage 1

	x2	+1		
14	7	6		
3	6	1	S	2 Segment
3		1	S	
3		1	S	
3		1	S	
X	X	1	Leg Ass S	
X	X	1	S Pres Ex	
2	1		Excepted $\frac{2}{14} = \frac{1}{7}$	

Stage 2

	x2	+1	
86	**43**	**42**	**=6x7**
21			**S**
21	42		**S**
21			**S**
21			**S**
2	**1**	7	**Leg** 1/6 **By Subtract 7−6=1**
X	**X**	6	**Exception** 1/7 **The real share for the legatee**
		1	**Resultant share of the legatee**

Stage 3

The whole number of the *Masala* is the product of multiplying the denominator of the share of the legatee by the denominator if the excepted share 6 x 7 = 42.
For the legatee from the whole number = 42 +6 = 7.
For the exception from the whole number = 42 + 7 = 6.
Subtracting the exception share from the legatee's share the difference will be the real share of the legatee 7 − 6 = 1.
The grand total = 1 + 42 = 43.
For the legatee from the whole number = 42 ÷ 6 = 7.
For the exception from the whole number = 42 ÷ 7 = 6.
42 + 4 = indivisible.
The *Tashih* = 2 x 43 = 86.
The legatee's share = 2 x 1 = 2.
The share of the four sons = 86 − 2 = 84.
The share of each son = 84 ÷ 4 = 21.
See Fig. 49.

	x2	+1		
86	43	42	=6x7	
21			S 1	
21	42 {		S 2	2
21			S 3	Segment of the fraction
21			S 4	
X	X		S Pres 5	
2	1	7	Leg 6 = 1/7	7 − 6 = 1
X	X	6	Excep 7 = 1/6	
		1		

Fig. 49

The approach of Ibn Qudama, in his famous book, *Al-Mughni* on which the book called the Great Commentary was based, the above two *Masalas* were different from the approach taken by a great number of Hanbali jurists. In the latter *Masala*, for instance, he considered the legatee's share to be the result of excepting or say, subtracting 1/6 from 1/5 of the *Masala*. However, such a result can only be conceived by the entire deletion of the assumed heir, replacing him by the legatee as the fifth son and bringing the exception as the sixth son. This is similar to al-Shafi'i's way of calculating such problems.

In an excellent and comprehensive scrutiny of such an approach and a review of all the Hanbali opinions related to this point, Al-Mirdawi[22] has concluded that the famous opinion of Ibn Qudama in his *Masala* was ambiguous to rules set up, by the companions (Hanbali jurists), and inconsistent with their method in this *Masala* and in similar ones. He also added that, if we were to compare the above *Masala* with the views of the companions (the Hanbali jurists), the testator would have been bequeathing the 1/6 of his property with the exception of 1/7. So the legatee will get one share from forty two shares.

BEQUEST OF A PORTION OF THE TESTATOR'S ESTATE

This kind of bequest consists of two types: A bequest of an unspecified portion, and, a bequest of a fixed portion.

The bequest of an unspecified portion is subdivided into a negligible portion and a general portion.

The bequest of a negligible portion

This is a bequest of unspecified and an insignificant portion such as the testator saying 'Give *X* something or some of my property'. This has been interpreted as if the testator has instucted a trivial amount to *X*. The value of this sort of bequest is left to the discretion of the heirs to define.

The bequest with a general portion

This bequest is considered effective and can be enforced by law, unlike that of a negligible bequest. The value of the general portion has been defined by the Hanbalis as coming from a precedent set by the Prophet (peace be upon him) in which a man was reported by Ibn Mas'ud to have bequeathed a general portion. The Prophet gave (the legatee), a sixth. The Hanbalis have also supported such view by quoting the reported *Fatwas* or legal decisions of the two companions Ali and Ibn Mas'ud that 'The general portion equals a sixth'. And also that that Iyas b.Mu'awiyah was reported to say that the general portion in the Arabic colloquial language is a sixth. Moreover, they say, the sixth is the lowest portion allocated to a blood relative heir, accordingly, they say, the general portion bequeathed will be treated as a sixth just as if it were a portion fixed by the *Quran*.
Illustration:

If a person bequeathed a general portion and dies leaving his father and son his *Masala* will be calculated as follows:

Applying the rules of calculation the whole number of the *Masala* is 6.
$\frac{1}{6}$ of the whole number $= 6 \div \frac{1}{6} = 1$ or $6 \div 6 = 1$ for the father.
$\frac{1}{6}$ of the whole number $= 6 \div \frac{1}{6} = 1$ or $6 \div 6 = 1$ for the legatee.
The residue $= 6 - (1 + 1) = 4$ for the Son. See Fig. 50.

Fig. 50

6		
1	**F**	**⅙**
4	**S Res**	
1	**Leg**	**⅙**

Another illustration:

A limitation to the general portion bequeathed is that the legatee will not be eligible to gain more under the doctrine of *Radd*, return since it is only the right of the blood relation. Thus, in the case when a person bequeaths a general portion dies leaving only his mother, the legatee will be allowed only one sixth while the rest will go to the mother as such:

6 is the whole number of the *Masala*.

⅓ of the whole number = 6 ÷ ⅓ = 2 or 6 ÷ 3 = 2 for the mother.

⅙ of the whole number = 6 ÷ ⅙ = 1 or 6 ÷ 6 = 1 for the legatee.

2 + 1 = 3. The shares withdrawn from the whole number of the *Masala* by the mother and the legatee according to their allocated portions.

6 − 3 = 3. The unexhausted shares of the *Masala*.

Applying the doctrine of *Radd* the unexhausted share will be added to the mother's shares since she is the sole blood relative in the *Masala* so her share will become 2 + 3 = 5. Thus giving as a final distribution 1 = ⅙, to the legatee and 5 = ⅚ to the mother.

See Fig. 51.

Fig. 51

6	6		
3+2= 5	2	M	⅓
1	1	Leg	⅙

6 − 3 = 3 This remnant augments the share of the mother as the sole heir.

A third illustration:

The general portion bequeathed will still be eligible to be satisfied even when the basic portions of the heirs have already exhausted the shares of the *Masala*. This is to be worked out by letting the legatee compete with ⅙ against the heirs through the application of the doctrine of *'Awl* or increase as follows:

If a woman bequeaths a general portion to someone and then dies leaving a husband and a sister, the *Masala* will be worked out as follows:

6 is the whole number of the *Masala*.

½ of the whole number = 6 ÷ ½ = 3 or 6 ÷ 2 = 3 for the husband.

½ of the whole number = 6 ÷ ½ = 3 or 6 ÷ 2 = 3 for the sister.

⅙ of the whole number = 6 ÷ ⅙ = 1 or 6 ÷ 6 = 1 for the legatee.

3 + 3 + 1 = 7 the aggregate of the beneficiaries shares form the *Masala*

6 ÷ 7 = the whole number is indivisible by the aggregate of shares drawn from it thus we apply the doctrine of *'Awl* by placing the aggregate as the *Masala* instead of the indivisible whole number thus to refer the shares to the *'Awl* 7 and not to the *Masala* 6.

3/6 of the husband is reduced to 3/7 to agree with the *'Awl*.
3/6 of the sister is reduced to 3/7 to agree with the *'Awl*.
1/6 of the legatee is reduced to 1/7 to agree with the *'Awl*.
3/7 + 3/7 + 1/7 = 7/7 = 1
See Fig. 52.

Fig. 52

+1			
7	**6**		
3	**3**	**H**	**½**
3	**3**	**Sis**	**½**
1	**1**	**Leg**	**⅙**

7 − 6 = 1 deficit

A fourth illustration:

The general portion bequeathed will also be allowed to compete against the heirs' portions as in the above *Masala* even though the basic portions of the heirs have not only exhausted the shares of the *Masala* but have already exceeded it as in the case when a woman who bequeaths a general portion to someone dies leaving a husband a mother, a father and two daughters.

Applying the rules of calculation the whole number of the *Masala* is 12.
1/4 of the whole number = 12 ÷ 1/4 = 3 or 12 ÷ 4 = 3 for the husband.
1/6 of the whole number = 12 ÷ 1/6 = 2 or 12 ÷ 6 = 2 for the mother.
1/6 of the whole number = 12 ÷ 1/6 = 2 or 12 ÷ 6 = 2 for the father.
2/3 of the whole number = 12 ÷ 2/3 = 8 or 12 ÷ 3 = 4 x 2 = 8 for the two daughters.
1/6 of the whole number = 12 ÷ 1/6 = 2 or 12 ÷ 6 = 2 for the legatee.
3 + 2 + 2 + 8 + 2 = 17. The aggregate of the shares from the *Masala* is exceeding that of the whole number and by the application of the doctrine of *'Awl* the aggregate is to replace the whole number, as such:
3/12 of the husband is reduced to 3/17 to agree with the *'Awl*.
2/12 of the mother is reduced to 2/17 to agree with the *'Awl*.
2/12 of the father is reduced to 2/17 to agree with the *'Awl*.
8/12 of the two daughters is reduced 8/17 to agree with the *'Awl*.
2/12 of the legatee is reduced to 2/17 to agree with the *'Awl*.
3/17 + 2/17 + 2/17 + 8/17 + 2/17 = 1
See Fig. 53.

+5

Fig. 53

17	**12**			
3	**3**	**H**	**¼**	
2	**2**	**M**	**⅙**	
2	**2**	**F**	**⅙**	
8	**8**	**2 D**	**⅔**	**four shares each daughter**
2	**2**	**Leg**	**⅙**	

17 − 12 = 5 deficit

The idea of this was instigated by the Hanabalis' tendency to compare the bequest of the general portion to the minimal basic portion inherited by an heir, that is ⅙ which led them to impose it on the *Masala* in order to compete with the allocated portions of the heirs rather than being given a ⅙ outright as we have already seen above.

The bequest with a specific portion

The specific portion bequeathed could involve either one share or more in the *Masala*. For each type the jurists have recommended a special method with which to ensure a fair distribution between the legatees and heirs, as we shall see in the following.

1. *Bequest with one specific portion*

The denominator of the fraction of the bequest with one specific portion is to be made the whole number of the *Masala*. Thus, if the testator bequeaths one fourth of his estate to someone and then dies leaving three sons, 4 the denominator of the fraction is to be the whole number so to give the legatee 1 out of the whole number 4 ÷ 4 = 1 and the rest of the whole number (4 − 1 = 3), is the share of the three sons from the whole number (3 ÷ 3 = 1), so to give one share to each son. See Fig. 54.

To make a precise distribution we should take as a pattern in all cases of similar sort, model charts of the latter jurists. We suggest such cases to be worked out in the same way as we have done in the cases of *Radd* or return (the doctrine of *Radd*), where a husband or wife survives with blood relatives, placing the bequest *Masala* inside the recommended chart instead of the spouse *Masala*. (Next to it is the succession *Masala* and then the

4		
1	**Leg**	¼
1	**S**	
1	**S**	
1	**S**	

Fig. 54

comprehensive *Masala*.) Thus we make three *Masalas*, the bequest *Masala* is (the denominator of its fraction), the succession *Masala* (containing the heirs), and then the comprehensive *Masala* (the product of multiplying the bequest *Masala* by either the entire or the *Wifq* (factor), according to the result of comparing the succession *Masala* with the collective share of the heirs from the bequest *Masala*, whether they be *Mutabayyn* or *Mutawafiq* only. The comprehensive is where each one of the legatees and heirs will take their final shares).

Accordingly, the above *Masala* with a bequest of ¼ and three sons will be worked out as follows:

4 is the whole number of the bequest *Masala* as it is the denominator of the fraction bequeathed.

¼ of the whole number = 4 ÷ ¼ = 1 or 4 ÷ 4 = 1 for the legatee.

The residue = 4 − 1 = 3 the collective share of the sons.

3 is the whole number of the succession *Masala* as it is the number of sons who inherit equally per capita shares.

3 ÷ 3 = 1 for each son.

The comprehensive *Masala* is usually the product of multiplying the bequest *Masala* by the whole number of the succession *Masala*. But since the succession *Masala* and the collective share of the heirs from the bequest in this case are *Mutawafiq* by ⅓. So the comprehensive *Masala* is 1 x 4 = 4.

The share of the legatee from the comprehensive *Masala* is the product of multiplying his share from the bequest *Masala* by the *Wifq* or factor of the succession *Masala* 1 x 1 = 1.

The share of each son from the comprehensive *Masala* is the product of multiplying each one's share from the succession *Masala* by the *Wifq* or factor of their collective share from the bequest *Masala*.

1 x 1 = 1 for the first son.

1 x 1 = 1 for the second son.

1 x 1 = 1 for the third son. See Fig. 55.

Comp M	Suc M	Beq M	
4	3	4	
1		1	Leg ¼
1	1		S
1	1	3	S
1	1		S

Fig. 55

Our suggested method is more useful when the specific portion bequeathed is a fraction bigger than the bequeathable one third (or when the bequest contains more than one fraction as we shall see later), where the bequest needed the approval of the heirs to the excessive part if it is to be operative.

Illustration:

If a person who had bequeathed ½ of his property to a person dies leaving his mother and two uterine brothers, his *Masala* will be calculated differently acccording to the approval or the disapproval of his heirs to the excessive bequest, using the suggested method as follows:

Calculation when the excessive bequest is approved.

2 is the whole number of the bequest *Masala* (the denominator of its fraction).

½ of the whole number $= 2 \div \frac{1}{2} - 1$ or $2 \div 2 = 1$ for the legatee.

The residue $= 2 - 1 = 1$ the collective share of the heirs.

6 is the whole number of the succession *Masala* and by applying the doctrine of *Radd* or return, the *Masala* is 3.

From the *Radd Masala* there is 1 for the mother and 2 for the two uterine brothers.

The comprehensive *Masala* is $3 \times 2 = 6$ (the bequest *Masala* multiplied by the succession *Masala*).

$3 \times 1 = 3$ (the legatee's share by the succession *M.*) for the legatee.

$1 \times 1 = 1$ (the remnant from the bequest *M.* by the mother's share from the succession *M.*) for the mother.

$2 \times 1 = 2$ (the collective share from the bequest *M.* by the share of the two uterine brothers from the succession *M.*) for the uterine brothers.

$2 \div 2 = 1$ for each of the two uterine brothers.

See Fig. 56.

Fig. 56

Comp M	Suc M		Beq M		
6 = 3 x 2	3	6	2		
3			1	Leg	½
1	1	1	1	M	⅙
2	2	2		2 UB	⅓

1 + 2 = 3 This becoming the Radd Masala

But the calculation of the *Masala* when the bequest is disapproved of is as follows:

When the heirs disapprove of the excessive bequest where the bequest consists of one fraction only the whole number of the bequest *Masala* will be 3.

From the whole number of the bequest *Masala* 1 for the legatee equals the disposable third 3 ÷ 3 = 1.

From the whole number of the bequest *Masala* 2 for the heirs equals the remaining two thirds 3 − 1 = 2 which is called the remnant.

The whole number of the succession *Masala* is 6, but as the shares of the heirs 3, in the *Masala* are less than the whole number, the application of the doctrine of *Radd* is considered so the *Radd Masala* will be 3, which is divided as such:

1 share for the mother and 2 shares for the two uterine brothers.

Comparing the *Radd* in the succession *Masala* with the remnant from the bequest *Masala* we find them *Mutabayyn* or incompatible, so the comprehensive *Masala* becomes the product of multiplying the bequest *Masala* by the succession *Masala* 3 x 3 − 9.

From the comprehensive *Masala* the beneficiaries shares are
3 x 1 = 3 (the legatee's share by the succession M.) for the legatee.
1 x 2 = 2 (the mother's share from the succession M by the remnant from the bequest M.) for the mother.
2 x 2 = 4 (the share of the two uterine brothers from the succession M by the remnant from the bequest M.) for the two uterine brothers.
4 ÷ 2 = 2 for each of the two uterine brothers. See Fig. 57.

Fig. 57

Comp M	Suc M	Beq M	
9=3x3	3 6	3	
3		1	Leg ½
2	1 1	2	M ⅙
4	2 2		2 UB ⅓

1 + 2 = 3 Radd Masala

Comp M	Suc M	Beq M	
18=6x3	6	3	
12		2	Leg ⅔
3	3		D ½
1	1	1	S's D ⅙
2	2		F Res

Fig. 58

Another illustration:

If a person who has bequeathed ⅔ of his property to someone leaves a daughter, a son's daughter and a father, his *Masala* (when it is approved of) will be calculated as follows:

3 is the whole number of the bequest *Masala* as it is the denominator of the only fraction bequeathed.

⅔ of the whole number = 3 x ⅔ = 2 or 3 ÷ 3 = 1 x 2 = 2 for the legatee.

3 − 2 = 1 the remnant for the heirs collectively.

6 is the whole number of the succession *Masala*.

½ of the whole number = 6 x ½ = 3 or 6 ÷ 2 = 3 for the daughter.

⅙ of the whole number = 6 x ⅙ = 1 or 6 ÷ 6 = 1 for the son's daughter.

The residue = 6 − (3 + 1) = 2 for the father.

Comparing the succession *Masala* with the remnant from the bequest *Masala* we find them to be *Mutabayyn*. The comprehensive *Masala* will therefore become the product of multiplying the bequest *Masala* by the succession *Masala* 3 x 6 = 18.

The final beneficiaries' shares are:
6 x 2 = 12 for the legatee (his share from the bequest M. by the succession M.)
3 x 1 = 3 for the daughter (her share from the succession M. by the remnant).
1 x 1 = 1 for the son's daughter (her share from the succession M. by the remnant).
2 x 1 = 2 for the father (his share from the succession M. by the remnant). See Fig. 58.
But when the heirs disapprove of the excessive part of the bequest in the above *Masala* it will be worked out as follows:

As the disapproval of the heirs to the excessive part of the bequest leads to the confinement of the bequest within the disposable one third so the whole number of the bequest *Masala* will always be 3 as long as the bequest consists of one fraction only.
$\frac{1}{3}$ of the whole number = 3 x $\frac{1}{3}$ = 1 or 3 ÷ 3 = 1 for the legatee.
$\frac{2}{3}$ of the whole number = 3 x $\frac{2}{3}$ = 2 the remnant for the heirs.

The whole number of the succession *Masala* is 6.
$\frac{1}{2}$ of the whole number = 6 x $\frac{1}{2}$ = 3 or 6 ÷ 2 = 3 for the daughter.
$\frac{1}{6}$ of the whole number = 6 x $\frac{1}{6}$ = 1 or 6 ÷ 6 = 1 for the son's daughter.
The residue = 6 − (3 + 1) = 2 for the father.

The comprehensive *Masala* is calculated as follows:
Comparing the succession *Masala* 6 with the remnant from the bequest *Masala* 2, we find them to be *Mutawafiq* by $\frac{1}{2}$.
6 ÷ 2 = 3 the *Wifq* factor of the succession *Masala*.
2 ÷ 2 = 1 the *Wifq* factor of the remnant from the bequest *Masala*.
The comprehensive *Masala* will therefore become the product of multiplying the bequest *Masala* by the *Wifq* of the succession *Masala* 3 x 3 = 9.
The final distribution of the beneficiaries' shares will be done as follows:
3 x 1 = 3 for the legatee (his share from the bequest *Masala* by the *Wifq* of the succession *Masala*).
3 x 1 = 3 for the daughter (her share from the succession *Masala* by the *Wifq* of the remnant).
1 x 1 = 1 for the son's daughter (her share from succession *Masala* by the *Wifq* of the remnant).
2 x 1 = 2 for the father (his share from the succession *Masala* by the *Wifq* of the remnant). See Fig. 59.

Comp M	Suc M	Beq M		
9=3x3	6	3		
3		1	Leg	⅔
3	3		D	½
1	1	2	SD	⅙
2	2		F	Res

Fig. 59

Comp M	Suc M	Beq M		
48=12x4	12	4		
36		3	Leg	¾
2	2		GM	⅙
3	3	1	H	¼
7	7		S	Res

Fig. 60

A third illustration:

If a testatrix who has bequeathed three quarters of her estate to someone dies leaving a grandmother, a husband and a son, her *Masala* will be calculated when the excessive bequest was approved by the heirs as such:

The whole number of the bequest *Masala* is 4 (the denominator of the only fraction bequeathed).

¾ of the whole number = 4 x ¾ = 3 for the legatee.

The remnant = 4 − 3 = 1 for the heirs collectively.

Applying the rules of calculation the whole number of the succession *Masala* is 2 x 6 = 12.

⅙ of the whole number = 12 x ⅙ = 2 for the grandmother.

¼ of the whole number = 12 x ¼ = 3 for the husband.

The residue = 12 − (2 + 3) = 7 for the son.

Because the comparison between the succession *Masala* and the remnant from the bequest *Masala* confirmed them to be *Mutabayyn* the comprehensive *Masala* is to become the product of multiplying the succession *Masala* by the bequest *Masala* as follows: 12 x 4 = 48.

The beneficiaries' shares from the comprehensive *Masala* are 12 x 3 = 36 for the legatee (his share from the bequest *Masala* by the succession *Masala*).

2 x 1 = 2 for the grandmother (her share from the succession *Masala* by the remnant from the bequest *Masala*).

3 x 1 = 3 for the husband (his share from the succession *Masala* by the remnant from the bequest *Masala*).

7 x 1 = 7 for the son (his share from the succession *Masala* by the remnant from the bequest *Masala*). See Fig. 60.

But if the excessive part of the same *Masala* were to be disapproved of by the heirs the *Masala* will be calculated as follows:

Disapproval of the excessive bequest by the heirs acts to confine the bequest to the disposable one third so the whole number of the bequest *Masala* will, as always, be 3.

⅓ of the whole number = 3 x ⅓ = 1 for the legatee.

The remnant ⅔ of the whole number = 3 x ⅔ = 2 for the heirs collectively.

The whole number of the succession *Masala* is 2 x 6 = 12.

⅙ of the whole number = 12 x ⅙ = 2 for the grandmother.

¼ of the whole number = 12 x ¼ = 3 for the husband.

The residue = 12 − (2 + 3) = 7 for the son.

As the comparison between the succession *Masala* and the remnant from the bequest *Masala* 2 shows the two to be *Mutawafiq* by ½.

12 ÷ 2 = 6 the *Wifq* or factor of the succession *Masala*.

2 ÷ 2 = 1 the *Wifq* or factor of the remnant from the bequest *Masala*.

So the comprehensive *Masala* will be the product of multiplying the bequest *Masala* by the *Wifq* of the succession *Masala* 6 x 3 = 18.

The beneficiaries shares from the comprehensive *Masala* are:

6 x 1 = 6 for the legatee (his share from the bequest *Masala* by the *Wifq* of the succession *Masala*).

2 x 1 = 2 for the grandmother (her share from the succession *Masala* by the *Wifq* of the remnant from the bequest *Masala*).

3 x 1 = 3 for the husband (his share from the succession *Masala* by the *Wifq* of the remnant from the bequest *Masala*).

7 x 1 = 7 for the son (his share from the succession *Masala* by the *Wifq* of the remnant from the bequest *Masala*). See Fig. 61.

When the bequeathed portion was granted to two or more legatees, each of the legatees shall take his share from the calculated *Masala* without extra calculation when their share from the comprehensive *Masala* is divisible by the legatees number. But when such a share becomes indivisible each one's share will be defined by the ordinary means of *Tashih*.[23] By comparing the collective share of the legatees with their number (making use of the aforementioned rules of calculation) and then to multiply the result which is

18=6x3	12	3		
6		1	Leg	¾
2	2		GM	⅙
3	3	2	H	¼
7	7		S	Res

Fig. 61

called the segment of the fraction with the comprehensive *Masala* giving each beneficiary his share from the comprehensive *Masala* multiplied by the segment of the fraction (with the collective share of the legatees being divided between them). Thus if a testator who had bequeathed half of his property to three legatees, *X,Y,Z,* and left a wife and a son the calculation of his *Masala*, when the excessive bequest is approved, will be done as follows:
2 is the whole number of the bequest *Masala* as it is the denominator of the fraction bequeathed. ½ of the whole number = 2 x ½ = 1 or 2 ÷ 2 = 1 for the three legatees.
2 − 1 = 1 the remnant for the heirs collectively.
8 is the whole number of the succession *Masala*.
⅛ of the whole number = 8 x ⅛ = 1 or 8 ÷ 8 = 1 for the wife.
The residue = 8 − 1 = 7 for the son.

The comprehensive *Masala* is 2 x 8 = 16 (the succession *Masala* multiplied by the bequest *Masala*).

The beneficiaries' shares from the comprehensive *Masala* are:
1 x 8 = 8 for the three legatees.
1 x 1 = 1 for the wife.
1 x 7 = 7 for the son.

But as 8, the three legatee's share fom the comprehensive *Masala* is indivisible between them we resort to the doctrine of *Tashih*.
By comparing the legatee's share 8 with their number 3, we find the two are *Mutabayyn*. Thus we take 3 as the segment of the fraction to multiply the comprehensive *Masala* where the product will be divisible between the beneficiaries as follows:
3 x 16 = 48 the *Tashih* of the comprehensive *Masala*.
3 x 8 = 24 the legatee's collective share.
24 ÷ 3 = 8 for each of the three legatees.
3 x 1 = 3 for the wife.
3 x 7 = 21 for the son. See Fig. 62.

Fig. 62

Com Tashih	Com M x3	Suc M x2	Beq M		
48	16	8	2		
8				X	
8	8		1	Y	½
8				Z	
3	1	1		W	⅛
			1		
21	7	7		S	Res

Comprehensive Masala
Approved

As to the same *Masala* when the excessive bequest is disapproved of by the heirs it will be worked out as follow:

3 is the whole number of the bequest *Masala*, the denominator of the disposable one third.
3 x ⅓ = 1 or 3 ÷ 3 = 1 for the three legatees collectively.
3 − 1 = 2 the remnant for the heirs collectively.

8 is the whole number of the succession *Masala*, the denominator of the hereditable portion.
8 x ⅛ = 1 or 8 ÷ 8 = 1 for the wife.
The residue = 8 − 1 = 7 for the son.

The comprehensive *Masala* is obtained by multiplying the bequest *Masala* by the *Wifq* of the succession *Masala* and the product divided between the beneficiaries, as such:
3 x 4 = 12.
1 x 4 = 4 the collective share of the three legatees from the comprehensive *Masala*.
1 x 1 = 1 for the wife from the comprehensive *Masala*.
1 x 7 = 7 for the son from the comprehensive *Masala*.

Applying the *Tashih*, to the comprehensive *Masala* as the collective share of the three legatees 4 is indivisible by their number 3, thus we find the two *Mutabayyn*. This leaves 3 the number of legatees to be multiplied by the comprehensive *Masala* as it is the segment of the fraction 3 x 12 = 36.

Out of this *Tashih* the beneficiaries' final shares are:

3 x 4 = 12 the collective share for the three legatees from the *Tashih*.
12 ÷ 3 = 4 for each of the three legatees, from the *Tashih*.
3 x 1 = 3 for the wife (her share from the *Tashih*).
3 x 7 = 21 for the son, his share from the *Tashih*. See Fig. 63.

Fig. 63

Com Tashih	Com M x3	Suc M 4 x 3	Beq M		
36	12	8	3		
4				X	
4	4		1	Y	½
4				Z	
3	1	1	2	W	⅛
21	7	7		S	Res

Disapproved M

2. *Bequest with more than one specific portion*

The juristic method of solving cases with more than one fraction bequeathed is slightly different from their method of solving cases with only one fraction as we have seen in the previous cases.

The use of the table suggested for the doctrine of *Radd* (where one of the spouses existed as well as the blood relatives) can also be used in the new situation.

2a. Illustration

In the case of a person who has bequeathed ⅕ of his estate to X and ⅓ to Y dies leaving his wife, daughter and father, his *Masala* in the case of its being approved of or disapproved of by the heirs is calculated as follows:

Calculation where the excessive bequest is approved by the heirs.

The whole number of the bequest Masala (when the bequest was approved), is the product of multiplying the denominators of the fractions bequeathed 3 x 5 − 15.
⅕ of the whole number = 15 x ⅕ = 3 or 15 ÷ 5 = 3 for the legatee X.
⅓ of the whole number = 15 x ⅓ = 5 or 15 ÷ 3 = 5 for the legatee Y.
The aggregate = 3 + 5 = 8.
The remnant = 15 − 8 = 7 for the heirs collectively.

The whole number of the succession *Masala* is 8.
⅛ of the whole number = 8 x ⅛ = 1 or 8 ÷ 8 = 1 for the wife.
½ of the whole number = 8 x ½ = 4 or 8 ÷ 2 = 4 for the daughter.

The aggregate = 1 + 4 = 5.
The residue = 8 − 5 = 3 for the father.

Comparing the succession *Masala* (8) with the remnant from the bequest *Masala* (7) we find the two are *Mutabayyn* or incompatible. Accordingly the comprehensive *Masala* will be the product of multiplying the bequest *Masala* by the succession *Masala* 8 x 15 = 120.

The beneficiaries final shares from the comprehensive *Masala* are:
8 x 3 = 24 for the legatee X (his share from the bequest *Masala* by the succession *Masala*.)
8 x 5 = 40 for the legatee Y (his share from the bequest *Masala* by the succession *Masala*).
1 x 7 = 7 for the wife (her share from the succession *Masala* by the remnant from the bequest *Masala*).
4 x 7 = 28 for the daughter (her share from the succession *Masala* by the remnant from the bequest *Masala*).
3 x 7 = 21 for the father (his share from the succession *Masala* by the remnant from the bequest *Masala*). See Fig. 64.

Fig. 64

Com M	Suc M	Beq M	
120 = 8 x 15	8	15	= 3 x 5
24		3	X Leg ⅕
40		5	Y Leg ⅓
7	1		W ⅛
28	4	7	D ½
21	3		F Res

Approved

2b. But where the excessive bequest is disapproved of by the heirs then the calculation of the whole number of the *Masala* will be done in the same way as we have seen in the previous cases but will be the aggregate of the denominators bequeathed as follows:

The whole number of the bequest *Masala* is 5 + 3 = 8 being ⅓ of the estate.
8 − 5 = 3 for the legatee X is proportional by ⅕.
8 − 3 = 5 for the legatee Y is proportional by ⅓.

To get ⅔ share which is the remnant for the heirs jurists always, in such a case, multiply the whole number of the bequest *Masala* by 3 the denominator of the ⅓ as follows:
3 x 8 = 24
⅓ of the bequest *Masala* = 24 x ⅓ = 8 or 24 ÷ 3 = 8 out of it 3 for X and 5 for Y.
⅔ of the bequest *Masala* or the remnant = 24 x ⅔ = 16 or 2 x 8 = 16 for the heirs collectively.

The whole number of the succession *Masala* is 8.
⅛ of the whole number = 8 x ⅛ = 1 or 8 ÷ 8 = 1 for the wife.
½ of the whole number = 8 x ½ = 4 or 8 ÷ 2 = 4 for the daughter.
The aggregate = 1 + 4 = 5.
The residue = 8 − 5 = 3 for the father.

Comparing the succession *Masala* (8) with remnant from the bequest *Masala*(16), we find the two numbers to be *Mutawafiq*, having a *Wifq* or common factor. Accordingly, the *Wifq* of the succession *Masala* is 8 ÷ 8 = 1. The *Wifq* of the remnant from the bequest *Masala* is 16 ÷ 8 = 2.

The comprehensive *Masala* therefore will be the product of multiplying the bequest *Masala* by the *Wifq* of the succession *Masala* 1 x 24 = 24.

The beneficiaries shares from the comprehensive *Masala* are:
1 x 3 = 3 for X (his share from the bequest *Masala* by the *Wifq* of the succession *Masala*).
1 x 5 = 5 for Y (his share from the bequest *Masala* by the *Wifq* of the succession *Masala*).
1 x 2 = 2 for the wife (her share from the succession *Masala* by the *Wifq* of the remnant).
4 x 2 = 8 for the daughter (her share from the succession *Masala* by the *Wifq* of the remnant).
3 x 2 = 6 for the father (his share from the succession *Masala* by the *Wifq* of the remnant). See Fig. 65.

Fig. 65

Com M	Suc M	Beq M	x3 (= the disposable ⅓)	
24 = 1 x 24	8	24	8	= 3 + 5
3		3	3	X Leg ⅕
5		5	5	Y Leg ⅓
2	1	16 {		W ⅛
8	4			D ½
6	3			F Res

Disapproved

Fig. 66

Comp M	Suc M	Beq M	
560 = 4 x 140	4	140	= 4 x 5 x 7
140		35	X Leg ¼
112		28	Y Leg ⅕
80		20	Z Leg ⅐
57	1		H ¼
114	2	57	D ½
57	1		FB Res

Approved

Another illustration:

If a woman who had bequeathed ¼ of her estate to X, ⅕ to Y and ⅐ to Z, dies leaving her husband, daughter and full brother, her *Masala*, if the excessive bequest is approved by the heirs, will be calculated in the same manner as that of the above *Masala* as follows:

The whole number of the bequest *Masala* is the product of multiplying the denominators of the fractions bequeathed by each other, 4 x 5 x 7 = 140.
¼ of the whole number = 140 x ¼ = 35 or 140 ÷ 4 = 35 for the legatee X.
⅕ of the whole number = 140 x ⅕ = 28 or 140 ÷ 5 = 28 for the legatee Y.
⅐ of the whole number = 140 x ⅐ = 20 or 140 ÷ 7 = 20 for the legatee Z.
The aggregate = 35 + 28 + 20 = 83.
The remnant = 140 − 83 = 57 for the heirs collectively.

The whole number of the succession *Masala* is 4.
¼ of the whole number = 4 x ¼ = 1 or 4 ÷ 4 = 1 for the husband.
½ of the whole number = 4 x ½ = 2 or 4 ÷ 2 = 2 for the daughter.
The aggregate = 1 + 2 = 3.
The residue = 4 − 3 = 1 for the full brother.

The comprehensive *Masala* is the product of multiplying the bequest *Masala* by the succession *Masala* since the succession *Masala* and the remnant from the bequest *Masala* are *Mutabayyn*. 4 x 140 = 560.

The final beneficiaries' shares from the comprehensive *Masala* are:
4 x 35 = 140 for X (his share from the bequest *Masala* by the succession *Masala*).
4 x 28 = 112 for Y (his share from the bequest *Masala* by the succession *Masala*).
4 x 20 = 80 for Z (his share from the bequest *Masala* by the succession *Masala*).

1 x 57 = 57 for the husband (his share from the succession *Masala* by the remnant from the bequest *Masala*).
2 x 57 = 114 for the daughter (her share from the succession *Masala* by the remnant from the bequest *Masala*).
1 x 57 = 57 for the full brother (his share from the succession *Masala* by the remnant from the bequest *Masala*). See Fig. 66.

But when the excessive part of the bequest as above has been disapproved of by the heirs, the case will be calculated as follows:

The whole number of the bequest *Masala* where the excessive bequest has been disapproved is the aggregate of the denominators of the fractions bequeathed 4 + 5 + 7 = 16 = ⅓ the disposable.
Of the whole number 7 for X is proportional by ¼.
Of the whole number 5 for Y is proportional by ⅕.
Of the whole number 4 for Z is proportional by ⅐.

As the whole number of the bequest represents only ⅓ of the *Masala* then to get the other ⅔, which is called the remnant we multiply the whole number by 3, the denominator of the ⅓, to be 3 x 16 = 48.
⅓ of the bequest *Masala* = 48 x ⅓ = 16 or 48 ÷ 3 = 16 for the legatees.
The remnant ⅔ of the bequest *Masala* = 48 x ⅔ = 32 or 2 x 16 = 32 for the heirs.

The whole number of the succession *Masala* is 4.
¼ of the whole number = 4 x ¼ = 1 or 4 ÷ 4 = 1 for the husband.
½ of the whole number = 4 x ½ = 2 or 4 ÷ 2 = 2 for the daughter.
The aggregate = 1 + 2 = 3.
The residue = 4 − 3 = 1 for the full brother.

The comprehensive *Masala*: The comparison of the succession *Masala* with remnant from the bequest *Masala* shows the two to be *Mutawafiq* or comparative by ¼. The *Wifq* of the succession *Masala* is 4 ÷ 4 = 1, while the *Wifq* of the the remnant from the bequest *Masala* is, 32 ÷ 4 = 8. The comprehensive *Masala* therefore will be the product of multiplying the bequest *Masala* by the *Wifq* of the succession *Masala* 1 x 48 = 48.
The final beneficiaries' shares from the comprehensive Masala are:
1 x 7 = 7 for the legatee X (his share from the bequest *Masala* by the *Wifq* of the succession *Masala*).
1 x 5 = 5 for the legatee Y (his share for the bequest *Masala* by the *Wifq* of the succession *Masala*).
1 x 4 = 4 for the legatee Z (his share from the bequest *Masala* by the *Wifq* of the succession *Masala*).
1 x 8 = 8 for the husband (his share from the succession *Masala* by the *Wifq* (¼) of the remnant from the bequest *Masala*).
2 x 8 = 16 for the daughter (her share from the succession *Masala* by ¼ of the remnant from the bequest *Masala*).
1 x 8 = 8 for the full brother (his share from the succession *Masala* by ¼ of the remnant from the bequest *Masala*). See Fig. 67.

Fig. 67

the disposable third

Comp M	Suc M	Beq M	x3	
48 = 1 x 48	4	48	16	= 4 + 5 + 7
7		7	7	XL : ¼
5		5	5	YL : ⅕
4		4	4	ZL : ⅐
8	1			H ¼
16	2	32 {		D ½
8	1			FB Res

2c. The variations of approval and disapproval of bequest in one case:

It is a fact that the collective approval of the excessive bequest by the testator's heirs reduces their shares from the estate of the deceased thus the legatees may take the maximum shares bequeathed. But however, the heirs disapproval of it confines the legatees' shares from the deceased's estate to the disposable one third only. In the light of this, it is also a fact that the right is reserved for each individual heir freely, without prejudice or undue influence, to prove or disapprove an excessive bequest. It is each individual's right too, if there are a number of bequests, to approve of some of the bequests while disapproving of the others.

The adherence of the Saudi Courts to the above freedom of choice granted to the heirs is clearly illustrated in the case where a house was bequeathed to be held in trust for the underage children of the deceased. The value of the house amounted to more than one-third of the bulk of the estate. The deceased's brother-in-law brought the case before the Court on behalf of his sister. he disputed the legality of such a disposition on the grounds that 'the value exceeded the one-third, and further was made in favour of only his minors.' The judge after examining the case thoroughly informed the wife through her brother (agent) that she would not forfeit her right to the bequest because it was within her right if she wished to withhold her consent on the accessive portion. Therefore, she would receive her full share in the estate from the two thirds and he (the judge) would order the shares of the others who gave their ratification to be reduced proportionately to meet the accessive bequest.

The wife who was then satisfied by the judge's explanation gave her consent to the execution of that testamentary trust of the minors.[24]

For instance, in the case of a person who has bequeathed ⅓ for X and ½ for Y dies leaving two sons, the calculations of his *Masala* taking into consideration all the distinct possibilities in relation to the calculation of the excessive bequest being approved or disapproved by all or some of the heirs to all or some of the legatees will leave us with six different processes which represent seven possibilities as such:

i. Calculation of the *Masala* where the excessive bequest has been approved of for both legatees by both heirs (sons).

ii. Calculation of the *Masala* where the excessive bequest has been disapproved of for both legatees by both heirs (sons).

iii. Calculation of the *Masala* where the excessive bequest has been approved of by both heirs (the two sons), to only one legatee, X.

iv. Calculation of the *Masala* where the excessive bequest has been approved of by both heirs (the two sons), to the other legatee Y only.

v. Calculation where the excessive bequest has been approved of to both legatees by one heir (one son), only.

vi. Calculation of the *Masala* where only one of the two sons approves of the excessive bequest to only one of the legatees.

vii. Calculation where each of the two sons approves the excessive bequest to one of the legatees only.

Each of the above processes possibilities will be calculated consecutively as follows:

2c.i. Calculation of the *Masala* where the excessive bequest has been approved of for both legatees by both heirs (the two sons), will be exactly the same as we have done in the previous *Masalas* as follows:

The whole number of the bequest *Masala* when the excessive bequest has been approved of is the product of multiplying the denominators of the two fractions bequeathed by each other 2 x 3 = 6.

⅓ of the whole number = 6 x ⅓ = 2 or 6 ÷ 3 = 2 for X.

½ of the whole number = 6 x ½ = 3 or 6 ÷ 2 = 3 for Y.

The aggregate = 2 + 3 = 5.

The remnant = 6 − 5 = 1 for the heirs (the two sons), collectively.

The whole number of the succession *Masala* is 2 equal to the number of the two sons. Their share is 2 ÷ 2 = 1 for each son.

The comprehensive *Masala* is the product of multiplying the bequest *Masala* by the succession *Masala*, (since the succession *Masala* (2) is *Mutabayyn* with the remnant (1)) 2 x 6 = 12.

The beneficiaries' final shares from the comprehensive *Masala* are:

2 x 2 = 4 for the legatee X (his share from the bequest *Masala* by the succession *Masala*).

2 x 3 = 6 for the legatee Y (his share from the bequest *Masala* by the succession *Masala*).

1 x 1 = 1 for the first of the two sons (his share from the succession *Masala* by the remnant from the bequest *Masala*).
1 x 1 = 1 for the second son (his share from the succession *Masala* by the remnant from the bequest *Masala*). See Fig. 68.

Fig. 68

Comp M	Suc M	Beq M	
12 = 2x6	2	6	= 2x3
4		2	XL ⅓
6		3	YL ½
1	1	1	S Res
1	1		S

Approved M

2c.ii. Calculation of the *Masala* where the excessive bequest has been disapproved of for both legatees by both heirs (the two sons), will be exactly the same as we have done in the previous *Masalas* as follows:

The whole number of the bequest *Masala* when it has been disapproved of by the heirs is the sum of the denominators of the two fractions bequeathed 2 + 3 = 5 = the disposable ⅓.
2 for X is proportional by the bequeathed ⅓.
and 3 for Y is proportional by the bequeathed ½.

As (5) represents the disposable ⅓ then to get the remnant ⅔ for the heirs we multiply the bequest whole number by (3) the denominator of ⅓ and then subtract the whole number from the product as follows:
3 x 5 = 15 the bequest *Masala*.
15 − 5 = 10 the remnant for the heirs equal to ⅔ of the estate.

The whole number of the succession *Masala* is the number of sons in the *Masala* (2). 2 ÷ 2 = 1 for each of the two sons.

For the comprehensive *Masala* we compare, first, the succession *Masala* (2) with remnant (10 from the bequest *Masala*. As the two numbers are *Mutawafiq* by 2 (2 ÷ 2 = 1 and 10 ÷ 2 = 5), we multiply the bequest *Masala* by the *Wifq* of the succession *Masala* 1 x 15 = 15.

The final beneficiaries' shares from the comprehensive *Masala* are:
1 x 2 = 2 for X (his share from the bequest *Masala* by the *Wifq* of the succession *Masala*).
1 x 3 = 3 for Y (his share from the bequest *Masala* by the *Wifq* of the succession *Masala*).

1 x 5 = 5 for the first son (his share from the succession *Masala* by the *Wifq* of the remnant from the bequest *Masala*).
1 x 5 = 5 for the second son (his share from the succession *Masala* by the *Wifq* of the remnant from the bequest *Masala*).
See Fig. 69.

Fig. 69

		the disposable ⅓		
Comp M	**Suc M**	**Beq M**	**x3**	
15=1x15	**2**	**15**	**5**	**=2+3**
2		**2**	**2**	**XL : ⅓**
3		**3**	**3**	**YL : ½**
5	**1**	**10**		**S** **Res**
5	**1**			**S**

Before we proceed to consider the calculation of the other possibilities we think it is necessary to start by working out an inclusive *Masala* from the above two comprehensive *Masalas* for both approved and disapproved cases by multiplying the two *Masalas* by each other if they are regarded *Mutabayyn* or by multiplying the *Wifq* of one of the two by the whole of the other if the two are *Mutawafiq*, since the final result of the beneficiaries' shares depends on it.

The Inclusive Masala

Comparing the two comprehensive *Masalas* of the approved and the disapproved cases we find that the two are *Mutawafiq* by third.
The *Wifq* or common factor of the approved one is 12 ÷ 3 = 4.
The *Wifq* or common factor of the disapproved one is 15 ÷ 3 = 5.

Since the two *Masalas* are *Mutawafiq*, the inclusive *Masala* will be the product of multiplying the *Wifq* of one *Masala* by the other as such: 4 x 15 = 60 or 5 x 12 = 60.

Knowing the *Wifq* of the two *Masalas*, when they are *Mutawafiq*, is very important too when we turn to calculate the share of every beneficiary from the inclusive *Masala*. For instance, the share of each legatee, whose share has been approved of, from the inclusive *Masala* is his share from the approved *Masala* by the *Wifq* of the disapproved *Masala*, and vice versa. Also the share of each heir who has approved the bequest from the inclusive *Masala* is his share from approved *Masala* by the *Wifq* of the disapproved, and vice versa.

The inclusive *Masala* when it is approved of. See Fig. 70.

Fig. 70

Incl M = 4 x 15	Disapd M	Apprd M	
60	15	12	
4 x 2 = 8	2	4	XL ⅓
4 x 3 = 12	3	6	YL ½
4 x 5 = 20	5	1	S Res
4 x 5 = 20	5	1	S

Incl M = 4 x 15	Disapd M	Apprd M	
60	15	12	
5 x 4 = 20	2	4	XL ⅓
5 x 6 = 30	3	6	YL ½
5 x 1 = 5	5	1	S Res
5 x 1 = 5	5	1	S

Fig. 71

2c.iii. Calculation of the *Masala* when the excessive bequest has been approved of by both heirs (the two sons), to the legatee X only.

The inclusive *Masala* as we have said is the disapproved *Masala* by the *Wifq* of the approved *Masala* 4 x 15 = 60 or vice versa.

The beneficiaries' shares from the inclusive *Masala* are:
5 x 4 = 20 the share of X who has got the approval of both sons being his share from the approved *Masala* by the *Wifq* of the disapproved *Masala*.
4 x 3 = 12 the share of Y (his share from the disapproved *Masala* by the *Wifq* of the approved *Masala*).

The share of each of the two sons who approved the excessive bequest for X only is the inclusive *Masala* minus the aggregate of the legatees' shares divided by two since the sons agree and receive the same ratio, as such:

20 + 12 = 32 the aggregate of the legatees' shares.
60 − 32 = 28 the collective share of the two sons.
28 ÷ 2 = 14 the share of each son from the inclusive *Masala*. See Fig. 72.

Incl M = 4 x 15	Disapd M	Apprd M	
60	15	12	
5 x 4 = 20	2	4	XL ⅓
4 x 3 = 12	3	6	YL ½
* 14	5	1	S Res
* 14	5	1	S

* 20 + 12 = 32
60 − 32 = 28
28 ÷ 2 = 14

Fig. 72

Incl M = 4 x 15	Disapd M	Apprd M	
60	15	12	
4 x 2 = 8	2	4	XL ⅓
5 x 6 = 30	3	6	YL ½
* 11	5	1	S Res
* 11	5	1	S

* 8 + 30 = 38
60 − 38 = 22
22 ÷ 2 = 11

Fig. 73

2c.iv. Calculation of the Masala when the excessive bequest has been approved by both sons to the legatee Y only.

The inclusive Masala, as we have said, is the disapproved *Masala* by the *Wifq* of the approved *Masala* 4 x 15 = 60.

The beneficiaries' shares from the inclusive *Masala* are:

4 x 2 = 8 for X (his share from the disapproved *Masala* by the *Wifq* of the approved *Masala*).

5 x 6 = 30 for Y which has been approved, (his share from the approved *Masala* by the *Wifq* of the disapproved *Masala*).

The share of the two (heirs) sons is the inclusive *Masala* minus the aggregate of the legatees' shares divided by their quota or ration (2), as such:

8 + 30 = 38 the aggregate of the legatees' shares.

60 − 38 = 22 the collective share of the heirs (the two sons).

22 ÷ 2 = 11 the share of each son from the inclusive *Masala*.

See Fig. 73.

2c.v. Calculations when the excessive bequest has been approved to both legatees by one son only. The inclusive *Masala* is 4 x 15 = 60.

When we calculated the above *Masala* where the excessive bequest has been approved by both sons to one legatee only, we started by working out the shares of the legatees and then we followed by working out the shares of the two sons. But here, just the opposite from the above occurs: we start by working out the sons' shares and then we follow with the legatees' shares, since the realization of their shares depends on the realization of the difference between the shares of the son who approves the excessive bequest to both legatees and the ratio of shares for each legatee from such difference.

So we say, the beneficiaries' shares from the inclusive *Masala* are:

4 x 5 = 20 for the son who did not approve the excessive bequest (his share from the disapproved *Masala* by the *Wifq* of the approved *Masala*).

5 x 1 = 5 for the son who approved the excessive bequest (his share from the approved Masala by the *Wifq* of the disapproved).

The share of the legatees from the inclusive *Masala* is the inclusive *Masala* minus the aggregate share of the sons divided by the ratio of the legatees' shares from the one third (5), multiplied by each one's share from the ratio as such:

5 + 20 = 25 the aggregate of the sons' shares.

60 − 25 = 35 the difference between the inclusive *Masala* and the sons' shares.

35 ÷ 5 = 7 equal to each part of the ratio.

2 x 7 = 14 the share of the legatee X.

3 x 7 = 21 the shares of the legatee Y. See Fig. 74

Fig. 74

Incl M = 4 x 15	**Disap M**	**Appd M**	
60	**15**	**12**	
14*	**2**	**4**	**XL ⅓**
21†	**3**	**6**	**YL ½**
5 x 1 = 5	**5**	**1**	**S approving** **Res**
4 x 5 = 20	**5**	**1**	**S disapproving**

Aggregate of 2 + 3 = 5 called ratio	**5 + 20 = 25** **60 − 25 = 35** **35 ÷ 5 = 7**
from the Disapp M	**2 x 7 = 14 *** **3 x 7 = 21†**

2c.vi. Calculation when only one of the two sons approves the excessive bequest to only one of the legatees.

a. In the case of one son (a) approving the excessive bequest to *X* only then the final share of the legatee *X* will be dependent on how many shares he extracts from the sons' share as a result of his approval to *X's* bequest. Accordingly, to define the final share of both the son and *X* we apply the following steps:

4 x 5 = 20 the share of the son when he disapproves the excessive bequest to both legatees.

5 x 1 = 5 the share of the son when he approves the excessive bequest to both legatees.

20 − 5 = 15 the difference between the sons' share in the case of his disapproval of the excessive bequest to both legatees and in the case of his approval of it to both legatees.

15 ÷ 5 = 3 (the difference above divided by the ratio of the legatees' shares, who take on the ratio of 2:3), equal to each part of the ratio of the legatees' shares.

4 x 2 = 8 the share of *X* when the excessive bequest has been disapproved
2 x 3 = 6 *X's* quota to be extracted from the difference between the share of the son when he approves and disapproves the bequest, (his rate from ratio by the quota of each part of the ratio).
6 + 8 = 14 the sum of the final share of the legatee *X* (his share when the bequest has been disapproved plus the extracted quota).
20 − 6 = 14 the final share of the son who approved for *X* after his quota has been extracted from the son's share.
4 x 3 = 12 the share of the legatee *Y* from the inclusion *Masala*.
4 x 5 = 20 the share of the son who has disapproved the bequest for both legatees. See Fig. 75.

Incl M = 4x15	Disap M	Appd M	
60	15	12	
(4x2) = 8 + 6 = 14	2	4	XL ⅓
4x3 = 12	3	6	YL ½
(4x5) = 20 − 6 = 14	5	1	S (a) App to X
			Res
4x5 = 20	5	1	S Disapp to X & Y

Fig. 75

b. In the case of one son (b) approving the excessive bequest to *Y* only then the final share of such legatee *Y* will be dependant on how many shares he extracts from the son's share as a result of his approval to *Y's* bequest.

Accordingly, to define the final share of both the son and *Y* we apply the following steps:
4 x 5 = 20 the share of the son when he disapproves the excessive bequest to both legatees.
5 x 1 = 5 the share of the son when he approves the excessive bequest to both legatees.
20 − 5 = 15 the difference between the sons' share in the case of his disapproval of the excessive bequest and in the case of his approval of it to both legatees.
15 ÷ 5 = 3 (the difference above divided by the ratio of the legatees' shares, who take on the ratio of 2:3), equal to each part of the ratio of the legatee's shares.
4 x 3 = 12 the share of the legatee *Y* when the excessive bequest has been disapproved.

3 x 3 = 9 Y's quota to be extracted from the difference between the share of the son when he approves and disapproves the excessive bequest, (his rate from the ratio by the quota of each part of the ratio).
9 + 12 = 21 the sum of the final share of the legatee Y (his share when the bequest has been disapproved plus the extracted quota).
20 − 9 = 11 the final share of the son, who has approved the bequest for Y after his quota has been extracted from the son's (b) share.
4 x 2 = 8 the share of X from the inclusive *Masala*.
4 x 6 = 20 the share of the second son (a) who disapproved the bequest to both legatees, from the inclusive *Masala*. See Fig. 76.

Incl M = 4 x 15	Disapp M	Appd M		
60	15	12		
4 x 2 = 8	2	4	XL	⅓
(4 x 3) = 12 + 9 = 21	3	6	YL	½
(4 x 5) = 20 − 9 = 11	5	1	S (b)	App to Y
				Res
4 x 5 = 20	5	1	S	Disapp to X & Y

Fig. 76

2c.vii. Calculation when one son approves of only one legatee and the other son of the other legatee.

It is known from the previous cases that the share of the son from the inclusive *Masala* when he disapproves of the excessive bequest to both legatees is 4 x 5 = 20.

It is also known that the share of the son from the inclusive Masala when he approves of the excessive bequest to both legatees is 5 x 1 = 5.
20 − 5 = 15 this is the difference between his shares when he approves or disapproves the excessive bequest.

As in this particular case each of the two sons has approved the excessive bequest to one or other of the legatees the final share of both the sons and the legatees will not be known before we determine how many shares each legatee gets from 15, being the difference, in addition to his original share from the disposable one third. This is solved by dividing the difference (15) by the ratio of the legatees' *Masala* (5), who share their *Masala* by the ratio of 2:3 (2 of it to the legatee X and 3 of it to Y).
15 ÷ 5 = 3 equal to each part of the ratio.
2 x 3 = 6 the quota to be taken by the legatee X from the 15.
4 x 2 = 8 *X's* original share when his bequest has been disapproved.
6 + 8 = 14 *X's* final share from the inclusive *Masala*.

3 x 3 = 9 the quota to be taken by the legatee Y from the 15.
4 x 3 = 12 Y's original share when his bequest has been disapproved of.
9 + 12 = 21 Y's final share from the inclusive *Masala*

Thus the final share of the two sons is:

20 − 6 = 14 the final share from the inclusive *Masala* for the son who had approved the bequest for *X*.

20 − 9 = 11 the final share from the inclusive *Masala* for the son who had approved the bequest for Y. See Fig. 77.

Incl M = 4 x 15	**Disapp M**	**Appd M**			
60	**15**	**12**			
(4 x 2) = 8 + 6 = 14	**2**	**4**		**XL**	**⅓**
(4 x 3) = 12 + 9 = 21	**3**	**6**		**YL**	**½**
(4 x 5) = 20 − 9 = 11	**5**	**1**	**S**	**Res**	**App to Y**
(4 x 5) = 20 − 6 = 14	**5**	**1**	**S**		**App to X**

Fig. 77

The position of having specific and unspecific portions in one Masala

In the past we have discussed separately each of the two elements, the specific and the unspecific portions when being made the subject of bequest, but here we are to show the possibility of having the two elements together in one Masala and the recommended method of solution.

Illustration:

If a person who has three sons as his prospective heirs bequeathed to *Zaid* one half of his estate and to *'Amr* an equivalent share as that of one of his sons, his *Masala* will be calculated by defining in the first step the bequest of *'Amr* which is the equivalent share of one of his sons. The result, whatever it is, say: ⅓, ¼, ⅛, 1/12, will be taken as one of the elements upon which we base our calculations in the second step. This will contain the heirs and the two legatees since Ibn Qudama preferred it and called it the *Hanbali Madhhab* or doctrine as follows:

Applying the rules of calculation the whole number of the *Masala* of the three sons and a legatee (*'Amr*), taking an equivalent share as one of his sons will be 4, by counting *'Amr* as a sharer with the three sons.

From the whole number each of the sons and the legatee will get one share 4 ÷ 4 = 1.

So *'Amr's* (the legatee's) share is equivalent to the ¼ of the whole estate. See Fig. 78.

4		
1	**S**	
1	**S.**	**Res**
1	**S**	
1	**Amr Leg 1 = ¼**	

Fig. 78

Accordingly, with the ¼ of *'Amr* in hand we are to calculate the whole *Masala* as follows:

1. Calculations when the excessive bequest has been approved of to both legatees by all sons.

The whole number of the bequest Masala when it has been approved of by all heirs is supposed to be the product of multiplying the denominators of the fractions allocated to the legatees when they are *Mutabayyn* but when the denominators are not *Mutabayyn* as in this *Masala* then we consider applying the other rules of calculation, *Mutamathil*, *Mutadakhil* and *Mutawafiq* 2 and 4 are thus *Mutadakhil* or concordent, so as it is the rule we take the highest of the denominators to form the whole number of the bequest *Masala* (4).

½ of the whole number = 4 x ½ = 2 or 4 ÷ 2 = 2 for the legatee *Zaid*.
¼ of the whole number = 4 x ¼ = 1 or 4 ÷ 4 = 1 for the legatee *'Amr*.
The remnant = 4 − (2 + 1) = 1 for the three sons collectively.

The whole number of the succession *Masala* is 3 the per capita number of the three sons 3 ÷ 3 = 1 for each son.

The comprehensive *Masala* is the product of multiplying the bequest *Masala* by the succession *Masala*, since the succession *Masala* is *Mutabayyn* with the remnant 3 x 4 = 12.

The final shares of the beneficiaries from the comprehensive *Masala* are:
3 x 2 = 6 for the legatee *Zaid* (his share from the bequest *Masala* by the succession *Masala*).
3 x 1 = 3 for the legatee *'Amr* (his share from the bequest *Masala* by the succession *Masala*).
1 x 1 = 1 for the first son (his share from the succession *Masala* by the remnant from the bequest *Masala*).
1 x 1 = 1 for the second son (his share from the succession *Masala* by the remnant).
1 x 1 = 1 for the third son (his share from the succession *Masala* by the remnant). See Fig. 79.

Comp M = 3 x 4	Suc M	Beq M	
12	3	4	= 4
3 x 2 = 6		2	ZL ½
3 x 1 = 3		1	Amr ¼
1 x 1 = 1	1		S
1 x 1 = 1	1	1	S Res
1 x 1 = 1	1		S

Fig. 79

2. Calculations when the excessive bequest has been disapproved of to both legatees by all sons.

The whole number of the bequest when it has been disapproved of is the sum of aggregating the denominators of the fractions bequeathed, (which is here 2 and 4) 2 + 4 = 6 = the disposable ⅓.

Out of it 4 for *Zaid* is proportional by ½ and 2 out of it for *'Amr* is proportional by ¼.

To get the remaining ⅔ of the bequest *Masala* for the heirs we multiply the bequest whole number by the denominator of ⅔. 3 x 6 = 18.

⅓ of the bequest *Masala* = 18 x ⅓ = 6 or 18 ÷ 3 = 6 For *Zaid* 4 and 2 for *'Amr*.

⅔ of the bequest *Masala* = 18 x ⅔ = 12 or 2 x 6 = 12 the remnant for the three sons.

The whole number of the succession *Masala* is 3.

3 ÷ 3 = 1 for each of the three sons.

Before we work out the comprehensive *Masala* we compare the succession *Masala* 3 by the remnant 12 from the bequest *Masala* using either the *Mutabayyn* or the *Mutawafiq* rules of calculation as we have seen in the doctrine of *Tashih*.

3 and 12 are *Mutawafiq* by a third. The *Wifq* of 3 is 3 ÷ 3 = 1.

The *Wifq* of 12 is 12 ÷ 3 = 4.

Thus the comprehensive *Masala* is the product of multiplying the bequest *Masala* by the *Wifq* of the succession *Masala*. 1 x 18 = 18.

The shares of the beneficiaries from the comprehensive *Masala* are:

1 x 4 = 4 for *Zaid* the legatee (his share from the bequest *Masala* by the *Wifq* of the succession Masala).

Simplification

Comp M ÷ 2		Suc M	Beq M x 3	
9	18 = 1 x 18	3	18 6	= 4 + 2
2	4 (= 1 x 4)		4 4	ZL ½
1	2 (= 1 x 2)		2 2	AL ¼
2	4 (= 4 x 1)	1		S
2	4 (= 4 x 1)	1	12	S Res
2	4 (= 4 x 1)	1		S

Fig. 80

1 x 2 = 2 for *'Amr* the legatee (his share from the bequest *Masala* by the *Wifq* of the succession Masala).
4 x 1 = 4 for the first son (his share from the succession *Masala* by the *Wifq* of the remnant).
4 x 1 = 4 for the second son (his share from the succession *Masala* by the *Wifq* of the remnant).
4 x 1 = 4 for the third son (his share from the succession *Masala* by the *Wifq* of the remnant from the bequest *Masala*).

To simplify the comprehensive *Masala* still further we divide the comprehensive *Masala* as well as the shares of all beneficiaries by a common divisor (2).

18 ÷ 2 = 9 The comprehensive *Masala*.
4 ÷ 2 = 2 for *Zaid*, the legatee.
2 ÷ 2 = 1 for *'Amr*, the legatee.
4 ÷ 2 = 2 for the first son.
4 ÷ 2 = 2 for the second son.
4 ÷ 2 = 2 for the third son. See Fig. 80.

NOTES

1. Jedda Katib al-'adl, Case No. 200, Vol. 1 (1382H).
2. *Al-Mughni*, Vol. 6, 449.
3. *Sharh al-Muntaha*, Vol. 2, 565.
4. *Al-sharh al-Kabir*, Vol. 6, 538.
5. *Al-mughni* Vol. 6, 452.
6. *Al-Mughni*, Vol. 6, 452.
7. *Al-Sharh al-kabir*, Vol. 6, 538.
8. *Sharh al-Muntaha*, Vol. 2, 565, and *Al-furu'*,(*Al-furu' wa Tashihuh*) Vol. 2, 947.
9. *Al-Sharh al-Kabir*, Vol. 6, 533.
10. *Al-kashshaf*, Vol. 4, 381.
11. Jedda Katib al-'adl, No. 200, Vol. 1 (1382H).
12. *Al-Mughni*, Vol. 6, 450-451, and *Al-sharh al-kabir*, Vol. 6, 533-535.
13. *Al-adhb al-fa'id Sharh Umdat al-farid*, Vol. 1, 125.
14. *Quran*, Al-ahzab (the clan), 30.
15. *Sharh al-muntaha*, Vol. 2, 565, and Kashshaf, Vol. 4, 382.
16. N. Ibrahim. *Al-adhb al-fa'd sharh Umdat al-farid*, Vol. 2, 193.
17. *Al-adhb*, Vol. 2, 194.
18. Jedda Katib al-'adl No. 974, Vol. 3, (1379H).
19. Jedda Katib al-'adl No. 889, Vol. 3, (1379H).
20. *Al-mughni*, Vol. 6, 452.
21. *Al-kashshaf*, Vol. 4, 383, *Sharh al-muntaha*, Vol. 2, 566.
22. *Al-Insaf*, Vol. 7, 276-278, (*Al-Furu'* and its commentary), Vol. 2, 948-949.
23. I. A. Ibrahim, *Al-Adhb al fi'id sharh umdat al-farid*, Vol. 2, 197.
24. Jedda Grand Court, Case No. 776, Vol. 6, (date 2/12/1389H).
25. *Mughni*, Vol. 6, 455.

CHAPTER III
THE DISTRIBUTION OF ESTATE

One should bear in mind that ali the previous mathematical processes and rules of calculation, though undoubtedly a major step forward towards the final solution of inheritance problems, should not be regarded as an objective in themselves. It must be remembered that all the previous calculations are considered no more than a preliminary attempt towards the distribution of the deceased's estate out of which we are only to be provided with a hypothetical proportion upon which the final and most important step is to be based. This, of course, is the distribution of the estate to those who are entitled to it whether they are heirs, legatees or otherwise. This is, in fact, what we can rightly call the ultimate objective of both the law of inheritance and the law of bequest.

To achieve this objective the mathematical jurists divided the estate into two distinct parts according to the characteristics of each part. That is to say, whether the estate to be distributed is divisible or indivisible.

The divisible estate can be defined as being of countable objects which can be enumerated by using dry measure, weight, counting or measuring length or distance or money, etc. Or in other words, it is the estate which has divisible units,[1] such as money, sacks of grain, etc. While the indivisible estate can be defined as having uncountable objects such as land, farms, houses and animals.

For each of these two distinct parts, the jurists have developed appropriate methods of distributing such estates in full or in part. The jurists have also developed a third method of distribution capable of being applied to distribute all kinds of estates divisible or indivisible.

However, although the judges usually stop short of applying such methods themselves, they delegate such a task to the court's auditor called *Mamur Bait al-Mal*, as their agent to arrange the distribution of estates on their behalf guided by the calculation of the primary *Masala*.

An illustration of this tendency is seen in the case of S^2 who died leaving an estate of SR27,824 Q.12 to his wife *N* and two maternal cousins, *M* and *A*. There were, in effect, three maternal cousins. His wife was also the daughter of his maternal uncle. The deceased also left a bequest of one third for good deeds.

In this case, the judge, after confirming those who were entitled to benefit from the deceased's estate, used as a guidance to the definition of their entitlements from the estate, the calculation of the succession *Masala* according to the inheritance fixed portions only, but without taking steps to distribute the remaining estate in accordance to such shares. Thus making the whole number of the succession *Masala* 4. This gave the wife 1 share, the three maternal cousins the residue 3 to be distributed equally between them as their inheritance stems from their being *Dhawi al-arham* heirs. Therefore, *N* (the maternal cousin) received a share from the residue equalling ¼ in addition to the ¼ share she took in her capacity of the deceased's wife making the total of ½; giving *M* (the maternal cousin) 1 from the residue equalling ¼ of the *Masala* and a similar share to the other maternal cousin *A*. On the basis of his distribution of the succession *Masala*, the judge ordered the head of Bait al-Mal to distribute the deceased's estate between the heirs after he had handed over the bequeathed ⅓ to the *Wasi*. See Fig. 81.

	4		
½ =	2 { 1	**W**	¼
	1	***N***	
¼ =	1	***M*** **M Cousins Res**	
¼ =	1	**A**	

Fig. 81

Although such calculation appears to be sensible, as the bequeathed one third is not difficult to work out, one could appreciate the other method we previously applied by calculating the bequest alongside the succession *Masala* in one table with a comprehensive *Masala* of the two which results in a proportional share upon which the distribution of the estate should be based.

That is, 3 is the whole number of the bequest Masala, as it is the denominator of the bequeathed share.

3 x ⅓ = 1 or 3 ÷ 3 = 1 the bequeathed share.

3 − 1 = 2 the remnant from the bequest *Masala* for the heirs collectively.

4 is the whole number of the succession *Masala*, as it is the denominator of the only fixed portion inherited.

4 x ¼ = 1 or 4 ÷ 4 = 1 for the wife.

4 − 1 = 3 for the other three heirs called *Dhawi al-arham*, as they were the deceased's maternal cousins, equally between them.

3 ÷ 3 = 1 for each of the three cousins (*M*, *A* and *N*), equalling ¼ of the whole number.

N (the maternal cousin) being also the deceased's wife, gave her the right to acquire ¼ of the whole number in addition to the ¼ share she had taken as a wife, making her share total ½ = 2 of the whole number.

Comparing the succession *Masala* 4 with the remnant from the bequest *Masala* 2 we find the two numbers *Mutawafiq* by half 4 ÷ 2 = 2 the *Wifq* of the succession *Masala* 2 ÷ 2 = 1 the *Wifq* of the remnant. Thus we take the *Wifq* of the succession Masala 2 only to multiply the bequest *Masala* 3 making the product to form the comprehensive Masala 2 x 3 = 6.

The beneficiaries' shares from the comprehensive *Masala* is calculated as follows:

1 x 2 = 2 the bequeathed third, (the bequeathed share from the bequest *Masala* by the *Wifq* of the succession *Masala*).

1 x 1 = 1 for the wife, (her share from the succession *Masala* by the *Wifq* of the remnant from the bequest *Masala*).

1 x 1 = 1 for *N* (the wife) her share from the succession *Masala* by the *Wifq* of the remnant from the bequest *Masala*).

1 + 1 = 2 the total of the dual share for *N* who is also the deceased's wife, from the comprehensive *Masala*.

1 x 1 = 1 for *M* (his share from the succession *Masala* by the *Wifq* of the remnant from the bequest *Masala*).

1 x 1 = 1 for *A* (his share from the succession *Masala* by the *Wifq* of the remnant from the bequest *Masala*).

See Fig. 82.

Comp M	Suc M	Beq M		
6=3x2	4	3		
2		1	Beq ⅓	
2	1		W ¼	
	1	2	Nur	M Cousins
1	1		Moh	Res
1	1		Abdul	

Fig. 82

The three methods of distribution are to be explained in the following.

THE METHOD OF DISTRIBUTING THE DIVISIBLE ESTATE

To distribute a divisible estate, whether it is money or any other kind of estate with a number of equal parts and pieces, one may apply the following steps.

We compare the amount of the estate with the succession Masala or with the comprehensive or inclusive *Masala* if there is any bequest allocated using as a criteria two of the four rules of calculation i.e. *Mutawafiq* or compatible and the *Mutabayyn* or incompatible. If the divisible units of the estate and the *Masala* are *Mutawafiq* then work out the *Wifq* of both numbers.

To distribute the estate amongst the beneficiaries, heirs and legatees, firstly multiply the *Wifq* of the estate by the share of each heir from the *Masala*. Secondly divide the above multiplication product by the *Wifq* of the *Masala* where the quotient will thus become the final share of the heir or legatee from the distributed estate.

But when the two compared numbers (of the estate and the *Masala*), are *Mutabayyn* then multiply the entire estate by the share of each heir or legatee from the *Masala*, then divide the product by the entire *Masala*. Thus the quotient will be the final share of each heir or legatee from the estate.

However, to demonstrate such a method a table which will make distribution seem simple and easier for comprehension, we recommend the drawing of a four sided table. There should be some horizontal lines, equal to the number of heirs and legatees, drawn inside it. As to the vertical lines, only the three basic lines are to be drawn inside the table thus forming four columns in all inside the table.

From right to left inside the first column we put the description, the status and the basic portion of either heirs and legatees, and on top of such a column we put the components of the *Masala* number. Inside the second column we put the share of heirs and legatees from the *Masala* and on top of it we put the final number of the *Masala* which, in short we call the *Masala*. Inside the third column we put the final share of each heir or legatee when it is a whole number from the estate distributed and on top of it we put the entire number of the estate. Inside the fourth column we put the final share of each heir or legatee when it is a fraction from the estate distributed and on top of it we put the *Wifq* of the *Masala* if the estate and the *Masala* are *Mutawafiq* or we put the entire number of the *Masala* where whatever is put underneath it will be considered to be fractions of it. To apply the above method as we have described here are some illustrations:

First illustration

A woman dies leaving an estate of £900 to a husband, two daughters and a full brother. The estate, according to the above method, will be distributed amongst the heirs as follows:

The whole number of the *Masala* is 3 x 4 = 12.
$\frac{1}{4}$ of the whole number = 12 x $\frac{1}{4}$ = 3 or 12 ÷ 4 = 3 for the husband.
$\frac{2}{3}$ of the whole number = 12 x $\frac{2}{3}$ = 8 or 12 ÷ 3 = 4 x 2 = 8 for the two daughters.
The residue = 12 − (3 + 8) = 1 for the full brother.

As to the method of distribution of the estate, we start as follows:

Comparing the estate with the *Masala* we find them to be *Mutawafiq* by a third. The *Wifq* of the estate is 900 ÷ 3 = 300, and the *Wifq* of the *Masala* is 12 ÷ 3 = 4 or by factorizing method $\frac{12}{900} = \frac{4}{300}$.

The final share of each heir from the estate is:
For the husband 3 x 300 = 900 (his share from the *Masala* by the *Wifq* of the estate), 900 ÷ 4 = 225, (the product on the *Wifq* of the *Masala*).
For the first daughter 4 x 300 = 1200, (her share from the *Masala* by the *Wifq* of the estate), 1200 ÷ 4 = 300, (the product on the *Wifq* of the *Masala*). The same is also for the second daughter.
For the full brother 1 x 300 = 300 (his share from the *Masala* by the *Wifq* of the estate), 300 ÷ 4 = 75 (the product on the *Wifq* of the *Masala*).
See Fig. 83.

Masala *Wifq*	**Estate**	**Estate *Wifq***	**The *Masala***	
4	**£900**	**300**	**12**	
0	**£225**		**3**	**H ¼**
0	**£300**		**4**	**D** } **⅔**
0	**£300**		**4**	**D**
0	**£75**		**1**	**FB Res**

Fig. 83

Second illustration:

A man dies leaving an estate of £1155 to a wife and a consanguine brother. The estate will be distributed amongst the heirs as follows:

The whole number of the Masala is 4.
$\frac{1}{4}$ of the whole number = 4 x $\frac{1}{4}$ = 1 or 4 ÷ 4 = 1 for the wife.
The residue = 4 − 1 = 3 for the consanguine brother.

As to the method of distribution of the estate, we start as follows:

Comparing the *Masala* with the estate, we find them to be *Mutabayyn* or incompatible so to remain as they are to be used accordingly.

The final share of each heir from the estate is to be calculated as follows.

For the wife 1 x 1155 = 1155 (her share from the *Masala* by the estate).
1155 ÷ 4 = £288¾ (the product divided by the *Masala*).
For the consanguine brother 3 x 1155 = 3465 (his share from the *Masala* by the estate) 3465 ÷ 4 = £866¼ (the product divided by the Masala).[3]
See Fig. 84.

Fig. 84

M	**Estate**	**Estate having no *Wifq***	**The *Masala***	
4	**£1155**	**1155**	**4**	
3	**£288¾**		**1**	**W ¼**
1	**£866¼**		**3**	**CB Res**

4 ÷ 4 = 1

Third illustration:

A person leaves an estate of £1845 to a son, a wife and a bequest of a share of one of his heirs. The estate will be distributed amongst his beneficiaries (the heirs and the legatee) following the view of the majority of jurists to give him a share similar to the share of the lowest sharer as follows:

The estate £1845 is *Mutawafiq* with the *Masala* 9 by one third.
The *Wifq* of the estate is 1845 ÷ 3 = 615. The *Wifq* of the Masala is 9 ÷ 3 = 3 or by factorizing method they are 9/1845 = 3/615.

The share of each beneficiary from the estate according to this method is calculated as follows:

Firstly, to multiply the *Wifq* of the estate by the share of each heir or legatee from the *Masala*. Secondly, to divide the product of the above multiplication by the *Wifq* of the *Masala* so the quotient becomes equal to each beneficiaries' share from the estate which is distributed as follows:

1 x 615 = 615 615 ÷ 3 = 205 for the wife.
7 x 615 = 4305 4305 ÷ 3 = £1435 for the son.
1 x 615 = 615 615 ÷ 3 = £205 for the legatee.
See Fig. 85.

An apparent application of this method is seen in the distribution of the allowance of *Al-Sh*,[4] who died leaving his wife *F*, his daughter *T* and his three sons, *A*, *At* and *Kh*. As a result of an action brought by *F* against *M*, who earlier received an arrear allowance for the deceased from the government amounting to SR 4,451.90, she appealed to the court to order the shares for herself and the children *T*, *A* and *At*, who were her only wards from such an amount to be paid to them.

Fig. 85

MW	Estate	Estate W	Masala	
3	£1845	615	9	=8+1
0	£205		1	W 1/8
0	£1435		7	S Res
0	£205		1	Leg

The Masala

+1

9	8	
1	1	W 1/8
7	7	S Res
1		Leg=1

In conformity to the judge's order the estate (allowance) was distributed between the legal heirs according to each one's share from the succession *Masala* with impressive accuracy in regard to the amount paid to each one as follows:

8 is the whole number of the succession *Masala* 1 for the wife, 1 for the daughter (*T*) and 2 for each of the three sons (*A*, *At*, and *Kh*).

Comparing the allowance to the *Masala*, the two numbers are *Mutawafiq* by half 4451.90 ÷ 2 = 2225.95 becoming the allowance *Wifq*, (estate).
8 ÷ 2 = 4 becoming the *Masala Wifq*.

The heirs' shares from the allowance are extracted by multiplying the share of each heir from the *Masala* by the allowance *Wifq* and the product is divided by the *Masala Wifq* making the quotient to become the final share of each heir from the allowance as follows:
1 x 2225.95 = SR 2225.95 (the share of *F* from the *Masala* multiplied by the allowance *Wifq*).
2225.95 ÷ 4 = SR 556.48¾ for *F*, (the product of the above multiplication divided by the *Masala Wifq*).
1 x 2225.95 = SR 2225.95 the share of the daughter from the *Masala* multiplied by the allowance *Wifq*.
2225.95 ÷ 4 = SR 556.48¾ for the daughter, (the product of the above multiplication divided by the *Masala Wifq*).

2 x 2225.95 = SR 4451.9 the share of *A* from the *Masala* multiplied by the allowance *Wifq*.
4451.9 ÷ 4 = SR 1112.97½ for *A*, (the product of the above multiplication divided by the *Masala Wifq*).
2 x 2225.95 = SR 4451.9 the share of *At*. from the *Masala* multiplied by the allowance *Wifq*.
4451.9 ÷ 4 = SR 1112.97½ for *At*, (the product of the above multiplication divided by the *Masala Wifq*).
2 x 2225.95 = SR 4451.9 the share of *Kh*. from the *Masala* multiplied by the allowance *Wifq*.
4451.9 ÷ 4 = SR 1112.97½ for *Kh*, (the product of the above multiplication divided by the *Masala Wifq*).
See Fig. 86.

Fig. 86

Masala Wifq	**Allowance on death**	**Allowance *Wifq***	***Masala***		
4	4451.90	2225.95	8		
3	556.48¾ SR		1	WF	⅛
3	556.48¾ SR		1	*T*	
2	1112.97½ SR		2	*A*	Res
2	1112.97½ SR		2	*At*	
2	1112.97½ SR		2	*Kh*	

(3 + 3 + 2 + 2 + 2) ÷ 4 = 3 SRQ

THE METHOD OF DISTRIBUTING THE INDIVISIBLE ESTATE

To distribute an indivisible estate, whether it is land, a farm, a house or otherwise, one may apply what the justists call 'The method of *Qirat*, (singular), *Qararit* (plural)', which they have devised as a way of calculation in the case of indivisible estate. They have defined the *Qirat* to be one unit of twenty four 1/24 and the total of *Qirat* is to always be 24. This method is of no use of course beyond the indivisible estate and the real estate in particular. To distribute an indivisible estate between heirs and legatees according to this method, one should apply the following steps:

Divide the *Masala* (whether succession *Masala*, comprehensive *Masala* or inclusive *Masala* which consists of heirs and legatees), by the denominator of the one *Qirat* 1/24. The quotient is called the *Masala Qirat*. If the *Masala Qirat* is more than five, such as 6, 8, 12 etc, then one must break the *Masala Qirat* into its components. For instance, one breaks 6 into 2 and 3 or 8 into 2 and 4 or 12 into 3 and 4.

To give each heir or legatee his share, one is to take his share from the *Masala* and divide it by the *Masala Qirat* if the *Masala Qirat* is bigger than 5 and is seen to be breakable into its components. Then the share of the heir or legatee from the *Masala* is to be divided by the components of the *Masala Qirat*, which is to be called the fractions of the *Qirat*, one after the other starting with the smallest component. However, if the quotient of such division consists of a fraction and a whole number, then one is to keep the fraction and move on to divide the whole number of the quotient alone by the bigger fraction of the *Qirat and so on.*

The last quotient, whether a whole number, a fraction or the combination of both in addition to any fraction we kept in hand from the previous division, will combine together to form the share of the heir or legatee from the indivisible estate. The same operations are to be repeated for each of the beneficiaries in the *Masala*.

To avoid repetition of the process, doctrines and methods of calculating the heirs' and legatees' Masala in the following cases, we shall be referring only to the final Masala and the final share of either heirs and legatees from such *Masala*. This means to make all the preliminary calculations, whether *Radd*, *'Awl*, *Tashih*, comprehensive *Masala* and inclusive *Masala*, on a separate table before we start the distribution of the estate.

To demonstrate such a method in a table makes the distribution of the estate simpler and easier for calculation. We recommend the drawing of a four sided table with horizontal lines. Inside it we draw as many lines as the number of heirs and legatees. If the *Masala Qirat* is unbreakable into its components, then three basic vertical lines are to be drawn inside it too. But if the *Masala Qirat* is breakable into its components, then as many vertical lines as necessary is to be drawn inside the table in addition to the basic three lines. Thus basically forming four columns in all. From right to left inside the first column, we put the heirs and legatees and on top we put the components of the *Masala*. Inside the second column we put the share of the heirs and legatees from the *Masala* and on top we put the number of the *Masala* which we will be calling the *Masala*. Inside the third column, we put the share of each heir or legatee from the *Qirat* when it is a whole number and on top we put the symbol (24) of the estate, being the denominator of one *Qirat* 1/24 to represent the indivisible estate. Inside the fourth column we put the fraction of the beneficiaries' shares and on top we put the *Masala Qirat*, i.e. the quotient of dividing the *Masala* by the *Qirat*.

If the *Masala Qirat* is breakable into its components then more columns are to be drawn, inside which we put the fractions and the subfractions of the shares of the heirs or legatees from the *Qirat* and on top of each extra column we put the components of the *Masala Qirat* placing the biggest component in the column next to the *Qirat* and next to it we place the smaller component and next to it we place the smallest component and so on. Accordingly, each heir or legatee shall be considered to have as a final share from the distributed estate an equivalent share to the numbers opposite him inside the other columns. It should be noticed that all the small components of the *Masala Qirat* and any numbers put underneath them are considered to be subfractions of the biggest fraction or component of the *Qirat*. To apply this method as we have described here are some illustrations.

First illustration:

Here we illustrate the *Masala Qirat* when it is an unbreakable number.

If a person dies leaving a real estate to a mother, a uterine brother, a uterine sister, two full sisters and three full brothers, then the deceased's real estate will be distributed between his heirs, following the above method as follows:

The Masala Qirat is the quotient of dividing the *Masala* by the *Qirat's* denominator $48 \div 24 = 2$.

The *Masala Qirat* as we can see is unbreakable so it has to be left as it is where the share of each heir from the real estate will therefore be the quotient of dividing each heir's share from the Masala by the *Masala Qirat* as follows:

$8 \div 2 = 4$ *Qirats* for the mother.
$8 \div 2 = 4$ *Qirats* for the uterine brother.
$8 \div 2 = 4$ *Qirats* for the uterine sister.
$3 \div 2 = 1\frac{1}{2}$ *Qirats* for the first full sister.
$3 \div 2 = 1\frac{1}{2}$ *Qirats* for the second full sister.
$6 \div 2 = 3$ *Qirats* for the first full brother.
$6 \div 2 = 3$ *Qirats* for the second full brother.
$6 \div 2 = 3$ *Qirats* for the third full brother.

Total = 24 *Qirats* = the real estate.

See Fig. 87.

Second illustration:

Here we illustrate the *Masala Qirat* when it can be divided into its components.

If a person dies leaving a real estate to his two wives, mother, daughter, and his three full brothers, his real estate will be distributed between his heirs as follows:

The *Masala Qirat* is the quotient of dividing the *Masala* by the *Qirat's* denominator $144 \div 24 = 6$.

The *Masala Qirat* as we can see is a divisible number. Its components are (2 and 3). $6 \div 3 = 2$ and $6 \div 2 = 3$. The components (2 and 3) are to be named the fraction of the *Masala Qirat*.

The share of each heir from the real estate is to be reached from the succession *Masala* by:

Fig. 87

MQ	Qirats den	The Masala	
2	= 24 ÷	48	6x8
0	4	8	M ⅙
0	4	8	UB ⅓
0	4	8	US
1	1	3	FS
1	1	3	FS
0	3	6	FB Res
0	3	6	FB
0	3	6	FB

2 ÷ 2 = 1
The Masala

x8

48	6	
8	1	M ⅙
8	1	UB ⅓
8	1	US
3		FS
3		FS
6	3	FB Res
6		FB
6		FB

1. Dividing the heir's share from the succession *Masala* by the components of the *Qirat* one after the other commencing from left; being the lowest, to the right.
2. If the result of the division by the smallest component is a fraction and a whole number, the fraction is left below and the whole number is carried forward to be divided by the second component and so on.
3. If in the last division, a whole number remained, it will be put below the *Qirat* denominator.
4. The share of each heir from the estate will be found horizontally.

To test the viability of the calculation, we add the numbers below the lowest component and then divide the result by the component. The result of this will be carried forward to be added to the numbers below the second component and so on. This total is then divided by the second component and so on and the final result is added to the numbers below the *Qirat* denominator.

If the result is 24, then the calculations are correct.
1st component 24 ÷ *2* = 12.
2nd component 12 ÷ *3* = 4 *Qirats* for the mother
1st component 9 ÷ *2* = 4½ In this situation where a fraction occurs in the calculation we leave the fraction and carry forward only the whole number.
2nd component 4 ÷ *3* = 1⅓ *Qirats* in addition to the above held-back fraction which is considered as a subfraction equal to ½ x ⅓ = ⅙ of a *Qirat* all of which are equivalent to one *Qirat*, one third of a *Qirat* and one half of one third of a *Qirat* 1⅓ and ⅙ *Qirat* are given to each of the two wives.

It must be remembered that each component is a fraction of the component preceding it (left to right), i.e. ⅓, ½ x ⅓ = ⅙.
1st component 72 ÷ 2 = 36
2nd component 36 ÷ *3* = 12 *Qirats* for the daughter.
1st component 10 ÷ *2* = 5.
2nd component 5 ÷ *3* = 1⅔ *Qirats* for the first full brother.
1st component 10 ÷ *2* = 5.
2nd component 5 ÷ *3* = 1⅔ *Qirats* for the second full brother.
1st component 10 ÷ *2* = 5.
2nd component 5 ÷ *3* = 1⅔ *Qirats* for the third full brother.
See Fig. 88.

MQ

Fig. 88

Fractions of the MQ		**Q den 6 = 24 ÷ 144**	***Masala***		
2	**3**	**24**	**144**	**= 24 x 6**	
0	**0**	**4**	**24**	**M**	**⅙**
1	**1**	**1**	**9**	**W**	**⅛**
1	**1**	**1**	**9**	**W**	
0	**0**	**12**	**72**	**D**	**½**
0	**2**	**1**	**10**	**FB**	
0	**2**	**1**	**10**	**FB**	**Res**
0	**2**	**1**	**10**	**FB**	

2 ÷ 2 = 1 + 8 ÷ 3 = 3

x 6

Fig. 88 cont.

144	**24**	
24	**4**	**M ⅙**
9	**3**	**W** } ⅛
9		**W**
72	**12**	**D ½**
10	**5**	**FB**
10		**FB Res**
10		**FB**

Third illustration:

Here we illustrate a *Masala Qirat* when it consists of a fraction only. To have a fraction as the *Masala Qirat* requires a different method of calculation as was used in the two previous illustrations. This is due to the fact that we need to convert the shares of each heir from the *Masala* into a fraction to suit the *Masala Qirat* which is a fraction in itself. This can be exemplified as such:

If a person dies leaving a real estate to his wife, a full brother and a full sister, it will be distributed between his heirs as below:

The *Masala Qirat* is the quotient of dividing the *Masala* by the *Qirat's* denominator 4 ÷ 24 = ⅙.

The *Masala Qirat* as we can see is a fraction. So to make the division of the share of each heir from the *Masala* by such a fraction possible, we have to convert the share of each heir into a fraction similar to the *Masala Qirat*. It will then be possible to go on with the intended division of the quotient which will be the final share of each heir from the real estate as such:

1 ÷ ⅙ = 1 x 6/1 = 6 *Qirats* for the wife.
2 ÷ ⅙ = 2 x 6/1 = 12 *Qirats* for the full brother.
1 ÷ ⅙ = 1 x 6/1 = 6 *Qirats* for the full sister.

An alternative for those who find difficulty in working out common fractions the above steps will be simplified by multiplying the denominator of the fraction of the *Masala Qirat* by the share of each heir from the *Masala* and then to divide the product on the numerator of the same fraction thus to get the same result which we have got above by the ordinary means of arithmetic as we see below:

1 x 6 = 6 ÷ 1 = 6 *Qirats* for the wife.
2 x 6 = 12 ÷ 1 = 12 *Qirats* for the full brother.
1 x 6 = 6 ÷ 1 = 6 *Qirats* for the full sister.
See Fig. 89.

MQ	Q den	The Masala	
1/6	24	4	
0	6	1	W 1/4
0	12	2	FB } Res
0	6	1	FS } Res

Fig. 89

Fourth illustration:

Here we illustrate the *Masala Qirat* when it consists of a whole number and a fraction. There is one more difference in this case from the latter (where the *Masala Qirat* was a fraction only). Such a differnece will be in the shape of converting the whole number of the *Masala Qirat* into a fraction with a similar denominator to the existing fraction in the *Masala*. But from then on we follow the same method as we have done in the previous cases; that is to say to convert the share of each heir from the *Masala* into a fraction to suit the converted *Masala Qirat*. This case can be exemplified as such.

If a woman dies leaving a real estate to her father, mother, husband, son and daughter, her real estate will be distributed between her heirs in the same way as follows:

The *Masala Qirat* is, as always, the quotient of dividing the *Masala* by the *Qirat's* denominator 36 ÷ 24 = $1\frac{12}{24}$ = $1\frac{1}{2}$.

The *Masala Qirat*, as we can see, consists of a whole number and a fraction. Therefore, in order to make possible the division of the share of each heir from the *Masala* by the *Masala Qirat*, we have to convert, firstly as we said, the whole number in the *Masala Qirat* into a fraction to liken it to the denominator of the already existing fraction. Secondly we have to convert the share of each heir from the *Masala* into a fraction to suit the fraction of the *Masala Qirat* thus to be able to go on with the usual division. The quotient of such a division will be considered the final share of each heir from the real estate as we shall see below:

$1\frac{1}{2} = 1 \text{ x } \frac{1}{2} = \frac{3}{2}$ The *Masala qirat* as it has been converted into a fraction.
$6 \div \frac{3}{2} = 6 \text{ x } \frac{2}{3} = 4$ *Qirats* for the father.
$6 \div \frac{3}{2} = 6 \text{ x } \frac{2}{3} = 4$ *Qirats* for the mother.
$9 \div \frac{3}{2} = 9 \text{ x } \frac{2}{3} = 6$ *Qirats* for the husband.
$10 \div \frac{3}{2} = 10 \text{ x } \frac{2}{3} = \frac{20}{3} = 6\frac{2}{3}$ *Qirats* for the son.
$5 \div \frac{3}{2} = 5 \text{ x } \frac{2}{3} = \frac{10}{3} = 3\frac{1}{3}$ *Qirats* for the daughter.

An alternative for those who are not familiar with the calculations of the common fractions, the above steps will be simplified by multiplying the denominator of the fraction of the *Masala Qirat* by the share of each heir from the *Masala* and then to divide the product by the numerator of the same fraction (of the *Masala Qirat*), thus to give the same result which we have got above as follows:
$6 \text{ x } 2 = 12 \div 3 = 4$ *Qirats* for the father.
$6 \text{ x } 2 = 12 \div 3 = 4$ *Qirats* for the mother.
$9 \text{ x } 2 = 18 \div 3 = 6$ *Qirats* for the husband.
$10 \text{ x } 2 = 20 \div 3 = 6\frac{2}{3}$ *Qirats* for the son.
$5 \text{ x } 2 = 10 \div 3 = 3\frac{1}{3}$ *Qirats* for the daughter.
See Fig. 90.

Fig. 90

MQ	Q den		
$1\frac{1}{2} = \frac{3}{2}$	24	36	= 12 x 3
0	4	6	F $\frac{1}{6}$
0	4	6	M $\frac{1}{6}$
0	6	9	H $\frac{1}{4}$
2	6	10	S Res
1	3	5	D

$3 \div 3 = 1$

Masala x 3

36	12	
6	2	F $\frac{1}{6}$
6	2	M $\frac{1}{6}$
9	3	H $\frac{1}{4}$
10	5	S Res
5		D

Fifth illustration:

If a person dies leaving a real estate to a daughter and a son's daughter and has also bequeathed to someone a share similar to the share of his presumed full brother at the same time, his real estate will be distributed between his beneficiaries (the heirs and legatees), according to the methd of the *Qirat* as follows:

The *Masala Qirat* as is always, the quotient of dividing the *Masala* by the Qirat's denominator $16 \div 24 = {}^{16}\!/_{24} = {}^{2}\!/_{3}$.

The *Masala Qirat* as we can see is a fraction. Therefore, in order to make possible the division of the share of each heir or legatee from the *Masala* by the *Masala Qirat*, we have to convert such a share into a fraction with the same denominator to the *Masala Qirat* where we will then be able to go on with the usual division. The quotient of such a division will be the final share of each heir or legatee from the real estate as we shall see below:

$9 \div 2/3 = 9 \times 3/2 = 27/2 = 13\frac{1}{2}$ *Qirats* for the daughter

$3 \div 2/3 = 3 \times 3/2 = 9/2 = 4\frac{1}{2}$ *Qirats* for the son's daughter.

$4 \div 2/3 = 4 \times 3/2 = 12/2 = 6$ *Qirats* for the legatee.

An alternative for those who find difficulty in working out common fractions, the above steps will be simplified by multiplying the denominator of the fraction of the *Masala Qirat* by the share of each heir from the *Masala* and then to divide the product by the numerator of the same fraction (of the *Masala Qirat*), thus to get the same result which we have got above by the ordinary means of arithmetic as follows:

$9 \times 3 = 27 \div 2 = 13\frac{1}{2}$ *Qirats* for the daughter.

$3 \times 3 = 9 \div 2 = 4\frac{1}{2}$ *Qirats* for the son's daughter.

$4 \times 3 = 12 \div 2 = 6$ *Qirats* for the legatee.

See Fig. 91.

Fig. 91

MQ	**Q den**	***Masala***	
⅔	**24**	**16**	**= 12 + 4**
1/	**13**	**9**	**D ½**
1/	**4**	**3**	**SD ⅙**
0/	**6**	**4**	**Leg**

2 ÷ 2= 1

+4

16	**12**	**= 2 x 6**
9	**6**	**D ½**
3	**2**	**SD ⅙**
X	**4**	**FB (pres) Res**
4		**Leg**

Note that in the above chart where the *Masala Qirat* is a fraction only and the numerator of such a fraction is more than one (in order to avoid confusion we recommend the drawing of a diagonal line in the column below the fraction between the numerator and the denominator so to indicate the connection of whatever number we put inside the column on either side of the diagonal line to the number above it), thus to form a separate fraction within it

Sixth illustration:

If a woman who left a real estate had bequeathed a general portion to someone and then died leaving her husband and a sister, her real estate would be distributed between her beneficiaries (heirs and legatees), according to the jurists as follows:

This case has been worked out in exactly the same way as we have done in the latter case because of their similar processes as we shall see below:

The *Masala Qirat* is as always the quotient of dividing the *Masala* by the *Qirat's* denominator, $7 \div 24 = \frac{7}{24}$.

The *Masala Qirat* as we can see is a fraction. Therefore, in order to make possible the division of the share of each heir or legatee from the *Masala* on the *Masala Qirat* we have to convert such a share into a fraction with the same denominator as the *Masala Qirat* where we will then be able to go on with the usual division. The quotient of such a division will be the final share of each heir or legatee from the real estate as we shall see in the following:

$3 \div \frac{7}{24} = 3 \times \frac{24}{7} = \frac{72}{7} = 10\frac{2}{7}$ *Qirats* for the husband.

$3 \div \frac{7}{24} = 3 \times \frac{24}{7} = \frac{72}{7} = 10\frac{2}{7}$ *Qirats* for the sister.

$1 \div \frac{7}{24} = 1 \times \frac{24}{7} = \frac{24}{7} = 3\frac{3}{7}$ *Qirats* for the legatee.

An alternative calculation of the final step without the use of common fraction is worked out as follows:

$3 \times 24 = 72 \div 7 = 10\frac{2}{7}$ *Qirats* for the husband.

$3 \times 24 = 72 \div 7 = 10\frac{2}{7}$ *Qirats* for the sister.

$1 \times 24 = 24 \div 7 = 3\frac{3}{7}$ *Qirats* for the legatee.

See Fig. 92.

Fig. 92

MQ	**Q den**	**The *Masala***		
7/24	**24**	**7**	**=6+1**	
2/	**10**	**3**	**H**	**½**
2/	**10**	**3**	**Sis**	**⅙**
3/	**3**	**1**	**Leg**	**⅙**

7 ÷ 7= 1

The *Masala* +1

7	**6**		
3	**3**	**H**	**½**
3	**3**	**Sis**	**½**
1	**1**	**Leg**	**⅙**

7 − 6 = 1 (deficit)

THE METHOD OF RATIO

The method which the jurists call *Al-Tariqa al-nisbiyah*, covers a wider range than the previous two methods. This method is intended to be used to distribute all kinds of estate whether divisible or indivisible. Such a method is based on giving the beneficiary, whether he is an heir, a legatee or otherwise, a ratio of the share of the estate to be distributed similar to the share he or she is entitled to from the *Masala*.

The actual distribution of estate is done by dividing the amount of estate whatever it is whether currency, sheep, kilos or sacks of grain etc, or the denominator of the one *Qirat* 1/24 which is to be taken as to represent the indivisible property such as the real estate by the *Masala*. The quotient of such division will be called the Ratio of estate. Then in order to calculate the share of each beneficiary from the estate we multiply the above quotient (the Ratio of estate), by the share of each beneficiary from the *Masala*.

However, to demonstrate such a method in a chart which will make distribution look simpler and easier, we recommend the drawing of a four sided table with horizontal lines inside equal to the number of heirs and legatees. As to the vertical lines we only draw two inside thus forming three columns in all.

From right to left, inside the first vertical column we put the beneficiaries with their description and basic portions and on top we put the components of the *Masala*. Inside the second vertical column we put the share of each one from the Masala and on top we put the number of the *Masala*, called the *Masala*. Inside the third vertical column we put the share of each beneficiary from the distributed estate represented by the amount of it if it is a divisible estate or represented by the beneficiary's share from the maximum amount of the *Qirat* if it is an indivisible property. We then divide the top into two parts; inside the left part we put the estate and inside the right part we put the Ratio of the estate. To apply the method of Ratio as it has been described above here are some illustrations:

First illustration:

If a person dies leaving £4000, to his surviving mother, uterine brother, uterine sister and a full brother, his property will be distributed according to the method of ratio as follows:

The Ratio of the estate is to be the quotient of dividing the estate value by the *Masala* £4000 ÷ 6 = 666⅔.

The share of each beneficiary from the estate is to be the product of multiplying his or her share from the *Masala* by estate Ratio as follows:
1 x 666⅔ = £666⅔ for the mother.
1 x 666⅔ = £666⅔ for the uterine brother.
1 x 666⅔ = £666⅔ for the uterine sister.
3 x 666⅔ = £2000 for the full brother.
See Fig. 93.

Estate Value	Estate Ratio	The *Masala*		
£4000 ÷ 6 =	666⅔	6		
£666⅔		1	M	⅙
£666⅔		1	UB	⅓
£666⅔		1	US	
£2000		3	FB	Res

Fig. 93

Second illustration:

When this method (the ratio method), is also to be applied to the distribution of a real estate, then instead of putting the value of the estate, we put the denominator of one *Qirat* or what we might call the maximum amount of *Qirat*, i.e. 24 to represent the indivisible estate.

The estate ratio is to be the quotient of dividing the maximum amount of *Qirats* which is to be equal to the real estate by the *Masala*. The share of each beneficiary from the real estate is to be the product of multiplying the estate ratio by the share of each beneficiary from the *Masala*. To apply this, here is an example:

If a woman dies leaving a real estate to her husband, daughter, mother and full brother, her estate will then be distributed between her heirs as follows:

The estate ratio is 24 ÷ 12 = 2.

The share of each beneficiary from the estate is:

3 x 2 = 6 *Qirats* for the husband.
6 x 2 = 12 *Qirats* for the daughter.
2 x 2 = 4 *Qirats* for the mother.
1 x 2 = 2 *Qirats* for the full brother.
See Fig. 94.

Third illustration:

If a woman who has bequeathed a general portion to someone dies leaving a husband, a mother, a father and two daughters with a divisible estate of £25874, her estate will be distributed between her beneficiaries, i.e. heirs and the legatee, as follows:

The estate ratio is the quotient of dividing the estate value by the Masala £25874 ÷ 17 = 1522.

Estate Q den	Estate Ratio		
24 ÷ 12 =	2	12	
	6	3	H ¼
	12	6	D ½
	4	2	M ⅙
	2	1	FB Res

Fig. 94

The share of each beneficiary (heirs and legatee), from the estate is to be the product of multiplying the estate ratio by the share of each beneficiary from the *Masala* as follows:
3 x 1522 = £4566 for the husband.
2 x 1522 = £3044 for the mother.
2 x 1522 = £3044 for the father.
8 x 1522 = £12176 for the two daughters.
12176 ÷ 2 £6088 for each of the two daughters.
2 x 1522 = £3044 for the legatee.
See Fig. 95.

Fig. 95

Estate Value	Estate Ratio	*Masala*	
£25874	1522	17	= 12 + 5
£4566		3	H ¼
£3044		2	M ⅙
£3044		2	F ⅙
£12176		8	2D ⅔
£3044		2	Leg ⅙

+5

17	12	
3	3	H ¼
2	2	M ⅙
2	2	F ⅙
8	8	2D ⅔
2	2	Leg ⅙

17 − 12 = 5 (deficit)

Fourth illustration:

In this illustration two things are to be dealt with; the excessive bequest and the appproval of it by the heirs. For instance, if a person who has bequeathed one half of his estate to someone dies, leaving his mother and two uterine brothers a real estate, his estate will be distributed according to the ratio method of distribution between his beneficiaries as follows:

The estate Ratio is the quotient of dividing the estate by the *Masala* 24 ÷ 6 = 4.

The share of each beneficiary (heirs or legatee), from the estate is the product of multiplying the estate Ratio by the beneficiary's share from the *Masala*.

3 x 4 = 12 *Qirats* for the legatee whose excessive bequest has been approved of by the heirs.
1 x 4 = 4 *Qirats* for the mother.
2 x 4 = 8 *Qirats* for the two uterine brothers.
8 ÷ 2 = 4 *Qirats* for each of the two uterine brothers.
See Fig. 96.

Fig. 96

Estate Q den	**Estate Ratio**	**The *Masala***	
24	**4**	**6**	**=3x2**
	12	**3**	**Leg ½**
	4	**1**	**M ⅙**
	8	**2**	**2 UB ⅓**

Comp M	**Suc M RM**		**Beq M**	
6=3x2	**3**	**6**	**2**	
3			**1**	**Leg ½**
1	**1**	**1**	**1**	**M ⅙**
2	**2**	**2**		**2 UB ⅓**

1 + 2 = 3 This aggregate becoming the Radd M.

Fifth illustration:

In this illustration we recall the same problem of the fourth illustration where the deceased is to have bequeathed to someone half of his estate with the exception here that the heirs disapprove of such an excessive bequest. In this case the legatee will then be limited to the disposable third only, leaving the other two thirds for the deceased's heirs. A *Masala* as such will be calculated as follows:

The estate Ratio is the quotient of dividing the estate (represented by the denominator of the *Qirat*), by the *Masala*, $24 \div 9 = 2\frac{2}{3}$.

The share of each beneficiary (heir or legatee), from the estate is the product of multiplying the estate ratio by the beneficiary's share from the *Masala*.

$3 \times 2\frac{2}{3} = 3 \times \frac{8}{3} = \frac{24}{3} = 8$ *Qirats* for the legatee equal to the third of the estate because of the heirs' disapproval of the excessive bequest.

$2 \times 2\frac{2}{3} = 2 \times \frac{8}{3} = \frac{16}{3} = 5\frac{1}{3}$ *Qirats* for the mother.

$4 \times 2\frac{2}{3} = 4 \times \frac{8}{3} = \frac{32}{3} = 10\frac{2}{3}$ *Qirats* for the two uterine brothers.

$10\frac{2}{3} \div 2 = \frac{32}{3} \div 2 = \frac{16}{3} = 5\frac{1}{3}$ *Qirats* for each of the two uterine brothers.

See Fig. 97.

Fig. 97

Estate Q den	**Estate Ratio**	***Masala***	
24	**$2\frac{2}{3}$**	**9**	**= 3 x 3**
8		**3**	**Leg ½**
$5\frac{1}{3}$		**2**	**M ⅙**
$10\frac{2}{3}$		**4**	**2 UB ⅓**

Comp M	**Suc M *Radd* M**		**Beq M**	
9 = 3 x 3	**3**	**6**	**3**	
3			**1**	**Leg ½**
2	**1**	**1**	**2**	**M ⅙**
4	**2**	**2**		**2 UB ⅓**

1 + 2 = 3 (*Radd Masala*)

NOTES

1. I.A. b. Ibrahim, *Al-adhb al fa'd sharh umdat al-farid*, Vol. 2, 114.
2. Makkah Grand Court, Case No. 142, Vol. 1, date 8/5/1381H.
3. Muh. Najib Khayat, *Al-rawdah al-bahiyah 'ala matn al-rahabiya*, 92-93.
4. Makkah Grand Court, Case No. 72, Vol. 17. Special Reg. of Sharh Al-Amr. Date 19/5/1391H.

BIBLIOGRAPHY

ARABIC SOURCES

Abdulbaqi, Mohammad Fu'ad.
Al-Mu'jam al-Mufahras li-alfaz al-Qur'an, Dar matabi' al-Sha'b, Kitab al-Sha'b.
Abu Zahrah, Mohammad.
Sharh Qanun al-Wasiya, Mitba'at al-i'timad, Egypt, 1947.
Al-'ittihad al-Umami lil-majami' al-ilmiya.
Al-Mu'jam al-Mufahras li-alfaz al-Hadith al-Nabawi. Maktabat Brill, Leiden, Holland, 1936.
Al-Bajuri, Ibrahim.
Hashiya 'ala-Sharh al-Shanshuri 'ala-Matn al-Rahabiya fi'ilm al-Fara'id. Al-Mitba'ah al-Bahiya, Egypt.
Al-Bahuti, Mansur b. Yunus b. Idris.
Sharh Muntaha al-Iradat. Al-Maktaba al-Salafiya, Al Madina al-Munawwara, Saudi Arabia.
Kashshaf al-Qina' 'an Matn al-'iqna'. Maktabat al-Nasr al-Haditha, Riyadh, Saudi Arabia, 1388H/1968AD.
Al-Banna, Ahmad Abdulrahman.
Al-Fath al-Rabbani fi-Tartib al-Musnad (a commentary and a re-arrangement of Al-Musnad of Ibn Hanbal). 1st Edition. 1353. Al-Ghuriya, Egypt.
Al-Bardisi, Mohammad Zakariya.
Al-Mirath wa-al-Wasiya fi-al-Islam. Al-dar al-Qawmiya li-al-Tiba'ah wa-al Nashr. Cairo, 1384H/1964AD.
Al-Futuhi, Taqi al-din Mohammad b. Al-Najjar.
Muntaha al-Iradat. Maktabat dar al-'Urubah, Cairo, 1961-1962.
Al-Hakeem, Abdulmajeed.
Al-Wasit fi-Nazariyat al-'Aqd. Sharikat al-Tab' wa al-Nashr al-Ahliya, Baghdad, 1387H/ 1967AD.
Al-Hasri, Ahmad.
Al-Tarikat wa al-Wasaya fi al-Fiqh al-Islami. Maktabat al-'Aqsa, Amman, Jordan, 1391H/ 1972AD.
Al-Wisaya wa al-Wilaya wa al-Talaq. Maktabat al-Kulliya al-Azhariya.
Al-Hijjawi, Abu al-Naja Sharaf al-din Musa.
Al-'iqna'. Edited by Abdullah al-Sabki. Al-Mitba'ah al-Misriya bi- al-Azhar.
Al-Huqail, Abdulkarim b. Hamad.
'Alaqat al-Muwatin bi al-dawa'ir al-Shar'iya. 1st Edition 1387H/1967AD. Maktabat al-Ma'arif, Taif, Saudi Arabia.
Ibn Badran, Abdulqadir b. Ahmad.
Al-Madkhal ila Madhhab al-Imam Ahmad b. Hanbal. Al-Matabi' al-Tijariya al-Kubra, Egypt.

Ibn Daqiq al-Eid, Mohammad b. Ali.
Ahkam al-Ahkam Sharh 'Umdat al-Ahkam. Mitba'at al-Sharq, Cairo, 1344H.
Ibn Ibrahim, (Al-Shammari), Ibrahim b. Ibdullah.
al-'Adhb al-Fa'id Sharh 'Umdat al-Farid. By the order of King Faisal.
Ibn Jarir al-Tabari, Abbu Ja'far Mohammad.
Tafsir al-Tabari (Jami' al-Bayan 'an Ta'wil al-Qur'an). Edited by Mahmud Mohammad, Shakir and his brother Ahmad. Dar al-Ma'arif, Egypt.
Ibn Muflih, Mohammad.
Kitab al-Furu' (Al-Furu' wa Tashihuh). 1st Edition 1341H. Mitba'at al-Manar, Egypt.
Al-Nukat wa al-Fawa'id al-Saniya. Mitba'at al-Sunna al-Mohammadiya, Cairo, 1369H/1950AD.
Ibn al-Qayim (Ibn Qayim al-Jawziyah), Shams al-din Abu Abdillah Mohammad b. Abi Bakr.
'Alam al-Muwaqqi'in 'an Rabb al-'Alamin. Dar al-Kutub al-Haditha, Cairo, 1389H/1969AD.
Al-Turuq al-Hukmiya fi al-Siyasa al-Shar'iya. Mitba'at al-Madani, 1381H/1961AD.
Tuhfat al-Mawdud. Maktabat dar al al-Bayan, 1st Edition 1391H/1971AD, Damascus.
Ibn Qudama, Muwaffaq al-din, Abdullah b. Ahmad.
Al-Mughni. Mitba'at al-Manar, 1348H. Egypt.
Al-Kafi. 1st Edition 1382H/1963AD. Al-Maktab al-Islami li al-Tiba'ah wa al-Nashr, Damascus.
Rawdat al-Nazir. Al-Mitba'a al-Salafiya, Cairo, 1385H.
Ibn Qudama (Shams al-din), Mohammad b. Ahmad b. Abdulhadi.
Al-Sharh al-Kabir. Mitba'at al-Manar, 1348H. Egypt.
Al-Muharrar fi al-Hadith. Mitba'at Mustafa Mohammad, *Al-Maktaba al-Tijariya*, Egypt.
Ibn Rajab, Abu al-Faraj Abdulrahman.
Al-Qawa'id fi al-Fiqh al-Islami. 1st Edition 1392H/1972AD. Maktabat al-Kulliyat al-Azhariya.
Ibn Taimiya (abu al-Barakat), Abdulsalam b. Abdullah.
Al-Muharrar fi al-Fiqh. Maktabat al-Sunna al-Mohammadiya, Cairo, 1369H/1950AD.
Ibn Taimiya (Shaikh al-Islam), Ahmad.
Fatawa Shaikh al-Islam Ibn Taimiya. Al-Maktaba al-Hukumiya, Mecca, 1386H.
Al-Musawwadah fi Usul al-Fiqh. Mitba'at al-Madani, Cairo, 1384H/1964AD.
Al-Khafif, Ali.
Ahkam al-Wasiya. Jami'at al-dowal al-Arabiya, Ma'had al-Dirasat al-Arabiya al-'aliya, 1962AD.
Khayyata, Mohammad Najib.
Al-Rawda al-Bahiya 'ala Matn al-Rahabiya. Mitba'at al-Nasr, Halab, 1382H/1962AD. Syria.
Al-Khiraqi, Umar b. Al-Husain.
Mukhtasar al-Khiraqi. 1st Edition, 1378H. Mu'assasat dar al-Salam li al-Tiba'at wa al-Nashr. Damascus.
Al-Kishki, Mohammad Abdulrahim.
Al-Tarika wa ma yata'allaqu biha min al-Huquq. Dar al-Nadhir, 1378H/1968AD. Baghdad.
Maghniya, Mohammad Jawad.
Al-Ahwal al-Shakhsiya. Dar al-Ilm li al-Malayin, 1st Edition, 1964. Beirut.
Al-Manqur, Ahmad b. Mohammad.
Al-Fawakih al-'Adidah fi al-Masa'il al-Mufidah. Manshurat al-Maktab al-Islami, Halbuni, 1st Edition, 1380/1960. Damascus.
Al-Mirdawi, Ali b. Sulaiman.
Al-Insaf fi Ma'rifat al-Rajih min al-Khilaf. Edited by Mohammad Hamid Al-Faqi. 1st Edition, 1375H/1956AD. Cairo.
Al-Tanqih al-Mushbi'. Al-Mitba'ah al-Salafiya, Cairo.
Tashih al-Furu'. (printed with Al-Furu'), 1st Edition, Mitba'at al-Manar, 1341H. Egypt.

Muhammasani, Subhi.
Al-Awda' al-Tashri'ya fi al-Duwal al-Arabiya Madiha wa Hadiruha. 3rd Edition, 1965 Dar al-ilm li al-Malayin, Beirut.
Musa, Dr Mohammad Yusuf.
Al-Tarikah wa al-Mirath fi al-Islam. 1960AD. Matabi' Dar al-Kitab al-Arabi bi Misr.
Al-Rasheed, Abdulaziz Nasir.
'Uddat al-Bahith. Riyadh, Maktabat al-Nasr al-Haditha.
Al-Ruhaibani, Mustafa al-Suyuti.
Matalib 'Uli al-Nuha fi Sharh Ghayat al-Muntaha. 1st Edition, 1380H/1961AD.
Al-Sabti, Abi Bakr b. Ahmad.
Kitab Sharh al-Rahabiya. Maktabat al-Nahda al-Arabiya, Mecca, Saudi Arabia.
Shalabi, Mohammad Mustafa.
Al-Waqf wa al-Wasiya bin al-Fiqh wa al-Qanun. 1st Edition, Mitba'at Dar al-Ta'lif. 1376H/1957AD. Egypt.
Al-Shanshuri, Abdullah b. Mohammad (Al-Ju'mi al-Faradi).
Fath al-Qarib al-Mujib. Maktabat al-Nahda al-Arabiya, Mecca, Saudi Arabia.
Sharaf al-din, Dr Abdulazim Abdulsalam.
Ibn Qayim al-Jawziya Asruhu wa Manhajuh. Maktabat al-Kulliyat al-Azhariya, 1387H//1967AD. 2nd Edition, Cairo.
Al-Siba'i, Mustafa.
Sharh Qanun al-Ahwal al-Shakhsiya. 1958. Damascus.
Al-Suyuti, Al-Minhaji.
Jawahir al-Uqud.
Al-Zarqa, Mustafa Ahmad.
Al-Fiqh al-Islami fi thawbihi al-Jadid, (Al-Madkhal al-Fiqhi al-'Amm.) 6th Edition. 1378H/1958AD. Mitba'at Jami'at Dimashq, Damascus.

ENGLISH SOURCES

Abdulrahim, M.A.
Muhammadan Jurisprudence. The Pakistan Educational Press, Lahore, 1970.
Bergel, Franz. & Davies, D.R.A.
All About Drugs. Barnes & Noble Inc., New York, 1st Edition, 1970.
Coulson, Noel James.
Succession in the Muslim Family. Cambridge University Press, 1971.
Fazee, Asaf, A.A.
Outlines of Muhammadan Law. Oxford University Press, 1964. 3rd Edition.
Islamic Law of Wills. Humphrey Milford, Oxford University Press, 1933.
Ibn S. Tung, al-Haj Mahomed Ullah.
The Muslim Law of Inheritance. S. Sultan, Law publisher, Allahabad, 1934.
James, Philip S.
Introduction to English Law. 6th Edition, Butterworths, London, 1966.
Kessel, Neil and Walton, Henry.
Alcoholism. Penguin Books, 1971.
Mellows, Anthony R.
The Law of Succession. Butterworths, London, 1970.
Parry, Sir David Hughes.
The Law of Succession. 5th Edition, Sweet & Maxwell Ltd., London, 1966.

Redmond, P.W.D.
General Principles of English Law. 4th Edition, M. & E. Handbooks, Macdonald & Evans Ltd., 1974.
Rumsey, Almaric.
Mohammudan Law of Inheritance. W.H. Allen & Co., London, 1880.
Al-Sirajiyyah or Mahommadan Law of Inheritance with notes and appendix. 2nd Edition, Thacker, Spink and Co., Calcutta, 1890. W.H. Allen & Co., London, 1880.
Russel, A.D. & Suhrawardy, A.A.
Muslim Law of Inheritance. Kegan Paul, Trench, Trubner & Co. Ltd., London.
Sandstöm, C.I.
Childhood and Adolescence.
Williams, Dr Lincoln.
Alcoholism Explained. Evans Brothers Ltd., London, 1967.

INDEX